African Worlds

STUDIES IN THE COSMOLOGICAL IDEAS
AND SOCIAL VALUES OF AFRICAN PEOPLES

AFRICAN WORLDS

STUDIES IN THE
COSMOLOGICAL IDEAS AND SOCIAL VALUES
OF AFRICAN PEOPLES

AFRICAN WORLDS

STUDIES IN THE
COSMOLOGICAL IDEAS AND SOCIAL VALUES
OF AFRICAN PEOPLES

Edited with an Introduction
by
DARYLL FORDE

Published for the
INTERNATIONAL AFRICAN INSTITUTE
by the
OXFORD UNIVERSITY PRESS

NOTE

In fulfilment of a resolution of the General Conference of U.N.E.S.C.O. at its fourth session, on the recommendation of the International Council for Philosophy and Humanistic Studies (Conseil International de la Philosophie et des Sciences Humaines), and in accordance with the decision of the Executive Board of U.N.E.S.C.O. at its twenty-first session, a grant was allocated towards the cost of the preparation and publication by the International African Institute of a study of the Cosmological Ideas and Social Values of African peoples.

The present volume has been prepared under the editorship of Professor Daryll Forde, Administrative Director of the International African Institute, and contains contributions by a number of distinguished ethnologists based on original field researches.

ISBN 0 19 724156 5

First Edition 1954
Eighth impression 1976

Printed in Great Britain by Clarke, Doble & Brendon Ltd., Plymouth

CONTENTS

INTRODUCTION

By DARYLL FORDE

I

IN this book an attempt is made to present in brief compass the world-outlook of a number of African peoples. Each study seeks to portray and interpret the dominant beliefs and attitudes of one people concerning the place of Man in Nature and in Society, not only as revealed in formal and informal expressions of belief but also as implicit in customs and ethical prescriptions in both ritual and secular contexts.

It is not to be assumed that the views and attitudes of a people concerning the duties of men among themselves and their relations to the universe are necessarily all of one piece. Anthropological studies of many cultures have shown that even in small and comparatively isolated societies, where differences of wealth, rank, and power are small, there need be no complete integration of belief and doctrine, still less the domination of conduct in all spheres by a single system of beliefs or basic ideas. For both the historical sources of knowledge and belief and the contexts of activity in which these are evoked are likely, even in a circumscribed world, to be diverse. On the other hand, there is reason to believe that a close relation exists between dominant attitudes towards social relations and the proper use of resources and established beliefs concerning the nature of human society and its place in a wider universe of cosmic forces. Between such beliefs, and the ethical standards of a people and their opportunities for action, there appears to be a continuous process of reciprocal adjustment.

The myths of the origin of a people, of the natural resources they exploit, of their cultural equipment and of their social institutions, express and sustain attitudes towards extra-human forces that are believed to control or intervene among them. Together these constitute a charter for the observance of customary patterns of activity and established social duties and privileges. It must be recognized, however, that the unique mobility and capacity for communication of the human species have nearly everywhere prevented any population from remaining long isolated and static, culturally or socially, in an unchanging environment. The history of all human communities has been one of recurrent, if irregular and uneven, change in response to local discovery or, more often, to external contacts; and the introduction of new ways of living in whatever sphere and by whatever means—from the spontaneous development of new tools or symbols to the imposition of external political power—generates, through wide repercussion, manifold adjustments of activity, new standards of conduct, and new mythological justifications.

At any given time, however, even in phases of extensive technical and social change such as the peoples of Africa, like many others, have experienced over the past century, traditional beliefs and standards continue to exert a powerful influence. For mythical charters and moral codes have their own cultural inertia whereby they can retard or guide adaptation in other fields. And, as we know from the history of ideas in the West, the reformulation of myth and code and the modification of social sentiments are slow processes as compared with the readjustment of particular items of technical activity or the mere acceptance of some new social relation. Hence the multifarious conflicts that arise between ideology and technical opportunity during phases of rapid cultural change. Even in such phases, while new techniques are adopted for reasons of individual or sectional self-interest, and new social relations are accepted as the distribution of economic power changes, traditional myths and codes may continue to claim allegiance. These may indeed appear, from one point of view—and one especially apparent to the outsider—to block obvious and important opportunities for general economic advance or social reorganization; but, from another, they can often be seen as preserving patterns of activity and social relations which are felt by the people to be of intrinsic and overriding value and so may in fact be indispensable to the preservation of their social cohesion and solidarity.

Such conflicts of values, both between peoples and between sections and individuals within a single society, are only too familiar from the history of the western world. It is, however, little appreciated that they have been and continue to be endemic in an acute form among the multitudes of small-scale societies as these have been brought increasingly within the orbit of an industrialized western civilization. Moreover, even when the nature of the conflict has been sensed, the problems of providing scope and time for adjustment have been made more difficult by virtual ignorance of the nature and the foundations of the traditional value systems that were being undermined by the introduction of new techniques of administration, production, and commerce.

The studies presented in this volume thus have both a theoretical and a practical bearing. They provide brief but comprehensive descriptions and analyses of the character and the contexts of the value systems of a number of African peoples. Painstakingly reached through prolonged field research, they make it possible to see how the varying material and cultural backgrounds of indigenous life in Africa have conditioned the beliefs and attitudes of its peoples. They show, too, how social and personal conflicts and disintegration are bound to arise if the foundations of such beliefs and attitudes are abruptly swept away without opportunity for adjustment.

The authors are professional field anthropologists, associated with the International African Institute, who have lived and carried out systematic studies among the peoples whose beliefs and social values they present. For some of them the investigation of religious beliefs and cosmological ideas as expressions of basic notions underlying cultural activities and social relations was a main objective. In all cases there was close concern with moral values and with the periodic rites and other ceremonies carried out on behalf of kin-groups, sects, communities, tribes, or states. For anthropologists realize, more fully, perhaps, than most other students of society, how much the study of religious observances may reveal of the strength of social bonds and cultural attachments which the superficial flow of everyday life, especially among peoples newly in contact with attractions offered by western institutions, might seem to gainsay.

For anthropologists and other students of human cultures and of the forces that mould them, this book should be of particular value as a first collection of brief but systematic studies of the cosmological, religious, and moral ideas of a number of African peoples in the context of their material environment and their social organization. Mary Kingsley, a pioneer field anthropologist, long ago wrote of the West African peoples to whom she was so devoted, that to understand them it was necessary to study their beliefs, fears, and ritual practices in the context of their own social and cultural situations. But systematic and scholarly studies of the religious ideas and moral values of African peoples have not kept pace with the advance of administrative control and commercial development, and have lagged behind the study of the political and economic aspects of the indigenous social systems. This is not to say that much has not been written by anthropologists and others over the past generation concerning African religious beliefs. But the few early studies of the religions and morals of African peoples,[1] in which prolonged critical study was combined with sympathetic insight, have not been followed, as might have been expected with the advance of both theory and field methods in anthropology, by an abundance of comprehensive studies of African religious systems and the values they express. Important aspects of ritual and belief in a number of African societies have, indeed, been most effectively described and analysed, but usually in the context of some specific problem of social structure or of cultural change. Notable advances have been made in this way in demonstrating the cohesive role of such religious institutions as ancestor or earth cults and first-fruit ceremonies, and the significance of witchcraft belief and accusation and the practice of sorcery as indexes of social stress. Evans-Pritchard,[2] in his study of divination and witchcraft among the Azande, has shown in detail, for one African people, how the occurrence of misfortune comes to be linked to socially generated fears and hatreds and so sustains an unformulated philosophy as well as moral sanctions for benevolent or circumspect conduct. Study of the religious beliefs of the Luba peoples of the southern Congo[3] has afforded Father Tempels the background for an arresting essay on the pervasive effects of belief in the

---

[1] Such as H. A. Junod's classic *Life of a South African Tribe* (the Thonga), 2nd edition, London, 1937; L. Tauxier, *La Religion bambara*, Paris, 1927.

[2] Evans-Pritchard, E. E., *Witchcraft, Oracles, and Magic among the Azande*, Oxford, 1937.

[3] Tempels, P., *La Philosophie bantoue*, Elisabethville, 1945.

permeation of nature by dynamic spiritual forces. Intensive field research has also revealed the hitherto unsuspected complexity and elaboration of cosmological ideas among some peoples of the Western Sudan, such as the Dogon, Bambara, and Akan, examples of which are provided in this volume.

But there remains the need to explore in the African field the significance of cosmological ideas as expressions of moral values in relation to the material conditions of life and the total social order. The value of such an attempt to discover and appreciate the *raison d'être* of those basic concepts which, though rarely explicit, so largely guide and give meaning to the conduct of a strange people in both trivial and momentous situations, was shown in such pioneer studies as those of Durkheim on Australian religion and Radcliffe-Brown on the Andamanese.[1] The contributors to the present volume have attempted, for the African peoples they have studied, to show this intricate interdependence between a traditional pattern of livelihood, an accepted configuration of social relations, and dogmas concerning the nature of the world and the place of men within it.

II

When these studies are considered together one is impressed, not only by the great diversity of ritual forms and expressions of belief, but also by substantial underlying similarities in religious outlook and moral injunction. In the first place in myth, ritual, and social code there is always a strong sense of direct dependence on local resources: on, for example, the rains and the harvest that they should bring forth or the grass to maintain the herds. There is often, too, an equally vivid expression of concern lest pestilence overtake men and crops and livestock. Primitive techniques in the production of food supplies, the small and localized scale of that production, and severe limitations on the accumulation, transport, and storage of surplus combine to render hazardous the very basis of subsistence for household and community. The practical measures that can be taken to combat disease and sickness whether individual or epidemic are equally limited. Where the natural processes involved in good fortune and in bad remain largely unknown and uncontrollable by practical means, men have at all times rationalized their fate by postulating mysterious forces and beings in nature, and mysterious powers among their fellows.

To all this Africans have been no exception. Gods, spirits, and magical forces beyond the community, together with witches and sorcerers within it, are postulated in explanation of the workings of the universe, of the incidence of benefits and misfortunes, and of the strains of life in society. Means are employed according to the situation and the diagnosis to enlist or avert the anticipated action of such beings and powers. Africans, in the

---

[1] Durkheim, E., *The Elementary Forms of Religious Life*, 1915, English translation by Swain, London, 1926; Radcliffe-Brown, A. R., *The Andaman Islanders*, Cambridge, 1922 (2nd edition 1933).

same way as Europeans, have appreciated and successfully based their routines of living on principles of causation linking events, on the logical implications of ideas, and on an understanding of mechanical and organic process. Their techniques of farming, fishing, and stock-raising, their procedures in training the young, their judgements of men and of social situations all reveal this at every turn. Where they have differed from the Europeans who have recently come among them has been in the depth and range of their collective knowledge of natural process and in the degree of control and security that they could thereby command.

Under primitive conditions of life and in the absence of a coherent body of scientific theory so much more lies beyond the reach of naturalistic explanation, so much more elicits interpretation and action in terms of the mysterious agents called into being in response to hopes and needs. Beliefs of this order are not capable of verification but neither do they require it. In such spheres the peoples of Africa, like those of the West and, indeed, all mankind save the tiny minority which is able to suspend belief, have adopted theories that project on to a plane of supernatural action the desires and aspirations that they know in the realm of human action. Passion and will, virtue and malevolence, compassion and indignation as they are known among men are attributed to unseen powers. The physical limitations on human action that are accepted in everyday life are thought no longer to restrict men who can command supernatural forces. Limitations of knowledge, and the absence of a tradition of critical inquiry and philosophic doubt, combine with the greater frequency of unforeseen distress to accentuate the universal dichotomy between explanations, commonsense or scientific, of processes directly involved in the occurrence of events and the desire to know why a particular chain of events should occur to particular people at a particular time.

Some educated Europeans in some situations are able to apply western knowledge concerning the complexity of causation, to maintain the distinction between *post hoc* and *propter hoc*. But there is a deeper propensity which tends to supervene outside fields of special training or knowledge— the tendency to seek the cause of any event which touches men closely in some antecedent and emotionally charged situation affecting themselves or other persons. The crops are known to wither for lack of rain, the cattle are known to flourish because the rains came early and in abundance; it is recognized that a man fell from a tree and died because he climbed out on a dead branch, that another is prosperous and has many children because he and his wives are healthy and able. But when the meteorological processes involved in fluctuations of rainfall are unknown, when the notion of chance is not applied to the occurrence of a dead branch, when the conditions of human well-being and ability can be so little analysed, what is to be the answer to the further questions: why should the rains fail or be abundant *now* for *us*? why should *my* kinsman and not another have fallen from the tree? why should one man and his wives enjoy prosperity while

neighbours sicken and lose their children? All these questions remain open
to explanation in terms of attendant emotions and the moral ideas of virtue
and guilt associated with them. In other words, success and prosperity, so
long as they are socially approved, may be seen as the rewards of virtue and
dependent on its continuance; misery and catastrophe are linked through
anxiety and anger to notions of wrongdoing or envy in oneself or others
and thence to the punishment or elimination of these faults.

So it is that in misfortune, not merely attendant circumstances, but
explanations in moral terms are sought and the consequences of human or
supernatural action divined. Where does the guilt or anger lie and how
may it be requited or expiated? And explanations in these terms take
different directions according to the actual or assumed locus of the emotions and desires in question and the moral status of the persons concerned.
Thus, for example, where guilt is ascribed to the sufferer of misfortune the
misfortune tends to be attributed to supernatural beings—to gods and
ancestral or other spirits, symbolic guardians of the moral order, whose
anger has inflicted punishment. But where the context of misfortune does
not elicit guilt on the part of the sufferer, then the injurious desires of
others, of evil spirits and malevolent human beings, tend to be invoked.
Where malevolence from other persons is feared, magical instrumentalities
—powers of witchcraft or sorcery—can be attributed without contradiction
from experience or in logic. Needless to say, the particular situations in
which persons consider themselves, or are considered, to be guilty and
those which arouse apprehensions of the evil intentions of others are so
judged neither abstractly nor capriciously, but in terms of accepted cultural
values and approved social conduct. Thus, as so many studies have shown,
and as is well illustrated in this volume, the reaction to misfortune and
apprehension is to take stock of the past conduct and social relations both
of those concerned and of others towards them. And, since there is always
wrongdoing to be observed, recalled, or feared, there is always opportunity
for the release of tensions by accusation and expiation or punishment,
whether through sacrifice to the supernatural custodians of moral values
and social obligations, or through denunciation of and vengeance on persons believed to be malevolent practitioners of witchcraft or sorcery.

Similarly, since there are always needs to be satisfied and doubts as to
the outcome of any venture, there is always anxiety to be stilled and assurance to be gained, whether by invoking the aid of supernatural guardians
of security and success, and thereby submitting to their authority and
accepting the code of conduct they enforce, or by seeking magical means
to harness supernatural forces that are supposed to aid men to gain their
ends. Thus the desire for protection and success where technical competence is lacking or in doubt reinforces the postulation and propitiation of
more powerful supernatural agents or the manipulation of hidden forces.

But while beliefs in supernatural action and in human ability to control
it through prayer and sacrifice, rite, and spell have their foundations in

universal features of human psychology, the forms they take, the contexts in which they are invoked, are related to the rest of the cultural pattern and to the social system. For the individual, for groups with important common interests, and for the community as a whole they are responses to the tensions and emergencies of life. Accordingly when analysed in this sense they reveal these tensions and emergencies together with the material situations and the frustrations or conflicts of values from which they arise. Furthermore, although they may not be rational and may lack empirical foundation, they must, to persist, be mutually adjusted or apportioned to different contexts of need and activity so that they do not explicitly contradict one another. Thus, collectively, they express both the general framework of ideas concerning the relations of men to one another and to the world they know and the articulation of different spheres of action and their degree of integration. Again, the extent to which cosmological ideas and social values are integrated in an explicit system affords insight into the degree of coherence of a cultural pattern and the stability of a social system, and correspondingly into the range of the repercussions and the disintegrations that are likely to follow from sudden change in any one field of social life. That there can be inconsistencies between dogma, ethic, and action in different fields will be as apparent in these studies as is the fact that cultural totalities and social systems do not automatically maintain equilibrium. The capacity for overall adjustment may well be exceeded by the impact of new forces, and it is to be expected that changes affecting techniques or the organization of society will be reflected in the spheres of cosmology and ethics.

III

Neither direct field observation nor the comparative study of the cosmologies and ritual patterns of African peoples are yet sufficiently advanced to attempt their systematic analysis and classification. We hope, however, that the studies presented here will afford material for a deeper understanding both of the religious ideas and social values which are widespread in Africa and also of the diversity of outlook that has existed among African peoples. This diversity is as understandable as it is obvious once it is realized that, although they have lived within the bounds of what western geographers have recognized as a single and distinct continent, and all derive in part from one branch of the human race, the geographical and cultural horizons of the hundreds of distinct African peoples were, until less than a century ago, necessarily restricted to small regions. And among these small, largely self-contained regions, the conditions of life, the material equipment, the accessibility to external influences of the various peoples have often been widely divergent. This will be immediately apparent, when, for example, the outlook of the Lele hunters of the forest margins of the Congo is contrasted with that of the Lovedu of the steppes of Southern Africa. Even among so distinctive a series of peoples as the cattle-keepers of Eastern Africa, nearly all of whom have acquired and preserved a common substratum of economic attachment and mystical attitudes towards their livestock, the social values actually associated with cattle differ greatly. As the studies in this volume show, the role of cattle in cult and their meaning in social relations are not the same for a Shilluk, for a Tutsi aristocrat, for a Hutu client, or for a chief or a commoner among the Lovedu.

The selection of African peoples represented here cannot claim to include or to distinguish a comprehensive range of indigenous African societies. No single cultural classification can take account of all the many variations in environment, economy, social structure, and ritual pattern. Further, any choice has, in practice, to depend on the availability of field studies germane to the questions under discussion.

It has, however, been possible to include accounts of peoples who not only differ widely from one another in their ways of life, but, taken together, illustrate the salient variations in the patterns of African life and the differences in outlook and social values that stem from them.

The interaction between the material and social conditions of life and their religious expression is analysed for two very different types of autonomous village communities in the African forests: the Lele of the Kasai and the Mende of Sierra Leone. In the small Lele communities, widely scattered in the forest, the age-old collective hunt, despite its meagre contribution to the food supply, has remained the repository of ritual values and, as Mrs. Douglas shows, the apparently unintended means of securing order and solidarity among the floating population of the village. Among the Mende, with a warrior tradition of raiding and slave-holding, a higher density of population, and greater stability of settlement, hierarchically ordered associations for men and for women support a secular chiefship and the patriarchal authority of the heads of large households in the organization of a more productive economy. The far-reaching effects on social attitudes and religious cults of the development in such forest regions of considerable states with centralized political institutions are exemplified in the Ashanti of the Gold Coast and the Fon of Dahomey.

Some of the wide variations in social organization and cultural values that exist among the cattle-keeping peoples of the grasslands of eastern Africa already referred to are to be seen in the studies of the Shilluk of the Upper Nile, the Kingdom of Ruanda, the Abaluiya in Kavirondo, and the Lovedu of the Transvaal. The Shilluk present a variant of the pastoral Nilotic culture pattern in which patrilineal kinship is the organizing principle for the many activities and interrelations of the local communities. But these people living along the banks of the Upper Nile are, as Dr. Lienhardt shows, unified by their beliefs concerning a first mythical being whose successors as sacred kings are believed to contribute powerfully to the harmony of society and the beneficence of nature on which pasture and crops depend. In Ruanda, as in several other great chiefdoms of the

Great Lakes Plateau of East Africa, where control of cattle has been a privilege of rank and a means whereby an aristocracy could organize labour and supplies on a considerable scale and thus maintain a centralized state, the notions of a good life for aristocrat and commoner differ as widely from those of the Shilluk as from those of the Abaluiya of Kavirondo, who never came under the control of a cattle-monopolizing aristocracy.

Beliefs and moral values operative in the comparatively long established and stable chiefdom of the Lovedu, as presented by Professor and Mrs. Krige, show how the patterns of mutual obligation among kinsfolk living or intermarrying in small communities can be extended to link together on kinship principles large bodies of originally separate people. The chiefship itself is conceived in terms of rights to receive and give women in marriage throughout the chiefdom. Girls of one group are fictionally married to the chief or chieftainess who then gives them in marriage to men of other groups thereby linking all districts to the chiefship by marriage and kinship. Thus basic domestic sanctions arising from the individual's need for support and approval among his kin are effectively extended to society at large, so that co-operative, unaggressive attitudes, which embody readiness to make compromises and to share benefits with others, are the qualities generally admired; and these qualities are, as far as possible, induced in the individual through fear of sickness or misfortune caused by the anger of his ancestors, the sorcery of his fellows, or conviction as a witch or sorcerer if he departs grossly from this norm.

Belief in the power of the chief to secure the beneficence of cosmic forces for the people—a notion which has been already noted among the Shilluk and is generally fundamental among the Southern Bantu—here takes on a special quality which reflects these conceptions of social relations. The Lovedu chief—the Rain-Queen—does not, as among some Southern Bantu peoples, stand apart as the possessor of a magically acquired power. Her power, we are told, is inherent in her position as one of a long line of ancestors to whom all Lovedu conceive themselves to be collaterally related; thus the 'establishment' of the seasons every year and the procuring of rain, which, as a source of moisture for crops and herbage, symbolizes general security, are regarded as the natural function and duty of the chief.

The account of the Dogon by Professor Griaule and Dr. Dieterlen concerns a culture very different in orientation. It affords an insight into one variant of the intricate cosmological ideas associated with the organization of husbandry and crafts which, with a ritually elaborate ordering of social relations, characterizes the many peoples who are heirs of the pre-Islamic civilization of the Western Sudan. Many of these fundamental ideas and ritual elements, as is evident from the accounts of belief and ceremony among the Ashanti and the Fon, are also found in the more complex societies of the forest lands of the Guinea Coast.

In his study of Dahomey, M. Mercier is able to show how remarkably the special features of the Dahomean pantheon and the role of ritual in social life were adjusted to the political and economic characteristics of this military kingdom, built up from the sixteenth century in the hinterland of one of the active trading areas of the Guinea Coast. Dahomey retained in its religious beliefs and cult forms many features, such as the androgynous or twin creators and the personification in *Dã* of a creative agent manifest in all vitality, that are widespread in West Africa. At the same time the military, bureaucratic, and commercial emphasis in its organization and the ethnic and economic diversity of its populations are reflected in special characteristics. Thus, the cosmological formulations vary according to ethnic groups or priesthoods; particular cults are given special status within a general but flexible scheme of creation; the political structure is reflected in the royal control of the many local cult organizations of priests and their devotees and in the insistence on the primacy of the royal cult in recurrent festivals. Notable also is the Dahomean attitude of acceptance towards the unforeseeable and the new, and their apparent readiness to adjust to new contacts and opportunities by innovation and assimilation in the field of belief and ritual. The Dahomean kingship and the cult of the royal ancestor harnessed underlying metaphysical notions of Fon religion to the prestige of the line of warrior adventurers and organizers. The spiritual power of the king as a moulder and supporter of the state is, for example, equated with that of the spirit *Dã* in building and sustaining the universe, and the dualistic doctrines embodied in the pantheon are reiterated in the ritual and in the organization of the court and government.

Thus, besides showing how different orientations in the means of livelihood are reflected in religious attitudes and codes of social obligation, these studies afford insight into the way in which differences in the type of political institutions affect the outlook of African peoples. Where, as among the Banyarwanda, the Lovedu, the Ashanti, and the Fon, there is a considerable concentration of power and a concomitant hierarchy of authority, beliefs concerning the role of the individual in society differ markedly from those found among such peoples as the Shilluk, the Lele, or the Abaluiya, in which political relations are those of give and take within and between kin- and residence-groups and where sex, age, and personality rather than inherited rank or appointed status determine the respect accorded to the individual. Among some African peoples as, for instance, the Shilluk or the Ashanti described here, the individual is offered security and protection by a dominant tribal or state cult which sanctions right conduct in all social relations and subordinates or curbs other magical or religious activities. Among others—for example, the Abaluiya and the Lele—although the pattern of belief concerning supernatural forces or personalities may be common to the people as a whole, the ritual units may be confined, according to context, to the household, kin-group, or local community. Although ancestral beings are believed to protect the living and sanction their conduct, these are not the ancestors of the tribe as a whole or of a royal line, but those of the several bodies of kin, each of which ascribes power and authority to its own. Belief and ritual tend, in other words, to mirror the scale and degree of social integration. The greater the economic self-sufficiency and the political freedom of action of localized groups, the greater the segmentation of ritual activity and the particularity of the objects of worship. On the other hand, the closer the integration of economic activity and of social control among such groups, the more extensive socially and the more firmly interconnected are the basic concepts and ritual forms.

IV

It has not been possible in this book to attempt the complex task of describing and analysing the multifarious social changes and the transformations of beliefs and morals that are so marked a feature of Africa today. But the study is of value, both scientifically and practically, for its portrayal of some of the backgrounds and points of departure from which African peoples are now making the extensive and often difficult cultural and social adjustments demanded by their progressive integration into the western world. And we hope that it will be of service, not only to those who are concerned with scientific problems in anthropology, but also to the growing number of people who are occupied in various ways with social and economic affairs in Africa today. Only a few of those who, as administrators, teachers, technical advisers, or traders, are participating in the economic and political transformation of Tropical Africa that has been going forward at an increasing rate over the last twenty-five years, have had any opportunity of living with Africans in their own communities and acquiring, through day-to-day experience of village life or chiefly courts, an appreciation of the attitudes and underlying beliefs which African peoples bring with them when they come under the influence of western institutions. The boy or girl going to a mission school, the youth who progresses to a college, the migrant labourer on farm or mine, the man who receives technical training in agriculture or forestry, the store clerk and the lawyer— all these, as well as their far more numerous fellows who have remained in their villages, bring to their manipulation of western tools and practice of western routines a background of ideas inculcated in childhood through their tribal culture. There can, as this book will show, be no single 'blueprint' that will apply directly to all African cultures and there is correspondingly no short way to the understanding of particular peoples. There are, however, recurrent themes and a number of main patterns of activity and interconnexion which are valuable guides to this understanding, and these are exemplified here.

THE LELE OF KASAI

By MARY DOUGLAS

THE Lele[1] are the western neighbours of the Bushongo[2] in the south-west of the Belgian Congo. The population of 20,000 has a density of about four to the square mile, but the total density of the district they inhabit is doubled by recent immigrants of the Luba and Cokwe tribes. The region is bounded on the north and east by the Kasai river, whose tributary, the Lumbundji, divides it into eastern and western sub-regions, each a separate chiefdom. It is with the western sub-region, lying between the Loange and the Lumbundji, that I am familiar and from which my observations are drawn. However, what I have learnt in the west is probably true also of the easterly chiefdom, which shares similar ecological conditions. There is a third group of Lele living to the south, whose country is predominantly savannah, instead of mixed savannah and forest. It is unlikely that my observations about the western Lele apply also to these southerners.

Lele country is at the extreme edge of the equatorial forest belt,[3] hence the great change of scene in the 150 miles from north to south. The Nkutu, their northern neighbours on the other bank of the Kasai, inhabit dense forest. Their southern neighbours, the Njembe, live in rolling grassland. Lele country has thickly forested valleys separated by barren grass-topped hills.

It is useless to discuss any aspect of Lele religion without first summarizing the material conditions of their life. This is not because these seem to have determined the bias of their religious thinking. On the contrary, the manner in which they have chosen to exploit their environment may well be due to the ritual categories through which they apprehend it.

Material Environment and Economy

A straightforward account of Lele material culture would not give the impression that hunting is their most important activity. By comparison with the Cokwe hunters, who have immigrated from the Kwango district into Lele country, they even seem inefficient in this pursuit. On the contrary, the culture of the raffia palm would seem to be their most vital economic activity, and if their ritual values were derived from their social and economic values, then we would expect the Lele religion to be centred

---

[1] The field-work on which this chapter is based was carried out under the auspices of the International African Institute and the Institut de la Recherche Scientifique en Afrique Centrale in 1949–50. For choice of tribe and much valuable advice I am indebted to Mr. G. Brausch, Administrateur Territorial in the Congo Belge.

[2] Described by Torday, 1908, *Les Bushongo*.

[3] J. P. Harroy, *Afrique, terre qui meurt*, 1944, p. 119.

round the cultivation of the raffia palm. Yet this is not so. Again, assuming that a people long settled[1] in their environment normally exploit it to the full, it is difficult to see why the Lele refuse to breed goats and pigs (which thrive locally), and why the cultivation of groundnuts is left entirely to the women. These problems find some solution, however, when they are seen in the context of their metaphysical assumptions and religious practice.

The Lele village, a compact square of 20 to 100 huts, is always set in the grassland. From each corner of the village, paths run down to the nearest part of the forest. They wind first through groves of palms which ring the village round, and then through the grass and scrub. The palm groves give shade to the men working at their weaving-looms. Each corner of the village belongs to one of the four men's age-sets, which has its own groves adjacent to its row of huts. Alternating with the men's groves are other groves used by their women-folk for pounding grain. Farther away still is another ring of groves where the women prepare palm-oil. The layout of the village shows a deliberate separation of the sexes. In all their work, feeding, and leisure, the women are set apart from the men. This separation of the sexes is a formality which they observe, a rule of social etiquette, not a natural principle derived from the nature of the work they perform, for in many of their economic activities there is a close collaboration between men and women. The separation and interdependence of the sexes is a basic theme of their social organization and ritual, and one which is reiterated in almost every possible context.

Their staple food is maize, cultivated in the forest by slash and burn methods. With such a scattered population no land shortage is recognized and no crop rotation is practised. Maize is only planted once in a forest clearing, and fresh clearings are made each year for the new crop.[2] The original clearing is kept open for several years, until the other crops planted in it have matured. The most important of these is raffia palm, and in recent years manioc has become nearly as important as maize. Small quantities of pineapples, red peppers, and hill rice are also cultivated.

The palm takes four or five years to mature, and is very carefully cultivated. All its products are used; its main ribs for hut wall and roof supports, its fibres as string in hut building and basketry, its smaller ribs as arrow shafts, its outside leaves as thatching for the walls and roofs of huts. The

[1] Torday considered the Bushongo and Lele to have been settled in their present home for many centuries and I found no evidence to conflict with his view in the ethnographic literature on the area, except in Dekerken, *Ethnie Mongo*, pp. 210, 261. See also Verhulpen, *Baluba et Balubaïsés*, pp. 51, 52. According to Dekerken the Bushongo and Lele chiefdoms were founded 150 years ago by conquerors from the north-east related to the Dekese and other Mongo. If this were so one would expect close political and cultural links to be still maintained between the Lele and their northern neighbours, but they regard the latter, whom they term collectively 'Nkutu', with mixed fear and contempt as having an alien and savage culture. It is more likely that their environment itself has changed in the last 100 years as there is evidence that the savannah has encroached considerably on the forest. See Harroy, op. cit.

[2] I speak of traditional methods only. The Administration now encourages two yearly sowings of maize in each clearing.

inner cuticle of the young leaf is the material from which they weave their raffia cloths. Finally, one of the most valued products of the palm is the unfermented wine, which forms the second staple article of diet. When the wine is all drawn off and the palm dead, its rotting stem harbours grubs which are a highly prized delicacy. When they have grown fat, and can be heard moving inside the stem, it is chopped open, and made to yield its last product.

This list of the uses of the raffia palm does not yet give an idea of its full importance in Lele culture. The Lele pride themselves on their skill in weaving, and despise the neighbouring Cokwe, Nkutu, and Dinga who are ignorant of the art, and who exchange their products for woven squares. The Dinga give fish, the Nkutu give lengths of red camwood, the Cokwe give meat in exchange. Although every Lele man can weave, they also use the woven squares among themselves as a kind of currency. There is no object which has not its fixed price in raffia squares—two for an arrow-head, two for a basket, one for a standard lump of salt. Moreover, they are required as marriage gifts, fifty to the father and forty to the mother of the bride. They are expected as mourning gifts, demanded in initiation fees, apprenticeship dues, fines, and payment for medical services. For diet, clothes, huts, and ceremonial gifts this is a culture heavily dependent on the raffia palm.

The palm and the banana are the only crops which, although they grow best in the forest's rich soil, are also planted around the village. Apart from these, and the groundnut, all good things come out of the forest: water, firewood, salt, maize, manioc, oil,[1] fish, and animal flesh.

The division of labour is based mainly on two principles. The first is that work which relates to cookery and the preparation of food is performed by women. They draw water, gather firewood, cultivate fish-ponds in the marshy streams, cultivate salt-yielding plants, and prepare salt from the ashes. They are excluded from certain other tasks for which they are held to lack the necessary skill, strength, or courage. On these grounds hunting and everything to do with the weapons and medicines of the hunt are men's work, although women cook the meat. Women cannot climb trees, so cutting oil-palm fruits and drawing palm wine, and preparing all the products of the raffia palm are men's tasks. All the complicated process of preparing raffia and setting up the looms, weaving, and sewing is performed by men, although there is no prejudice against a man's wife or sister helping if she is able. The men cut down the trees for the maize clearings, and are aided by their women-folk who clear away the undergrowth, and later take on most of the work of keeping the crops clear of weeds. Women help with the planting and undertake all the harvesting of crops.

From this it is clear that the division of labour is based on practical considerations, men and women taking their appropriate share of the burden.

[1] The Elaïs palm from which oil is made grows in natural plantations in the forest. The Lele do nothing to cultivate it.

Both are required to spend the major part of their time in the forest. Apart from the clearing and planting of crops there, which men and women share together, the time the men spend hunting and seeing to the raffia palms i paralleled by the time the women spend tending their salt and fish-ponds chopping firewood, fetching water, and washing their manioc. If the women did not work in the forest the economic life of the village would collapse. Yet the Lele regard the forest as almost exclusively a male sphere and women are frequently prohibited from entering it. On every third day they are excluded from the forest and must lay in their supplies of food firewood, and water the day before. On all important religious occasions such as mourning, birth of twins, appearance of the new moon, departure of a chief, in menstruation and childbirth, they are similarly excluded from the forest until proper rites have been performed by the men. This exclusion of women from the forest is one of the principal recurring themes of their religious practice.

The Forest

The prestige of the forest is immense. The Lele speak of it with almost poetic enthusiasm. God gave it to them as the source of all good things They often contrast the forest with the village. In the heat of the day, when the dusty village is unpleasantly hot, they like to escape to the cool an dark of the forest. Work there is full of interest and pleasure, work else where is drudgery. They say, 'Time goes slowly in the village, quickly i the forest.' Men boast that in the forest they can work all day without feel ing hunger, but in the village they are always thinking about food. For going into the forest they use the verb *nyingena*, to enter, as one might speak of entering a hut, or plunging into water, giving the impression that the regard the forest as a separate element.

But as well as being the source of all good things the forest is a place of danger, not only for women at the specified times but often for men. No mourner may enter the forest, nor one who has had a nightmare. A ba dream is interpreted as a warning not to enter the forest on the next day All kinds of natural dangers may hurt the man who disregards it. A tree may fall on his head, he may twist his ankle, cut himself with a knife, fall of a palm-tree, or otherwise suffer a fatal accident. These hazards exist at a times, but the risk on certain occasions is that inimical powers may direct them against him. The danger for a man is one of personal mishap, but woman who breaks the injunction against entering the forest may endang the whole village.

These risks, personal or general, can be warded off, or afterward remedied, by means of sacred medicines, which give men power to domi nate their environment, heal sickness, make barren women conceive, an make hunting successful. There seem therefore to be three distinct reason for the great prestige of the forest: it is the source of all good and necessa things, food, drink, huts, clothes; it is the source of the sacred medicine nd, thirdly, it is the scene of the hunt, which in Lele eyes is the supremely important activity. At this stage of description it would seem that two of these reasons are economic, not religious, but further examination shows that in reality the immense importance of the forest is derived from its role in Lele religion.

The attitude to hunting cannot be entirely ascribed to the importance of meat in Lele diet, although it is true that they have a craving for meat. Cooked maize, or manioc dough, would be unpalatable unless served with the appetizing sauces prepared daily by the women from vegetables, red pepper, salt, and oil. A purely vegetable diet is so much disliked that unless meat or fish can be served as well, people often prefer to drink palm wine and sleep unfed. Mushrooms, caterpillars, grubs, &c. are poor substitutes for fish, and even fish is second in their esteem to meat. In their ideal life the men would set traps and hunt regularly to provide their families with a daily supply of meat. To offer a vegetable meal to a guest is regarded as a grave insult. Much of their conversation about social events dwells on the amount and kind of meat provided.

The craving for meat has never led the Lele to breed goats and pigs, as do their southern neighbours, the Njembe. They profess to be revolted at the notion of eating animals reared in the village. Good food, they say, should come out of the forest, clean and wholesome, like antelope and wild pig. They consider rats and dogs to be unclean food, to which they apply the word *hama*, used also for the uncleanness of bodily dirt, suppurating wounds, and excreta. The same uncleanness attaches to the flesh of goats and pigs, just because they are bred in the village. Even plants which are used in sauces when gathered in the forest are left untouched if they grow near the village. This attitude does not seem to apply to poultry. Between men various social conventions cluster around the giving and receiving of chickens, but women are forbidden to eat their flesh or eggs. This prohibition, like most food taboos, is unexplained, but there may be greater danger to women from eating unclean food than for men, as in many contexts women are treated as if they were more vulnerable to pollution than men are.

Knowing of their craving for meat, and knowing that recent hunts had been unsuccessful, I was puzzled early in my visit to see a large pig carcass being carved up and carried some miles for sale to Luba and Dinga tribesmen. The Lele would not eat it. A few go-ahead men keep goats or pigs, but not for food. They rear them for sale to the rich Luba lorry drivers and mechanics of the oil company at Brabanta. The Lele owners make no attempt to feed or control their livestock, which does much damage to the palms and bananas near the village. This carelessness does not result from total ignorance of rearing animals, for the Lele keep poultry and dogs successfully. In particular, the dogs are objects of an elaborate veterinary theory and practice. It seems that if they wished to make a success of goat herding they could do so.

Livestock is not the only source of meat which the Lele overlook wh
they declare that the forest is the source of all good things, for the gra
land around the village harbours quantities of game. These duikers a
eaten with relish when they are killed, but the Lele hunt them only at c
season of the year—the short dry season when the grass is burnt, and t
animals are slaughtered as they rush out of the fire. Their normal hunti
techniques are not adapted to the pursuit of grassland game.

The way in which the Lele, in speaking of the forest, disregard other i
portant sources of meat and food can be explained only in terms of t
coherence of their religious concepts. To admit an alternative supply
meat, independent of the forest game, would be inconsistent with th
attitude to the forest as the source of all the best things of life. Their vi
of the village as totally dependent on the forest is fundamental to their p
ception of the relation between human life and the natural and spiriti
powers on which they depend. Ultimately, it appears that the prestige
the forest is entirely due to its place in Lele religion. It is the source
sacred medicines, but it need not be the only source of the material thii
of life. It is the scene of the hunt, but Lele hunting has primary religi
functions which outweigh its economic importance.

The distinction of the village from the forest is one of the princi,
themes of their ritual, which is constantly emphasized and elaborat
There is also a subtle interplay between this theme and that of the sepa
tion of the sexes mentioned above. The separation of women from m
of forest from village, the dependence of village on forest, and the exclusi
of women from the forest are the principal recurring elements of th
ritual, on which minor variations are embroidered.

The Grassland

The appropriation of the forest by the men is balanced by treatment
the grassland as the exclusive sphere of women. The grassland has
prestige like the forest. It is dry and barren. The only crop which thri
there, the groundnut, is exclusively cultivated by the women. Ritual sai
tions forbid a woman who has lifted the first sod of grass on her groundr
plot to have sexual intercourse until a month or six weeks later, when t
seedlings are well established. No man must even set eyes on the work
progress, to say nothing of helping in the heavy work of cutting down t
bushy trees on the plot. This is the only crop which women tend fr
start to finish, and the only crop which does not grow in the forest.

Most activities which custom allocates entirely to one or the other s
are similarly protected by sexual taboos, some lasting even longer than t
example. No hunting expedition is undertaken without one night of cc
tinence being imposed first on the whole village. A man making pit tra
may have to abstain from sexual relations for several months until cert:
specified animals have been caught. Most situations of ritual danger affe
ing the village as a whole are treated in the same way. The refrain "Tonig

ach woman her mat alone, each man his mat alone' is a regular announcement preceding important rites.

The groundnut crop is the most striking example of the appropriation of
he grassland by the women as their sphere. They often manage to find in
he grassland some substitutes for what they cannot get on days when they
re excluded from the forest. When they may not go fishing, other delicacies
nay be gathered in the grassland: grasshoppers in the dry season, caterpillars in the wet, or grubs from decaying palms planted near the village.
A woman who has run short of firewood may collect in the grassland enough
brushwood for the day's cooking. There are no ritual prohibitions connected with the grassland. As a neutral sphere between the two it is used
again and again in the prohibitions which separate the village from the forest.

At first view I was tempted to find a natural explanation of the allocation
of male and female spheres, the forest to the men, the grassland to the
women. It is obvious that women, in spite of their economic tasks there,
are at a disadvantage in the forest. Unarmed, and loaded with baskets, they
are defenceless against strange men or wild animals. They are afraid of the
dark. They do not understand the medicines which men find there and
administer to the village. Hunting is a man's task. On the face of it there is
something appropriate in regarding the forest as primarily the sphere of
men, particularly if we associate the prestige and danger of the forest with
male domination. But these considerations in themselves do not adequately
explain the strict ritual exclusion of women on so many occasions.

A more satisfactory explanation can be given in terms of their religious
concepts, according to which women hold a very complex status. Child-
bearing, their most vital function, is regarded as highly vulnerable. On the
other hand, sexual intercourse and menstruation are dangerous to all male
activities. These contrasted themes are handled with elaborate subtlety in
the treatment of marital and extra-marital relations, which do not concern
us here. It is enough to remember the complex ritual status of women when
trying to understand the separation of the sexes and the exclusion of
women from the forest. As women are both highly vulnerable and highly
polluting some separation of male and female spheres is indicated, and the
very neutrality of the grassland makes its allocation to the women more
appropriate.

Medicine

In Lele religion nearly all important rites are associated with the practice
of medicine. The idiom of medical healing has so dominated their religious
forms that it is often hard to distinguish two separate spheres of action.
This is consistent with Lele speculations about life and death, which they
consider to be controlled exclusively by God, *Njambi*. Such power of
healing and curing barrenness as may be exercised by humans is derived
only from God. Hence, the diviners must be at the same time healers and
religious experts. Whether they are trying to cure a fever, or to set right the

relation of a village to spiritual powers, the same vocabulary is used to
describe the treatment, and the same personnel and resources are employed.
To find the cause of the disorder they first use divination; then they prescribe and apply some herbal remedy with the proper formula, and impose
a number of restrictions on the patient.

Although up to this point the vocabulary is the same, yet beneath the
general similarity two categories are distinguished. The words used by the
sick man to describe his symptoms are not used to describe the state of
the village needing medical treatment. The man says he is feverish, sick, or
weak, but of the village they say that it is bad (*bube*) or spoilt (*wonyi*). If the
man is cured he says that he is strong (*bunono*) or that he has gained vigour
(*manyin*). But a village in a sound condition is said to be soft (*bolabolu*) or
peaceful, quiet (*polo*). The word for curing a sick man is *belu*; for setting
right a disordered village, *ponga*, to mend, set straight, arrange in order.
These important verbal differences show that there is a distinction between the two situations, and it may be only by analogy that they draw on
the same vocabulary in describing the treatment given to a sick person or to
a village.

The word for rites and medicines is *nengu*, which applies equally to healing and to village ritual. The practitioner who applies the medicine or performs the rite is in either case *ngang*, which in its widest application means
only 'expert'; in its narrowest it refers to members of the group of diviners.
As individuals they have each their own practice. As a body they have a
public responsibility towards their village. They administer its *nengu* for it.

I prefer to translate *nengu* as sacred medicine, whether in its medical or
its mainly religious sense, because the Lele themselves consistently identify
rite and medicine. I should point out a distinction which they make between these sacred medicines and a range of simple remedies called *bilum-
bela*, which are used to treat minor ailments. The latter work by virtue of
their natural properties, as wine intoxicates or food nourishes. They may be
applied for headaches, constipation, coughs, and colds. Knowledge of them
carries no prestige, for they are not worth a diviner's serious attention.
Consistently with what has been said so far, these simple remedies are
applied mainly by the women, not by the men, and significantly, they are
to be found in the grassland. Sacred medicines, by contrast with women's
remedies, are found in the forest. Diviners asking for a high fee remind
their clients that their calling imposes on them arduous expeditions through
the damp undergrowth.

Unlike simples, all sacred medicines, to be effective, require prohibitions
to be imposed on the patient. Their power depends largely on the control
the diviner has over them: according to whether he has undergone the
correct initiation and paid for the power to apply them and followed the
proper restrictions himself. It depends also on the recital of an address
which adjures the medicine to do its work, and on the goodwill between
the diviner and his client.

A man under medical treatment must accept restrictions on his way of living. He may be forbidden to drink palm wine, to eat certain kinds of fish, to enter the forest, &c. If a village is undergoing a course of medicines, it is similarly put under restrictions. The character of these gives us some further insight into Lele religious ideas. The favourite themes which are used over and over again have already been indicated: the separation of the two spheres, forest and village, the separation of the sexes, women's exclusion from the forest, the association of the forest with spiritual power, the neutrality of the grassland. To the Lele their rites do not appear as a series of disconnected and meaningless acts. The very economy and repetition of the themes they draw upon produces a kind of pattern which is intelligible in terms of their assumptions about the relation of God to men and animals.

Spiritual Beings: God

In writing about God and the spirits, and the sacred medicines which draw their power from them, it is convenient to use the word 'spiritual', although I do not know of a Lele word to cover this single category of things which are not human and not animal. They frequently dwell on the distinction between humans and animals, emphasizing the superiority of the former and their right to exploit the latter. When they feel that too much is being required of them by the Administration, they like to exclaim; '*Cung bahutu i?*' 'Are we animals then?' But there is no suggestion in their speech that God and the spirits belong to either of these categories.

Of God, *Njambi*, they say that he has created men and animals, rivers and all things. The relation of God to men is like that of their owner to his slaves. He orders them, protects them, sets their affairs straight, and avenges injustice. Animals of the forest are also under God's power, though they have been given to the Lele for their food. Game protection laws enforced by the Administration strike the Lele as an impious contravening of God's act, since he originally gave all the animals in the forest to their ancestors to hunt and kill.

The third class of beings under the power of God are the spirits, *mingehe*. In talking about them the Lele are careful not to speak in anthropomorphic terms. They insist that spirits are not and never have been men. They have never been seen by men. If one were to set eyes on a spirit he would be struck blind, and die of sores. If pressed for more details they are forced to give analogies from human behaviour, but they do not like talking of the spirits. It is obvious that they are held in fear in spite of their benevolent powers.

The spirits inhabit the deep forest, especially the sources of streams. They sleep in the day, but roam about at night. Hence the need to avoid loud noises in the village at night, lest a spirit walking in the fringe of the forest hear, and be tempted to come near. The day of rest is the one time when the spirits roam abroad in daylight. Spirits suffer no death or illness.

They control the fertility of women and prosper men's hunting. Or they may withhold the game, and turn aside the hunter's arrow. They may prevent women from conceiving. They can strike a village with sickness. In all their acts they do not behave capriciously. The study of their ways is the diviner's secret lore.

This is the official view of the spirits, held by the diviners, and which influences their practice of médicine. There are also popular fancies about them, told to children, or believed by the uninitiated. The thin wreaths of mist twisting up from the forest in the early morning are said to be smoke from the night fires of the spirits. A man walking alone in strange forest at night may find his hair stiffening, his body pouring with cold sweat, his heart beating madly. He suddenly comes on a clearing, where there was a bright light. He sees a smouldering fire, but no one there... a fire of the spirits.

The diviners regard the water pigs as the animals most highly charged with spiritual power, because they spend their days wallowing in the stream sources, which are the favourite haunt of the spirits. The ordinary man thinks of the pig as a sort of dog, owned by the spirits; he lives in his master's home, sleeps and feeds with him, obeys him like a hunter's dog. The spirits punish and reward hunters by giving or withholding game, but in the single act they control opposite destinies. For while they are rewarding a hunter with game, they are punishing the animal for some disobedience to their commands.

Natural Objects Associated with Spirits

Certain animals and plants show signs that they are associated with the spirits in a particularly close way; the pig, as I have said, because he frequents the sources of streams. Certain bush bucks, because, like the spirits, they sleep all day and move at night, are spirit animals, and for that reason their flesh is forbidden to women. Fish also, because they live in streams, are associated with spirits, and are therefore prescribed or prohibited in different medicines. A pregnant woman must not eat fish. Crocodiles are the subject of some controversy among the experts. In the south they are classed with fish, because they live in water, and are therefore forbidden to pregnant women. In the north the fact that they inhabit water does not make them fish, and so here, crocodile flesh, since it can be bought and dried, is considered to be the food *par excellence* for pregnant women forbidden to eat fish.

Certain plants are either forbidden or recommended in medical treatment, because they are associated with the spirits. The banana, for example, is a plant of the spirits because, when it has been cut down, it does not die, as would a palm, but sprouts and lives again. Only spirits do not die, so this characteristic marks the banana as the proper ritual food on certain occasions. These few examples show how the animal and vegetable worlds are studied and classified according to religious categories.

Spring water and rain water are spirit things, because they are essential to life. The moon is called a spirit for two reasons. First, it seems to die, and to disappear completely, but always reappears. Second, it is associated with fertility, because by it a woman reckons the nine months of her pregnancy. They say, 'The moon brings children'. The moon therefore shares with the spirits their immortality and their control over fertility. The appearance of the new moon is treated with characteristic rites. Sexual relations are forbidden, women are not allowed to pound grain, nor to enter the forest. No one may make loud noises in the forest, such as chopping trees. The next day the men go hunting and shed the blood of an animal. The hunt may be a pure formality, the death of one squirrel suffices. Then the restrictions are lifted. This rite is performed in order that the maize crop may thrive. It is highly characteristic of the bias of the Lele culture that the only rite which they perform to prosper their staple crop is a hunting rite. The taboos accompanying it are also characteristic: taboos on sexual relations, on women entering the forest, on noisy work. Further examples will make clear how the medical prescriptions draw constantly on the simple familiar themes which have been outlined above.

Fish, when freshly taken from the stream, are treated as if charged with spiritual power, or as if there were danger in their improper handling. They figure frequently in medical advice for this reason. There is a significant rite which must be observed before any fish can be brought into the village. A woman returning from her fishing expedition in the forest first sends a child ahead into the village to fetch a firebrand. The fish touched with the fire may then be carried into the village. Her fishing-baskets may not be brought in until they have been left for a night in the grassland outside the village. Special stakes are set up at the paths leading to the forest, on which fishing-baskets are always to be seen hanging. Similar rules apply to some other forest products, creeper-ropes and withies used in basket-making, but not to meat, nor to planted products, maize, manioc, or palm wine. I do not know the basis of the distinction which treats fish and certain natural forest products as dangerous in this way, while exempting meat and planted products, but Lele ritual seems to be so consistent that deeper research would probably explain the distinction.

These are rules of everyday behaviour, but particular medicines also treat the grassland as if it were a ritually neutralizing element. For example, a woman in childbirth who confesses her adultery is held to be in mortal danger. The appropriate medicine for her case prescribes among other things that she be first carried out of the village, so that the difficult delivery takes place in grassland. When medicines are being used to establish a new village, there is a period between the setting up of the huts and the killing of certain game in the hunt, during which it is forbidden for villagers to eat in the village. They carry their food to be eaten in the grassland just outside. Examples could be multiplied.

Rules of Behaviour towards God and Spirits

Some of the stock prohibitions concern noise. Noises associated with the day are always forbidden at night: for instance, women may not pound grain after dusk. Drumming, on the other hand, is a legitimate night-time noise, and dancing does not usually take place in the day. On all important religious occasions, such as the day of rest, at the new moon, in mourning, and in villages undergoing certain medicines, pounding is completely forbidden. A mourning village goes hungry for three days, and the closest relatives of the dead may not pound grain for two or three months. Medicines sometimes forbid pounding to be done in the village, so the mortars are carried to the grassland outside. Other medicines forbid any kind of loud noise in the village at night. In such a case, were a man to let out a loud, yodelling call in the dark in the village, he would have to pay the maximum fine for spoiling the medicine. In one village a medicine required that the women should not carry their full load of firewood into their compounds, lest they drop it with a loud crash. They were obliged to drop the load in the grassland outside the village, then bring in the logs in armfuls, a few at a time.

Dance drums may not be beaten in periods of mourning. If a man dies his village does not dance for three months. On days of rest and other religious occasions, all work in the forest which involves what they call a drum-like noise is forbidden to men and women. No trees may be cut, no clearing of the forest, no chopping of wood, no opening of dead palm-trees to extract the grubs. Noisy work seems to bring the village into a dangerous relation with the forest, except on specified occasions. On ordinary days the spirits are sleeping in the farthest depths of the forest, and would not be disturbed, but on the day of rest they come out, and may be near the village. They would be angry to hear chopping sounds in the forest, or pounding in the village. On the day of rest the rules are in part reversed where drums are concerned. The spirits are then abroad in daylight as if it were night, so no workaday noise of pounding or chopping is allowed; but this is the only day when the drums may be beaten in full daylight, and everyone dances.

These examples sufficiently illustrate the themes on which the ritual idiom is based. The prohibitions are acceptable to the Lele because they relate in an intelligible way to what they know of the spiritual and natural worlds. They provide a code of behaviour for men towards God and the spirits. They introduce order into the universe; regulations distinguish the day from night, one month from another, the day of rest from working days, forest from the village, males from females. They place the whole environment in intelligible categories. These categories have unquestionable validity, because they have been proved, from the beginning of Lele times to the present day, by the working of the sacred medicines. Any particular medicine may fail, for a number of possible reasons, but the whole theory and practice of medicine is not thereby jeopardized. On the other hand, any little cure, any successful hunt, testifies to the soundness of the basic hypotheses. The rites contain in themselves the proof of their own efficacy and of the truth of the assumption on which they are based.

The various medicines bring before the mind the kind of good relations which ought to exist between the spiritual, the human, and the natural worlds. But they do more than this. As well as demonstrating order in the universe, they also provide for order in social relations. They insist on a high degree of harmony between the persons undergoing and performing the treatment.

Harmony in Human Relations

I have not said so far what kind of interest the spirits in the forest are thought to take in the affairs of men, what acts are meritorious, and what are transgressions to be punished. They uphold all the regulations which I have mentioned concerning men's relation to the spiritual: observance of the day of rest, of the food privileges of cult groups, the taboos on workaday noise at night-time, the distinction of the sexes, and of the forest from village. In the second place, they require all persons living in a village to be at peace with each other. The village faces its own forest, and through it the spiritual world, as a single whole. In this the ritual corresponds to the political situation, in which each village is autonomous and potentially at war with other villages. In religion the solidarity of each village is such that an offence by one member affects adversely the whole village, and the barrenness of a woman or the failure of an individual hunter may be attributed to the general condition of the village in which they live. This spiritual condition is constantly discussed in the terms I have given: the village is either *polo*, soft and quiet, or *bube*, bad. The exchange of greetings with a visitor usually includes a question; 'Is your village quiet?', to which the answer may be that they are in mourning for a dead person, or that they are undergoing hunting medicine, or that all is well and quiet, wild pig having recently been killed.

Good hunting is the clearest sign that all is well with the village. The small amount of meat which each man, woman, and child may receive when a wild pig is killed cannot explain the joy which is shown in talking about it for weeks afterwards. The hunt is a kind of spiritual barometer whose rise and fall is eagerly watched by the entire village. This is one of the reasons why hunting carries more prestige than any other activity.

It is impossible not to be struck by the way in which child-bearing and hunting are coupled together, as if they were equivalent male and female functions. A village which has had a long series of bad hunts will begin soon to remark how few pregnancies there have been lately, or a village suffering from an epidemic or frightened by a recent series of deaths will send for a diviner to do medicines for them, saying that the village is spoilt, hunting has failed, women are barren, everyone is dying. Diviners themselves do

not confuse the two symptoms. They perform distinct medicines for the
separate disorders, but the grateful village whose hunting has been set on a
sound basis will praise the medicine, saying, for example; 'Our village is soft
and good now. Since the diviner went home we have killed three wild pigs
and many antelopes, four women have conceived, we are all healthy and
strong.' These are the accepted signs of a generally prosperous condition.

In a small village changes in the fertility of women are not easily observed. It is by watching the hunt, in the way that the Lele do, that we can
see what kind of harmony between its members is rewarded by the spirits,
and what dissensions are punished by hunting failure.

The concept of peace within the village receives a profound interpretation. The success of the hunt requires that internal solidarity be real in the
fullest sense. Bloodshed, striking of blows, tearing of hair, scratching, or
any violence spoils the village, but so also do hard words and insults.
Whether the offender is a resident or a temporary visitor makes no difference. Villagers naturally resent violent behaviour by outsiders more acutely
than they mind quarrels between residents. On the other hand, within the
village itself the higher the ritual status of the persons quarrelling, the
more fatal their ill will may be. The officially appointed diviner of the village
may spoil it by a rebuke to his wife, whereas a more open show of anger
from an ordinary man might escape notice. The village seems to be specially
sensitive to any breach of marital peace. A wife who runs away in anger,
even if she returns penitent the same evening, has spoilt the village, and
both she and her husband owe a fine before hunting can be resumed. The
anger of an old man, whether just or unprovoked, is highly dangerous. A
simple rite performed usually before any hunt illustrates their interpretation of ritual peace. Each man, as he sets out, takes the matchet or knife
from his girdle and gives it silently to his neighbour, who completes the
exchange with his own knife. The meaning of this action is explained as if
one were saying: 'My age-mate, you take the matchet with which I may
have been hitting my wife', and the other replying: 'And you take my knife,
in case I have struck my children with it.' At the end of the hunt the
weapons are returned to their owners, for the need for covering all secret
breaches of peace is over.

Organization of Villages

Village solidarity is evidently a major preoccupation. This is intelligible
in view of the lack of strong internal village organization. Although the village is united politically against all other villages, and although it acts as a
single unit in face of the supernatural, yet, apart from their religious institutions, it is difficult to see any underlying principle which is capable of
producing this unity.

The men of the village belong to age-sets, but these do not perform any
obvious function in regulating village life. They are the basis of a form of
gerontocracy. Old men of the senior sets enjoy considerable prestige, but

they only dominate the village in subtle, unformalized ways, through esoteric knowledge, and reputation as sorcerers. The principle of seniority is carried so far that it even prevents any strong leadership emerging in the person of the village chief. The man who carries this title is qualified by being the oldest man in the village. Since by definition he is approaching senility, he has little real power.

There is no centre of authority in the village and, moreover, it is customary to avoid public responsibility. Most men shun conspicuous roles for fear of exciting jealousy. The Lele ideal of a man fitted to hold public office is not a dominating personality, but one who is modest, gentle, self-effacing. There are several posts in the village to which young men of this character are appointed, by the old men in some cases, by their age-mates in others, but they are junior executives of the village and not in any way its leaders.

To make internal cohesion more unlikely the population of the village fluctuates constantly. Of twenty or more men in the oldest age-sets, only two or three will have been born in the village. Every ten or fifteen years the village itself changes its site. There is no closely knit kin group forming the core of the village. The matrilineal clans are weak and scattered, and a man's tie with his father's people generally lasts only during the father's lifetime. From the standpoint of social organization alone it is surprising that such a heterogeneous collection of people can form a village highly conscious of its identity, and capable of carrying on historic feuds with other villages. Their very real corporate unity evidently derives from their religious institutions, and from the way these are related to the communal hunt.

Hunting: a Communal Activity

It is the communal hunt, and not the private hunter's or trapper's success, which is the anxiously scanned indication of spiritual health. The method is to set a cordon of men armed with bows and arrows around a section of the forest, which is then combed by beaters and their dogs. Young boys and old men who can barely walk try to join the hunt, but the most valued members are the dog-owners, who have the heavy work of scrambling through the undergrowth, shouting to control and encourage their dogs. The game startled by them rushes out on to the arrows of the waiting hunters. This is probably the most effective method of hunting in dense forest. It depends on surprising the game and on quick shooting at very short range.

What is strange in a people proud of their hunting is the general lack of individual skills. A man going into the forest for any purpose carries his bow and a few arrows, but these are intended for birds or squirrels. He does not expect to take large game by himself. They know none of the specialized techniques of the single hunter. They do not stalk, do not know how to imitate the calls of animals, do not camouflage or use decoys, seldom penetrate into deep forest alone. All their interest is centred on the communal hunt. I was often struck by the lack of confidence an individual hunter would have in his own aim. A range of 40 feet or more is outside their power, and they expect to hit at 10 or 15 feet. A man walking in the forest might come on a herd of pig wallowing in a marsh, creep up to them so close as to hear their breathing, then, rather than risk a long shot, he will tiptoe away agog to call out the village.

These weaknesses of the Lele style of hunting I attribute to their having specialized in techniques suited to the dense forest. Their inefficiency is noticeable by comparison with the Cokwe hunters, who are immigrants from true savannah country, and have what I suppose must be the characteristic skills of savannah hunting. They hunt in pairs or singly, stalk and call their game, and have such success that they decimate the animals of the forest in a few months. Admittedly, the Cokwe have for many generations been used to firearms, since the Portuguese used them as slave raiders, whereas very few Lele villages possess more than two or three guns.

The Lele have specialized in the communal hunt of the forest to such a degree that they only hunt the grassland when the same techniques are applicable, that is, in the dry season when they fire the grass. On this annual occasion several villages combine to ring around the burning countryside. This is the time when young boys expect to make their first kill, for the slaughter, I am told, is terrific.[1] This is the only occasion when the hunting unit is more than the male population of one village, as it is in all forest hunting. Ultimately the village is a political and a ritual unit because it is a single hunting unit. It is not surprising that the Lele think of theirs as a hunting culture first and foremost.

An account of a month's wet season hunting in one village will illustrate the points which have been discussed so far. Unfortunately, the period covered by the hunting journal gives a poor impression both of their skill in the hunt and of the efficacy of their medicine. It is only fair to mention that a party of Cokwe hunters had been for the previous three months staying in the village, killing the animals and selling the meat to the villagers at exorbitant prices. Finally, their funds of cash were as depleted as the game in the forest, and they chased the Cokwe away from the village when bargaining for lower prices had failed. However, for the purpose of illustrating an account of their ritual, a series of bad hunts is more illuminating than successful ones.

A village has sometimes to undergo a long course of medicine, extending over several months. At various stages of the performance a specified kill may be required. Until the pig or the right type of antelope is brought home and the dedicated parts eaten by the appropriate cult group, the medicines cannot be continued. An example of such a series of medicines is the one called *Kinda*, which is usually set up in a village after it has been

---

[1] This form of hunt has now been ended by the Administration, in an effort to stop erosion of the land and extinction of the game.

moved to a new site. It ensures fertility for the women and good hunting. In these medicines the hunt becomes an essential part of the ritual which makes for the prosperity of the village.

Hunting Journal[1] *of Yenga-Yenga.*[2] February–March 1950

18 February. Fruitless hunt. The failure was generally attributed to the refusal on the eve of the hunt of one of the diviners, Ngondu, a fiery tempered man, to co-operate with his colleagues. In the middle of their consultation he had suddenly burst out complaining that his wife's groundnuts had been stolen, and that when the Administration came to inspect the crop he would be sent to prison, though it was no fault of his that an enemy had stolen them. He flung out of the meeting and someone whispered: 'See the diviner is spoiling the village.' The hunt was fruitless, in spite of the medicines prepared.

19 February. The whole day was taken up in discussing the cause of failure. Ngondu's sister's son, who had overheard the whisper against his uncle, told him that he was suspected of having spoilt the hunt. Quarrelling went on in the centre of the village about this, Ngondu shouting with tears of rage that he was the injured party. He brought up all his old grievances: one of his wives had died the year before, allegedly killed by the poison of the catechist. Ngondu had actually been building her a new hut, and its unfinished framework still stood in the village. He declared that every time he saw it he felt bitter in his heart, for no food cooked by his remaining wives tasted so sweet to him as hers. This brought up all his concentrated dislike of the catechist. Now his other wife was in distress because her child had been beaten for playing truant from the catechism class. If this were reported to the missionary he, Ngondu, would be sent to prison, and for none of his own fault. And not for the first time. He could not speak the language of the white men, and did not understand their ways, so it was he, and no others who got sent to prison for avoiding road-corvée work, when others had been slacker than he. And so on. He brought up complicated histories reaching far back into the past. His friends tried to calm him, his enemies insisted that none of this was a reason for spoiling the hunting medicines; a diviner should feel more responsibility for his village. Finally, the matter was settled by a summing-up from a visitor, Bikwak, a famous diviner, who had been invited from another village to set up the *Kinda*, the fertility medicine which every new village should have. He suggested that the matter be dropped; Ngondu was in the wrong in having left the diviners' meeting in a rage, but he had been sorely provoked by the theft of his wife's

---

[1] For translating the Lele names for animals I am much indebted to Mr. J. Jobaert, who has been for many years game-warden in the Kasai region, and to Mr. H. Hoofd, Administrator of Basongo, who obtained Luba translations for most of the Lele words. As the result depends on translation through three languages, there is a wide margin of uncertainty for which they are not in any way responsible.

[2] Yenga-Yenga is the name given by the Administration to the southernmost of three villages called Homba.

groundnuts. No one knew who had stolen them. Perhaps it was some un-thinking child. Let the matter rest there.

20 February. Bikwak, the visiting diviner, together with two important local diviners, Ngondu and Nyama, prepared the medicine for the next day's hunt. In the night Bikwak sang in a trance, during which he was visited by spirits, who told him where game would be found the next day.

21 February. The medicines were finished at dawn. Bikwak, as superin-tending diviner, directed the hunters where to go, but he had to stay in the village all day. Women were forbidden to pound grain or to cut wood until he gave the all-clear.

The kill was disappointing: one little blue duiker and one red duiker. In all, seven antelopes had been put up by the dogs, so the spirits had not deceived Bikwak. The village was undoubtedly spoilt, as they had only killed two instead of seven.

At night Bikwak sang again, and divined in his singing the cause of the failure to kill seven animals. The spirits were protesting at the prolonged absence of the *Kinda* medicine in the village. The village was over two years old, but after the *Kinda* had originally been set up with full rites by Nyama, it had been maliciously stolen by an unknown thief. The catechists and the young Christians of the village had been suspect. Bikwak learnt in the night's trance that it had been stolen by the men of Hanga, a rival village, which had been defeated in war many years ago by Yenga-Yenga and which, ever since, had been trying to be revenged by underhand means. Hunting would continue to fail so long as the *Kinda* was not set up. So they began at once to make preparations for it.

24 February. Bikwak sang again in the night, after announcing that men and women should sleep apart, as next day there would be hunting.

25 February. In the morning he streaked each man's leg with charcoal and white clay. But it rained, and the hunt was postponed. As the medicine for the new *Kinda* had been started, no visitors were allowed to eat in the vil-lage. A man and his wife from Mbombe were turned away, as, if they had taken food, they would have had to spend the night in the village. Taking food in the village brings the stranger under the full ritual prohibition affecting residents. Were he to eat, then go away, and have sexual relations while the village was still under the ban, he would be charged with having spoilt the medicine and be obliged to pay a heavy fine.

26 February. The hunt was successful. One blue duiker, one red duiker, and one big yellow-backed duiker. Bikwak ordered that the backs, heads, feet, and intestines should be set aside to be eaten by the cult groups of the village.

28 February. Bikwak still needed wild pig before he could proceed with the next step in the *Kinda* medicines. He announced that today everyone must get on with their usual work, for tomorrow he would send the men off on a hunt.

In the afternoon a bloody fight broke out between two road-menders and their wives. As the villagers gathered to watch the fight, the scratching and tearing of women's hair and head-wounds, nose-bleeding and insults, they were unanimous in their indignation: 'Fancy spoiling the village for other people! Disgusting! They are ruining tomorrow's hunt.' After the fight Bikwak, with the other diviners, ordered a fine of two raffia cloths and a chicken from the initiators of hostilities. They pleaded for time to pay. In order not to delay the hunt the village went bail for them, notching the ears of a goat in token of their payment. Bikwak did new medicine to cancel the effects of the fight, and announced in the evening: 'Tonight each woman her mat, each man his mat. Tomorrow we hunt.'

1 March. Rain. No hunt. The fighters were reported to the Tribunal, and taken away by the police. At night, Bikwak again announced: 'Woman, her mat, man, his mat.' &c.

2 March. Rain. No Hunt. Announced: 'Woman, her mat, man, his mat,' &c.

3 March. Hunt: killed three: one red duiker, one blue duiker, one bay duiker. No pig killed. At this hunt they drew cover four times:

1st draw. Blank. Consultation held. Agreed that the village must still be spoilt by the road-menders' fight. The fine asked could not have been heavy enough for so much violence. In token of a bigger fine, one man gave his matchet to another.

2nd draw. Blank again.

3rd draw. They put up an antelope, one man shot and wounded it, another fired his gun and killed it.

4th draw. One blue duiker killed, one bay duiker.
End of hunt. Still no pig. At this stage, Bikwak, the diviner in charge, went away temporarily, and the medicines were suspended until his return.

5 March. A hunt without medicines, undertaken because they wanted to taste meat. One red duiker only killed. This time failure to kill more was not ascribed to moral or religious conditions. The two best dog-owners were absent, and neither of their two juniors knew the forest so well. Several animals had been put up by the dogs, but had slipped between the waiting hunters. Too many were missing for the communal hunt to be effective. A thunderstorm finally broke up the hunt, and they decided to postpone further attempts until the leading dog-owner returned.

10 March. The leading dog-owner returned, so they went hunting. Nothing to do with medicine, just to chase up some little blue duikers for food. No game.

16 March. Wild pig spoor reported very near the village. The men went off quickly. A fruitless expedition, the pig had passed by in the night. A few young men were in favour of going on in the hope of rounding up some little blue duikers. Then one of the dogs fell suddenly sick, and the owner had to prepare medicines for it. As the dog looked like dying, the hunt was abandoned.

18 March. Another impromptu hunt. A man reported fresh wild pig tracks. The men were called in from their work. They met at the grove of one of the chief diviners, Ngondu. The plan of the hunt was decided upon. Then a matter was raised by one of the other diviners. He mentioned the rumour that when Bikwak, the visiting diviner, had been at work, he had not been given the help of his colleagues of the village. Was it right that he should have been left to collect medicines by himself? Was it true? In reply Ngondu asked scornfully, when was a visiting diviner ever left unaided? Of course they had all collaborated. Another diviner suggested that the rumour might have arisen because Bikwak had sent one of them to look for herbs in one direction, the other in another direction, and had set off himself in a third, so giving the impression of working alone. This settled the matter, and the man who had raised it took one of the dog bells, and breathed over it, in sign of goodwill. He then swopped his matchet with that of Ngondu and the hunt moved off.

No kill, as the herd of pig had escaped behind the place where the dogs were sent in.

23 March. Bikwak still absent. A local diviner, Nyama, prepared hunting medicines in the evening. He shouted his orders: no one was to sleep on Cokwe woven mats, but only on traditional Lele beds; no one to sleep in European blankets; no one to smoke European cigarettes or to wear European clothes, only Lele raffia loin-cloths; each man to sleep on his mat alone, each woman alone. Next morning at dawn, before the hunt, they were all to meet and to bring up their grievances, lest any secret grudge should spoil the hunt.

24 March. At the meeting, the first man called upon to speak was the village chief. A few days ago, on the morning of the impromptu hunt (18th), the tax-collectors and policemen were going away, and ordered him to provide men to carry their boxes. Just before the hunt the village chief went round pathetically pleading for volunteers. The young men laughed at his anxiety, and promised that after the hunt they would carry the luggage. But when they got back they said they were too tired, and would first sit down and rest. The village chief, though goaded by the police, could persuade no one. Finally, in despair, though so weak in the knees that he could hardly walk, he and his nearest age-mate (nearly as decrepit as himself, and even more a by-word for senility) prepared to lift the load themselves. Loudly complaining of aching backs, they staggered a few feet, and two young men were shamed into taking the load. This disrespect and indignity was felt to be very disgraceful to the village, so the chief was asked to breathe out a blessing on the hunt, to show that he harboured no ill will.

The next to be asked for a blessing was Nyama, one of the principal diviners, and he who had prepared the medicines for that day. He said that he felt very bitter because, two years ago, he had made the *Kinda* medicine for the new village, and it had worked well: seven women in all had conceived, hunting had been good. Then someone had come in the night and stolen it away. It was useless their asking him to make it anew. Someone else could, but he felt too angry in his heart. However, he would not let his grief spoil the day's hunt, and he breathed out a blessing.

Then someone brought up the question of Nyama's wives who had been bickering for some time. On the previous day one of them, Ihowa, had been so stung by the taunts of her co-wife that she had run away to her mother's village. Was not this likely to spoil the medicine of the hunt? Nyama replied that the quarrel had not been serious, and Ihowa had not left in anger, she had merely paid a normal visit to her mother.

This completed the agenda, the meeting ended, and the hunters moved off. The first two coverts they drew were blank. They consulted and decided to swop matchets. In the next draw the dogs put up a duiker but it got away with a surface scratch. They consulted again, and decided that something should be done at once about Nyama's wife, in case her running off to her mother's village had been in anger after all. Nyama's sister's son, representing him, gave a knife to a man representing the village elders. At the next draw they put up a duiker again, but the arrow missed it altogether. The fifth draw was a blank. Decided it was useless to pursue the hunt. Someone must have been fighting secretly in the village. They would have to have an inquiry to find out what was wrong. No good hunting until it was set right.

24 March. Oracles were consulted. Nyama's wife was convicted of running away in anger. She was ordered to pay two raffia cloths and a chicken, and to destroy the skirt she had worn while running away. That evening all the diviners co-operated in a medicine for the next hunt.

25 March. They went hunting and killed two antelopes. Nyama's wife paid the fine, protesting her innocence.

30 March. Bikwak, the visiting diviner, came back at last, and took up again the series of medicines he had begun in order to replace the stolen *Kinda* medicine. Orders were given for men and women to sleep apart and to stay in their huts next morning until the all-clear was given. At dawn next day all the men, lined up in a single file, went slowly out of the village, the women behind them bent double sweeping the ground. At the diviner's grove he gave medicines to the men, smearing their chests with it. The women were sent back to their huts and told not to pound grain until the word was given. The hunt went off.

It was quite fruitless. The three gun-owners fired and missed. Three arrows were shot, and three blue duikers escaped unhurt. All that was brought home in the evening was one half-grown duiker, which was reserved entirely for the cult group whose privilege it is to eat the young of animals. The rest of the village prepared to go to bed meatless again. Talking over the reason for the failure, Nyama was almost jubilant. He felt that the blank day proved that it had never been the quarrel between his wives which had spoilt the village in the first place. He kept saying: 'Look, we paid a chicken and two raffia cloths, and Ihowa's skirt has been burnt. All in vain. They accused us falsely. Someone else has been fighting and has hidden it.'

One theory was that Bikwak himself had been at fault. Medical convention required that after he had done the medicine he ought to have stayed in the village all day, ensuring by his presence there that the medicine worked successfully. But he had gone to set his wife and children on their homeward journey, about an hour's absence.

Another theory was soon circulated: that the official diviner of the village, who had been on bad terms with his wife for some time, had, on the day before the hunt, refused to eat what she had cooked for him. When her friends reproached her, she denied there had been a quarrel. Her husband had merely refused to eat because he could not stomach another vegetable meal. In spite of her denials she seemed to welcome the attention drawn to her domestic affairs. While she was sitting with her friends in the compound of the senior official diviner of the village, her husband came in. Without a word he gave a raffia cloth and two chickens to his colleague, who took them in silence. An official diviner cannot be even mildly annoyed with his wife without spoiling the village.

The journal ends at this point as I had to leave. Bikwak told me frequently that when he had finished the course of medicines and set up the *Kinda*, he would ask no payment for his services, but would simply take with him a haunch of meat to give to his wife. He had been born in the village, but had left it after his father's death. Now he belonged to a village to the north of Yenga-Yenga which had the same traditional name, Homba, and which recognized a common origin with it. As he counted himself a son of the village, and as he was resident in a 'brother village', he felt he could not charge the usual fee for his medicines.

Diviners

The lending and borrowing of diviners is a very important aspect of inter-village relations, particularly when it takes place between villages which do not acknowledge a common origin. One of the obligations to each other accepted by 'brother-villages' (i.e. those which have at some time split off from each other or from another parent village) is the supply of expert help in religious matters for a fee smaller than would be demanded from an unrelated village. But the borrowing of a diviner from a 'brother village' is a much less interesting affair than a visit from a stranger village.

Any diviner imposes a ban on fighting in a village undergoing his medicines. But if he is only a local expert the village itself exacts fines for breaches of the peace and takes the proceeds into its own treasury. If fighting breaks out while a visiting diviner is at work it is he and his village which will demand payment for the spoilt medicine, and the fine will be much greater. He is temporarily a 'chief' in the village which has invited him. A village which lends its official diviner or one of its Pangolin men to another village does not allow him to appropriate the whole of the fees paid. He should show his colleagues at home what he has been given, and a certain amount is taken from him as 'things of the village'. As few important village medicines can be completed in less than three months, the visiting expert is put to much inconvenience, and a fee of 100 raffia cloths and a bar of red camwood is not thought to be excessive.

If he brings the rites to a successful conclusion, after the last hunt, say when wild pig has been killed the specified number of times, his grateful clients send all their young men, dressed in finery and playing drums, to escort him to his home. He first sends word to his wife that on the day of rest after the next moon he will be returning. She then should spend all her spare time catching and drying fish against his arrival. The whole village is warned to expect the visitors, and the young men practise wrestling and summon their age-mates from other 'brother-villages' of the same cluster. When the diviner's escort arrives, the two villages contest with each other in a wrestling match, the home team supported by all its 'brother-villages'. This wrestling match does not take place when the diviner has been lent by a 'brother-village', for villages which have a common name and origin are not allowed to wrestle against each other. Then the visitors are feasted on fish provided by the diviner's wife, and he, to thank them for escorting him home, gives them a present of say twenty or thirty raffia cloths. If, however, something has gone wrong in the course of the expert's visit, if he is judged for some reason to have failed to achieve the results he promised, then he is sent home without pay, without escort, and is ridiculed by songs invented to mock his name. Some diviners acquire a country-wide fame and can list ten or more villages to which they have been called. Without doubt, this feature of Lele religious organization exercises a strong unifying influence on the scattered villages, for it is the most important form of friendly intercourse between them.

Cult Groups

The full role of the hunt in Lele religion is not made clear without a description of the cult groups. There are three of these, the Begetters, the Pangolin men, and the Diviners. The second and third have important duties in preparing medicines for the village, but the first seems to have no function more important than that of defending and enjoying its food privileges. Membership of all Lele cult groups is defined by a food privilege enjoyed by initiates, and forbidden to outsiders on pain of grave illness. The Begetters are entitled to eat the chest of game and the meat of all young animals. The Pangolin men are so called because only they are allowed to

eat the flesh of the pangolin. The Diviners as a group may eat the head of
wild pig and its intestines. The fact that in each case the cult privilege relates to the division of game gives the final clue to the religious importance
of the hunt.

The Begetters' group is composed of men who have qualified by begetting a child, of either sex, and who have undergone a painful and expensive
initiation. Within this group there is a subdivision of men who have begotten a male and a female child. From the latter are selected the candidates
for the Pangolin group, the leading religious experts of the village, who are
also diviners. Initiation into the Diviners' guild depends on other criteria
altogether. They are supposed to be called to their status by spirit-posses-
sion or by a dream summons. A candidate has to undergo a novitiate of a
year or more of restrictions on his life, and to pay crushing fees to his future
colleagues. Once initiated he is bound to share the councils of the other
diviners on village matters. One of the group is selected by the village to
be its official diviner, a post to which various special functions are attached.
He, together with the Pangolin men and the Diviners, performs all the
rites of the village.

Nearly all major rites, such as those for setting up the *Kinda* for a new
village, or for installing the official diviner, or for initiating a new diviner,
require that the whole of the game taken in the hunt be reserved to the
Diviners, or to the Begetters, or that certain additional parts be eaten by one
of the cult groups. This very common practice could be regarded as simply
derived from the interest of the cult groups in extending their gastronomic
advantages. It is not clearly stated that these extensions of normal privilege
are in themselves effective for the future of good hunting, and the enthusiasm with which breaches are punished could perhaps be attributed to the
natural desire to protect privileged status. But similar practices in the field
of gun- and trap-medicines show more clearly the general implications
of food taboos in Lele hunting rites.

Hunting Medicine

A man who buys a medicine to make a trap more effective undergoes
various restrictions on his life. He may have to refrain from sexual intercourse, avoid various foods, &c., until a certain number of animals have
been killed in the trap. These restrictions are in the same spirit as those
accompanying any medicine, but trap-medicines generally specify a particular treatment for the first three or five animals caught in the trap. In some
cases certain parts, such as the head, liver, and feet, must be eaten by the
trapper himself alone. In others these parts must be eaten by the trapper
and his wives. After the given number of animals has been killed and eaten
in this way, the medicine is completed, and the trap fully established to
take game to which no further restrictions apply. But if any other person
were to steal and eat the parts indicated by the medicine, he would spoil
the trap, and be made to pay a fine to the trapper for interfering with his

medicine. In this case it is quite clear that the trap will not perform its work unless the food privileges are enjoyed by the owner of the medicine. The eating of the first meat, alone or with his wives, is itself a rite which completes the action of the medicine.

Guns are a relatively new weapon in Lele hunting. They replace bows and arrows, but no traditional medicine exists for rendering these more effective. They were assumed to profit from the general effects of the village medicines. The gun, therefore, has been treated as if it were in the same category as the trap. Trap-medicines have been adapted to guns, suitably enough in one way, as the gun is like the trap in being primarily the weapon of the individual hunter. However, unlike the trap, the gun is taken on the communal hunt, and hence arises a conflict of medicines. An uninitiated man who trapped a big animal would always give the chest to be eaten by an uncle or other relative belonging to the Begetters' group. No trap-medicine would require him to eat the chest of game, only the head, liver, or other parts not usually reserved to the Begetters except on special communal hunts. But the gun-owner, having bought a similar medicine for his gun, may find that the specified part of the game he has killed on a communal hunt has been reserved by village medicines to a cult group to which he does not belong. In such a case of conflicting medicines the gun-owner must give way to the village, but his medicine can be saved by payment of a fee to him by the village.

This is the situation which arose on 26 February in the hunt described above. A man who had bought a medicine for his new gun shot on the communal hunt the big yellow-backed duiker. The parts of the kill which the medicine prescribed should be eaten by himself alone, were reserved, by the village *Kinda* medicine, to the cult group of Begetters of which he was not a member. He was not paid for forgoing his rights. On 3 March he joined the hunt again, and a bay duiker was put up by the dogs. It came towards him, but not within what he considered to be the range of his gun. After it escaped the hunters consulted, and asked why he, usually so successful, was not shooting on that day; he replied that his gun-medicine had evidently been spoilt. After he had shot the yellow-backed duiker he had not eaten the meat reserved to him by his gun-medicine, nor had any of those who had eaten it paid him. His friends admitted the justice of his complaint, and then and there one gave him a franc in token for the part of the head which he had eaten. In the next draw they put up an antelope; one man shot and wounded it with his arrow, and the gun-owner fired the final shot that brought it down. He killed nothing else that day, and remarked that if only everyone had paid a fine to satisfy his gun-medicine he would undoubtedly have killed a whole beast by himself.

Food Privileges of Cult Groups

The food privileges of the cult group demonstrate the same spirit as that shown in the eating of special parts of game prescribed by gun- or trap-medicines. The shared feast of cult initiates is in itself spiritually efficacious for the hunting of the village. It is not an object in itself, but a rite which brings to a climax the series of preparatory medicines and taboos which are undergone to ensure a variety of ends. Sometimes the object is good hunting, at other times the fertility of women, at others to establish a new village site, or to initiate a diviner. The dedication of certain parts of game has an aspect which completes the analogy between healing medicines and village rites. In the former case the private practitioner imposes on his patient food restrictions necessary for the working of the medicine. In the latter the body of diviners imposes on the uninitiated in favour of the cult members sacrifices which are necessary to the efficacy of the rites.

At first it seemed difficult to understand how a cult group so important as that of the Begetters should exist solely in order to enjoy its privilege of eating the chest of game and young animals. But as all cult privileges relate to the division of game, the result is that no big animal can be killed without being the object of a religious act. Only birds, squirrels, and monkeys are not counted as game and can be eaten by any man, woman, or boy. Of all animals the wild pig has most significance. The head and entrails are reserved to the Diviners, the chest to the Begetters, the shoulders go to the men who carried it home, the throat to the dog-owners, the back, one haunch, and one foreleg belong to the man who shot it, the stomach goes to the group of village-smiths who forge the arrows. This division is made for all animals except that the Diviners only claim the head of the pig.

Religious Significance of the Hunt

It is because it provides the feast of the cult groups that the hunt is the supreme religious activity, around which all the paraphernalia of medicines, divination, and taboos cluster. And it is to these religious aspects of the hunt that the forest owes its pre-eminent place in the Lele estimation of their environment. Without its central religious functions the hunt would not be able to sanction as effectively as it does the social solidarity of the village.

It is not difficult to account for the Lele tendency to regard hunting as the supreme male activity, more vital to the general prosperity than the equivalent female role of child-bearing. It provides the field in which Lele traditions are constantly validated. For when it is successful, and equally, as we have seen, when it fails, it shows that the relations of God and spirits to men and animals are in fact what the Lele ancestors have taught. It is the sign of the spiritual condition of the village, the test of orderliness in human relations, and in the relations of the village to God. It is itself an essential act in the rites which establish the desired religious condition in which the forest yields its products, and the fertility of women is assured.

THE ABALUYIA OF KAVIRONDO

By GUNTER WAGNER

THE subject to which this essay is devoted can, for obvious reasons, be studied directly only to a limited extent. The field-worker, bent on discovering the world outlook of the people whose culture he is studying, can hope to achieve his aim by scrutinizing the various aspects of that culture for any traits which, directly or indirectly, reflect their views of the world and of the principles that govern it, including their own social order and the forces that affect, or are thought to affect, their social and in-dividual well-being. But in doing so he will encounter two major difficulties: the first of these is that he is almost certain to meet with contradictory or mutually incompatible evidence. Few, if any, native cultures will be so well integrated that all ideas bearing on a certain phenomenon, e.g. death, as expressed in mythology, in ritual, in professed belief, in linguistic usage, in proverbs and sayings, &c., will tally with one another. Every culture has various 'levels of reality', and only a very intimate knowledge of it will enable the investigator to differentiate between them. The second difficulty, related to the first, is that in the endeavour to synthesize the various ex-pressions of native belief, sentiment, and custom into a coherent and con-gruous system of thought, he can scarcely avoid imposing to some extent his own way of thinking. The concepts and sentiments of our own culture with which we must in the last resort operate when presenting our data (or even when trying to comprehend them) will, at best, only approximately render the meaning for the people themselves of the native ideas and senti-ments with which we are dealing. Moreover, our task involves the constant need to interpret and correlate our facts, and as long as our knowledge of the culture which we are analysing is still fragmentary—and this applies even to those cultures on which we have comparatively ample data—the evidence on which we have to base our interpretations and correlations will seldom be conclusive.

In the face of these two difficulties inherent in our task, the presentation of the world outlook of a tribal people cannot claim to possess the same objectivity as a straightforward description of observable custom, but must remain of a tentative nature.

Cosmogonic and Cosmological Ideas

The views held by the Abaluyia[1] on the creation of the world are very

[1] The Bantu tribes of North Kavirondo (now North Nyanza) district, Nyanza Province, Kenya, are now officially known as 'Abaluyia', cf. Wagner, *The Bantu of North Kavirondo*, vol. i, London, 1949, p. 20. The Abaluyia consist of the following tribes: The Vugusu (including the closely related Tadjoni), Hayo, Marach, and North Wanga, all of whom live north of the Nzoia river. To the south of it live the Nyala (also known as Kabras and

closely linked with their belief in a high god who is called *Wele* or *Nyasaye*.[1] The idea of God as the creator both of the world and of man finds such numerous expressions in stereotyped prayers and sayings that there can be no doubt that it is a very firmly established belief and of basic significance for the whole world view of the Abaluyia. Nevertheless, most people with whom I discussed their idea of God and of his role as the creator of the world were rather vague as to the manner in which God is believed to have proceeded with his task. Some said that he created the world in several successive stages but were uncertain about the order in which he did so. Others maintained that he created the whole world in a single day or 'like lightning' but that 'nobody knows how'. Only from the Vugusu, the northernmost sub-tribe of the Abaluyia, did I obtain a creation myth which goes into some detail. It runs as follows;

The world was created by *Wele xakaba*, the granter or giver of all things. Before he created the whole world with everything in it, he made his own abode, heaven. To prevent heaven from falling in, he supported it all round by pillars just as the roof of a round hut is propped up by pillars.[2] *Wele xakaba* created heaven alone, without the assistance of anyone else. In a miraculous way, *Wele xakaba* then created his two assistants, *wele muxove* and *wele murumwa* [according to other versions the latter is called *wele mu oma*].

Heaven, being the dwelling-house of God and his two assistants, is said to be always bright (i.e. during day and night). It is a place of everlasting scintillation. God created it like lightning and in a mysterious way. Also, the substance of which heaven is made is a mystery.

After God had created heaven, he decided to put certain things in it. First, he made the moon and put it into the sky, and then he created the sun. In the beginning the moon was larger and more luminous than the sun, who is his younger brother. Being envious of the moon and its scintillating power, the sun went to assault the moon. The two brothers wrestled with one another and the sun was knocked down by the moon and asked for mercy. The moon yielded to his brother's plea and left him alone. Later, the two brothers wrestled again. This time it was the sun who knocked down the moon, throwing him into the mud. Then he splashed the moon all over with mud to stop him from being resplendent. While they were still wrestling, God came to separate them. After he had done so he said that from thence forward the sun was to possess light and be brighter than the moon and that it was to shine for kings, leaders, and all other things, whether good or bad. This would be day. The moon was to shine only for thieves, witches, and things at night.

The moon was deprived of his resplendence because he was so stupid as to grant mercy to his younger brother, the sun. Rather than show pity, he should

Kakalelwa), Tsotso, Marama, South Wanga (with a recent offshoot, the Mukulu), and Holo, and still farther south the Isuxa, Idaxo, Kisa, Nyole, Logoli, and Tiriki (cf. also pp. 16 sq.).

[1] The term *Wele* is common to the northern tribes of the district (esp. the Vugusu and Wanga) while the term *Nyasaye* prevails among the southern tribes.

[2] Often the roof of the larger living-huts rests not only on the circular wall but on a circle of pillars erected around the eaves of the hut at intervals of several feet. It was, however, never suggested to me that the shape of the hut is a symbolic representation of the universe.

have beaten the sun and not waited until God himself came to stop them from fighting.

After having created the sun and the moon, God made clouds and put them into the sky. He then created a big rooster from which lightning originates. This rooster (*engoxo enjahi*) is of reddish colour and lives among the clouds. Whenever it shakes its wings there is lightning, and whenever it crows there is thunder.

God also created the stars to assist the sun and the moon. First, he created the two large stars, called *tsisulwe* (sing.: *isulwe*), the one to shine in the east and the other one in the west. The eastern *isulwe* shines before dawn, and the *isulwe* in the west lights the earth after the sun has set. Other stars were created after these two.

God then decided to put something into the clouds. So he created rain and put it there. Later, rain became the source of all water on earth. Next, God thought of something that would stop the rain from falling whenever it was not needed. So he made two rainbows, a male one which is narrow and a female one which is wider. The male one alone cannot prevent the rain from falling, but the male and the female one together can do so. To stop the rain the male rainbow appears first and the female one follows.

Next, God created both air and 'cold air'. It is this cold air which makes some of the water in the sky form into hailstones (*kamararara* or *amatjina*).

It is said to have taken God two days to create heaven and all the things in it.

After God had created heaven and everything in it, he wondered where his two assistants, *wele muxove* and *wele murumwa*, and all the other things he had made could do their work. He therefore decided to create the earth. Again he did so in a mysterious way, providing the earth with mountains, valleys, and larger depressions.

Having created the sun and given it the power of resplendence, he asked himself, 'For whom will the sun shine?' This led to God's decision to create the first man. The Vugusu believe that the first man was called Mwambu. Because God had created him so that he could talk and see, he needed someone to whom he could talk. God therefore created the first woman, called Sela, to be Mwambu's partner.

These two people wanted to have water to drink. So God released water for them from the sky. The water that fell from the sky filled all the valleys and large depressions and troughs on earth, thus forming large and small lakes, rivers, and streams of all sorts.

After God had provided the surface of the earth with water, he created all plants. He then said to himself that all those plants were useless unless there was something to eat them. So animals, birds, and other creatures living in the water, on the surface of the earth, and in the soil were created.

The first animals were a buffalo, an elephant, a hippopotamus, and a rhinoceros. Then all the other beasts followed. God told Mwambu and Sela to eat the flesh of certain animals only but not that of others. He instructed them to eat only the flesh of beasts with two hoofs as well as all fish found in rivers and lakes. He ordered them to refrain from eating the animals that crawl, such as snakes, lizards, and snails. He also forbade them to eat scavenger birds, such as vultures and hawks.

Cattle originated from buffaloes. Once, when a buffalo cow had young ones, God came upon them by surprise. The buffalo cow ran away, leaving her young ones behind. *Wele* then took the calves—a male and a female one—with him and gave them to Mwambu and Sela. They took care of them until they became what today we know as cattle. It is also said that Mwambu and Sela fed the buffalo calves on an ant-hill. That is why some people maintain that cattle sprang from an ant-hill.

The first human couple, Mwambu and Sela, lived at a place called Embayi. Their house did not stand on the earth but in the air, supported by poles. So whenever Mwambu and Sela wanted to walk on the earth, they had to descend from their house by means of a ladder. When back in their house, they pulled the ladder up so that no one could climb into their house. This was because there were monsters (*amanani*) on earth who might have come to attack them.

At first, Mwambu and Sela lived together without having any children, for 'Mwambu did not know his wife'. But later, when he knew her, she became pregnant[1] and gave birth to a son, called Lilambo. Mwambu and Sela were very much astounded when they saw their first child. Later, Sela bore another child, a daughter, whose name was Nasio.

When Lilambo and Nasio had grown up, they did not live together with their parents but down on earth. They too, had children, but these were in constant danger of being eaten up by the *amanani* that were still haunting the earth. After having borne Lilambo and Nasio, Sela gave birth to two further daughters, called Simbi and Nakitumba. These were later married to the sons begotten by Lilambo with his wife Nasio. In this way human beings began to multiply on the surface of the earth.

God completed the whole work of creation in six days [*sic*]. On the seventh day he rested because it was a bad day (*inyana ye musafu muvi*). The Vugusu have all sorts of beliefs and taboos (*gimisilu*) referring to this day and the number seven.

Other data which I obtained, either in the form of myths, folk-tales, prayers, or detached utterances, on the cosmogonic and cosmological ideas of the Abaluyia agree in most essentials with this myth of origin. I shall therefore discuss only those additional data which either enlarge upon the themes dealt with above or present different versions.

In a text dictated to me by a Logoli elder on the various celestial bodies, the sun is praised for lighting up the earth, so that people can work in the fields and go about their daily tasks, as well as for enabling them to divide the day into morning, noon, afternoon, and evening.[2] Significantly, this latter function of the sun was also the only comment which my informants had to make on the fact that it travels from east to west across the sky: 'It does so to help us know the time of day.'

At night the sun is believed to travel back from west to east, though not across the sky but underneath the earth. This, at least, is what the sun is supposed to do in accordance with the 'normal order of things'. A story relates, however, that once a man woke up in his hut at night and went outside to urinate. There he saw the sun quickly speeding across the sky back

[1] According to a widespread story, the first human couple lived for many years without knowing how to have sexual intercourse. Cf. Wagner, op. cit., p. 169.

[2] The Logoli distinguish the different times of the day by the various activities they have to perform.

to the east, a most inauspicious experience which necessitated an elaborate rite of lustration.[1]

In another myth, the sun figures as a powerful and very wealthy chief who lives in the sky and looks very red and shiny like lightning. The myth relates how a girl, who had refused all the young men of her village, was carried up to the sky by a rope. There she was received by the mother of the sun, who told her that her son wished to marry her. When the sun came back from the gardens where he had been working, he duly courted the girl and offered her many presents, such as eleusine, sorghum, and everything else that grows on earth. But the girl cast her eyes down and refused all the presents offered her. Only when the sun presented her with his rays did she agree to become his wife. The sun-rays were given to her shut up in a pot, which she kept in her hut without opening it and thus releasing the rays.

After she had given birth to three sons, she asked her husband for permission to visit her parents. Together with her three sons and her servants she descended to earth by the same rope which had lifted her up into the sky. Her parents were very happy when they saw her again, but before they could salute her they had to kill a cow for her (as a rite of purification necessitated by her long and unusual absence). Her father selected a black cow, which the girl refused. Only when, after choosing cows of various other colours, he selected a white cow did she agree by nodding her head. On the following day her father killed two more white cows for her to take back to the sky. On the third day the girl returned home with her sons and servants, accompanied by her parents as far as the place where the rope was hanging down from the sky. After she had arrived at the chief's (i.e. the sun's) place, she opened the pot containing the rays so that they could shine down upon the earth. 'There were many cows in the rays, and they all fell down on her father's homestead. The whole earth was warmed by the rays of the sun, and things began to grow well. Now all people could live well and in plenty.'

The 'social value' of the sun which finds such striking expression in this myth is evident also from its importance in ritual. Though the sun is clearly not conceived as a deity, the Abaluyia pray to God every morning 'to let the day dawn well and spit his medicine upon the people, so that they may walk well'. While offering this prayer they spit in the direction of the rising sun. Among the Logoli, on the occasion of the first sacrifice offered for a new-born child, the child's parents sit in the doorway of the hut and the 'blower of *ovwanga*' (see below, p. 50) stands in front of them holding a calabash filled with *ovwanga* (a thin paste or gruel consisting of eleusine mixed with water). Facing the rising sun, he takes a small sip of the *ovwanga*, spits it towards the sun, and cries: 'When the sun rises in the east it brings milk and health with it, and when it sets in the west may it take the evil along with it.' Then he spits the remaining *ovwanga* on all the members of the family, including the new-born child.

---

[1] Cf. Wagner, op. cit., pp. 245 sq.

References in myths to the moon deal exclusively with the fact that 'he'
is so much less brilliant than the sun. The story that the sun and the moon
wrestled together, with the result that the moon got splashed with mud,
seems to be common to all the sub-tribes of the Abaluyia, but the creation
myth quoted above is the only version of this theme in which the moon is
said to be the elder brother of the sun. According to the other versions
which I obtained, he is the sun's younger brother or clansman and, as the
two wrestled with one another, they both fell into the mud. They agreed
to clean each other and, as befits a younger brother, the moon washed the
sun first. When it was the sun's turn to perform the same service for the
moon he refused to do so. The common element in both versions is that
the sun owes his present resplendence and his advantage over the moon to a
trick which he played on his brother.

Strangely enough the phases of the moon do not seem to have formed
the subject of an explanatory myth. They figure, however, in a number of
magical rites. Thus, a mother whose child has been in poor health for a long
time throws *kitatula* sticks (thought to be vehicles of the child's illness) at
the full moon. After having done so she quickly returns to her hut without
looking back at the moon. The interpretation given of this rite was that the
sickness would now gradually disappear just as the moon was getting smaller
from night to night.

An analagous magical virtue is attributed to the waxing moon by stut-
terers, who try to cure their disability by talking to the new moon (i.e. on the
night when the new crescent is first visible). The magical efficacy of this
rite is evidently based on the principle of sympathy: as the moon waxes, so
the stutterer's power of speech will increase.

Apart from the significance attached to the moon in connexion with
these rites it is praised 'because it shines upon the people at night and
helps them to make love. It is also helpful to women as it enables them to
know when they will have their menstrual period or, if it has failed to come,
how long it will take for them to be delivered of a child.' Another text
dealing with the 'helpfulness of the moon' describes at some length how
the phases of the moon enable people to say when a pregnant cow will
calve, and states only as an afterthought that 'it helps women in the same
way'.

The stars seem to occupy only a very minor place in the scheme of
things as viewed by the Abaluyia. In spite of frequent inquiries, I failed to
obtain any names for stellar constellations, and those which I pointed out to
my informants seemed never to have struck their imagination or even their
attention. Nor does it ever seem to have been observed that there is a difference between the planets and the fixed stars. The only star which the
Logoli distinguish from all the others is the evening star, which they refer to
as the 'chief of all stars'. They also say that when it sets it defecates all the
other stars. According to some people, the stars are spirits of persons who
died very long ago and are now 'stuck on the sky'. As distinct from the sun

and the moon, the stars do not figure in any of the rites which have been described to me or which I have witnessed.

The appearance of a comet is regarded as an evil omen, a sign of impending and ill-fated war. If a comet had been sighted, a prophet (cf. p. 46) used to be consulted on behalf of the tribal community. He kindled a ritual fire (*ovwali*) over which he roasted a white fowl.[1] He then observed which side the smoke rose and predicted that fighting would break out on that side. It was believed that if people disobeyed this warning sent to them by God and allowed themselves to get involved in any fighting in that part of the country towards which the smoke had blown, they would stand no chance of escaping from the enemy.[2]

Rainbows are everywhere looked upon as instruments sent or wielded by God to stop the rain, for 'whenever a rainbow appears in the sky, the rain ceases to beat down hard and becomes a mere drizzle'. Though rain and wind are thought to be either sent or withheld by the rain magicians (see p. 37), their power is not believed to extend to the control of rainbows.

Of the four quarters of the sky, the north and the south are treated with indifference, whereas the east is in various ways identified with life, health, and wealth, and the west with illness, evil magic, misfortune, and death. Not only is this idea expressed in the words uttered in connexion with the ritual spitting towards the sun (see p. 31), but also, in a number of rites performed for sick people, the illness is implored 'to go west'. Similarly, a text on earthquakes states that 'when the country begins to shake, a man with a high-pitched drum is sent out to drive the earthquake away, beginning in the eastern portion of the tribal lands and proceeding towards the west'. In the semi-annual tribal sacrifice of the Logoli, which is performed to ward off drought and disease, &c., the assembled warriors of the tribe used to stand on the top of a hill facing west and brandishing their spears in that direction where the Luo, the principal enemies of the Logoli, happen to live. The country of the dead, too, is said to be not only below the earth but in the west. Incidentally, in Kavirondo not only does the sun rise in the east, bringing 'milk and health' with it, but the rain, too, comes from that direction, and all major streams flow from the east or north-east. The symbolic meaning attached to east and west thus receives support from the nature of the local environment. However, the points of the compass do not, nowadays at least, determine the layout of homesteads, cattle-kraals, sacrificial shrines, or graves.

Turning now from the sky and the celestial bodies to the earth, we find that its various phenomena command interest only inasmuch as they directly affect the well-being of the individual or the tribal community. Such striking sights as the broad massif of Mount Elgon, which extends over the

---

[1] All animals offered as a sacrifice to God must be white.

[2] The smoke oracle was consulted in connexion with a number of family and public rites; cf. below p. 52.

northern horizon and is seen from every point of the district, or the Kavi-rondo Gulf of Lake Victoria, which is clearly visible from many hills in the southern part of the district, seem to arouse little interest, for they figure in none of the myths or stories which I collected nor in rites or ceremonies. The only exception is that among the Logoli the waters of Lake Victoria serve as a dumping-ground for witchcraft medicine (*elilogo*). A person who believes he has been infected with *elilogo* must immediately set out for the Lake and throw all his clothes into the water, as this is thought to be the only effective means of getting rid of the *elilogo*.[1]

Place-names seem to be given chiefly to human settlements, either past or present, and they are identical with the personal name of the founder or present owner of the homestead or village. A systematic study of native geographical, botanical, and zoological lore would probably reveal more clearly which objects and features of the natural environment possess 'social value' and which are ignored. Unfortunately, my own observations along these lines have been too casual to permit a discussion of this aspect of the Abaluyia's world view.[2]

The extent of the geographical 'horizon' of the various sub-tribes in pre-European days I found very difficult to discover. The traditions of some tribes refer to places which are hundreds of miles away from their present homes. The Wanga, for instance, claim to have come from 'West Africa', that is to say, from somewhere west of Lake Albert, whence they migrated through Unyoro, Buganda, and Busoga to Kavirondo; the Logoli say that their ancestors lived on the eastern shore of Lake Victoria near the present town of Shirati and that on the way to their present abode they crossed Kavirondo Gulf in boats. I have, however, found it impossible to determine whether, and to what extent, these traditions are genuine and how far they have been modified in the light of the recent extension of geographical knowledge. As most sub-tribes of the Abaluyia maintained either friendly or hostile relations only with their immediate neighbours, their direct knowledge of the outside world does not seem to have extended more than a few miles beyond their tribal boundaries.

In native folk-lore it is a frequently recurring theme that a herd-boy in search of lost cattle arrives in the country of giants and monsters (*amanani*), but apart from such themes in folk-lore little thought seems to have been given to the nature of the world that lay outside their own tribal area and those of their immediate neighbours.[3] I searched in vain for any ideas as to the 'end of the world' or 'the place where earth and sky meet'.

The sphere beneath the earth is vaguely referred to as the 'country of the dead' (*emagombe*). Folk-tales, proverbs, and sayings referring to the *ema-gombe* endow it with quite contradictory characteristics: a person suffering

---

[1] The idea is that if an evil substance is buried it will reappear in the plants growing in the soil where it was buried; if burnt, it will reappear in the smoke.

[2] Cf., however, the last section of this essay.

[3] In pre-European days there seems to have been very little trade or any other form of communication between the more distant tribes.

from serious illness is admonished to eat while he is still alive, for 'there are no gardens in the country of the dead'. Analogously, people often told me, in explanation of their custom of putting offerings of beer, gruel, or meat into their ancestral shrines, that the ancestral spirits had neither grain nor meat on which to live and therefore had to be given occasional offerings, of which they only inhaled the smell, for being 'like shadows' they would not need substantial food. In folk-tales, on the other hand, the land of the dead is always described as an exact replica of the land of the living.

The View of Society—Patterns of Prestige and Status

The order of the social world in which the Abaluyia live is determined to a large extent by their system of patrilineal clans and lineages and the principle of seniority as an integral part of that system. Each tribal community (particularly its male half) derives its 'group consciousness' first and foremost from the belief that all or the large majority of its constituent clans have descended in an agnatic line from a mythical tribal ancestor. An exception is provided by the Wanga, among whom only twelve out of a total of thirty clans claim to be direct descendants of Omuwanga, the alleged founder of the tribe. The remaining eighteen clans are said to have joined the tribal community on various subsequent occasions after having seceded from surrounding tribes. Significantly, the Wanga are the only tribe among the Abaluyia that, even in pre-European times, had hereditary chiefs and an apparently well-developed institution of chieftainship, a fact which seems to have been instrumental in bringing the extraneous clans into the original tribal community.

The individual tribes which together form the Abaluyia have, until recently,[1] been independent political units whose internal cohesion was, in most cases, extremely weak. Not only did the majority of tribes in pre-European days lack the institution of chieftainship, but groups which still claim descent from a common ancestor and also culturally consider themselves as one tribe, have in some cases split up into politically independent units that today form separate chieftaincies. Thus the tribe of the Vugusu has split up into the three chieftaincies of North Kitosh (Kimilili), Malakisi, and South Kitosh, and that of the Logoli into the chieftaincies of North and South Maragoli.

The only tribal group which attained a certain political ascendancy over some of their neighbours was the Wanga. Their ascendancy was, however, rather limited, and it is even doubtful whether it existed before the opening of the direct trade route from the coast to Uganda, which passed through the residence of the Wanga chiefs.[2] Their political influence over their neighbours was further strengthened when the British Administration

---

[1] The setting up of divisional native courts to replace the former chief's courts has been one of the principal factors in the creation of larger political units.

[2] Until the end of the last century all trade from the coast to Uganda followed the southern route which led through Tanganyika and round the southern tip of Lake Victoria so as to avoid the Masai country.

established its first headquarters and a small garrison of Sudanese soldiers
in the Wanga country, and when, in recognition of the loyalty shown by the
Wanga chief, it bestowed upon him the honorary title of paramount
chief. This was, however, not much more than a gesture, for the various
tribal chiefs appointed by the Administration from 1902 onwards were not
actually subordinate to the Wanga chief.

The essential equality of status enjoyed by the various tribes is reflected
in their traditions. These refer chiefly to the routes of migration followed
by each group before it settled at its present abode as well as to intermediary
places of residence. There are no accounts of conquests on which claims to
political domination over other tribal groups or sub-groups might be based.
All the tribal communities in which I carried out detailed inquiries base
their unchallenged claims to their present tribal lands on the right of first
occupation, but none of them assert that these lands are their original
tribal home.

Until the beginning of this century, the various Bantu tribes of North
Nyanza waged periodical 'wars' against each other. These seem, however,
to have been little more than cattle raids on their immediate neighbours or
demonstrations of prowess to reassert the title to their tribal lands. Since
the establishment of the British Administration and the pacification of the
whole area, the various tribes have gradually developed a consciousness of
forming a unit on a higher level. This tendency has recently[1] led to the
official recognition of the name 'Abaluyia' as the common designation for all
the Bantu tribes of North Nyanza. It is the result of a growing consciousness
of their close cultural and linguistic affinity which is accentuated by the
fact that they are surrounded on all sides by non-Bantu-speaking neighbours.[2] The process of integration was, of course, greatly aided by the
numerous intertribal contacts and common interests which resulted from
the fact that they all came under the same district administration, with a
joint Local Native Council (established in 1924), a joint Native Appeal
Court (1926/7), and, more recently, the establishment of 'Divisional Native
Courts' (1936), which replaced the former chiefs' courts and cut across tribal
boundaries. The higher status enjoyed by the Wanga chiefs, on the other
hand, seems to have been a factor of only minor, if any, importance in this
process.

Within each tribal unit the patri-clans that claim descent from the
senior line of the 'house' founded by the tribal ancestor enjoy a somewhat
higher rank than those descended from the junior line, or than the smaller
sub-clans which split off only a few generations ago or are only now in the
process of establishing their independence which, above all, is marked by
their asserting themselves as an exogamous group of their own. Thus, among

---

[1] The new term was apparently adopted during or after the last war. Cf. *The Liguri and
the Land*, by Norman Humphrey, Nairobi: Government Printer, 1947.

[2] viz. the Nilo-hamitic Nandi, El Konyi, and Sabei in the east and north-east, the Nilo-
hamitic Teso in the north-west, and the Nilotic Luo in the west and the south.

the Logoli the priests officiating at the semi-annual tribal sacrifice all belong to the Nondi sub-clan of the Mavi clan. This sub-clan enjoys the highest rank of all, for omuNondi is said to have been the eldest son of omuMavi, who, in turn, was the eldest son of omuLogoli, the tribal ancestor. Even in the present-day political life of the tribe the Mavi clan and its immediate sub-clans[1] play a more important part than all the other clans. It has, for instance, provided the tribal chiefs appointed by the Government as well as the chairman of the Native Appeal Court (which serves the whole district).

The principle of seniority (both in age and in descent) on which rank as well as authority and prestige are based is carried right through to the smallest social group, the individual family. Both as regards succession and inheritance, seniority sets an order of precedence. A man's rights and privileges, as well as his estate, are passed on upon his death first to his brothers as his senior relatives and then to his eldest son, who acts as the guardian of his younger brothers.

Seniority, however, is not the only factor which confers rank or authority. A large family, the possession of wealth, and a 'gentle' character are contributing factors of major importance. Wealth, of course, in any community may enhance a man's status by conferring power; but from the native point of view wealth, numerous offspring, and a gentle character are looked upon as an integral complex because they offer visible proof that a man who possesses them enjoys a higher 'ritual status' (cf. below, p. 48) than less fortunate persons. A man whose wife is cursed with barrenness, whose cattle die, whose crops are devastated by hailstorms, and whose character betrays those qualities which, if extreme, are attributed to witches, must obviously have a poor ritual status and hence cannot command authority or enjoy prestige. He is, therefore, also debarred from holding the office of chief or priest (*omusalisi*) or other functionary in the ancestral cult.

Of the various 'departmental experts' only rain magicians, dream prophets, diviners, certain sorcerers (*avavila*) and, to some extent, also iron-smelters and smiths enjoy a marked degree of prestige which is based on the belief that they wield superior powers.

The status of the rain magicians in the northern part of the district did not differ materially from that of the other experts, for they could be hired by individual clients and were occasionally given a good beating if there was a major drought; but the family of rain-makers in Bunyole[2] enjoyed such a widespread fame that tribal delegations came from far and wide to offer them tribute. A text on this tribute states:

The people go to the rain-maker once every season. They take presents to him

---

[1] They are called avaNondi, avaLogovo, avaGonda, and avaMutembe, after the four sons of omuMavi.

[2] Name of the tribal territory occupied by the avaNyole, who live in the south-western corner of the district.

because the heat is very great. They go to him at the *ekimiyu* time (end of December). Then the big elder of the clan sends someone to fetch a pot from the hill where the person lives who is making pots. He must make a very big one indeed, and they also prepare tobacco which they take to the rain-maker's place at Vudjigwi. He who is carrying these things is an old man called Amambia, and he is a chief (*omwami*) in the country of the Logoli. He must go with three people only, and when they have arrived there they must sleep at the rain-maker's place because Amambia is a great person in the country; he is one of the rich people like the rain-maker. If he were to send his elders (only), they would not get there a thing [i.e. they would not get rain for the people]. Then they leave again, for the rain-maker cannot take them to see the place where he is making the rain.

In the course of time, it is said, this tribute increased:

One day, a man from another clan went to the rain-maker and said to him: 'Ah, *omugimba*, you are like a chief who is watching the earth and the sky. Why do you allow the people to bring you tobacco only? You are indeed a person who.ought to be given cows and goats.' From then on the people began to fatten the goats, and for a few years they brought him goats. Then again, when they saw that the rain did not fall for many days, they thought, 'perhaps the rain-maker refuses to let the rain fall because we are not giving him cattle'. Then they began to fatten cattle.

Despite the outstanding tribute rendered to the rain-magicians of Bunyole,[1] they were no more than local experts, that is, they possessed no political authority nor did they exercise priestly functions in the strict sense of the word. Their prestige was based solely on their alleged power to control the rain. Their reputation for doing so was backed by a widely known myth explaining how this particular family came to acquire the knowledge of rain magic.

The salient features of this myth are:[2]

In the beginning of this country, very long ago, the people saw the rain falling and wondered only. They did not know where it came from, nor did they know if there was anyone who owned the rain. Thus the rain would either stop or it would go on raining. The word 'rain' was there from long ago.

This state of affairs changed when one day a woman who had been 'lost to her clan' wandered about and, in the course of her travels, visited various people, to whom she demonstrated her knowledge of how to make rain. When she began to bring 'thunder and lightning' into the house as well as 'poisonous snakes and all the other creatures that crawl',[3] they got afraid and chased her away. At last the old woman went to live with a man called Nganyi of Evutjigwi (in Bunyole) who did not drive her away 'even though he did not understand quickly'. She taught him the art of rain-making.

Eventually, people came to hear about her knowledge and they went to Nganyi's place to ask for rain. Then they were told that they could not get the rain for nothing but had to pay for it. So they held council and decided to send presents.

---

[1] This tribute was all the more remarkable as it was rendered not only by members of the Nyole tribe but by delegations from a number of surrounding tribes as well.

[2] For a full account cf. Wagner, op. cit., pp. 153 sq.

[3] Snakes and crawling animals are associated with rain. Cf., however, below p. 52.

In an analogous manner the diviners, prophets, sorcerers, circumcision operators, &c., are believed to be the 'owners' of their particular art, which they hand on either to their own sons or sisters' sons or, in some cases, to strangers if they submit to instruction and pay for it. The underlying idea is that no occupation which involves the possession of 'secret knowledge' can be practised successfully by outsiders because, in addition to mere technical mastery, the right of ownership acquired by birth—or, in exceptional cases, by a payment—is an integral part of the profession. When a smith hands the smith's hammer and the other implements of his craft to his apprentice after he has completed the period of instruction, he emphasizes that 'the hammer is ours from long ago (*enyuli yefwe exale*)'. A diviner will impress on his client the fact that he is fully entitled to practise his art, as in the following song which I took down in the course of a consultation:

> It is ours since a long time ago;
> We have bought it from no one,
> it is ours.
> It came with us from the Lake;
> With us, the uncircumcised ones of the Lake.

The members of a clan which owns a certain art or occupation are, in fact, not only entitled to practise it but are even under an obligation to do so. Thus, the son of a diviner, a smith, or an *omuliuli*,[1] will be seized by a sudden spell of insanity which is said to be caused by the ancestral spirits 'who grumble that it is time for him to practise the art of his clan'. Such a spell of insanity is, in fact, the most common indication whereby an expert judges which one of his sons (or sisters' sons) has been chosen by the ancestors to become his successor.

The more common crafts such as pottery, basket-making, wood and leatherworking, &c., do not seem to carry particular prestige, apparently because they are not associated with the notion of magic or 'secret knowledge'. They are not 'owned' by certain clans or families; anyone may learn them without having to be specially selected by the ancestral spirits or ritually initiated by his teacher. The origin myths which I was able to obtain on them are rationalistic explanations rather than 'mythical charters', as is the myth dealing with the origin of rain magic. A typical origin story of this rationalizing type is the account of the invention of pottery among the Vugusu:

Before people knew how to make pots, they carried the water in calabashes which they plucked from certain wild plants. When the children saw that calabashes were used by their mothers for carrying water, they tried to make their own calabashes by moulding bits of clay into the shape of calabashes. Somehow or other they put these imitation calabashes into the fire, where they hardened and thus became impervious to water. In that way the first pot was made by a child. The mothers then imitated their children and likewise began to mould pots. The

---

[1] i.e. the expert who detects hidden witchcraft substance.

first pots which they made they did not fire, and so they collapsed. Only when they put them into the fire, as their children had done, they succeeded in making real pots.

Similarly, the origin of basket-making is explained as a series of efforts leading from rough bundles of grass (such as are still used to bundle grain) to the finished baskets of today.

Nevertheless, even in the ordinary crafts the idea of professional prestige is not wholly lacking. This idea is reflected, for instance, by a story which tells how women came to be freed from the burden of housework:

There were two sisters, one of whom spent all day making pots without doing any work in the house. This annoyed the other one so much that she broke all the pots which her sister had made. The girl who had made the pots thereupon ran away from her parents' home, walking for three days till she came to a great lake. Right in the water she saw a tall tree called *kumurumba*. When the tree noticed the girl, it came up to the shore and she climbed it, whereupon the tree returned to the water. After a while, her parents, who had been searching for her, reached the lake and saw their daughter sitting in the crown of the tree away from the shore. They implored her to descend from the tree and come back to the shore but the girl refused to do so. Only when her lover came and begged her, too, she agreed to return to the shore. When they were all home again, her people made some new pots for her. From then on she never had to work in the house again.

As opposed to the various categories of people whose prestige is above the average because they are believed to possess 'superior powers' there are people who suffer from an inferior social status because they are regarded as witches (Lurogoli: *omulogi*, pl. *avalogi*), active or latent, of one type or another. In some cases the reputation of being an *omulogi* derives from a person's character—that is to say, from various expressions of anti-social behaviour, though not everybody who has an unpleasant personality is on that account suspected. As most people are reluctant to accuse a particular individual outright of being an *omulogi*, discussions on this point remain as a rule hypothetical. On the other hand, the charges levelled against the person concerned may be so fantastic that they could not possibly have a factual basis. People would say, for instance, that so-and-so is known to be an *omulogi* because he keeps a leopard in the loft of his hut as a pet, or because he has repeatedly been seen dancing in front of other people's houses at night, behaving exactly like an *omulogi* is supposed to behave. Some informants insisted that they could recognize an *omulogi* by his 'queer look' or by his 'rasping voice'. It is probable that diviners, who in cases of illness or misfortune are consulted to detect the responsible agent, will hint at certain persons as having caused the illness through practising witchcraft; thus they will either arouse the beginnings of suspicion against a certain person or strengthen an already existing suspicion. In other cases a mere coincidence might cause a person to be suspected of being a witch, as, for instance, if one has quarrelled with somebody and shortly afterwards is seized by a violent attack of gastric influenza, or if a woman with a small child meets another woman who 'talks sweet words to the child' and the latter then suffers from diarrhoea.

Not only individuals but entire clans may be reputed to be afflicted with witchcraft, or at least with a latent disposition to it. My informants suggested that the members of such a clan started many generations ago to practise their evil art, and as a man or a woman cannot help passing on the disposition to all descendants, these people came to be regarded as at least potential witches. The behaviour adopted towards a suspected *omulogi* is described in the following text:

Who is an *omulogi*? He lives like other people but everybody knows, 'indeed, this one is an *omulogi*'. The people know him to be an *omulogi* because he has been found outside at night without wearing any clothes. You must fear him very much and cannot talk to him; only in the daytime can you stand together with an *omulogi*, but not when it is dark. You must fear him because, since long ago, a person who has become an *omulogi* cannot walk together with his friends, nor can he offer you food without eating of it himself. Only after he has eaten first can you begin to help him eating. You must watch everything carefully lest he might give you food like grain (?). If he has given you something [and you have not yet touched it] you must wait until he is not there. Then you must call a woman and she must touch [what he has given you] with her hand. Then you may begin to eat or touch the thing which he has given you.

Also, when you know for certain, 'this man is an *omulogi*', and he has a daughter, and you are a person whom they call a *milongo* [a person free from witchcraft], you cannot wish to marry the daughter of that man. You must fear to marry her, because he is an *omulogi*. If you have already married a girl and then you hear that there is an *omulogi* at the girl's place, you refuse, indeed [to stay with her] for nobody wants to be married to the daughter of an *omulogi*.

Besides the factors already discussed, which determine prestige and social status, there is a marked sex dichotomy. Some aspects of this appear as a direct expression of the cultural emphasis placed on patriliny: namely, residential arrangements after marriage (patrilocality), the laws of property,[1] and, hence, the rules of inheritance.[2] As regards succession, the sex cleavage is strictly maintained (i.e. a man can only be succeeded by a man, and a woman by a woman) but the principle of patriliny is not, for any male 'departmental expert' may pass on his knowledge either to his son or to his sister's son. In the activities of everyday life there is a sharp division of labour as well as a far-reaching segregation of the sexes in most other respects: men and women take their meals separately, they dance in separate groups (though on the same dancing-ground), and on festive occasions they do not mingle but enjoy themselves in separate groups. In the magico-religious sphere the sex cleavage is expressed in the belief that the spirits of male ancestors have power only, or primarily, over male persons, and those of female ancestors over female persons. Similarly, a male witch is thought to harm only a male person, and a female witch only a female

---

[1] Women can own neither cattle nor land.

[2] A man's property can only be passed on to a man, and a woman's only to a woman.

person. A logical inference from this belief is the notion that the 'stream of magic' which is thought to flow from a male witch to his victim can be rendered ineffective if, as prescribed above, a female person touches the object which is intended to convey the evil magic.

In view of these beliefs it is surprising that the sex dichotomy does not, at least to any marked degree, extend to ritual occasions and to ceremonial in general. Male and female members of the same family submit jointly to the various rites that aim at restoring ritual status (for instance, sacrifices and purification ceremonies), and even in connexion with the circumcision and initiation rites which the young men of the tribe undergo, there are only a few phases from which women are debarred. Though women cannot officiate as priests (*avasalisi*) in the ancestral cult, even when the sacrifice is offered on behalf of a woman and thus addressed to her female ancestors, they can be diviners. Even the art of making or controlling the rain, which carries with it such high prestige, is said to have been originally owned by a woman (cf. p. 38). In a number of magico-religious rites women may perform minor duties, as in the Logoli's semi-annual tribal sacrifice to God, where they collect and carry the firewood for kindling the sacrificial fire (*ovwali*); but these must either be girls 'who have not yet joined a man' or old women who no longer have sexual intercourse.

These facts suggest that the sex dichotomy is primarily the result of the social structure, with its stress on patriliny, and only to a minor degree an expression of the idea of ritual uncleanness associated with a woman's sex life, though ultimately the two ideas are probably related.

Summing up this discussion of the Abaluyia's view of society and their patterns of prestige and social status, it must be stated that despite marked differences in prestige and social status the tribal society is essentially 'democratic', at least as far as its male members are concerned. The fact that all members of the tribal community consider themselves descendants from a common tribal ancestor carries more weight than the principle of seniority, for, with the possible exception of the Wanga, the senior clans of the tribal community (cf. p. 36) cannot be said to have formed an aristocracy. Nor has the prestige derived from the possession of 'secret knowledge' ever led to the assumption of political power or other concrete rights and privileges. Among the Abaluyia we should search in vain for any of those features which are characteristic of a stratified society.

A discussion of the Abaluyia's view of society should, properly, be extended to comprise the dead as well as the living. For, as has already been indicated, the dead are believed to possess the power of affecting the health and general well-being of their living relatives. They are, accordingly, thought to be a source of potential danger to them. This notion, which appears to be largely derived from the psychological reaction to the phenomena of death and bereavement, will become more comprehensible when viewed within the wider context of the native concept of the natural and social order and the forces that are believed to threaten its maintenance.

The Natural and Social Order: Notions of the Normal and the Abnormal

In the first part of this essay we have seen that God did not merely create the world and man but he also established an order which enabled man to live in this world. God provided man with a woman so that he might multiply, with air to breathe, a sun to shine for him in the daytime and a moon to light up the night, with water to drink, plants and animals to eat, and so on. From discussions on the nature of God's creation it emerged quite clearly that the order as ordained by the Creator God is not thought to embrace the disruptive forces in nature and society which interfere with man's happiness, that is, with the 'normal course' of his life and activities. In other words, God did not create the evil along with the good, but the order of the world as established by him was perfect, endowing man even with the blessing of eternal life.

Such an interpretation of God's creation as conceived by the Abaluyia seems to be incompatible with their belief that God has the power to alter the order ordained by him, a belief which is, however, implied in the custom of offering prayers to God imploring him 'to let things take their normal course', 'to let the sun rise and shine as usual', and 'to spit his medicine upon the people so that they may walk in peace'. God is also supposed to have said: 'It is I who made the people; whom I love he will thrive, and whom I refuse he will die.'

However, the significant point is that God is not believed to vary the 'normal order of things' out of spite but only to punish people if they themselves deviate from the order established by him. Thus, among the Vugusu, God is said to punish a woman for committing adultery by letting her previous children die. He will then appear to her in a dream and say: 'I have given you these children from your husband. Why have you left him and joined another thigh? Now I shall take these children back to me.' Similarly, God is said to have given man a number of rules or taboos (Lurogoli, *emigilu*; Luvugusu, *gimisilu*). If these are violated and misfortune ensues, the diviner may attribute it to an act of punishment sent by God. People who contemplate committing a bad deed and then have to sneeze repeatedly are said to have been sent the sneeze as a warning (*engani*) from God. These beliefs[1] suggest that the conception of the Creator God is modelled on the pattern of a benevolent father who also would punish his children or curse them if they did wrong; they do not contradict the basic notion that the natural and social order as established by God does not include evil and disruptive forces as an integral part of that order.

Misfortune, evil deeds, illness, and death must thus be due to forces that are opposed to the natural order. A widespread myth relates that man became mortal only when he was cursed by the chameleon after he had repeatedly refused its request for a share of his food.

According to the Vugusu version of this story, the chameleon came one day to

[1] The circumstances in which these beliefs were recorded make it appear very unlikely that they are influenced by Mission teaching.

the homestead of one of the sons of Maina, the eldest son of the tribal ancestor. He was sitting in front of his hut eating his evening meal. The chameleon begged him for food, but Maina's son refused. It kept on begging until he grew impatient and drove the chameleon away. Before leaving, the chameleon uttered the following curse: 'I am leaving now, but you all may die.' Then the people started to breathe the air [*sic*], get ill, and die. Later, the chameleon visited the snake and begged it for food as well. The snake willingly gave the chameleon what it had asked for, and as a reward the chameleon uttered a blessing, saying that the snake should live on for ever. So, when it gets old, it merely casts its skin but does not die unless it is killed by force. Antelopes, too, if not killed, will live for ever.

The themes of eternal life and resurrection from death occur in a large number of folk-tales. One of them, entitled 'Why people never rise from death', tells that long ago people who died came back to life after four days. Once, however, a boy who had died and later returned to his parents' homestead was driven away by his mother, who told him that he had died and should stay in the grave. Thereupon the boy went away but cursed the people, saying that henceforward people who had died should never come back to life again.

Among the Vugusu all evil things in life are ultimately ascribed to the 'black god', the opposite of the Creator God or—as he is also called— the White God. The black god, *wele gumali* or *wele evimbi*, is never described as a tool used by the White God but as an independent, though weaker, force. In prayers, the White God is implored to drive away the black god; for example:

> *Wele*, you who made us walk in your country,
> You who made the cattle and the things which are in it,
> You may spit the medicine on your person,
> He may recover and walk well,
> He may plant his gardens.
> Drive away the black god,
> He may leave your person,
> He may move into the snake
> And into the abandoned homestead;
> He may leave our house.

Among the other tribes I did not find such an explicit belief in a parallel to the Creator God, but rather a very pronounced belief in a dichotomy of good and evil forces. Everything which deviates from the normal order of things, both in the natural and in the social world, is regarded as a manifestation of these evil forces and, hence, as dangerous. Among the Logoli, all 'abnormal' phenomena are classed under the two concepts of *luswa* and *kiragi*, the former referring to human beings and the latter to animals. That is to say, if a person shows abnormal physical characteristics or behaves in a way which is in striking contrast to the norm of custom, he or she is said to 'fall *luswa*' (*okugwa luswa*); and if an animal behaves in a way which deviates from its normal behaviour or which leads to some unusual happening, it 'falls *kiragi*'. These 'abnormalities' comprise a wide range of phenomena, as will be seen from the following examples:

1. If an infant cuts its upper teeth first.
2. If a small child cries excessively without having any apparent reason for doing so.
3. If a circumcised person rides on an ox or a cow (as small boys often do when herding cattle).
4. If a woman climbs upon the roof of a hut. (Roofs are thatched and repaired exclusively by men.)
5. All forms of ritually prohibited or incestuous sexual intercourse are regarded as manifestations of *luswa*.
6. If a man sees a widow or his mother-in-law naked.
7. If a person commits an act of gross indecency in the presence of a person of the opposite sex.
8. If a beard grows on a woman's chin.
9. If either men or women indulge in homosexual practices.
10. If a hen 'crows like a cock'.
11. If a cow twists its tail round the trunk of a tree.
12. If a person unwittingly eats of the crops growing on a neighbour's field before the first-fruit rites have been performed.
13. If a bull calf jumps on a person's back.
14. If a certain bird, called *efurusi*, drops its excreta on a person.

In addition to events grouped under the two concepts of *luswa* and *kiragi* there are a number of other deviations from the normal order of things which are likewise thought to be fraught with dangers of a mystical nature: for example, the birth of twins—a highly welcome event among some tribes, though others consider it a great misfortune—is everywhere hedged about with elaborate rites and ceremonies which aim at neutralizing the *vuxwana*, a word which means, literally, twinship, but refers also to the inherent dangers of twinship.

Birth and death, too, evoke reactions which outwardly resemble those caused by abnormal phenomena: a woman who has given birth, a widow, and a warrior who has slain an enemy are all considered to be in a state of ritual impurity, which in the first case is referred to as *vusixu* and in the others as *vuxutjakāli* and *ovukāli* respectively. All these persons are in the same situation in that their ritual status has been impaired, thus rendering them dangerous to others, while they themselves will either get ill and die or become insane or else 'turn pale'—that is, develop a fatal skin disease.[1]

Obviously, the three situations of *vusixu*, *vuxutjakāli*, and *ovukāli* differ from each other as well as from those of *luswa* and *kiragi*, but they have a number of elements in common. Both the widow and the warrior who has slain an enemy have become contaminated through their association with death. In the case of a young mother and a widow the common denominator of their ritual status is more difficult to see. They are, of course, both passing through a critical and, as it were, 'abnormal' phase of their life, but

---

[1] The skin is said to rot like that of an over-ripe banana.

the primary source from which the danger emanates is, in the one case, the new-born child and, in the other, the person who has died. Now both the new-born child and the recently dead are referred to as *avasinde* (sing., *omusinde*), 'persons who have not yet been sacrificed for'. This is tantamount to saying that they are not yet members of the community—either of the living or of the dead. Both the new-born child and the recently dead are thus in a state of transition which is somehow felt to be critical and thus akin to the various manifestations of abnormality which we have discussed above.[1]

These notions of the normal and the abnormal provide a clue also to an understanding of the Abaluyia's idea of witchcraft (*ovulogi*). The notions of *ovulogi* and *luswa* are undoubtedly related. If we compare the various types of witches and the practices ascribed to them, we find that they are thought to be a threat to other people's lives, health, or property, not merely because they wish them evil and therefore concoct harmful medicines and utter spells, but also (or even primarily) because they themselves are freaks of nature, deviations from the normal, 'cursed people' with perverse habits and thoughts. My informants were all very emphatic that witches are not free agents but victims of an evil force that has taken possession of them or is congenital.

Since persons who become involved in any of the situations discussed above suffer from an impaired ritual status (cf. p. 48), the conclusion seems to be warranted that all these situations are believed to be at variance with the natural and social order as ordained by God. They derive their harmfulness from this very fact, for if not checked they would threaten to destroy this order.

Those specialists, on the other hand, who wield mysterious powers of a positive nature are thought to have had those powers bestowed upon them by God. The diviner, for instance, who consults various oracles to detect hidden causes, frequently invokes the help of God. After his client has left him he will pray:

> *Wele*, may you help me in my divination
> Together with *Muxove* and the ancestral spirits.
> May this man go home and everything turn out right.
> It is this which is my food.[2]

Similarly, the dream prophet is said to derive his powers from a blessing bestowed by God on him or his ancestors, who passed their special gift on to him. The same applies to the rain magician. Although he is often referred to as the 'owner' of the rain and is believed to possess the power of sending or withholding rain, my informants were unanimous in declaring that the 'real owner' of the rain is God and that 'he merely allows the rain magician to control the rain for the people'. I could not discover whether he,

[1] It must be borne in mind that our own conceptions of what is normal and what is abnormal probably differ considerably from the corresponding native ones.

[2] i.e. he makes his living by divining for other people.

also, prays to God to make his rain magic work, but there can be no doubt that according to the present world-view of the Abaluyia, his powers are believed to have been delegated to him by God and thus to form part of the scheme of things as ordained by God.

Though the powers of these experts are 'supernormal' in that they are beyond the reach of the average human being, they are not 'abnormal' in the sense in which *ovulogi*, *luswa*, and related phenomena are abnormal and hence fraught with danger.

An attempt to determine the relation between the concept of *ovuvila* (sorcery) and the two notions of the normal and the abnormal as outlined above presents greater difficulties. The sorcerer (*ombila*) also wields super-normal powers, for he is thought to be capable of curing and killing people at will by uttering magical spells or performing magical rites (based on the principles commonly encountered in magic), as well as of neutralizing the magic wielded by his fellow sorcerers or, in some cases, by witches. But just as the nature of his magic is ambivalent, so is his place in the natural and social order. My informants either denied that he derived his power ultimately from God, or they felt uncertain on this point. At the same time there is no doubt that the powers of *ovuvila* and *ovulogi* are thought to be of an opposite, or at least a fundamentally different nature. The *ombila* is feared but respected, and while he does not practise his art openly as do the diviner, the rain magician, and the dream prophet, he would never flatly deny the possession of the powers attributed to him, as would an *omulogi*; he would, however, challenge anyone who, in a concrete case, accused him of having made a person ill, or perhaps even of having killed him, with his *ovuvila*. All, then, that can be said on the available evidence is that *ovuvila* is a force *sui generis* which cannot be assigned a definite place in the scheme of things as envisaged by the Abaluyia.

The power which the ancestral spirits are believed to wield over their living relatives appears to be of a complex nature. For the first few months after death a spirit is still afflicted with the 'smell of the living' and there-fore is not yet accepted into the community of the spirits.[1] He is accord-ingly said to be in a restless, spiteful mood, bearing a grudge against all his living relatives, whom he is inclined to hold responsible for his death. This state of transition is thought to spell danger to the living in much the same way as danger emanates from a witch. Moreover, since it is generally be-lieved that a spirit retains the same character which it had as a living person, the spirits of 'bad' persons (especially those of witches) are feared more than those of 'good' persons.

As the spirit 'cools off', that is to say, becomes reconciled to his fate, his dangerousness is thought to subside and his attitude towards the living to become gradually one of benevolence. As time goes on, the offerings and prayers addressed to the spirit of a dead person acquire more and more the

---

[1] A new-born baby is said to be afflicted with a similar smell; cf. Wagner, op. cit., pp. 304–5.

character of invocations for help and lose the aspect of appeasement. Nevertheless, the spirit still retains power over the living which—though conceived as a much weaker force—resembles in quality the power ascribed to God. The spirits of the tribal and the clan ancestors especially are thought to act as guardians of tribal law and custom, punishing people who deviate from these customs, just as God punishes those who infringe the rules he has given them (cf. p. 43).

This power which the spirits are thought to have over the well-being of the living seems to be associated with the idea of seniority and thus to be related to the power ascribed to curses and blessings uttered by aged persons.[1]

The Maintenance of Social and Natural Harmony and the Expression of Social Values in Ritual

The idea of an order of things ordained by God and of deviations from that order which we have described as 'abnormal' on the one hand and as 'supernormal' on the other gives rise to a notion which may be expressed as ritual status. The starting-point of any discussion of ritual status must be the 'neutral ritual status' which a person enjoys so long as he and his dependents are in a normal state of health, so long as he lives in harmony with his relatives, friends, and neighbours, and the various activities in which he engages produce the normal results, i.e. are neither frustrated nor unduly successful.[2]

Similarly, a social group (a clan, an age-set, a village community, or the whole tribe) enjoys a neutral ritual status so long as it lives in peace with other groups and is spared such disasters as an epidemic, a drought, or similar misfortunes affecting the whole group.

Now, the ritual status may, as we have seen, be impaired by any of the mysterious disruptive forces which have been discussed above. Common symptoms which are held to indicate such impairment are illness and major or persistent misfortune in the pursuit of one's usual activities. Other symptoms at least as frequent in daily life are the various deviations from the normal (cf. pp. 44 sq.), many of which we might be inclined to regard as trivial but which to the Abaluyia are signals of serious danger. Finally, a person's ritual status is threatened by any disharmony in his social relations: for example, a matrimonial quarrel or a dispute over property.

Conversely, one's ritual status is thought to be enhanced or promoted by persistent good fortune, especially by such blessings as wealth and numerous and healthy offspring, as well as by increasing age. Old age carries with it prestige and authority, not only because seniority is one of the basic principles of the social order, but also because people who have grown old have successfully held their own against all the disruptive forces of life, and have succeeded in maintaining their ritual status at a high level.

[1] Cf. Wagner, op. cit., pp. 101 sq.
[2] While, generally speaking, persistent good fortune enhances a person's ritual status, any 'abnormally' good luck tends to render his ritual status ambiguous.

According to native belief, neither the individual nor the social group should adopt a passive attitude towards the level of its ritual status, for the Abaluyia have evolved an elaborate system of magico-religious rites and observances designed to promote, maintain, or restore the ritual status of the individual or the group. Next to the activities which aim at the satisfaction of material needs and those serving to maintain and promote social relations (hospitality, observance of kinship duties), the maintenance or restoration of the ritual status occupies the most important place in the life both of the individual and the community.

The ancestral sacrifices offered on certain occasions in the course of an individual's life[1] all serve to *promote* his ritual status, for they invoke the blessing of the ancestral spirits and of God. They also contain elements of promotive magic. Analogously, the occasional feasts staged by age-sets or by the clan community, and the semi-annual sacrifices performed by the Logoli on a tribal scale, are considered to strengthen the age-set, the clan, or the tribal community respectively.

The observance of signs and omens as well as of ritual prohibitions and avoidances (food taboos, avoidances between in-laws, rules of continence, &c.) aims at *maintaining* one's ritual status, for these enable one to steer clear of any dangers that may loom ahead or that are involved in particular situations or relationships. The initial avoidance between in-laws (it is usually lifted after the birth of the first child), for instance, seems to be based on the idea that the newly established relationship between two groups of persons belonging to different clans contains numerous latent points of friction which, like any social disharmony, imply ritual dangers. It has, accordingly, the function of a social quarantine and is based on the same idea as the avoidance observed between husband and wife after a matrimonial quarrel or between two clans that carry on a feud and therefore have also to avoid each other ritually.[2] The only difference is that the in-law avoidance is a preventive measure, while that observed after a quarrel or during a feud comes into operation only after the ritual status of the two parties concerned has been impaired by the state of social disharmony existing between them.

Ancestral sacrifices performed in cases of illness or misfortune, rites of lustration in connexion with *luswa, vuxwana, vusixu*, and similar states of ritual contamination, rites of reconciliation between individuals or groups (including peace-making ceremonies) and the various forms of counter-magic which aim at destroying or neutralizing the evil magic of an *omulogi* or an *ombila*, all finally aim at *restoring* an impaired ritual status to its normal level.

As the symptoms from which an individual or a social group suffers do

[1] e.g. the *liswakila* rite performed for a new-born child, the naming rites, various sacrifices offered in connexion with the circumcision and initiation ceremonies, with marriage, and with the setting up of a new homestead.

[2] That means that any members of the two groups must refrain from social intercourse, since this would involve ritual dangers if a rite of reconciliation had not been performed.

not in all cases indicate automatically to which one of the various agents or forces they are due, it is often necessary to consult a diviner. His oracles will identify these and also advise as to the particular magico-religious rites his client must perform to remedy the situation—that is, restore his ritual status and thereby remove the symptoms.

The principle features of the ritual pattern in all these magico-religious rites are:

1. An animal (a sheep, goat, fowl, or, in exceptional cases, a bull calf or ox) is killed by strangling.
2. Part of the animal (the entrails of a goat or sheep, the 'breast meat' of an ox, or a wing of a fowl) is hung round the neck of the person (or persons) on whose behalf the rite is performed.
3. Strips of the skin of the slaughtered animal are tied round the right wrist of all the persons whose ritual status needs to be restored. This skin wristlet is usually worn for four days (the number four figuring prominently in many rites).
4. The meat of the slaughtered animal is consumed jointly by all the persons concerned. Great importance is attached to the presence of all persons whose status has been directly or indirectly impaired. For instance, when a rite of reconciliation is performed or a curse lifted, participation in the ritual meal carries a ritual sanction with it. No one who has shared in the meal may continue to harbour ill will (or practise evil magic) against the other party without thereby coming to grief himself. No meat must be left over from such a meal.
5. Some blood of the slaughtered animal is sprinkled all over the homestead, and sometimes also over the persons submitting to the rite.
6. In all rites which serve to appease or invoke the blessing of the ancestral spirits, meat of the slaughtered animal is offered to them (it is placed either inside or on top of one of the sacrificial shrines erected in the yard of the homestead).
7. The person or persons for whose benefit the rite is performed are stroked with a live fowl (Lurogoli: *okweya nengoko*).
8. The stomach contents (Lurogoli: *ovose*; Luvugusu: *vuse*) of the slaughtered animal are trodden on by the persons concerned, or smeared on their bodies; the stomach contents are also smeared or sprinkled on any objects or parts of the homestead which may be involved, and a portion is always kept in the house so as to be available when a rite of minor importance has to be performed.
9. *Ovwanga* (a paste of eleusine flour mixed with water), or sometimes beer kept in a new gourd, is spit or blown on the chest of everyone who undergoes the rite.

It must be emphasized in this connexion that ritual killings are by no means always, or even predominantly, of a sacrificial nature. On numerous occasions a goat, a sheep, or a fowl is ritually killed and eaten (with all the other observances that form part of the ritual pattern) without any meat or blood being offered to the ancestral spirits or prayers being addressed to them. Even where the sacrificial aspect of the rite appears to be its primary feature, the magical aspect is always combined with it.

In addition to the basic features of the ritual pattern there are others which occur only in some rites or are of only marginal significance. From our own point of view they might be classed as symbolic expressions of purity, virtue, or goodness, but they are more than mere symbols. They form an integral part of the rite itself, for they are believed to possess the magic virtue of producing good or counteracting evil. The more important of these features are:

1. The colour white, which is an attribute of the Creator God, *Wele*. According to one version, this colour is associated with God because 'his dwelling-house, the sky, is very white, (i.e. bright and luminous).' Hence, sacrificial animals offered to God must be white (see also p. 31).

2. The right-hand side of anything. This figures not only in omens but also in numerous rites. Thus the skin wristlet cut from a ritually slaughtered animal must always be put on the right arm; in everyday activities, too, the right-hand side is considered the lucky and the left-hand the unlucky side.

3. Even numbers. Whenever numbers figure in rites of promotive magic they must be even numbers (cf. above, p. 50).

4. Honey (of wild bees) is licked ceremonially in many rites; for example, when performing a rite of lustration over a girl who has committed incest, when lifting a curse uttered against a thief, or when two clans ritually terminate a feud.

5. The early morning. Before sunrise 'the country is clean'. Important sacrifices must, therefore, be performed in the early morning. The same applies to quasi-ritual activities, such as visits to a diviner.

6. Virginity. In a number of rites in which girls perform minor ritual duties it is important that they should be virgins (cf. p. 42).

7. Flowing water is regarded as a purifying agent 'because it carries the evil things away'. Warriors cleanse their bloodstained spears by dipping them into a swift-running stream, and evil magic is sometimes thrown into a running stream to be carried away. Circumcision candidates and brides take a ritual bath in a swift-running stream.[1]

8. Certain wild plants, e.g. *elisazi, elilande* (a creeper), and *elineke* (a variety of saxifrage). The *elineke* plant is considered a symbol of peace: a concoction of the pounded leaves of this plant mixed with wild honey and the stomach contents of the slaughtered animal is drunk when performing rites of reconciliation. In connexion with many ritual observances persons, animals, and objects are decorated with the

[1] Unfortunately I failed to ascertain whether and in what way such a ritual bath is distinguished from an ordinary bath.

leaves of the *elilande* creeper. On the occasion of the tribal sacrifice
a number of plants and grasses (*elisazi, oluvinu, ekisugi, omuguluka,
omusundzu,* and *ekilusu*) are burnt in the ritual fire, as their smoke
is said to please God. Dried *oluvinu* plants are also burnt in the
ritual fire kindled in front of the centre post of the hut after the first
sacrifice has been offered for a new-born child.

9. Fire. As a feature of certain rites addressed to the ancestral spirits and
to God, a ritual fire (*ovwali*) is kindled either in the hut (at the base of
the centre post) or, on the occasion of the tribal sacrifice, outside a
cave which contains a sacred drum and is looked upon by the Logoli
as their tribal shrine. If the smoke from the fire rises straight to the
sky, this is auspicious; if it rises sideways, it is a bad sign.

10. Butter (ghee). When a new-born child is presented to its kindred for
the first time, both the child and its parents are ritually anointed with
ghee. Circumcision candidates who make a round of visits to their
various relatives are rubbed by them with ghee and have simsim
seeds sprinkled over their bodies. The same rite is performed over a
bride before she pays her first visit to the bridegroom's homestead.
Ghee and simsin seeds appear to be symbolic expressions of wealth.

11. Shaving the hair. At the end of a woman's confinement she and her
child are ritually shaved immediately before the child is shown to its
kindred. Circumcision candidates have their heads shaved the day
before they appear before the operator, a bride (and the bridesmaids)
before they set out to visit the bridegroom's homestead; widows and
everybody else who has come into contact with the dead are shaved
three days after the death has occurred.

Opposed to these symbols of purity, virtue, wealth, peace, and safety are
others that are thought to possess magical efficacy of a destructive nature.
They occur in the comparatively rare rites of counter-magic which are
directed against witches. Thus the *elitembe* tree (*erithrina tomentosa*) and
the *eligaka* bush (a variety of aloe) are 'bad' plants which one would throw
at the door of a suspected witch 'to return his evil magic.'[1] Further, all
poisonous plants and roots, crawling animals (snakes, lizards, worms, &c.),
birds that feed on carrion, faeces of men (but apparently not of animals—
at least, not of cattle) and any decaying matter, eggs (because they rot) and
objects of a similar nature are looked upon as 'evil substances' which are
used, or alleged to be used, by witches and sorcerers in the preparation of
their evil magic.

The various elements of the ritual pattern clearly reflect the social
values of the Abaluyia. Their domestic animals (cattle, goats, sheep, and
fowls) are their principal source of wealth and well-being, while eleusine,
though not their main staple food, is their most highly valued grain crop; it
has, so they say, a much sweeter taste than sorghum. Hence eleusine (in

---

[1] Cf. Wagner, op. cit., p. 266.

the form of *ovwanga* or beer) and the meat, blood, skin (or feathers) and, above all, the stomach contents of their domestic animals play by far the most prominent part in their magico-religious rites. It appears to be the intrinsic value for the people's well-being possessed by these objects which endows them with magical efficacy, that is, with the power to promote or restore the ritual status of those persons or things that are brought into intimate contact with them.

However, not only material objects possessing social value but also aspects of the Abaluyia's social order, such as the principle of seniority or the value attached to solidarity within the various groups, or the idea of reciprocity, find expression in ritual. It might, of course, be argued that this is self-evident and therefore without particular significance. However, the emphasis placed, for instance, on the rule that a family sacrifice must be performed by an elder brother (real or classificatory) of the head of the family and never by the latter himself (not even if he is an old man of high ritual status) seems to show that social relations through their enactment in ritual become a force which directly contributes to the efficacy of the rite. Similarly, nearly every text describing ritual procedure insists that the rite cannot be performed unless 'everyone' is present. 'Everyone' means, in any given case, all persons having a common interest in the situation which calls for the rite to be performed. The fact that all these people assemble is in itself an integral part of the rite. Thus, even in connexion with the tribal sacrifice performed by the Logoli, it is deemed an essential condition of its success that all members of the tribal community are present or at least stop working in their gardens.[1] The notion that an enactment in ritual of social relations and the principles of the social order has in itself a magical virtue finds expression also in a spell of promotive magic which enumerates a number of 'good' things and includes among them the 'coming together of people for a sacrifice' as well as 'mutual help'.[2]

The preceding discussion has shown that, according to the world view of the Abaluyia, the maintenance of the natural and social order hinges on the two notions of God as the supreme guiding and controlling principle in the world and of magical power which manifests itself in a great variety of ways. In every society religion and magic coexist, but in many they do so at different levels. Among the Abaluyia, however, the worship of God and practice of magical rites coexist on the same plane. They are, in fact, so closely interwoven that in analysing the magico-religious phenomena it seems difficult to separate the sphere of religion from that of magic. We have seen that the purification rites performed on countless occasions to restore the ritual status of an individual or a group, and the sacrifices offered both to the ancestral spirits and to God are outwardly almost identical; yet the former are evidently magical, and the latter religious rites. Ritual

---

[1] A text states: 'If they still find any one on the field, they catch him and take his hoe away from him.'

[2] Cf. Wagner, op. cit., p. 334.

killings are either rites of magic (cf. p. 51), or of religion, or both combined. Religious prayers and magical spells are recited in such similar conditions and circumstances that it is difficult to draw a clear dividing-line between them. The power of uttering curses or blessings which is attributed to living people is evidently of the same nature as the power of spirits to affect, either positively or negatively, the well-being of the living. Yet the former would be commonly classed as magic (curses and blessings are clearly spells), while the latter is usually considered a religious phenomenon. It appears, therefore, that in Abaluyia custom and sentiment the two concepts of religion and magic are not clearly differentiated into two distinct spheres but still form one integral complex.

THE LOVEDU OF THE TRANSVAAL

By J. D. and E. J. Krige

The World View of the Lovedu

THE Lovedu are a South Bantu tribe ruled by a divine queen. They live amid fertile foothills and forest-clad ravines below the Drakensberg escarpment in the north-eastern Transvaal. Their country, of which the present Mujaji Reserve is but a small portion, is situated near the frontiers of the main masses of Sotho-Tswana, Venda, Tsonga, and Nguni peoples; and it was important for the development of Lovedu institutions that the great migratory movements of these major groups skirted round this geographically insulated area.

Before the coming of the Lovedu the population of this area appears to have been predominantly Sotho not unmixed with Karanga, Tsonga, and Nguni elements. Then, about three centuries ago, a small group of Karanga immigrants from the crumbling empire of Monomatapa in Southern Rhodesia arrived and gradually incorporated the local population. From this group the royal house of the Lovedu traces its descent, and it was these people who introduced the complex of royal institutions which eventually became crucial for the world view of the Lovedu tribe. For two centuries, the formative period of their development, they enjoyed peace during which they came to dominate the area and to establish firmly the conception of the divine kingship which they had brought from the north. The situation was complicated at first by the numerical weakness of the nuclear group and the diversity of the incorporated alien groups; and a major challenge was later presented by the influx in the first half of the nineteenth century of great numbers of refugees fleeing from the depredations of Shaka, Moselekatse, and others, and seeking sanctuary in the inviolable realm of Mujaji, the rain queen of the Lovedu. They responded to this challenge by an adaptation of the pattern of the sacred kingship that facilitated incorporation of alien elements, and the result has been a remarkably coherent and well-integrated way of life.

Some Aspects of Lovedu Social Structure

Despite some unique emphases, Lovedu culture is not atypical of the South Bantu. They practise a mixed economy of hoe-culture and cattle-rearing with, however, less reliance upon cattle than Nguni or Tswana. They cultivate a fair variety of crops, most important of which are maize, millet, pumpkins, and groundnuts, and their exploitation of the rich, natural sub-tropical vegetation for purposes of nutrition, economic pursuits, and medico-magical practices is exceedingly thorough. The few cattle that are reared are significant, not for subsistence or as wealth, but for creating and maintaining the all-important social relationships and re-alignments in the social structure that arise from marriage. Cattle are not 'gods with the wet nose' as among Tswana, but they may be dedicated to the ancestor spirits.

The economy is largely a subsistence one. A man should have enough for his family's needs as well as to entertain friends and neighbours with beer to maintain his good name and reputation for liberality, and to fulfil his kinship obligations. But accumulation of goods is frowned upon: in any case, in the absence of markets or methods of preservation of the crops, an economic incentive is lacking. Payment for most services, even that of a doctor, is made in beer. Exchanges on the whole are usually not motivated by differential needs but by goodwill, the obligations of kinship, and the general emphasis upon long-run reciprocity; they are for the most part not business transactions but gift exchanges. Kin and neighbours co-operate in work parties for weeding, reaping, building. Helpers are honoured as workers (*vashumi*) and treated to beer at the end of the day, yet they cannot be said to receive any specific reward, for the gate-crashers (*vahobedi* or beggars), who join the party when it repairs to the home of the host for beer, drink calabash for calabash with the workers. In ploughing partnerships, in which each of the parties contributes his services or some commodity, there is complete disregard of equivalence between what is contributed by a partner and the service he is entitled to. Reciprocity operates through the instrumentality of economic goods, but it owes its significance as a moral force to the interdependences that arise from the social and political structure.

The society is patrilineal and marriage patrilocal, but cognates, agnates, and affines are not segregated into distinctive groups; each category over-laps to such an extent with the others, through cross-cousin marriage and other factors, that both structurally and functionally it is the bilateral kin-groups that are significant.

One of the basic features of the social system is the linking of brother and sister whereby the cattle (*munywalo*) coming in from the marriage of a sister are allocated to her brother to enable him to marry a wife. This cattle-linking of brother and sister is co-ordinated with cross-cousin marriage and an alignment of lineages into wife-providers and wife-receivers. That a man is expected to marry where his father has married or, more accurately, where his mother's marriage cattle have been used to establish a 'home', is the inevitable consequence, according to Lovedu conceptions, of the right of a sister to her cattle-linked brother's daughter as a daughter-in-law, who will cook and stamp for her and care for her in her old age. The arrangement implies that this girl should marry the son of the cattle-linked sister of her father, but should there be no such son her paternal aunt may never-theless 'marry' her, in which case she will bear children by some person appointed by the aunt to act for her non-existent son or 'pick them up' as she wishes.

A sister's cattle-providing capacity gives her a pivotal position in the social structure. It is the cattle accruing from her marriage that 'build' a house for her brother and 'beget' children to her lineage. Over this house she has rights that can be legally and mystically enforced. She settles disputes in it, and distributes its possessions when its owner dies. She invokes the gods on its behalf; no one, not even her brother himself (the husband and head of the house), can ill treat the wife of this house without having to reckon with her, and any breach of the marriage relationship is void without her consent. It will be evident that no judgement of the Lovedu courts in regard to a marriage has much chance of being carried out without the assistance and co-operation of this sister. For this and other reasons women are prominent as intermediaries and conciliators in the society. It should also be no surprise that any woman may marry wives, whose children call her 'father'; that many women are kraal heads and some of them the most important districts heads in the country. As chief officiators in offerings and sacrifice women play an important role also in religion.

Structurally the agnatic group, of which the cattle-linked brother is a member, is a minor lineage three to four generations deep, which supplies wives to the lineage into which his sister has married. The obligations of providing wives on the one hand and returning cattle on the other cannot, indeed, be enforced beyond the actual houses concerned and their lineal descendants, but the relationships of reciprocity and the behaviour patterns of helpfulness on the part of the wife-receivers, and of honouring and periodically bringing beer on the part of the wife-providers, are usually extended beyond these houses to the whole minor lineage and, where the relationships have been long established and are kept alive as part of the political structure, they may embrace major lineages five to eight generations deep. The wife-providers are called either maternal uncles (*vamalume*), since a man's mother's brother (*malume*) is ideally his wife's father, or grandparents (*vamukhulu*), since his maternal grandfather is the male representative of his wife's agnatic group (being her paternal grandfather). Conversely, the wife-receivers are called either sons-in-law (*vatsεzi*), because the lineage into which a man's sister marries is also the lineage into which his daughter marries, or *vaḍuhulu* (grandchildren or sister's sons), a man's sister's son being the same person as his daughter's husband or his father's granddaughter. It should be noted that, even though these wife-providing and wife-receiving lineages are related through marriage, the relationships between them are not merely affinal. The wife-providers and wife-receivers are not merely brothers-in-law but also cognates—wife-providers being maternal uncles and grandparents, and wife-receivers being children of paternal aunts, sisters, or daughters. A man's maternal kin are also his affines, while the maternal kin and sororal affines are merged with the paternal kin.

This merging of various types of kin is perhaps the reason why all four lines of kin—father's father, father's mother, mother's father, mother's mother—are important in ancestor worship. Any of these forebears may seize a man and make him ill, require a dedicated animal or a shrine in his or her honour, and, in fact, one may find shrines in one village or kraal to kin of several different lineages. In practice the mother's mother is an ancestor who most often causes illness in her grandchildren because of her great love for them.

The core of a large kraal or village (20 to 80 huts) is usually the minor lineage, but there are always also affines and cognates, quite apart from the spouses of agnatic members of the lineage who themselves are usually cognates. In kraal matters it is by virtue of being not an agnate, but a member of the kindred (muloɔ), that a man has a voice. The core of the district is sometimes also the lineage of the district head, but the lineage is not a political group and the influence and authority of its head are not a function of his relationship, agnatic or other, to the people living in the district. Districts, of which there are 140—with an average area of 1 square mile and population of 250—are linked to the queen on the pattern of cattle and wife exchanges. Districts are either held by descendants of one of the original agnatic lineages of the nuclear ruling group, or they have been allocated to vaṭanoni (wives of the queen) or to immigrant alien groups. They all send wives to the queen, who thereby becomes their son-in-law (muḍuhulu) and, by allocating them to other district heads and to royal relatives, she becomes parent-in-law (vamakhulu) to the latter. Those lineages of the royal nuclear group who send wives to the queen are both 'brothers' (agnates) and relatives-in-law (affines) to her. The use of the mechanism of the social system to align groups into reciprocal relations forges a great network of ties radiating from the queen to all strategic points in the society. It was in this way that large numbers of alien refugees were incorporated into the tribe and became related to one another. Payments of tribute and services to the queen are thus looked upon as the fulfilment of kinship obligations, in return for which the queen not only gives land and protection from enemies, but also transforms the clouds into rain and so frees men from fear and uncertainty.

Thus the kinship ties that bind subjects to the rain queen are interlocked with the values and institutions supporting her divinity. The homage in wives that is paid to her for giving men the blessings of rain, is also the means of forging the network of kinship ties. The kinship ties, again, convert political tribute and services due to the queen into morally sanctioned ceremonial exchanges between relatives-in-law; and just as there is no need for military virtues and military organization to deter enemies, since the queen, merely by withholding rain, can secure the defeat of the foe, so also there is no need to rely upon force to secure the willing allegiance of subjects who are treated to the beer that they bring, ostensibly as tribute to a sovereign but in reality as gifts from parents-in-law.

The queen is accordingly the pivot of the nodal institutions of the society. The benevolent forces in the universe are, as the Lovedu sometimes say, equally divided between the ancestors and the rain queen. And it is she also who controls, in the interest of social well-being, that half of the cosmic order upon which men's life and happiness are conceived most vitally to depend. This dependence upon her and the moral imperatives of the kinship obligations between her and her subjects are the main factors conditioning the Lovedu outlook upon the world and upon society. Their ritual ideology, linking the queen's mystical powers to the welfare of society, expresses their most important conceptions of the ordering of the natural world; their kinship ideology, incorporated into the political system and converting political into moral obligations, provides the main principles governing men's relations to one another. Agreement and mutual adjustment between individuals become ultimate values which have an overriding validity in determining the rights and duties of man to man. The Lovedu political pattern follows that of the centralized states of the South Bantu; yet it is not force but reciprocity, not administrative machinery but ties of sentiment, not inflexible rules but agreement, that are the great principles of social and political obligation.

Myths and Origins

The Lovedu are not given to speculation about first beginnings or final causes. There is no world-dawn or far-off mythical event when the order of nature and of society was irrevocably instituted. There is not even a sky-god to account for lightning and thunder or to furnish men with an explanation of stellar phenomena, such as the movement of heavenly bodies. Some of the larger stars are named, for example the Pleiades which are associated with hoeing time, but the association seems to be a vestige diffused from another culture and has no real significance, whether pragmatic or mystical. A vague, hardly ever invoked myth attributes the creation of the world and man to *Khuzwane* who left his footprints on certain rocks in the north when they were still new and soft. But the act of creation, like *Khuzwane* himself, is too remote, too unrelated to present realities, to be of any concern to men; and they find no place in, nor do they in any way influence, the Lovedu philosophy of the cosmos or of society. The Lovedu apparently feel the need to posit a first or final cause, but such a cause has not continued to operate as a force. An inexplicable affliction such as sterility appears sometimes to be attributed to *Mudimo*, the creator-god of the Sotho, who, according to Lovedu thought, is identical with *Khuzwane*; but *Mudimo* in this context is to be equated with a conditional destiny, and thus does not imply belief in fatalism since the course of events can be deflected by man-made medicines. Nor is there any supplication of the creator, for the Lovedu do not conceive of any link between their ancestor spirits and the creator: *Khuzwane* cannot be approached through the ancestors.

Thus origins of the cosmic order and wonders of celestial phenomena do not exercise the Lovedu mind. When Simeon, a close relative of the queen, whom we had interested in these things, asked the old men about them, they deprecated his lack of practical sense and wondered whether he was losing his reason. What is significant to the Lovedu is not the origin but the maintenance of the order of nature. Interest in the continuity of natural forces centres, however, not on an abstract system, but on the benefit of man or rather of the Lovedu people. Among these forces the most important are those governing the auspicious movements of clouds and their transformation into rain. But they stand in no relation to the forces that brought the world into existence. Among Lovedu, in contrast for example to Oceanian peoples, there is consequently complete discontinuity between mythological origins, or the forces that operated at the dawn of the world, and present realities or the forces maintaining the existing order. Even the ancestor gods do not bridge this gap, and man's dependence upon them—and hence the force of religious sanctions—derives not from their relationship to the beginnings of things but from kinship principles.

Myths play an insignificant part in Lovedu life. Almost the only myths are legends of the institution of the present political order which give a generalized account of the migration of the royal nuclear group from Rhodesia and of the reigns of the various chiefs. There is no attempt in them to intensify the beliefs or validate the institutional arrangements underlying the sacred kingship. It is not these myths that give warranty to the queen's mystical credentials and to the complex of customs that supports them. Indeed today scant credence is accorded by the younger men to the legendary royal ancestry which traces the descent of the nuclear group to the Karanga of Monomotapa in Southern Rhodesia, for the Lovedu find it difficult to believe that they are related to a people who now appear to them to be inferior, lacking the prestige and aristocratic pretensions of their reputed ancestors. In one version of the myth the Lovedu broke away from Monomotapa under the younger 'chosen' son to whom the previous chief had given the rain-charms. He fled south as a result of his conflict with the eldest brother who had legal precedence. In another, it is a daughter who, having committed incest with her brother, escapes with the rain-charms and her infant son from her outraged father.

The legends are further concerned to explain the settlement of the Lovedu in their present environment: their choice was determined by the absence of red earth which would soil their loincloths and the abundance of *murula* trees and mounds of edible termites, both of which are valued and ritually significant items in their diet. A later dissension between two claimants to the throne is presented as a conflict between chief son and chosen son, and again the victory of the chosen son vindicates the divine right of the rain-maker against legal precedence, and in that way appears to justify the present flexible system of succession as against the challenge of the Northern Sotho emphasis on primogeniture and certainty. Just as the title to becoming ruler of a new tribe is in one version validated by the incest of brother and sister, so the later and equally momentous change from kings to queens is brought into relation with father-daughter incest.

But the whole cycle of myths merely emphasizes in very general terms the importance of rain-making as a prerequisite of the claim to chieftainship and for the well-being of the tribe; it does not concern itself with justifying the validity of the various institutional arrangements that are the main support of the beliefs and values of the queen's mystical credentials.

Conception of the Natural Order

The Lovedu do not oppose man and nature. There are no explicit formulations of the nature of the universe, but a natural order inexorably going its ordained way is implicitly rejected in their conceptions. The assumption is that cosmic forces are controllable and, in fact, controlled at every turn by man for his own benefit. Since nature is of interest and importance only so far as it is or can be used by society, there is no such conception as a world order unrelated to man's activities and desires. The order of nature is a controlled one. There are various ways in which man is able to use and control powers in nature—by *vuɲaga* (the evil aspect of which is *vulɔi*), i.e. by the use of power concentrated in certain persons and objects; by appeal to the ancestor-gods upon whom are projected the powers that the child experiences in relation to its parents; through the mysteries of the *digɔma* which are associated with initiation and the fertility cult; and through the divinity of the queen whose concern it is to control nature in the interests of the tribe as a whole. This idea of the control of nature by the chief on behalf of the tribe is not unique; it is common among the Bantu tribes of South Africa. But the Lovedu emphasis is on the divine origin and special affinity with nature of the queen herself, whereas in tribes such as the Zulu and Tsonga, where the mystical relation of the chief to his people and his powers over nature have to be achieved by magical strengthening on his accession and to be renewed periodically, it is largely by means of the magic of the royal regalia that the chief is able to exercise control. Among all, including Lovedu, one of the most important factors in the powers and position of the chief is the fact that he is the living representative of the long line of royal ancestors (tribal gods). There is considerable overlapping of these four categories among the Lovedu. Thus ancestors are kept satisfied and happy by a charm placed in their shrine; the queen controls rain not only through her divinity but also by means of medicines and charms and appeals to her ancestors who can prevent her from making rain. Let us consider these means for the control of nature in greater detail.

Vuɲaga (skilled use of power concentrated in persons and objects)

The forces of nature may be manipulated through properties intrinsic in various objects, animate and inanimate. The substances in which these attributes or powers (*maaɖa*) reside are mainly *melimo* (medicines) or *mɛre* (plants). But the term medicines in this context has a wider connotation than the parallel term among us; it includes both medicine and magic, and is a medico-magical conceptual category which to the Lovedu is quite distinct from the supernatural. While anyone who knows a cure for an ailment is manipulating the forces of nature and using *vuŋaga*, there are doctors who, by virtue of long training, know many medicines, have learnt how to divine and have been imbued with additional perspicacity and powers as a result of a special initiation. Medicine functions by virtue of the properties, actual or ascribed, of matter; the principles underlying the operation of medicines assume mechanical cause and effect and even the divining bones are read according to rule.

There are, however, two types of doctor who fall into a different category: the *lelɔpɔ* doctor, directly possessed and guided by an ancestor spirit, who largely confines his activities to curing possessed people, and the *mugɔme* or 'smeller-out' who is generally a foreigner. People using the forces of nature for evil purposes are *valɔi* (witches and sorcerers) and are dealt with in another context. *Uuŋaga*, it will be seen, is the use of impersonal power inherent in matter, which is extracted by the expert (*ŋaga*) and applied in the interests of the health and well-being of men; it is also the exercise of personal qualities or skills, either inherited or acquired through spirit possession or guidance.

Ancestors

Ancestors can influence for good and evil the fortunes only of their own descendants, who in the case of the chief's ancestors are taken to include the whole tribe. Their control over the forces of nature is not explicitly formulated; and what is expressly stated is not always confirmed in Lovedu religious practices. The ancestors are clearly conceived to exercise an overall control. A man will always assert that no harm or illness can befall him if his ancestors are watchful enough, for they have power to ward off all evil and misfortune. It is said that even witches cannot, without the will of the ancestors, enter a village or deliver the last fatal blow that kills a man. But in practice the will of the ancestors either is not interposed, for no ascertainable reason, or is ineffective to ward off attacks. If some great sorrow overtakes a man, it is said that 'his ancestors have had an accident' implying that he has been temporarily deprived of their protection and is at the mercy of his enemies. Even medicines are said to be ineffective without the co-operation of one's ancestors, the conception being not merely that their goodwill is essential but also that *vuŋaga* belongs to the ancestors. In fact, however, the ineffectiveness of medicines is never in any concrete case attributed to the lack of such co-operation.

Ancestors are appealed to and thanked for good crops, fertility, plenty, and all manner of good fortune and success. The desire to be remembered and given tendance is attributed to them, and they may themselves cause harm and sickness to descendants who neglect them; but somewhat inconsistently a man may with impunity neglect them for many years and give them tendance only when misfortune overtakes him. Ancestors may be approached and propitiated or thanked by means of offerings and prayer and the use of *dithugula*, objects such as beads which have once been in their possession; but they can also be constrained by medicine or the properties of matter.

Ancestors are capricious: their complaints as seen in the divining bones are usually about being neglected; but they may cause illness to those they love most in order to receive recognition, have their name perpetuated, or their beads worn. They are said to 'hold' the woman experiencing difficult labour, to afflict children with sore eyes, and even to prevent the queen from making rain. Their complaints need imply no omission or neglect on the part of the afflicted descendant, but merely some special desire that could not have been anticipated. The degree of either neglect or tendance bears no relation to their satisfaction or dissatisfaction, since the ascription of misfortune to the ancestors is always *ex post facto*: hence the paradox that a family that is assiduous in its tendance of the ancestors may suffer more ill health and misfortune than one that has neglected the ancestors for a long time.

Dithugula are instrumental in controlling nature not only indirectly through the ancestors but also directly by virtue of the substances used in them. A *thugula* may be a shrine to an ancestor (male or female), an animal dedicated to him, old beads or objects of iron to which, owing to their having once been in his possession, power to influence him is attributed. But a *thugula* may also be any charm of herbs concocted by a doctor and worn for protective purposes. The queen's rain-medicines are *dithugula*. The most important religious ceremony of the year, the annual offering of beer to ancestors as thanksgiving for the harvest, is also called *thugula*. *Dithugula* thus constitute a category of objects, usually closely associated with the ancestors (though they may be made by a doctor), through which they may be approached, and which have special virtue particularly to give health and protection against ills and epidemics.

Dithugula are found in every lineage which, through its shrines, dedicated animals, and charms, secures the general welfare of its members. The queen's *dithugula*, her rain-medicines, sacred objects, and shrines through which she intercedes with the royal ancestors, are the ultimate symbols of her power and the safeguards of the welfare of the country; and just as certain medicines (*diphaba*), which are used in shrines or offerings to make the ancestors forget their complaints, are pegged round the village by the paternal aunt or sister of its head to protect it against witches, so also the queen may *thugula* the whole country by sending boys to peg medicated sticks on its boundaries as a protection against evil, particularly epidemics that might threaten it from outside.

The queen's control

The basis of the queen's control over nature is her divinity. So bound up is she with nature that her very emotions affect the rain. The complex of royal institutions includes the conceptions that she must be without physical imperfections, not susceptible to the ills that befall ordinary men; that she cannot die a natural death but departs only by her own volition; that succession to the throne is uncertain since the choice of a ruler must in the last resort be made by the spirits of the tribe; that though she may not have a husband, lest political control become concentrated in him, yet she must bear the heir by a secret consort (a royal classificatory brother) specially chosen to maintain untarnished the purity of the royal blood; that she ensures the regularity of nature and the changing of the seasons; and, more particularly, that her death dislocates the rhythm of nature, bringing drought and famine, the abrogation of law and order. People today still speak with horror and fear of the years (1894–6) following the death of the previous queen, Majuji II. They were years, as we know from documentary sources, when drought, locusts, rinderpest and, in their wake, unprecedented famine and desolation, wiped out practically all the cattle and perhaps a third of the human population.

The preservation of the queen's sanctity requires that her life be subject to observances which shield her from the public eye and restrain her movements. She is 'the huckster in the hut' (*mushava-ndoni*) who sells her rain-medicines from the seclusion of her abode, and may not move about freely or leave the district of the capital. She was the only chief in the Union who, a few years ago, could not go to the Native Commissioners' Office to exercise the vote of her people in the election of a representative to the Native Representative Council. She cannot attend large assemblies of men, and is generally inaccessible except to her close relatives and great councillors. But otherwise her activities are not restricted, nor is her life a continuous ritual and, unlike other Divine Kings, there are no elaborate safeguards surrounding her every movement.

Tradition decrees that chiefs may have no physical defect, but not that they must die while still young and strong. Ritual suicide of the queen is by Lovedu conceptions not a means of guaranteeing a timely death lest failure of physical powers should upset the regularity of nature, but rather a symbol of her divinity, for it proves that she is not heir to the weaknesses of ordinary man. It is mystically connected with the fourth circumcision school in her reign: she must see the boys going in but not coming back. The Lovedu queen is believed to be immune from disease, but age does not diminish—it even increases—her mystical powers over nature. The only disqualification to rule is inability to make rain in the early period of her reign. Once she has demonstrated, by her ability to make rain, that the rain-charms have been entrusted to her and that she has been divinely chosen, irregularities in the seasons are attributed not to weakness of her powers but to some extraneous factor, such as contraventions of rules associated with keeping the country cool, disobedience to the chief, and the anger of the ancestor spirits.

Arrangements connected with succession of a new queen also emphasize her mystical relations with the cosmic order. The death of her predecessor

was not announced for a year, while, as the body decomposed, such vital in-
gredients of the rain-medicine as the skin and body-dirt were carefully collected; after the announcement a period of anarchy often supervened as rival
claimants marshalled their armed forces for the struggle for the throne. At
the end of this year of mourning all the fires of the country were put out with
purificatory rain-medicine (*mufugɔ*) from the official keeper at the capital.

This fire rite symbolizes purification of the country as well as a transition
from one order to another. At any time when the country is not right (*naha
a e loge*), as when there is severe drought, the fires are put out 'to usher in a
new year' (i.e. a new order or period of operative forces). But the fire rite also
symbolizes the means through which the allegiance of subjects and the
authority of the queen are asserted. Finally, the beating out of the fires with
cooling medicine is part of a complex of practices connected with heat and
cold, symbolizing respectively dysphoria and euphoria. The 'earth is hot'
(*mavu a fesa*) on the death of the queen and a new cosmic order has to be
inaugurated by cooling it in preparation for the new rain-maker.

After the fire rite there follows the divine identification of the successor
by the rite of opening the door. The rival claimants, one of whom, chosen
by the inner royal council and the deceased queen, has been secretly prepared for his office, pass the hut in which the queen has died. They announce their identity to the spirit of the deceased, lightly touching the door
of the hut, which yields to the chosen successor.

In and around the inner secret council where the choice is actually made
centre serious tensions, not only between the present ruler and the heir-
elect for whose sake and succession she must poison herself, apparently not
always willingly, but also between those who depend for their position and
prestige upon the patronage of one or the other. The 'chosen' heir always
goes to live far away, ostensibly to conceal his or her identity but in reality
also owing to a serious conflict with the reigning sovereign.[1]

For the regulation of cosmic forces the queen relies not only on her
divinity but also upon the royal rain-medicines and, in the last resort, on
the agreement of the royal ancestor spirits. To prevent the weakening of
the rain-medicine it must be revitalized by being given the first termites and
first-fruits each year, and occasionally parts of a black sheep or, in the old
days, a human being.

Rain-charms are liable to weaken (*figɛhɛla*) or become defiled (*khuma*) by
certain deviations from the normal course of nature unless special precautions are taken. Twins, babies cutting their upper teeth before their lower,
women dying in pregnancy, abortions and miscarriages, men dying from
dɛrɛ, a deadly coughing disease believed to be contracted by having sex
intercourse with a woman who has had a miscarriage or abortion or whose
child has died before weaning—all these are deviations which contaminate
the earth, causing it to be 'hot', and therefore have to be buried in wet soil or

---

[1] Males are not debarred from succession; indeed the early rulers were all men. But a
definite preference for women rulers seems now to be firmly established.

cooled with rain-medicine. The polluted corpse (called *pukudi*, the opposite of *fuga*) is thought of as thrusting up an arm and waving it about to disperse the rain.

It is the duty of the queen each year to *thea* or 'establish' the season propitiously for her people. Certain district heads who are close relatives of the queen have rainpots which they revitalize every year with medicine from the queen and stir them up at the queen's command to ensure a propitious season. In the old days the year was 'established' also by the beating of the sacred drums (*gɔmana*) and a visit to the royal ancestor graves, but this has fallen into disuse.

If there is drought or if the rain does not come at its appropriate time, people say the queen has not changed the year properly and steps are taken to approach her. Royal relatives may approach her personally or complain in her hearing that she is killing her people by withholding rain; district heads may formally pay homage (*hu lova*) with gifts of £1 or a head of cattle, or may bring a troupe of dancers to please her and invoke her pity at the spectacle of people dancing when they should be hoeing. The songs (*lesugu*) are associated with offerings to the ancestors and with rain. If these efforts are of no avail diviners are consulted to determine the cause of drought— the rain-charms may have been 'weakened' or evil practices of witches may have prevented rain. In 1937 the people were told at a tribal gathering to report lightning 'sent' by witches, and shortly afterwards, when lightning had struck a tree near a village, boys were sent to sprinkle every house in the area with *mufugo* to 'cool' the lightning. Witches may also disperse rain by hanging up medicated branches which sway in the air. If it is an ancestor that is 'holding the queen's hands' he or she has to be propitiated by the sacrifice of a black beast or sheep on the grave.

When winds frustrate the efforts of the queen to make rain, especially when a gale disperses auspicious black clouds, people come to condole with her as if she had lost a relative, and it is taboo to work in the fields the next day, just as it is on the day after the first rain of the season and on certain other occasions.

The queen is 'Transformer of the Clouds', the changer of the seasons, and guarantor of their cyclic regularity, but she can exercise her powers auspiciously only in certain conditions and in 'agreement with the ancestors'.

Digɔma

The fourth category of forces by which nature is regulated in the interests of man consists of *digɔma* which are associated more especially with changes in the status of man. A *gɔma* is primarily a drum, but as an abstract concept it is particularly identified with the power concentrated in the drum cult. This cult includes the large complex of institutions connected with rites of transition, of which the year-long *vyali-vuhwera* (fertility cult) is one. A *gɔma* is thought of as something mystical and secret, awesome and esoteric. The circumcision 'school' for boys is called a *gɔma* which is said to 'bite' the initiates. It is something mystically powerful which transforms boys into men. But if the initiation as a whole is a *goma*, so also are the secret formulae, objects, and mummeries that form part of the ceremony.

With the *vyali-vuhwera* fertility cult, which is at the same time also an initiation for girls (*vyali*) and for boys (*vuhwera*), are associated many *digɔma*, in the form of masked figures in costumes made of grass, reeds, and leaves, or plays and mummeries emphasizing the value of certain foods. But the greatest of all is *Khiudogane*, Bird of Muhale (the royal founder ancestor), ruling spirit of the *vyali*, which is believed to emerge from a pool on moonlight nights, leave mists behind it when it departs, and upon which much of the ritual centres. It is the link between two aspects of sacred forces, that conceived as mysterious, fearful, approached only through elaborate symbolism, and that represented by ancestors and directly approached. For the bird is both a great *gɔma* and a symbol of the royal ancestors.

Revived in 1938, after an interval of twenty years, the *vyali-vuhwera* with its great *digɔma* is thought to promote abundance and rain, the welfare and happiness of the people. While it lasts it is the main national interest to which all energies are bent and all activities subordinated. Marriages are held up, the normal judicial machinery is at a standstill, and anything that might compete with the ceremonial is interdicted. Since initiates spend only early mornings and evenings at the secret enclosure, they sleep at home and are able to carry on essential domestic tasks for the greater part of the day.

The sacred drums of the tribe (*digɔma*), four in number, are kept and cared for by the people of Ravothata, a lineage that came from Phalavorwa, where the drum cult is more intimately connected with the chief than among the Louedu. These drums, which are said to contain under the resonator a human skull and, in the case of the smallest, the facial skin of a councillor, are mystically linked with the life of the queen and the welfare of the tribe. The heir sits on the smallest drum while being taught the rain ritual and it must accompany the queen if ever she is forced to flee from her enemies. The sacred drums are spoken of as *vadimo* (gods) as well as *digɔma*, and they were beaten twice a year in the old days in a ceremony known as *gɔmana* as an appeal to the ancestors for rain and to thank them for the harvest. The latter took the form of an initiation into the secrets of the cult at which boys were given certain cuts on their faces.

Associated with the sacred drums and also classed as *digɔma* are the *zwidajani*, the weird whistling ancestor spirits of the royal lineage who come to earth in the guise, it is said, of half-men with one eye, one arm, and one leg, to take part in the rites connected with the sacred drums and in the annual harvest *thugula* ceremony in all royal and certain other lineages. They are, in fact, as is known to those initiated in the *gɔmana*, old men masquerading as spirits. They appear in the bush near the village and join in the singing of *lesugu* songs which are sung, on these occasions, through specially constructed secret whistles.

The *gɔmana* drums are no longer used by the queen to appeal to the
ancestors for rain, but she permits boys from the royal village to attend
gɔmana initiation ceremonies held occasionally, with her permission, by an
outsider. The *gɔmana* concept, despite the support it gives to the mystical
attributes of the queen, appears to represent a conceptual pattern that is
autonomous and more fully developed in some neighbouring tribes, where
the moments of the agricultural year were signalized by the sounding of the
drums which were thought to bring rain and fertility, to bless the crops and
cattle, and to safeguard the country from disease and enemies. In some
tribes today the cult is a recent innovation in the form of initiation schools
managed by outsiders who have their own drums and *zwidajani* visitors
from tribes where the cult is better known.

Evil and how to avoid it

It has been shown that the Lovedu conceive the order of nature as
something essentially man-controlled through the power of medicine and
magic (*vuŋaga*), through the ancestors, through the divinity and powers of
the queen, and through the mysterious forces associated with *digɔma*. The
seasons and the rain have to be established by the queen for the crops to
prosper; the baby 'grows by medicines' which guard it from harm and
sickness and imbue it with health and strength; adulthood is achieved
through initiations and *digɔma*; and over and above all, there is the watchful
care of the gods. The natural order accordingly can and must be manipulated by utilizing benevolent and nullifying malignant forces, in order to
further man's good fortune or to prevent evil from befalling him.

The Lovedu have elaborated some interesting concepts of impersonal
evil powers which are concentrations of forces brought about by certain
concatenations of conditions or events. These concepts are found over a
much wider area, but have received special emphasis among the Lovedu.
To them the ultimate good is rain. Rain is regarded as not merely the
material source of life and happiness and the physical basis of man's sense
of security; it is also a symbol of spiritual well-being and a manifestation
that the social order is operating smoothly. Hence coolness denotes a state
of euphoria: man and matter to be in order and to function properly have
to be kept cool; angry ancestors must be cooled by means of medicine; even
witches can be cooled and so made to forget their evil purposes. On the
other hand, heat as the antithesis of the main basis of man's security, the
cooling, life-giving rain, is conceived as a destructive force leading to a
state of dysphoria.

'Heat' is a concept suggested by the physical properties of heat; it may
sometimes be sensed, for example, as an important factor in fever, one of
the most prevalent illnesses. But actually its operation is inferred from conditions of which 'heat' is clearly the cause, such as droughts and the desic-
cation of the crops. Here the generation of heat is ascribed to the effect upon
the earth of disturbances of the regular course of nature by the burial in it

of twins, abortions, miscarriages, and women dying in childbirth, or by the
cosmic chaos resulting from the death of the chief. 'Hot blood' is one of the
commonest causes of illness. *Leswa* (burning) is primarily a physiological
condition of a woman resulting from abortion and it may be transmitted to
the man who has intercourse with her, who then contracts the dreaded and
fatal *dɛrɛ*, a coughing disease considered to be quite different from con-
sumption (*lefiha*). 'Heat' affects the physical potency of medicines and
charms, the mental repose of the gods, the mysterious powers of *dithugula*,
and the welfare of the whole country. It stirs (*dzusa*) the gods to anger and it
activates the criminal propensities of witches.

'Heat' and 'cold', then, are all-important conceptual categories which are
brought into relation with the functioning of the physical, mental, and
emotional forces in man, in the ancestors, and in nature. Wherever 'heat' is
considered to be generated, the proper antidote is the administration of
'cooling' medicines, i.e. substances which have the property of counteracting the heat or soothing the burning. The remedy is to put right what is
wrong (*hu logisa*), to secure a return to normal conditions by cooling
agencies. If the whole country is in an abnormal condition (*a e loge*, literally,
is not right) all the fires must be sprinkled with *mufugo* medicine (*hu fuga*
means to blow upon with a cool breeze). Sources of heat to the earth, e.g.
twins, abortions, must be buried in wet soil; ancestor spirits aroused by
'heat' (anger) have to be calmed by squirting water (*hu phasa*) on objects
once in their possession or over their graves. Cooling medicines likewise
counteract that burning of the fingers which constrains witches to do evil,
while charms protecting the village against witches are often called
mashɔthɔjɔ (things causing coolness). In all these cases the active reagent
in the medicines is some substance having 'cooling' properties, such as the
river stones guarding the entrance to villages or built into shrines of
ancestors, the succulent bulbs used in the rite for the removal of the 'dirt'
(*khitshila*) of death, the great overhanging fig-trees shading shrines, the
green undigested chyme from a sheep or goat's alimentary canal that figures
prominently in ritual. Much medical ingenuity goes into the manufacture
of powders and decoctions which, owing to their special cooling properties,
will counteract heat; and it is not surprising that the Lovedu way of curing
malaria is to seek drugs that will drive out the 'heat' by means of profuse
perspiration. 'Heat' is most commonly caused by abnormalities associated
with the procreation and the actual or threatened destruction of human
life—hence the close association of 'heat' with sex, reproduction, and death.

Another malignant force, *muridi* (shadow), is conceived as evil cast by
certain conditions. It infects those upon whom it falls, but if they are
healthy, the effect upon them is invisible and harmless, though they become
carriers who may transmit the contagion to others with whom they come
into contact, especially those whose resistance is weak, such as new born
babies and sick people. 'Shadow' thus explains the spread of contagion, not
by direct contact but through an intermediate unaffected carrier. *Muridi* is

not a real or mystical shadow in our sense of the term, but an evil and contagious force conceptualized, on the analogy of a shadow, as an invisible counterpart of certain conditions. The sources of 'shadow' are such conditions or events as death, activities connected with human reproduction, including sex intercourse, the early stages of pregnancy, birth of twins, miscarriage (regarded as death), women during confinement, irregular appearance of the teeth, e.g. upper incisor before lower or molar before incisor. 'Shadow' is accordingly connected with many of the same kind of irregularities as generate 'heat', but it appears to be differentiated as an independent concept for the purpose of dealing with its effects on the health of people who are peculiarly susceptible to defilement.

Precautions are taken to protect the sick against the influence of *muridi*. A sick person is smeared with medicines or quarantined like a new-born child by means of a medicated stick placed across the entrance to his hut to warn off carriers of 'shadow' and counteract the 'shadow' of anyone unaware of his condition. If there is an epidemic in a village and the general vitality and resistance consequently are lowered, people may be told to refrain from sex intercourse lest *muridi* make the illness worse. In the small-pox epidemic of 1938 people cohabiting were said to have the disease in a worse form than others. When a child is ill, its parents refrain from sex intercourse. A warrior who slept with his wife the night before battle would be easy prey to the enemy. A man sleeping with his wife may not approach a slaughtered animal before its stomach has been pierced nor help skin it without first smearing his hands with (usually cooling) medicine, lest *muridi* affect the meat and cause stomach trouble (*makhuma*) to those eating it. Children whose teeth appear irregularly (*lesheга*) are full of *muridi* and were killed in the old days. But today they are treated by a doctor and have to be careful never to bite others, for the wound will not heal and there is always difficulty in obtaining the necessary antidote, namely, scrapings from the teeth of the *lesheга*. Cross-roads and river fords are secondary sources of *muridi* since the 'shadow' carried by unsuspecting hosts infects these places. For this reason pregnant women are not supposed to go on long journeys from home.

Muridi is a much more limited concept than 'heat'; it is invoked mainly to account for the aggravation of illness or the susceptibility to illness or other injury of persons contacting defilement. It does not affect the country generally, and it furnishes an alternative to witchcraft as an explanation of the aggravation of ailments or the failure of illnesses to yield to ordinary remedies.

Muridi in a more virulent form is called *leridi* (ominous or menacing shadow), which infects a warrior who has killed an enemy and who is in grave danger of becoming mad or very quarrelsome unless purified. An allied concept is that of *letala* (sinister track) derived from the idea that, if a woman is cohabiting with two men one of whom gets ill, the track of the other, should he approach near or within earshot of the sick person, will cause the latter to die by aggravating his illness. Similarly a man's mistress must avoid coming near the hut of his wife when she is ill or in childbirth, lest the mistress's sinister track endanger the life of the wife.

Makhuma (from *hu khuma*, to mix) is a concept which uses the analogy of contamination by mixture or contact to account for physical weakening, wasting away or enfeeblement (*hu fiɡɛhɛla*). The situations that constitute the chief source of *makhuma* are critical transitions in the life of the individual as well as serious crises such as severe illnesses. The evil contaminates or infects the person who has undergone the change or who, in the case of death, comes into contact with its baneful influence. He seems to suffer from loss of vitality, or to become dislocated because of the change in his condition.

The measures taken to combat *makhuma* are in the first instance preventive. Strengthening medicines are administered or inoculated to fortify the individual by anticipation; thereafter, under isolating conditions that are gradually relaxed, an adjustment is made to the new situation. Thus novices in the various initiations are medically treated in anticipation of their susceptibility to *khuma* on entering their new condition. Babies are fortified (*hu thuswa*, to be helped) by scarification and steaming before they leave the hut of confinement; kin and other inmates of the village must after a death be readjusted by means of medicines and other treatment to the change caused by the death lest they *khuma*. *Makhuma* also affects possessed people who fail to use medicine with the first-fruits. A man will *khuma* if he cohabits with a woman after the death of her child unless she has first been medically purified, and she must also be careful not to give food to other children before treatment lest they get ill and die. If one baby dies, any illness its successor may have is liable to be diagnosed as due to *makhuma*. Even cattle may *khuma* after a death in the village or if a woman enters the cattle fold.

By logical extension and the invocation of a further series of presuppositions the concept is applied to the bones of a diviner, which are liable to *khuma* (lose their diagnostic powers) every month—they are said to 'see their moons'—or when used to divine about a death, and must be washed in medicine before being used again. Similarly the queen's rain-medicine will *khuma* unless given the first termites and first-fruits, or when people neglect observances connected with the burial of those who are 'hot'.

The evils differently conceptualized in the notions of 'heat', *makhuma* and 'shadow' have this in common: they are all instances of a ritual impurity, generated by certain states or conditions, not because of their morally reprehensible nature but because of their abnormality or their relation to reproductive processes or critical changes in life. 'Heat' and 'shadow' appear to be different aspects of the same kind of ritual impurity, but 'shadow' is dangerous only to someone whose resistance is low because of illness or immaturity, while 'heat' may have deleterious effects not only on healthy people but on natural phenomena, on ancestor spirits, and on charms or *digɔma*. *Makhuma* which arises from critical transitions causes mainly stomach trouble and general debility in men and cattle; but it also causes weakening of the mystical powers concentrated in sacred objects. These ritual forces do not strike down the guilty person: it is, for example, not the husband who will be revenged if the adulterer approaches the hut of his wife; or when a woman has procured an abortion, it is not she but her innocent lover who will be affected with *dɛrɛ*, the most dreaded disease among the Loʋedu. The harmful effects of all these forms of impurity are not sanctions against the acts or events causing the impurity, but sanctions for taking the necessary precautions to remove the impurity and prevent it from spreading to others, or from causing some calamity not necessarily affecting the guilty person. And, as so often happens in Loʋedu society, it is generally *ex post facto*, and as an explanation of some illness or evil that these conceptions are invoked and steps are taken to put things right.

The concatenations of actions and conditions that must be avoided lest they bring about misfortune and evil to men are wider than what is included in the conceptions of 'heat', *muridi*, and *makhuma*. Many things or natural objects brought into relation with men have evil consequences and must be avoided: they are taboo (*hu ila*). Burning a certain kind of wood in the village causes quarrels; working in the fields the day after the first rain is taboo, not sanctioned by a penalty but the breach of which is a bane (*lesola*) that may portend evil. The breach of these taboos is disapproved but leads to no organized reaction or public indignation even where it affects the welfare of all, as in the case of a wrong burial. A man who sleeps with his wife while she is still suckling a child may thereby cause the death of his child; but it is his own foolish and inconsiderate conduct that causes the mother's breast to *khuma* (become polluted and weakened), and it is not the concern of outsiders. He is a fool rather than criminal.

Many things in nature are recognized as directly affecting man adversely; various foods and drinks cause stomach troubles; poisonous weeds may kill cattle which, like men, occasionally die of old age; many minor illnesses are attributed to natural causes, e.g. one may contract malaria by walking in the dew in the early morning. Epidemics may be brought about naturally by the air or wind (*phɛfo*). 'Ward off from us these winds' is a constant plea in prayers to the ancestors. Hot, dry winds which drive away rain-bearing clouds or dissolve them in thunderstorms or gales are thought to be specially detrimental to the rain, and it is the duty of the ancestors to keep away such winds. Even anxiety or worry wears a man down (*hu seḍa mutho a homɛlwa*, lit., scrapes a man thin). A woman who is prone to break her pots is not bewitched; she has *khifyaisa*, a natural propensity for breaking, which can be cured by medicine.

The Loʋedu also have the conception of natural accident (*gozi*) and of luck (*leshuto*), though bad luck is sometimes attributed to breach of obligations to kin, to malicious gossip, or to the misconduct in one's absence of one's wife.

An omen or bane (*lesola*) presages death or disaster, but it may itself be the cause of the evil that follows. An owl hooting outside a hut, cats crying plaintively (not caterwauling) at night, presage disaster, for cats have uncanny insight; a mountain snake can be a *lesola*, and so can a *leshega*, i.e. a person whose teeth have appeared in the wrong order. A person will *tola* another, i.e. cause misfortune or death to descend upon a member of the latter's family, by swearing badly at him, especially if the words are out of all proportion to the offence or provocation.

These concepts of natural luck, accident, and omens are thus also linked with human relationships. Good relations with near relatives may bring you good luck, bad relations, especially with your father or father's sister, bad luck or illness to your children. In fact any man who despises the great, particularly his father, will, it is said, see him in the bones as the cause of his misfortune, especially if the old man dies before a reconciliation has been effected. An old man's scolding or curse is an omen (*vusola*) which portends and causes misfortune to a near relative of the person scolded, and the grievance of one's sister or father's sister, even if it is unconscious, generates a force (*mahava*) which brings illness upon one's children and which can be neutralized only by a religious rite. The exact relation between *mahava* and the ancestors is not very clear. The Lovedu conceive *mahava* as following automatically from the bad relationship between important kin. Yet reconciliation, which removes the source of the *mahava*, is not enough for putting matters right. It is the ancestors that must remove the illness at the request of the aggrieved party.

Witchcraft and Sorcery (*Uulɔi*)

The evils that have so far been mentioned are either inherent in nature or only vaguely brought into relation with the conduct and relationships between men. Their effects except in a few cases are mild, rarely ending in death. In a completely different category is the greatest and most devastating source of evil *vulɔi* (witchcraft and sorcery), brought about directly by man. *Uulɔi* is, by Lovedu conceptions, always due to the conscious, evil practices of man and is directed at persons he has reason to hate.[1] *Uulɔi* is morally reprehensible, and witches and sorcerers are the arch enemies of society. The concept of *vulɔi* explains evil in terms of the malicious wickedness in men's hearts; it is criminality incarnate in man. The term *vulɔi* covers both witchcraft and sorcery; nevertheless the Lovedu make a clear distinction between witchcraft (*vulɔi vya vusiu*—night witchcraft) and sorcery (*vulɔi vya matsiare*—day witchcraft). The night-witch uses sinister inherited powers which extend beyond the ordinary course of nature. The sorcerer uses the natural, known powers of medicine for anti-social ends. Witchcraft implies possession of power to do evil transcending the under-

---

[1] Neighbouring Venda and Tsonga conceive the witch as constrained to evil by heredity but unconscious of his own evil acts.

standing of ordinary men; sorcery is the manipulation of lawful means for unlawful ends.

The night-witch belongs to an unholy fraternity whose members meet at night to dance to their drums and deliberate upon their deeds of darkness. She uses no medium of destruction and no medicine or spells, but has inborn powers to do what is physically impossible to ordinary men. She goes herself on her nefarious errands or uses familiars. Witches are almost invariably women, partly no doubt because it is difficult to conceive of women having the facilities to purchase medicines for purposes of sorcery, partly also because they are endowed with more mysterious powers than men. The sorcerer, usually a man, whose machinations involve the use of medicines and spells, is a day-witch because his power is derived from ordinary natural techniques 'of the day'. The essence of sorcery is the criminal use of the potency of medicines which can be, and usually are, used in the service of legitimate ends.

Many medicines are specifically good or bad and their use cannot traverse their intrinsic nature; but some of the most important are good and hence moral, or bad and hence immoral according as they are used for socially approved or socially disapproved ends. *Madabi*, for example, has the power to transmute the nature of things. It is right for a husband to manipulate *madabi* in a way that will cause wild animals to appear while his runaway spouse works for her lover, for in this way he may frighten her into returning to him. But a jilted lover who takes revenge upon a girl is guilty of sorcery if he uses *madabi* to change her sex when her child is about to be born and thereby endangers her life. Such an act is unlawful vengeance, which is sharply distinguished from lawful restitution; it reflects a desire to injure another for personal motives which are not in harmony with approved social values.

Witchcraft and sorcery can always be counteracted. A favourite method of dealing with a witch is the use of reprisal magic whereby the evil is sent back to him, but there are many charms and medicines, all relying on the power of *vuŋaga*, by means of which witchcraft can be combated or rendered harmless. Villages are protected against witches and sorcerers by charms circling the village or placed at strategic points, while the witch within the village is treated by *hu fera*, i.e. a drug is introduced into his food which has the power of making him forget his frustration and seek compensation in day-dreaming and doddering. After witchcraft or sorcery has been established by divination as the cause of an evil, and the culprit has been identified (the diviner mentions no name but gives certain attributes, such as sex, clan, locality), it is open to the victim to make an accusation and risk the legal proceedings that will inevitably follow. But resort to law is not entirely satisfactory since appeasement, not the hardening of animosities that accusations occasion, is the function of law. Moreover, the initiation of legal sanctions against a witch may spur him to greater activity.

Witch beliefs reflect the Lovedu notion that almost all the misfortunes that befall men, whether sickness, barrenness, lightning that strikes men, huts, or cattle, failure of an individual's crops, or death of his children, are caused by the hatred and envy in men's hearts.

There is no greater fear than the fear that gnaws at the heart of a Lovedu who suspects he has been bewitched. Yet he is not impotent before its onslaught. By ascribing destructive forces, disease, and other evil to witchcraft and sorcery, and at the same time believing in the power of magic (*vuŋaga*) to counteract witchcraft, a Lovedu is able to feel that he is master of his own fate. Evil in the world on this theory becomes intelligible, not arbitrary and capricious. This is an ordered and just world in which evil, being held to express itself largely in witchcraft and sorcery, is outlawed and criminal, and in which good ultimately triumphs. And if this projective system affords a convenient theory of failure, it also stresses the virtue of goodwill for human welfare.

Relationships of Man to Man

That the greatest source of all evil should be the envy and jealousies in men's hearts is in keeping with the emphasis everywhere in Lovedu social life on the importance of good relationships between man and man. Bad relations and non-fulfilment of obligations between kin may, as we have seen, cause not only bad luck, through ancestral displeasure, but even illness, through the automatic force of *mahava*. The dissatisfaction in a mother's heart, whether conscious or not, in connexion with her daughter's marriage may cause her sterility, just as the complaints of a sister may be the cause, as seen in the bones, of the illness of her brother's children. The queen's emotions, too, affect the rain and it becomes important, therefore, for the welfare of all that she should not be sad or displeased.

Dominating relations between individuals and between groups is the whole pattern of mutuality, co-operation, and long-run reciprocities in the social structure. 'One leg cannot dance a *gɔsha*' say the Lovedu; co-operation is essential for the tasks of life. Security is bound up with the mutualities of kin, cognatic, agnatic, and affinal. In a society where wealth cannot be accumulated, it is not surprising that men's efforts should be directed towards building up and maintaining through generations links of marriage and kinship with all that these imply. These reciprocities in the society are motivated by unavoidable necessity but they are long-run ones. There is no weighing up of one service against another, nor any attempt to seek prestige by lavishness. Moreover, it is sharing and helpfulness not the display of one's generosity that is wanted.

Side by side with the emphasis on give and take, the society provides in such a manner or the place and achievement of individuals that competitiveness is limited and aggressive traits are outlawed. The immediate goals of individuals are divergent, and men are not conceived as striving against one another for the attainment of the same end. There is no special prestige attached to possession and no socio-economic stratification of classes; for a great man, whether he be poor or rich, is first and foremost a royal relative, and the purpose of economic activities is self-sufficiency and independence. Trade is disliked and competition is absent even in craftsmanship. So marked is the disinclination to make comparisons that it is difficult to obtain any expression of opinion concerning the relative merits of things that Europeans quite naturally compare, such as the achievements of individuals or objects of craftsmanship.

Children are taught 'to be like others', not to strive to outdo them and precociousness is disliked. A child asking for sweets often says 'Give me also', even if no one else has been given any on that occasion. He begs for what others may receive, not a special advantage for himself. When favours are asked from the ancestors the prayer is quite often phrased, 'Give us also', or 'Let him have health like others'. To stress, before the ancestors, a desire for personal achievement in competition with or greater than that of others would be improper. Contrast with this the opportunities for and love of competition in Zulu society where every boy is constantly measuring himself against others, vieing with them in fights, in dress, in love-making, in dancing, for leadership and praise.

The give and take, absence of competitiveness, and lack of force in the social and political structure, make moderation the keynote of Lovedu social life. Outstanding individuals are not tolerated: a show of forcefulness on the part of a councillor one day, which appealed to us as an indication of efficiency unusual in the society, was apologized for with the excuse that he must have been drunk. Display of all kinds is disliked. The elaborate beadwork and interest in dress, so characteristic of the Zulu, are absent, and there is nothing to correspond to the institutionalized public boasting (*ukugiya*) —jumping and stabbing at an imaginary foe to the accompaniment of a string of praises—that plays so important a role in Zulu life.

Excess of every kind is deprecated. Speed is undignified. Things must be done *ga vuya*, slowly, at a regular pace, in a moderate and dignified manner. Excess in human relations, like heat in the cosmic order, is liable to bring disaster. The reaction to death is calm, quiet grief, not the funeral wail of the Nguni or the terror reaction of the Tsonga. Too much weeping by a mother is believed to call down evil upon the next child born to her. Mputa was born a cripple, because, so we were told, his mother, Makwadu, wept bitterly at the death of her first son. Even in scolding moderation has to be observed, for scolding out of proportion to the offence, can, as we have shown, bring evil, even death.

Quarrelsomeness is one of the worst offences. Congruent with this outlook, the murderer or the warrior who has killed an enemy must purify himself to avoid becoming quarrelsome, the threat of which is so unpalatable as to be a powerful sanction. But quarrels and conflicts do occur on account of temperamental qualities, conflicting interests, and other causes; they are also precipitated sometimes through imperfections in the social institutions or their inadequacy for meeting all situations. In the resolution of difficulties of this nature arbitration and compromise play an important role, both judicially and extra-judicially. The genius of the legal system even in its most formal aspects is the skilful use of the restitutive sanction, in its spiritual rather than its material sense. The fundamental objective is the re-establishment of relations that have become broken or strained, and that objective is achieved, not so much by vindicating rules as by reconciling the parties. There is indeed a tacit assumption that the social equilibrium will be maintained if personal relations are suitably adjusted. The primary task of the courts is therefore to smooth out personal difficulties rather than to settle legal issues. For in law as in life it is not the rule that is important but the personal and social relations. The cattle-linking of brother and sister from different 'houses', ordinarily disapproved, is an arrangement that agreement between the 'houses' makes possible, and if the parties agree, even murder can be compounded. Even when a diviner has found a man guilty of witchcraft, it is felt to be necessary that the culprit should 'agree' with the findings, i.e. accept the verdict of the bones. In judicial proceedings a defendant will be asked if he agrees to pay the award; if he disagrees, full latitude is allowed him to expostulate. Should the court sense a genuine grievance it will reopen the case and bring its decision more into line with an amicable adjustment. As laws and institutions exist for human beings, they are not ends in themselves, and even the most fundamental duties and obligations between individuals and groups are conditional upon the ever-invoked 'if they agree'. If people do not agree there can be no relationship. If they have to be coerced there cannot be genuine agreement. This is why the execution of a judgement is left to the parties. The whole social and political structure relies upon the maintenance of good relations without resort to compulsion. Hence the use of the mechanisms of marriage and bride-price to hold in willing allegiance a great diversity of alien groups, who outnumber the LoƲedu proper by nine to one; hence also the aversion from regimentation and military discipline.

Great importance is attached to the dignity of the individual. Every person has rights and obligations; even a child's rights to property are respected. If a man feels that he is not being given his due, it is right to complain (*vɛlaɛla*) just as the ancestors do when they have not received proper attention. Any indignity to the personality, such as corporal punishment, is socially disapproved. Perhaps it is for this reason that a LoƲedu soon becomes tractable if ordered by the court to carry stones or perform some other useless task when he has been guilty of 'despising' the court.

Suicide is not common, but when it is resorted to it is as a protest against wrongful accusations or as a result of the complete frustration of an individual forced against his will into an impossible situation, e.g. a girl forced to marry someone she dislikes.

A high value is placed on human life. An aspect of Western civilization that puzzles the LoƲedu is that we tolerate the loss of human life involved in the use of motor traffic. Are not people more important than speed? The need for even a chief to respect the wishes of his subjects upon whom he depends for a following is summed up in the saying, *Vuhosi gi vatho*, 'chieftainship is people'.

The qualities or virtues that are stressed, then, in the moral code of the Lovedu are moderation and temperance, compromise and agreement, humility, respect for the personality and rights of others. Courage is not rated very high in this non-military society. Perseverance is often enjoined and is especially necessary in the monotonous tasks of hoeing, carrying heavy loads of wood, walking up steep mountain slopes; but it is never carried out with the single-mindedness that a European might expect. Theft is condemned and there are ritual sanctions against it. If the object stolen has been magically treated, for example, a painful sore will develop on the finger which defies treatment until guilt has been confessed and restitution agreed to. 'Don't steal, always beg (*hobɛla*) for what you want', children are exhorted. But theft is not a problem in this economically undifferentiated society, though nowadays cases of theft, even if extremely rarely, do come before the tribal courts. Drunkenness is bad only if it leads to neglect of duties or fights and quarrels. To be drunk is in itself no disgrace, it is merely pleasant and perhaps exhilarating, not a condition to be ashamed of. Indeed everyone looks forward to the *murula* season when all become slightly intoxicated from the cider made out of the fruits.

Right conduct is relative always to the human situation and morality is oriented not from any absolute standards of honesty or truth but from the social good in each situation. Conduct that promotes smooth relationships, that upholds the social structure, is good; conduct that runs counter to smooth social relationships is bad. Courtesy and the respect due to age or seniority are thus of greater importance than truth. A son-in-law who, tired of always being imposed upon by his wife's father, truthfully signified his unwillingness to help him by providing a goat would be guilty, in view of the special mutualities between families related by marriage, of unpardonable behaviour which might jeopardize his marriage. The correct procedure is to agree to help but to be always 'still looking for it' when approached for the goat. It took us a long time to discover that the right way to deal with incessant begging was not to refuse however politely, but to say 'I have none' or 'It is not mine to give'. The polite lie even if palpable is better calculated to maintain smooth relationships than strict adherence to truth. Truth is not good in itself nor is a lie always evil. Lies are objected to when they are socially inconvenient. Yet not only is it expected that a man will lie to get out of difficulties but there are cases in which lying is prescribed, as when children are told to lie to strangers if asked about village affairs. To keep tribal secrets and the secrets of initiation schools is of far greater importance than to tell the truth.

The social orientation of morality is clear in Lovedu sex morality. Sex is not regarded as a temptation to be resisted by painful efforts of will.

There is nothing morally wrong in sex or the sex act; not only is sex play among small children connived at, but premarital sex relations are institutionalized. It is only having a child before marriage that is immoral. For adultery restitution must be made, yet a husband who is jealous and watches his wife too closely is despised, and most men and women have extra-marital lovers (*vatavo*). The Lovedu attitude is less strict than that of the Tsonga living among them, for Tsonga married women are expected to be faithful to their husbands, and the compensation and fine for adultery are far higher than among the Lovedu. The Lovedu attitude to sex is matter-of-fact, and obscenity in ritual does not have a prominent role. Sex is handled with moderation: men are warned against the dangers of promiscuity; they learn from their proverb that 'a woman's pubes may break up a family', but passion is not esteemed and sex techniques are undeveloped.

To anyone brought up in the West European culture, where every breach of the moral code is also a sin in the eyes of a God who may punish the wrongdoer either in this life or the hereafter, an arresting aspect of Lovedu culture is that there is only a vague connexion between the ancestor-gods and morality. It has been said for the South Bantu in general, and by more than one authority, that the ancestors 'are the guardians of the moral code, it is they in the first instance who are thought of as visiting on their descendants punishments for some omission or commission'[1] There is among Lovedu a vague idea that failure to carry out one's kinship obligations may bring ancestral displeasure in the form of bad luck, and there may also be some connexion between such displeasure and *mahava*, the force generated by complaints of living kin, which causes illness. But a careful study of Lovedu religious practices over a period of years has brought to light no single instance in which ancestors have complained about anything not immediately concerning their own personal relations with their descendants—their right to tendance, remembrance, and propitiation; the manner of their burial; their desire to be told of major events in the lives of living kin. No ancestor has ever been known to concern himself with the theft, witchcraft, murder, or adultery of any descendant, nor do they trouble about the breaking of taboos which prevent rain and vitally affect the welfare of all. Lovedu ancestors are not upholders of custom in general; they are concerned only with those customs and taboos which affect their own welfare and that of their kin. Even royal ancestors do not concern themselves with the breaking of taboos that lead to drought. This is not a reflection of their carelessness or supineness, for they are quick to complain if, for example their graves are desecrated. On one occasion in 1938, when two men had cut firewood in the bush near the royal burial grounds at Maulwi, the *zwidajani* wailed all night to indicate their displeasure. Again when Mologwane, deceased chief councillor and brother of the queen, 'held her

---

[1] A. W., Hoernlé, 'Religion in Native Life', in *Thinking with Africa*, edited by Milton Stauffer, 1928, p. 100. See also, W. C. Willoughby, *The Soul of the Bantu*, 1928, pp. 381–90.

arms' to cause drought in 1938, it was because he had for personal
reasons been buried, at his own express request made before death, in the
Christian cemetery instead of in the damp shade of the forest, like his
forebears.

It would appear that this lack of interest on the part of the ancestral gods
in the morality of their descendants is in conformity with the pattern of the
relationship between living parents and their children. Parental protection
and care are given not by virtue of the morality or conduct of their
children; it is one of the imperatives of the kinship bond. A parent loves
his wayward, bad son as much as, if not more than, his well-behaved,
virtuous children. It is only a bad personal relationship between parent
and child or neglect of filial duty that could cause a parent to withhold
his protection.

Sanctions for right behaviour are, first and most important, the pressure
of public opinion and of the reciprocal arrangements of the political and
social structure. A man conforms to the code because of his self-esteem and
the high regard he has for his reputation for fairness and moderation, wisdom and ability to get on with others, generosity and helpfulness, not
merely among his kin but in the wider circle of his friends and neighbours.
The next important group of sanctions are the pain and misfortune that
may follow if those he has injured use vengeance magic or resort to witchcraft and sorcery against him. Certain types of conduct carry their own automatic ritual sanctions which form a third group of deterrents, even though
there is little pressure of public opinion against the conduct and no necessary or immediate consequence to the person himself, unless indeed he is repeatedly guilty. Finally, duties towards the ancestors, such as tendance and
recognition, have the religious sanctions of ancestral anger in the form of
illness, or misfortune. Ancestral displeasure can also be inferred as a sanction
acting indefinitely and over a vague area of conduct to reinforce men's
obligations to kin, generally those kin who stand to them in a relation of some
authority. This inference may be made, not because ancestors ever directly
cause misfortune to a descendant for breaches of correct behaviour to kin
as they do in the case of neglect of themselves, but because bad luck may be
attributed to failure in one's duties to kin.

Ancestor worship of the Lovedu plays hardly any part, then, in uphold-
ing tribal morality. Nor are people so delicately conditioned to the values of
the society that they spontaneously react to conscience. Their moral code
is not markedly internalized and Lovedu have no sense of 'sin'. Since there
are few repressed fears the pressure of which on the mind can be removed
by confession and atonement, a sense of guilt seldom moves men, and
offenders very rarely repent merely at the dictates of conscience. Their
sense of shame is more delicately internalized, but it drives men to make
restitution only when the misdeed has been exposed or brought into relation with the system of reciprocities. Lovedu are sensitive mainly to the
intangible forces of the social system, and the moral code is upheld mainly

by the institutions and by the reciprocal duties and responsibilities between individuals and groups inherent in the social structure.

Effects of Culture Contact

This picture of the world view of the Lovedu presents living practices and conceptions, not a dead and reconstructed past. Christianity has, indeed, modified some aspects of the culture: Christians are prevented from performing their kinship obligations in the traditional manner; they have accepted European ideas of trade for profit and use institutions such as the work-party for the exploitation of their fellows; but witchcraft, which they are supposed to have rejected, is as a result of increased tensions even more rampant among Christians than pagans. Christians substitute God for the ancestors, but continue to believe that the queen makes rain, albeit by the will of God. They tend to discredit the powers of charms but not of *vuŋaga*, while 'heat', *makhuma*, and 'shadow' are still real forces, and the underlying conceptions of the causation of disease and misfortune still hold sway. Even these minor modifications have to be viewed in the light of the fact that Christians constitute only about 5 per cent. of the tribe and are relatively isolated.

The influence of Western culture as a whole is more insidious. The knowledge acquired by young men working in the towns and returning to the tribe holds implications as regards the nature of the universe and the destiny and purpose of man which they cannot harmonize with the traditional world view. They tend to despise what the old men cannot or will not make intelligible to them, such as the significance of the *digɔma* and the *zwidajani* which appear to them to be shams. This attitude and the inadequate response to it lead to lack of respect for their elders and for traditional values and institutions. But the total effect is minimized by the reassertion of the old values as the young men grow older, begin to play a part and to have a stake in the culture. Moreover, they are sensitive to insinuations that their doubts are due to the white man's insidious influences and soon repress them as unworthy and disloyal.

The younger generation tend to shirk unpleasant responsibilities. Thus Jim refused to take over the family office of keeper of the rain-medicine, fearing the risk of sterility which handling of this medicine entails. The absence of many adult men, who are away as migrant labourers, makes the organization of the great ceremonials difficult. Reconciliation and the restitutive sanction are no longer the great forces they used to be, since the closely knit system of reciprocities, everyone's dependence upon day-to-day mutualities and the imperativeness for social life of co-operation, no longer exert the irresistible pressure on the parties to carry out compromises reached in the courts. Aggrieved litigants, reluctant still to invoke European intervention, increasingly resort to magicians who have developed a whole new system of revenge magic to even up matters. The trend is to put their faith in magical retaliation rather than in the sanction of reciprocity.

But the rewards of participation in reciprocal give and take and the penalties of being denied these reciprocities are still strong sanctions.

On the whole, therefore, culture contact has not yet brought about profound changes in Lovedu conceptions of the order of nature or of the relations of men to one another. The old outlook is still intact, even though some of the values supporting it cannot be maintained for much longer at an intensity sufficient to make them effective forces.

THE DOGON

By MARCEL GRIAULE *and* GERMAINE DIETERLEN

Introduction

At the present stage of studies of the Dogon, and precisely because these studies seek to penetrate deeply into the mentality of the people, it is not possible to present a brief and clear-cut account of the relationship between their cosmogony and their social organization. The reader is warned from the outset, therefore, that he will not find here an exhaustive presentation of Dogon thought from the point of view with which this book is concerned; only certain institutions and concepts among those for which adequate documentation exists will be selected for discussion.

The ideas of the Dogon may perhaps best be understood by considering the forms in which they express them. The basis of their thought concerning the universe and man's place in it is the 'sign', most fully elaborated in the form of a 'table of signs'.[1] The Dogon hold that a 'sign' or symbol and that which it symbolizes are reversible; that signs, substitutes, and images constitute a vast system of correspondences, in which every term is interlocked within what seem to be specific categories. These categories in their turn, whether linked or opposed, are themselves correlated.

Social institutions and, in general, all organized human activities constitute a scheme of representations. By analogy, a parallel scheme of myths reproduces the former, but with persons, places, times, and functions transposed. This second scheme, whether esoteric or not, provides for the natives a system of references and explanations of their social institutions.

Among the Dogon exoteric myths correspond to a 'superficial knowledge'[2] common to the greater part of the population; on the other hand, esoteric myths, parallel to these, present other identifications and much wider connexions. Finally, within and beyond this totality of beliefs appears a logical scheme of symbols expressing a system of thought which cannot be described simply as myth. For this conceptual structure, when studied, reveals an internal coherence, a secret wisdom, and an apprehension of ultimate realities equal to that which we Europeans conceive ourselves to have attained. The Dogon, in this system of myths and symbols, are able to express a correspondence between their social organization and the world order as they conceive it. For them social life reflects the working of the universe and, conversely, the world order depends on the proper ordering of society.

Furthermore, the social order is projected in the individual, the indi-

---

[1] See M. Griaule and G. Dieterlen, *Signes graphiques soudanais*, Paris, 1951.

[2] For the knowledge possessed by the peoples of the French Sudan see G. Dieterlen, *Essai sur la religion bambara*, Paris, 1951.

visible cell which, on the one hand, is a microcosm of the whole, and, on the other, has a circumscribed function, like a cog in a machine; not only is a person the product of his institutions, he is also their motive power. Lacking any special power in himself, but because he is the representative of the whole, the individual affects the cosmic order which he also displays.

The Myths of the Dogon

In order to understand the Dogon view of their own social organization it is necessary to know their myths of creation, and a brief analytical summary of these will be given below. Their conception of the universe is based, on the one hand, on a principle of vibrations of matter, and on the other, on a general movement of the universe as a whole. The original germ of life is symbolized by the smallest cultivated seed—*Digitaria exilis*—commonly known as fonio and also called by the Dogon *kize uzi*, 'the little thing'. This seed, quickened by an internal vibration, bursts the enveloping sheath, and emerges to reach the uttermost confines of the universe. At the same time this unfolding matter moves along a path which forms a spiral or helix[1] (see Fig. 1). Two fundamental notions are thus expressed: on the one hand the perpetual helical movement signifies the conservation of matter; further, this movement, which is presented diagrammatically as a zigzag line (*ozu tonnolo*) on the façades of shrines, is held to represent the perpetual alternation of opposites—right and left, high and low, odd and even, male and female—reflecting a principle of twin-ness, which ideally should direct the proliferation of life. These pairs of opposites support each other in an equilibrium which the individual being conserves within itself. On the other hand, the infinite extension of the universe is expressed by the continual progression of matter along this spiral path.

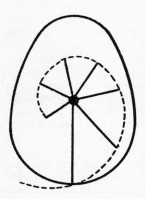

FIG. 1. *The first seven vibrations of the egg of the world*

These primordial movements are conceived in terms of an ovoid form—'the egg of the world' (*aduno tal*)—within which lie, already differentiated, the germs of things; in consequence of the spiral movement of extension the germs develop first in seven segments of increasing length, representing the seven fundamental seeds of cultivation, which are to be found again in the human body, and which, with the *Digitaria*, indicate the predominance of the Ogdoad or Divine Octet in this system of thought: the organization of the cosmos, of man, and of society (Fig. 2). At the seventh vibration

[1] The circular outward and/or upward motion is represented by a helical or spiral form in Dogon signs (Ed.).

the segment breaks its envelope. This segment is the symbol of the seed which plays a primary role in the life and thought of the Dogon—the *emme ya*, female sorghum, which represents life, the ideal food, immune from impurity.

Having broken its wrapping the creative process emerges to follow the predestined and predetermined movement of being. For inside the first seed, and forming its central core, was an oblong plate divided into four sectors in which lay the signs corresponding to the twenty-two categories into which the universe is classified, each placed under the direction of one of the four elements: air, fire, earth, and water. In the rotatory movement of creation this plate, turning on itself, flings off the signs into space, where they come to rest, each one on the things which it symbolizes and which till then existed only potentially. At their touch every being comes into existence and is automatically placed in the predetermined category.

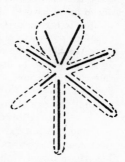

All these images seem to relate to an effort of discovery, an attempt to apprehend the infinitely small at its point of departure towards the immeasurably vast. In fact, the order of the heavens, as it is observed and conceived by the Dogon, is no more than a projection, infinitely expanded, of events and phenomena which occur in the infinitely small.

Fig. 2. *The prefiguring of man in the egg of the world*

The starting-point of creation is the star which revolves round Sirius and is actually named the '*Digitaria* star'; it is regarded by the Dogon as the smallest and the heaviest of all the stars; it contains the germs of all things. Its movement on its own axis and around Sirius upholds all creation in space. We shall see that its orbit determines the calendar.

Just as on the vegetal plane seven seeds came out of the first, so in the same way on the astral plane, from the first star came seven others bearing the names of the seven corresponding seeds. But from the moment when beings became conscious of themselves and capable of purposive action, the course of creation developed, in Dogon thought, in a less simple fashion. Personalities appeared who, after the chief person, the Creator God *Amma*, moved in a world of feeling, resembling man's ideas of himself and his own activities.

The preceding events, as already mentioned, took place inside an enormous egg (*aduno tal*), a world situated in infinite space and containing the appointed model of the creation, *Nommo*, the son of God. This egg was divided into two twin placenta,[1] each of which should have contained a pair

---

[1] In ordinary conversation the Dogon constantly use the term *me* for both the placenta and the amnion. We use 'placenta' here because their symbolic representations are mainly associated with that organ.

of twin *Nommo*, direct emanations and sons of God, according to the Dogon, and prefigurations of man. Like all other creatures these twin beings, living images of the fundamental principle of twin-ness in creation, were each equipped with two spiritual principles of opposite sex; each of them, therefore, was in himself a pair. We shall see how these images dominate the organization of society and of the family.

In one placenta, however, the male person, for reasons which are obscure, did not await the usual period of gestation appointed by *Amma* but emerged prematurely from the egg. Moreover, he tore a fragment from his placenta and with it came down through space outside the egg; this fragment became the earth. This being, *Yurugu*, brought the fonio with him intending to make a world of his own, modelled on the first but surpassing it.

This irregular procedure at the outset disorganized *Amma's* order of creation; the earth thus constituted was provided with a male soul only, since the being who made it was thus imperfect. From this imperfection arose the notion of impurity: earth and *Yurugu* were, from the beginning, solitary and impure. *Yurugu*, realizing that this situation would effectually prevent him from carrying out his task on earth, returned to heaven to try and find the rest of his placenta with his twin soul. But at his revolt, *Amma* had handed over this twin soul to the remaining pair in the other part of the egg, and had put her in their charge. *Yurugu* could not retrieve her; and from that time he has been engaged in a perpetual and fruitless search for her. He returned to the dry earth where now there began in the darkness to come into existence single, incomplete beings, offspring of incest; in fact he procreated in his own placenta, in the earth, that is, with his mother. Here we have the prefiguration of certain kinship ties and sentiments.

Seeing this, *Amma* decided to send to earth the *Nommo* of the other half of the egg, creators of the sky and the stars. They came down to earth on a gigantic arch, at the centre of which stood the two *Nommo* of the sky, who had assumed the guise of blacksmiths. At the four cardinal points were four other pairs of *Nommo*, avatars of the first and the ancestors of man. The four male ancestors were named Amma Seru, Lébé Seru, Binu Seru, and Dyongu Seru. The arch constituted a new, undefiled earth; its descent coincided with the appearance of light in the universe, which till then had been in darkness. Water, in the form of rain, purified and fertilized the soil in which were sown the eight seeds which the mythical ancestors brought with them—each bearing a seed; human beings, animals, and plants forthwith came into existence. The 8 ancestors first gave birth to 12 offspring consisting of 4 pairs of twins—3 of mixed sexes and 1 male pair—as well as 2 males and 2 females. Thus the first 3 mythical generations comprised 22 persons, 10 of whom were female and 12 male.[1] With the aid of the skills taught by *Nommo*, social life was organized. In this way everything which had been created in the egg was then made manifest.

The advent of the arch of *Nommo* denotes not only the delimitation of

---

[1] Totemism among the Dogon is closely linked with this descent system.

space but also the measurement of times and seasons: the year was linked to the apparent movement of the sun, avatar of the other portion of the placenta of *Yurugu*; days alternated with nights and the seasons followed each other.

This period of the ordering of creation extended over twenty-two years, during which all social institutions were established. The first four years correspond to the first four seed-times, which today are symbolized by the actions of the totem priests who, at the rituals of sowing, cast the millet seeds to the four cardinal points. These four sowings, which denote the planting of the whole world, were necessary to ensure the perennial resurgence of plant life, that is, symbolically, the procreation of human beings. From the fifth sowing onwards a rite was celebrated of which the name, *bulu*, indicates its purpose, for its meaning is 'to make alive again'.

Death made its appearance in consequence of events connected with the position of *Yurugu* in the new organization. In the myth the dry, uncultivated, uninhabited earth belongs to *Yurugu*, a being of night, whereas *Nommo*, a being of the day, associated with the sky, water, and fertility, rules the cultivated, habitable land.

Man

Man is the 'seed' of the universe: that is to say, he was prefigured in the seed *Digitaria*, the vibrations and extensions of which produced the world.

This notion is expressed in the interpretation of the first seven segmentary vibrations which occurred in the first envelope. The first and the sixth produced the legs, the second and fifth the arms, the third and fourth the head, the seventh the sex organs of man (see Fig. 2). The first movements of creation were thus the first prefiguration of the being around whom everything was to be organized. But the link between man and the first creative act does not end here. The original seed first produced the image of man; conversely, man in his own person presents the image of the seed; the seven segment-vibrations also represent seven seeds, to which should be added the original *Digitaria* itself. These eight seeds are to be found in man's clavicles and symbolize his substance as well as his sustenance. We shall see that this notion of a vegetal series, in its various modifications, plays a dominant part in human society.

Man is the image not only of creation's first beginning but also of the existing universe. The egg of the world is represented by a diagram in which it is shown filled with germinating cells, one of which extrudes downwards, while a second lies horizontally across the first at its point of exit; these two constitute the setting of the world and establish the four cardinal points. A third cell, pressing on the first, takes its place and forces it to curve on itself, forming an open egg-shape symmetrical in position with the first (Fig. 3).[1] The Dogon thus produce a diagram which they call 'the life of the world' and which is interpreted not only as the microcosmic

[1] See also 'Signes graphiques dogon' in *Signes graphiques soudanais*.

man but also as the heavenly placenta (the upper egg-form) and the earthly placenta (the lower egg-form) which are separated by the space represented by the cross. In this diagram there may also be seen a reference to the principle of twin-ness: the two egg-shapes and the two segments form two pairs of twins recalling the four primordial beings each possessing two souls. From this it follows that the supreme expression of the individual's identity with creation, the perfect creation, is a pair of twins.

Like these primordial beings, man possesses two souls of opposite sexes, one of which inhabits his body while the other dwells in the sky or in water and links it to him. The vital force (*nyama*), which flows in his veins with his blood, is associated with the eight seeds which are distributed equally between his two clavicles. These seeds, united in pairs, are the basis of various notions concerning human personality and the changes it undergoes and they also recall the original groups of four pairs of twins (cf. p. 86). The series so constituted, the terms of which may vary from one social group to another, does not occur in the same order for every individual in the same group. Thus, within the same family the order applicable to a man will be inverted in the case of a woman; some seeds are excluded for certain social ranks or functions; they are held to be the chief factors of social differentiation. Since the condition of a person mirrors the condition of the universe, everything which affects the one has repercussions on the other; that is to say, in some way all a man's actions and all his circumstances must be conceived as closely connected with the functioning of things in general.

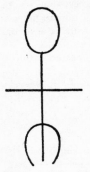

FIG. 3. '*The life of the world.*' *The heavenly and earthly placentas*

The seeds symbolize the food of mankind; they are the pivot on which turns the life of the cultivator, which depends as much on the seasonal renewal of vegetation as on the daily intake of food. They recall also the renewal of human life itself, which vanishes momentarily from its possessor only to be reborn in his descendants. Finally, the regular and appointed series attributed to the seeds is the sign of the universal order established on earth since the descent of *Nommo*.

Disorder among the seeds, which for an individual results especially from the breaking of the rules of life, prefigures the universal disorder which spreads by stages from the individual to his close kinsmen, his family, his clan, his people. But the disorder may be arrested and removed at any stage by appropriate rituals. Exact and complicated, they make it possible both for the individual to be restored and the general order to be preserved. Thus the individual, through his family and the society in which he lives, is linked in his structure and in his evolution with the universe; and this connexion operates in both directions.

A human being in his development manifests the development of *Nommo*, symbol of the ordered world. Thus the new-born infant at birth is the head of *Nommo*; when later he becomes a herd-boy, he is the chest, at betrothal the feet, at marriage the arms, and when fully adult he is the complete *Nommo*; as an elder and still more as a supreme chief he is both *Nommo* and the totality of the world and mankind.

The Tribe

According to their own accounts, the Dogon are all derived from one stock.[1] This they explain by the tradition that the original four pairs of twins gave birth to four tribes, Arou, Dyon, Ono, and Domno,[2] who in theory shared the universe among themselves, and in particular the stellar system.[3] Each tribe originally had its habitation at one of the four cardinal points and was associated with one element. Naturally, also, they divided between them the various social and economic functions.[4]

Their distribution is shown in the following table.

Ancestors	Tribes	Cardinal Points	Elements	Functions
Amma Seru	Arou	East	Air	Chieftainship, Medicine, Divination
Dyongu Seru	Dyon	South	Fire	Agriculture
Binu Seru	Ono	West	Water	Trade and Crafts
Lébé Seru	Domno	North	Earth	Trade and Crafts[5]

This 'organization of the earth' (*ganda yegru*) is not only applicable to the whole people; each tribe and smaller group must display the same divisions, and it is also believed that the system is reproduced in every individual. The Dogon express this idea by saying that in every group warfare is controlled by the male *Nommo*, whose shrine is placed in the centre; cultivation is under the protection of the female *Nommo*, whose shrines are built of the stones (*sogo*) of the fields; the shrines dedicated to divination are scattered over the flat, sandy land surrounding the village. The right conduct of affairs will need, first of all, the use of divination, the domain of *Yurugu*; then a visit to the shrines of cultivation and of war, the domain of

[1] This refers to the internal organization of the Dogon; there is also an international system in which the same notions are employed.

[2] It should be noted that on one level the Dogon regard three tribes as being superior in status: Arou, Dyo, and Ono. In accordance with their habit of thought it is necessary that even in the numbering of the tribes the numbers 3 and 4, symbolizing male and female, should appear. For the Dogon tribes and their present habitat see G. Dieterlen, *Les Ames des Dogons*. This study takes into account a fifth group, the Kor, which as far as our present knowledge goes seems to be connected with the Ono and Domno.

[3] Thus, for the purpose of making certain calculations bearing on the calendar, the sun is associated with Arou and the moon with Dyon. But through craftiness in juggling for precedence the Arou, who consider themselves the stronger, left the sun to Dyon and took the moon for themselves.

[4] This refers to the organization which existed before French occupation and which is, to a considerable extent, still preserved or recalled in certain circumstances.

[5] The Domno are coupled with the Ono in regard to functions.

the *Nommo*. Any other procedure, and particularly the omission of any of these stages, will produce disorder. On the other hand, the correct mechanism is so effective that even if it is set in motion by a stranger the results are always beneficial. 'If you wish to organize the country, the first (thing is) to practise divination, (then you must) sacrifice a chicken to Binu, a chicken to Pégu, a chicken to Lébé. If you do this (even) if you are a stranger, because of you there will be peace, rain, and ripe millet!'[1]

It should be noted that three chief functions are distributed among the four tribes; here may be seen the numerical expression of twin-ness applied in two different spheres, that of mankind and that of function; mankind as a whole (the four tribes) participates in the femininity from which it issues, and the number of which is 4; functions, which are activities, are male, and their number is 3. The number 7 (sum of the 3 and the 4) symbolizes human personality, which means, in this particular instance, that man organized in society must be active.

The hierarchy of the three functions denotes also a theoretical hierarchy of tribes which, however, is the subject of continual dissension on the part of those concerned, because at the same time each group in itself possesses the same powers. This hierarchical principle is projected into the realm of material objects; thus pots, according to their size, are associated with one tribe or another: the largest are assigned to Arou, the smallest to Dyon; but in the interests of precedence and tact, in practice the order is reversed. The same principle may be seen, among other examples, in the mounds built up in the fields at the base of the millet stalks, the largest being made in fact by the Dyon, the smallest by the Arou.[2] This hierarchy is still observed today in the institution of chieftainship; the religious and political chiefs of Dyon, Ono, and Domno recognize the supremacy of the single Hogon of Arou. Thus it may be shown that, in spite of historical upheavals, the social structure of the Dogon and its organization into tribes is still valid and meaningful.

Kinship

The corporate body of kin among the Dogon is an agnatic exogamous, patrilocal and patrilineal group, and totems are inherited in the paternal line. In marriage a widespread exchange is practised and marriage with the daughter of a maternal uncle is preferred. Family relationships are variously conceived according as one is concerned with the reciprocal relationships of uterine and paternal kin, the relations between one married couple, those of the uncle and maternal nephew, or those of the different generations, &c. The original couple formed by the male and female *Nommo*, the twins in the heavenly placenta, is represented by a brother and sister. Thus it was formerly believed that the ideal marriage was one contracted between

[1] *ganda yegru nammay woye pologo almaqa kana binu endye obo pegi endye obo lebe endye obo kokana boye u yerne wo kana kuwone dyam bębęniose ana di babamose yu ile bebémose.*
[2] In practice this rule only applies to the first mound to be made.

a brother and sister. The fact that the father is not actually the mother's brother leads to a complex series of ideas and patterns of behaviour in relation to the family. In order to understand the Dogon conception of their kinship system it will be useful to consider the mythical situation of the members of two consanguineous and uterine families on several different planes. On the simplest level and the one which accounts for the twofold kinship which every individual possesses, all the relatives on the father's side are *Amma* (God) and all relatives on the mother's side are *Nommo* (the Universe), thus indicating the first expression of the principle of twin-ness which equates God with his creation.

On the other hand, for any given individual, all his uterine kin represent femininity and all paternal kin masculinity. A man calls all women who are uterine kin, whatever their age, mother (*na*); he calls all adult men of his patrilineal kin father (*ba*).[1]

In another context, in which is envisaged the individual's situation in relation to the members of his father's and of his mother's family, the Dogon adjust their classification to the mythical personages and to the era of the creation: the two grandfathers are *Amma* and the individual is the offspring of two pairs of *Nommo*, like those which, in mythical times, occupied the original placenta. One of these is symbolized by the father and the father's sister, the other by the mother's brother and the mother. This is expressed in the terms by which members of the two pairs are addressed as well as by the behaviour of the individual in relation to them.

On a third plane, paternal and uterine kin groups may be considered in isolation. The paternal kin group is mythically connected with the twin *Nommo* who inhabited one of the two divisions of the world egg, and came down to earth after the adventure of *Yurugu*. In this line of descent the grandfather will be *Nommo*; all the sons and daughters will be the octet which includes, as we have seen, four pairs of twins of mixed sex; this justifies one of the principles of the extended family in which all the brothers and sisters are regarded as pairs of twins. Some of the names given to the first four sons are linked with the ordinal numbers which recall the series of male *Nommo* of the arch (see p. 86). Grandchildren represent the twelve descendants of *Nommo* (cf. p. 86) within the direct line, and so on. Associated with these representations is patrilineal descent, by which each individual is linked with four direct ancestors, the five generations involved symbolizing the five seed-times which followed the advent of the arch. No ancestor earlier than the great-great-grandfather is thought to affect directly the individual's personal existence. The head of the patrilineal joint family lives in the house of the family (*ginna*), which is that of the territorial founder of the lineage. In this house are the shrines of the ancestors to which new-born infants are presented. The patrilineal kin group is thus held to be a reflection of the first mythical family which

[1] See below, p. 93.

emerged from that part of the world egg (see p. 86) in which all events
unfold in order, the generations following one another in normal fashion.

A person's uterine kin group, on the other hand, reflects the situation in
that part of the original egg in which events unfolded in disorderly fashion
and where the generations were irregular. Here the maternal grandfather
symbolizes *Amma*; the next generation—that is to say, the mother and her
brother (the maternal uncle)—are the twin *Nommo*. The third generation—
that is, Ego—is, in relation to the two earlier ones, *Yurugu*.

Just as *Yurugu*, breaking too soon from the womb and bearing with him
a fragment of his placenta, is still, so to speak, a part of his mother—is, indeed, his mother, so every individual, even if his birth was perfectly normal,
is an integral part of the woman who bore him. That is to say, every individual is identified with his mother to the extent of belonging to her
generation rather than his own, as though the child, after leaving the
womb, continued to possess its pre-natal character as part of its mother's
body, and thus belongs to the older generation. If the child is a male,
he is regarded as the brother of his mother. He is therefore, as it were, a
substitute for his maternal uncle—the ideal husband of his mother.

Since, however, the child is in fact born into the generation following
that of his mother, a pattern of behaviour develops towards his elders and
his collaterals which is regulated by various beliefs. The fate of *Yurugu*,
emerging from the womb before he had attained his proper form, is to belong still to the older generation, from which resulted the incestuous union
of the myth.

In real life the child, even if born at full term, unconsciously preserves
towards its mother the attitude of *Yurugu*. But since she cannot commit
incest, the wife of the maternal uncle replaces the mother. This transfer-
ence is explained by the fact that the couple who engendered the child must
represent the original twin *Nommo*. That is to say, the genitors should be
brother and sister and the child can regard his real father as a stranger and
his maternal uncle, whose substitute he feels himself to be, as his ideal
genitor. In consequence the child regards the wife of his maternal uncle as
a substitute for his own mother; he addresses her as *yana mo* (my wife)
and she calls him *mu ige* (my husband); he jokes with her and takes liberties
(including sexual relations), thus recalling the act committed by *Yurugu*;
on the other hand, he is allowed to plunder and rob his uncle's goods and
household as much as he likes.

These attitudes may also be explained by the relative situations of the
souls of the people concerned regarded as reflecting the situations of the
souls of mythical personages. It should be remembered that *Yurugu*, prematurely born, was alone with the scrap of placenta he had carried away.
Moreover, he only had his male soul, for the female soul had remained in the
other half of the placenta. He tried to return and possess her, but she had
already been placed by *Amma* in the care of the *Nommo* in the other half of
the egg. *Yurugu* was unable to recover her and ever since then has been

pursuing a fruitless quest (cf. p. 86). The maternal nephew, in his early years, like *Yurugu*, lacks a wife; just as *Yurugu* is seeking his female soul, so the nephew is seeking a wife, a search which is concealed under the guise of thefts committed in his mother's brother's house. This situation comes to an end when the maternal uncle, who cannot give his own wife to his nephew, finds him a wife of his own who will be a substitute for the female soul he is seeking.

The wife, indeed, should be chosen preferably from among the daughters of the maternal uncle, and this is frequently done. Symbolically the girl is regarded as a substitute for her husband's own mother. Clearly there is a correspondence here between the maternal uncle's daughter, his wife, and his sister, who is the mother of the nephew. The marriage is thus, in some sense, a re-enactment of the mythical incest. It is also, however, re-garded as a caricature and is thus a kind of defiance hurled at *Yurugu*. For the existing order represents the reorganization, under the direction of *Nommo*, of an original situation characterized by the disorderliness of his enemy.

Another consequence of the situation just described is that, in theory, brothers should always marry their sisters. Any member of one generation therefore regards all members of the previous generation as his fathers (among paternal kin) and his mothers (among maternal kin).[1]

Not only is there tension between the individual and certain of his mater-nal kin, tension operates also between generations. There is rivalry between a son and his father. And, as with all the institutions of the Dogon, one must consider its mythical origin in order to discover the way in which this parti-cular mode of behaviour is understood.

We have seen how, in the original seed, there developed seven vibrations symbolized by the emerging segments of increasing size. The seventh seg-ment, which broke the enveloping sheath and set in motion external vibra-tions, divided itself into two unequal parts, the shorter of which might in some sense be regarded as an eighth vibration (Fig. 2). In another con-text this short segment is regarded as the tip of the male sexual organ of the being represented by the seed. It is thus the emanation of a human micro-cosm which is itself conceived as a pair consisting of a male and a female, as is twice indicated in the representation. In fact the ideal couple—repre-sented by the numbers 4 (female)+3 (male) making 7—is recalled, on the one hand in the number of the seven segments, on the other by the order (seventh) of the reproductive vibration. According to Dogon ideas, the frag-ment issuing from the seventh vibration is eighth in order and represents the first of a second series of seven. By virtue of being a beginning, it is incomplete in itself and for this reason is likened to *Yurugu*, who is essen-tially an incomplete being. It is to be expected, therefore, that the offspring will make demands on its genitors, and more particularly on the male, since,

[1] This attitude should be distinguished from that described above in which, in a different context, Ego regards *all* uterine kin as mothers and *all* consanguineous kin as fathers.

as the symbolism shows, it is the male sex organ which in this particular situation seems to emit a segment detached from itself.

This representation—at once mythical and metaphysical—of the primordial relationship between father and son enables the instructed to understand existing attitudes. The son bears his father a grudge on account of his initial incompleteness. At the same time he resents his father's part in begetting him, which clearly shows that he is not wholly the product of his mother, that he is not derived entirely from the maternal 'root' (*du*). It would be some consolation if he could regard himself as the son of his mother and his maternal uncle, that is to say, of two genitors springing from the same 'root'. Even so, he would be hostile to this genitor because the uncle, by begetting other children, would give him brothers like himself. The son, indeed, believes that at the moment of sexual intercourse his father implants in his mother a seed similar to that from which he himself was born; thus it seems to him that his father sets no store by the previous child since he wishes to make him over again. This feeling towards the father has repercussions on the sentiments which brothers feel for one another. Each in fact regards all the others as rivals, both in regard to property and to women.

Territorial Organization

Districts, countryside, villages

The country of the Dogon has been organized as far as possible[1] in accordance with the principle that the world developed in the form of a spiral. In theory the central point of development is formed by three ritual fields, assigned to three of the mythical ancestors and to the three fundamental cults. When laid out they mark out a world in miniature on which the gradual establishment of man takes place. Starting from these three fields, the fields belonging to the various kin groups, and finally individual fields, are sited along the axis of a spiral starting from this central area. The various shrines are similarly distributed according to the same plan and, in theory, sacrifices should be offered in the same order as the shrines, on the line of a spiral starting from the centre. The Dogon even say that, in accordance with the original rule, when land is to be cleared the cultivators must work with their backs to the edge of the last field and the area cleared must be of such a shape that the opposite side is much longer than the side from which they start. Thus each field will be an irregular and, as it were, twisted quadrilateral, two sides of which will form a very wide angle opening towards the fields which will subsequently be cleared. This angle symbolizes the continuous extension of the world.

Another form of organization is, moreover, embedded in the foregoing. Every extended family should possess eight fields grouped in pairs and

[1] In most cases the nature of the country, the contours, and the siting of watercourses necessitate compliance with the rule.

facing towards the four cardinal points; each of these pieces of land is associated with one of the eight original seeds.

As the theoretical arrangement of fields and the process of clearing the ground reproduce the primitive spiral form, so the method of cultivation recalls the more delicate vibratory movement of the axis of the spiral. This screw-like movement, which is represented on shrines and in caves by a zigzag line, is reproduced in the old method of cultivation which is like the technique of weaving; it consists in starting on the north side, moving

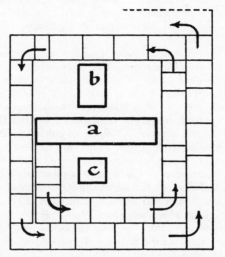

FIG. 4. *Theoretical layout of cultivated land around the three original fields*

from east to west and returning from west to east. Each line of millet planted is eight feet long, and a typical patch of planted land comprises eight lines, recalling the eight ancestors and the eight seeds.

Moreover, the cultivator advances along the line changing his hoe from one hand to the other at every pace, like the action of weaving, whereby the thread of the woof is fitted into the warp, which itself symbolizes cultivation and the advance of man's labour in uncultivated land.

The purposive repetition of the processes of creation is carried yet farther: the different tribes combine to work their land in accordance with the same detailed symbolism, each one, when cultivating, moving in the opposite direction from the next. That is to say, in theory each tribe observes its own rule in working on its own land so that the country as a whole is cultivated in every possible direction.

Just as the original vibration in the first seven segments (see Fig. 2) prefigured man, who is placed at the centre of the universe, so at the centre of the territorial organization, embedded in the three fields which constitute the point of departure, is situated the village, itself a symbol of man.

The village may be square like the first plot of land cultivated by man, or oval with an opening at one end to represent the world egg broken open by the swelling of the germinating cells. Whatever its shape it is a person[1] and must lie in a north to south direction; the smithy is the head and certain particular shrines the feet. The huts used by women at their menstrual periods, situated east and west, are the hands; the family homesteads form the chest, and the twin-ness of the whole group is expressed by a foundation shrine in the form of a cone (the male sexual organ) and by a hollowéd stone (female organ) on which the fruit of the *Lannea acida* is ground to express the oil.[2]

Not only is the village anthropomorphic but each part or section of it is a complete and separate entity and, so far as possible, must be laid out on the same pattern as the whole. Thus, individual families are fitted into a grouping which itself is a unity.

Finally, if such a group of habitations is seen from above or from a height, the fields shining in the sun on the one hand and the shadows cast on the earth on the other resemble hillocks of cultivated land casting their shadows into the hollows. And this is a picture of the little family homestead which bears on its façade eighty incised lines of shadow separated by bright surfaces. Furthermore, this façade is a substitute for the black-and-white checked blanket which resembles the appearance of cultivated fields and the alternation of light and shadow in the rows of hillocks.

Thus the settlement where men dwell close together is a representation both of man himself and of the layout of the fields outside the walls. This is a way of calling to mind the fact that the processes of germination and gestation are of the same kind.

In accordance with the principle of twin-ness, villages are built in pairs, one of which is often referred to as Upper and the other as Lower. A pair of villages of this sort is regarded as the heaven and earth (*Nommo* and *Yurugu*) united, and also as the representation of man (see Fig. 5).

The same pattern is repeated in the layout of the district which, at the present time, often coincides with the administrative unit (canton). This area is divided into two parts, one known as Upper and the other as Lower; it is also marked by an open space or public meeting-place in the village where the Hogon, the district chief, lives. In theory this open space should be round like the sky which it represents. The shrine of Lébé at its centre symbolizes the sun, and around it are various shrines belonging to the Binu of the founders, and representing the most important stars.

In fact, in the open space called *lebe dala* in Upper Ogol of Upper Sanga

[1] See M. Griaule, *Dieu d'eau*, Paris, 1948, p. 118.
[2] This, in theory, is the position of the male shrine (*pegu*); out of respect for the female sex, represented by the hollow stone, and for the women of the village, the male shrine is often built outside the walls.

there are nine shrines placed in three parallel lines, the central one facing south. The central shrine of Lébé, which in one sense is the first, also has the number nine which is associated with chieftainship. The other eight are substitutes for the shrines of the family fields, beneath which specimens of the eight original seeds are buried. They are also the eight ancestors of the arch of the world of which the meeting-place itself is a symbol. In a sense it might be said that the place known as *lebe dala* represents the coming down to earth of a new world, borne by the eight ancestors who have now assumed the form of the eight stone altars.

The Homestead

It is possible to go into yet more detail; the basic structure of the village consists of a group of dwellings, among which may be distinguished the big house (*ginu da*) of each lineage, the plan of which clearly demonstrates all that has been described above.

The big house comprises the *dembere* or 'room of the belly', that is to say, the central room, around which are placed a kitchen (*obolom*), three store-rooms (*kana*), a stable for goats (*ende*) and the *denna* or big room, flanked by the entrance (*day*) and another stable (*bel de*). On either side of the entrance and at the angles of one of the rooms are four conical towers surmounted by domes (*arsobo*).

The plan of the building is said to represent, on the one hand, *Nommo* in his human form, the towers being his limbs; on the other hand, the kitchen and stable are said to be the heavenly placenta and its earthly counterpart, together representing the head and legs of a man lying on his right side, whose other limbs also have their architectural counterparts: the kitchen represents the head, whose eyes are the stones of the hearth;[1] the trunk is symbolized by the *dembere*, the belly by the other room, the arms by the two irregular lines of store-rooms, the breasts by two jars of water placed at the entrance to the central room. Finally, the sex organ is the entry which leads by a narrow passage to the work-room, where the jars of water and the grinding-stones are kept. On these, young fresh ears of new corn are crushed, yielding liquid which is associated with the male seminal fluid and is carried to the left-hand end of the entry and poured out on the shrine of the ancestors (Fig. 5).

The plan of the house, then, represents a man lying on his right side and procreating.[2] This attitude has a logical consequence: the differences in height of the roofs over the rooms and sheds, whether or not there is more than one story, express the diversity of the beings which issued from the ejected seeds. Each part of the building represents an original being germinating and growing from its genitor. The whole plan is contained in an

---

[1] The hearth, which is also a symbol of breathing, is often made of two stones placed against the wall at the back of the kitchen. The round cooking-pot rests on the stones and leans against the wall.

[2] A dead body is placed in this position in the grave, and the same attitude is adopted by the man on the marriage bed.

oval which itself represents the great placenta from which have emerged, in course of time, all space, all living beings, and everything in the world.

Procreation is also expressed in the patronage under which the house is placed; while the *sirige* house, also called *tire gingi*, 'the house of the ancestors',[1] belongs to the Fox (*Yurugu*), the 'big house' is placed under the sign

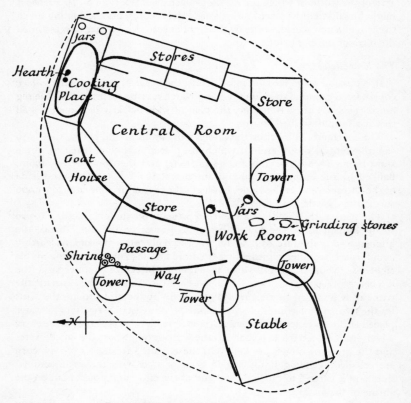

FIG. 5. *The family homestead and the man*

of *Nommo* the Demiurge, the reorganizer of the world. Thus the thunder stone (*andugo*) placed on the central terrace may be explained as a materialization of *Nommo*, who comes down in rain and fire. The stone itself is fire and water, and near it are placed the funerary urns of the ancestors, who are regarded as the human representatives of *Nommo* through the ages.

Thus the same pattern, continually repeated on an ever-expanding scale, leads from man to the cosmos, each stage of the process also representing

[1] See *Dieu d'eau*, pp. 102 sq.

the whole, while a series of material avatars leads from the world itself to smaller and smaller groupings—district, village, village-section, homestead.[1]

The Hogon

The chief of a district among the Dyon, the Ono, and the Domno is given the title of Hogon, and the same designation is applied to the single chief of the Arou.

Primarily the Hogon is the representative of his group, which is divided into seven age classes, he himself constituting an eighth. These eight classes symbolize the eight ancestors and are represented in each village by eight elders, who possess the necessary knowledge and who act as a corporate body, having been constituted as such by means of various rituals. Thus, the chief stands for the group as a whole; but the seven classes and the chief are represented by a chapter of eight notables who, to some extent and in specific situations, act in their name. That is, the chief does not rule alone, but is assisted by a council.

Every Hogon is the successor of Lébé Seru (see p. 89) and as such is responsible for one of the two seeds of which Lébé Seru had charge, to wit the female sorghum (*emme ya*), which is in some sort a substitute for all cultivated seeds and thus sustains the soul and the vital energy. It is the typical seed and the symbol of the cultivation which purifies the unclean soil of *Yurugu*.

The Hogon is also the head of the totem priests, who represent the other seven principal seeds. The motions of their souls are in harmony with the rhythm of all cultivated plants, and therefore the Hogon is ruler of all land laid out in cultivation and of all the rituals connected with it.

But since the seeds are the earthly images of the stars, the Hogon controls the cosmic rhythm, and is thus the personification of the universe and the regent of *Nommo* on earth. In consequence, all his material attributes and all the prerogatives attaching to his function represent the qualities and movements of the cosmic mechanism.

The Clothing of the Hogon

The usual dress of the Hogon consists of a tunic, trousers, a head-dress, and sandals. The tunic is made of strips of cotton cloth sewn together to form a long rectangle, which is folded over and sewn along the edges, leaving openings for the arms and a slit in the folded part for the head. This garment, which is the general dress of all the Dogon, resembles the Egyptian *calasiris*, but those worn by the Hogon and the notables, unlike the common style, have wide sleeves. The white threads of the warp are striped with the red, white, dark blue and light blue threads of the woof. These colours symbolize the four cardinal points, the elements, and, in general, the world; but the name of the garment, *arge bunugu* (lit. the tunic which has not

---

[1] See M. Griaule, 'L'image du Monde au Soudan', *Journal de la Soc. des Africanistes*, xix, 1949, pp. 81–88.

come), indicates that it cannot achieve the size or the diversity of the world owing to its limited dimensions and the small number of colours which compose it. To express the universal character of this garment, all the Arou contribute to the cost of their chief's dress, which is woven by a Dyon. Conversely, the tunic worn by a Hogon of the Dyon is woven by an Arou.

The trousers, which are white or dark blue, have on the front and back of the legs four coloured stripes to which the same significance is attached as to the colours in the tunic. The sandals represent the arch of *Nommo*, the point of the toe being the east. The moon is symbolized by the button which fastens them and the sun by a disk on the heel. This interpretation is valid for the Arou, while for the Dyon it is reversed. The button is ornamented with a cluster of twenty-four cowries, representing the twenty-two categories, with two added for the original *Nommo*. Finally, the sandal is the image of the Hogon, the point of the toe being regarded as the head, the heel as the feet.

The head-dress symbolizes even more clearly the function and the quality of its wearer, particularly in the case of the supreme chief of Arou. It is in the shape of a cylinder, slightly convex at the back, made of basket-work woven from the stalks of the seven sacred plants (millet, sorghum, hibiscus, &c.). The weaving produces a spiral pattern from the centre of the crown to the edge, which symbolizes the path followed by the original seed. Eight Hogons, representing the eight ancestors, share in its making. Not counting the female sorghum (*emme ya*), which is quite separate, the stalks of the seven other seeds used in the head-dress symbolize the seven colours of the rainbow.

In any serious emergency the chiefs assemble round the head-dress of the Hogon of Arou, who then invokes the god *Amma* and, before all the assembled company, speaks into his head-dress and places it on the ground, as if it were a world turned upside down which had to be restored to order. With this head-dress, whose shape suggests the moon, the chief indicates the position of the planet in its various phases.[1] So important is the head-dress (in which resides the female soul of the chief) that he may not go out wearing it on his head, for if he did the course of the moon would be disturbed and thereby that of the seasons. At the death of its owner the head-dress is deposited in a granary at his home, which is opened on this occasion only; it is regarded as the shell of the world-egg since it contains all the potency of dead chiefs and all the seeds symbolized by their head-dresses.

The Homestead of the Hogon

The house of the Hogon of Arou, paramount chief of the Dogon, is so built as to present a model of the universe. It portrays, either by figures made of millet pulp or in reliefs of puddled earth, the beneficent heavens. On the wall behind the platform or dais on which the Hogon sits are

[1] See p. 102.

painted the northern stars to the left, the stars of the south to the right.[1] This diagram is divided in two by a vertical row of four hemispherical earthen bosses, the topmost of which is level with the ceiling of the room above the platform. Each boss is decorated with a spiral of four coils, representing the descent of the world, and is itself the centre of four rays, with four intercalary rays. Each of the four sections of the three lower bosses on the wall represents a lunar month, while the boss at the ceiling symbolizes the head of the Hogon and the thirteenth month. In another context the four bosses are interpreted as the four seasons which, like the lunar months, serve to sustain the head-dress of the Hogon.

Facing the platform, the sun is represented on the wall between the two doors of the east. This egg-shaped relief is painted red and surrounded by twenty-two rays of the same colour symbolizing the twenty-two chieftainships of the Dogon world.[2] The solstices are represented by two smaller ovals placed to right and left of the doors. In the wet season the Hogon's pouch, called 'the pouch of the world', is hung on the left, while his staff, called 'the axis of the world', is placed on the right. In the dry season their respective positions are reversed.

The Hogon's platform is made of sun-dried mud, in which are embedded fragments of the dry stalks of eight varieties of millet; eight store-rooms set in the walls also represent these eight cereals. The house is entered by a flight of eight stairs representing the first eight chiefs; thus the Hogon follows in the steps of his predecessors. To the left of the entrance is the Hogon's own hut or shelter (*toguna*) which is also approached by eight steps. Beside it are eight stones, representing the eight mythical predecessors, which serve as seats when the Hogon sits in judgement. The whole arrangement of standing stones reproduces the great constellations, especially Sirius and its cluster. To the right of the entrance is the hearth where beer is brewed; a row of eight stones represents the Hogons of the future. By the side of these a hollow stone serves as altar where the spirits of dead chiefs come to drink.

The daily life of the Hogon is thus set against a background which presents the world in miniature, and in reference to which his ceremonial acts and movements symbolize the motive power which animates the whole. At dawn, seated with his face towards the east, he is present at the rising of the sun; he then proceeds to walk through his homestead following the order of the four cardinal points. At the end of the day he takes his seat facing towards the west. His walks abroad are similarly regulated: he may never go outside the homestead during the season of vegetal growth when his two souls are in close communion with the spirit of the corn. The beginning and end of this period are marked by libations of water, one from

[1] The diagram is here described as facing the observer; actually, for the Dogon left and right are reversed since the symbols are arranged with reference to the chief when seated on the platform facing the assembled company.

[2] In theory there are five Ono and five Domno chiefdoms. The Arou and Dyon each have six. In fact there is only one Arou chiefdom, which is, nevertheless, counted as six.

the first rains and the other from the last. In the dry season, however, when growth is suspended, the Hogon enjoys greater freedom of movement except at the time of the new moon—that is, when the moon is not yet 'out'.

Thus the Hogon by his clothing represents the world; by his movements about his home he participates in the universal rhythm of things, and in addition he controls the calendar through his links with the motion of the stars, and particularly the moon.[1] On the other hand, he is set at the midpoint of time, between two theoretically equal series of predecessors and successors, symbolized by the steps placed before his doorway and his judgement seat.

The Hogon and millet beer

Just as his clothing and his homestead are necessary elements in the exercise of the Hogon's power, and substitutes, in their particular spheres, for the whole universe, so also the large yeast-container belonging to the chiefdom is the image of the world. This vessel, of a different shape from those used for making beer in other cults, consists of a large cap-shaped container made of basket-work with four small tassels hanging from its rim, and represents the sun in the centre of the four cardinal points. When the beer is being brewed, it is dipped in the boiling liquid in which the grains of millet have lost their vitality; this signifies the plunging of the sun, with its rays and the world which depends on it, into a state of death in preparation for the renewal of spring and in order to set in motion again the phases of creation. The baobab fibre of which the vessel is made is a substitute for all vegetation and, in particular, for the original seed; the bubbling of the fermenting beer recalls the movements of living beings struggling to emerge from the enclosing sheath. Finally, the pattern of its weaving resembles the chief's head-dress woven from the stalks of eight grain plants, and signifies the moment when men first obtained possession of seeds.

At the *sigui* ceremony, which is held every sixty years and at which one of the chief ritual actions is the drinking of fermented liquor, the Hogon makes the first brew of beer and reserves a portion of it which is distributed to every family and mixed with their own beer.

In this way the chief signifies his control of all brewing, and this has many important consequences which it is impossible to discuss here.[2] It

[1] Each Hogon, in the territories within his jurisdiction, and with due regard to arrangements in neighbouring areas, fixes the dates of the various rites and ceremonies. So great is his authority in this sphere that he can omit an important feast without anyone daring to remind him of it. Some chiefs often do so intentionally to display their power. Thus the procession of leaf masks in Sanga was not held at all in 1949 and took place very late in 1950.

[2] We cannot touch on its connexion with the primordial placentas or with copper or with numerology, nor yet its function in the purification of the earth, in drunkenness, in pregnancy, or the part it plays according to the different kinds of beer used in the various cults, or the influence of the varieties of cereals used, &c.

may be pointed out, however, that everyone must be seated when drinking, because the seated position symbolizes founding and planting and thus to drink while seated is to found villages and set plants in the earth. On the other hand, the liquor purifies the man who drinks so that he becomes, as it were, the scene of a resurrection. The living seeds, which died in the boiling liquid, were restored to life in the process of fermentation and finally live again in man. The drinking of the beer causes the seeds to come in contact with the living grain with which the human clavicles are filled; the beer passes out of the body again in the urine which makes its contribution to the family dunghill. The dung, containing dry straw which once was living, will itself distribute the ferment of life to the fields.

The economic functions of the Hogon

The Hogon controls all trade. Before the arrival of the French, and until quite recently, this control was exercised through his regulation of markets. Until 1932 the Hogon's drums, on the eve of a market, beat out instructions for the population as to the procedure to be followed on the morrow. But even at that date this was no more than a gesture, the relic of an institution of which the chief ceremony used to be celebrated by the supreme Hogon of Arou. At the time of the first-fruits sacrifice, an assembly of all the chiefs was held on the parade-ground of the court on which was drawn the 'diagram of the world'—a human figure whose head lay to the south and whose arms were indicated by a triple row of dots symbolizing cowries. This figure, on which the assembled chiefs stood, represented, among other things, the accounting system required for trading. Thus the three rows of 20 dots forming the arms gave the number 60, known as the 'Mande reckoning', which was formerly used in the West Sudan.[1] The circle formed by the head and the open circle of the two legs, symbols of the male and female *Nommo*, each represented 10, the whole and perfect number.[2] The sum of 20 (that is, 10×2) and 60 gives 80, the basis of the later system of reckoning in French Sudan. But to the value of each *Nommo* may be added the unity which it represents; thus, if only the one pair is taken into account, the result will be $(10+1)2 = 22$, the number of the original categories in which all things and living beings were classified.

This arrangement of numbers on the Hogon's parade-ground was not accidental; in theory the Hogons of Arou formed series of sixty, reckoning by their funerary urns. At the same time the parade-ground is, as it were, the site of a great market square on which are displayed the cowries represented by the sixty dots marked out in millet pulp. But the cowries themselves, on which the assembled chiefs stand, are an avatar of the finger-nails

[1] For the system of reckoning based on 60 see G. Dieterlen, *Essai sur la religion bambara*, Paris, p. 27, n. 1.

[2] The number 10 is a repetition of unity. See D. Zahan, 'Aperçu sur la pensée théogonique des Dogon', *Cahiers internationaux de sociologie*, vi, 1949, p. 117; G. Dieterlen, op. cit., p. 213.

of one of the cult ancestors which he left in his grave;[1] they signify, therefore, finger-tips counting out money and handing it over in payment.

Totemism

Totemism among the Dogon emphasizes the fact that men belong to twenty-two categories, and demonstrates the links which bind them to the universe, all the elements of which are similarly classified. In theory, and on one plane, the Dogon believe that the eight original ancestors sprang from eight families each of which ruled an eighth part of the universe (see p. 89). Each family was united in substance with that whole and thus all animals and plants in the corresponding series were taboo to it, while each individual in the family was linked to one specimen of each animal and plant. 'When a man is born, because he is their head, all the tabooed animals are born at the same moment.'[2]

But because this situation was burdensome and man was entangled in too complex a mesh of prohibitions, the rule was applied only to some animals and plants.

The cult of Binu, which may be described as totemic, is associated with with that of Lébé, one of whose attributes is the female sorghum (*emme ya*) brought to earth by the monitor of the arch called Lébé Seru, who died and returned to life after cleansing the soil. When the arch arrived on earth, another monitor, Binu Seru, made war on *Yurugu*, who had stolen the seven seeds intended for man. Twenty-two animals took part in this struggle, seven of which were on the side of the victorious *Nommo*, Binu Seru.[3] To mark the recovery of the stolen goods, he handed on to his successor Dewa the stone *duge*, symbol of the seven seeds, and on it the cult of Binu was founded. Dewa, whose name was given to the totem of which he became the priest, divided his goods, his attributes, and his functions among twenty-two original cults, each of which is attached to a particular Binu with its own special name; this division corresponded to the order of the universe, itself divided into twenty-two categories. The seven animals who had been the allies of *Nommo*, and the seven plants associated with them, were all taboo for the priests of the twenty-two Binu, acting as substitutes for their groups.

---

[1] See M. Griaule, *Dieu d'eau*, p. 66. It should be noted that here there is another reference to the basic 80. Actually, the ancestor put down 8 cowries with 5 fingers, thus indicating that the first great unity was 8 tens. (According to Dogon thinking, 8 must here be multiplied by 5, giving 40 for each hand and 80 for the 2 hands considered as instruments for counting with.) These two bases of reckoning—60 and 80—are complementary, for Dogon as for various other West Sudanese peoples. Sixty represents 3 times the number of a man's fingers and toes and therefore is male (see p. 90); 80 represents 4 times the number of the human person and so is female. Moreover, and this shows how the maximum use is always made of symbols, 6 is twice the number 3 which represents masculinity; 8 is twice 4, the feminine number. These two numbers sum up the primordial situation in the world-egg where two pairs of twins developed simultaneously.

[2] M. Griaule, *Dieu d'eau*, p. 155.

[3] The fifteen other animals were allies of *Yurugu*; they became unclean and died and are now portrayed by the first fifteen animal masks.

The division into 22 Binu corresponds to the 22 members of the first 3 mythical generations which comprise, first, the 2 original *Nommo*; second, the 8 *Nommo* ancestors of the arch; third, their 12 human descendants—4 pairs of twins and 4 single individuals. But as the families of the Dogon increased in number and expanded territorially, the 22 original Binu divided into as many segments as were necessary, and as they divided their names were changed, the segments often adopting other taboos to distinguish them from the original group;[1] all the priests, however, continued to observe the basic double series of seven taboos.

Every individual is attached to the Binu of his father and therefore belongs to an exogamous agnatic group wider than his major lineage.[2] This affiliation is indicated by the name of the Binu which is given to him by the priest at his birth.

Rules of endogamy and exogamy applied to clans and smaller groups are expressed in terms of the compatibility of the symbolic contents of the clavicles of each group. As we have seen, the clavicles are thought to contain a series of seeds, eight in theory, peculiar to each people. It is also accepted that, as regards the Dogon, each tribe is distinguished from the others by the particular order in which the same series of seeds is placed. It has not yet been possible to study fully the variations in the series of seeds in relation to what might be called the totemic clan.

The cult of Binu, integrated as it is with that of Lébé, is primarily aimed at promoting growth in the widest sense of the term; that is to say, it is concerned to secure the well-being not only of the crops but also of men, the bearers of the seeds and partakers of their substance. During the period between the harvest and the next seed-time, the totemic shrines house the spirit of the corn embodied in ears or clusters gathered under certain specified conditions. The seeds from these are put into circulation again by the priests at the next sowing; during the rains they throw them down from the terrace to be gathered up by the women and mixed with the new seed.

As regards men, the Binu guardian of the clan bestows on each the clavicular seeds associated with his two souls. A breach of the Binu taboo deprives the offender of his seeds, which the Binu takes away; the purification ceremony proper to the Binu cult consists in restoring these seeds to the one who has lost them. It thus appears that the Binu dispenses the seeds of the clan, and that he is concerned with the sustenance of its members and with the substance proper to them. It follows that the Binu preserves the special character of each person as member of a particular clan, tribe, and people.

---

[1] This is why, though they have different names and different taboos, all the Binu of the Kamme district are derived from one single Binu, which was that of the founders.

[2] Cf. Tait, 'An Analytical Commentary on the Social Structure of the Dogon', *Africa*, xx, 3, 1950, pp. 175–99.

Technology

Iron-working

Among the Dogon, as among all the peoples of the Western Sudan, iron-working is one of the most important crafts. Iron-workers are, in a sense, a separate race, whose members, in some localities no more than a single family, are found all over the Sudan. Among the Dogon only the *dyemme na* (lit. great skin—an allusion to the bellows) are regarded as iron-workers by origin; the *irin* are Dogon who practise the craft by permission of the former and after the requisite initiation. In fact, however, they perform the same functions as if they were craftsmen by origin.[1] Iron-workers are an endogamous group in relation to the rest of the Dogon, the prohibition of sexual relations being based, as has already been said, on differences in the symbolic contents of the clavicles. In theory these craftsmen own no land nor do they receive any direct payment for the agricultural implements which they make or repair. At harvest-time they are given a portion which constitutes their recompense. The special position occupied by these men, a state of economic and cultural symbiosis, derives, in Dogon belief, from the fact that they are the culture heroes of agriculture who came to earth on the arch. In addition to the clavicular seeds, the original iron-worker had in his hammer eight others intended for men. The violent collision with the earth when he arrived there broke his limbs, providing him with joints enabling him to do his work; at the same time his anvil buried itself in the ground, thereby cleansing the earth and giving it—and men—cultivable grain. The iron-worker, as a result, suffered a diminution of energy, but this put him on an equality with other men. According to Dogon notions, this enfeeblement constituted a kind of uncleanness, though of a different sort from ordinary impurity. The situation of iron-workers is characterized by a diminution of vital energy[2] which excludes them from the category of ordinary 'living' men (*omo*). But this diminution is not comparable to that of death, which also divides them from men who are by destiny 'unclean' (*puru*). Neither are they to be ranked with 'white' men, such as leather-workers, witch-doctors, basket-makers, wood-workers, &c. In one sense they are diminished, but in another sense they are increased, because they have given their energy for the common good.

Along with this ambivalent position there is a recognition of the unquestioned superiority of the craftsman who, in relation to the exercise of his ritual functions, is thought to possess all the seeds which were his at the time of his arrival on earth.

Weaving

The Dogon make a large range of narrow lengths of cloth, plain-coloured and striped, the most usual colours being indigo, white, and red; these are used chiefly to make clothing and blankets. Weaving is held to be one of the

---

[1] This is admitted to be a fiction but it is universally accepted.
[2] Cf. *Dieu d'eau*, p. 105.

original crafts, and innumerable symbolic images are associated with it. It is said that 'cloth is the centre of the world', that it expresses everything, since the originating signs of all things were traced in it. The *Nommo* who invented weaving used his jaw-bone for loom and his tongue for shuttle. He wove into the cloth the words which were bringing in a new order.[1]

In another way the weaver imitates the *Nommo* who, springing from the clavicles of God, forthwith wove together the four elements contained therein and made from them the whole universe. Just as he drew the four elements from the clavicles of God, so the weaver draws his threads—that is, the four elements—from the spindles, the clavicles of the loom.

In some sort, textiles form seven 'families' comprising twenty-two principal strips corresponding to the categories of the universe. It seems that the total number must, in theory, be equal to the number of signs inscribed in the original seed (see p. 85). For the strip of cloth is itself a sign and connotes a myth, partial or complete—a material or spiritual image. To wear a particular cloth,[2] to possess a certain blanket, is therefore to display a symbol which, in practice, corresponds to the physical or moral condition of the wearer, to his social and religious functions and his ordinary activities, which are themselves in harmony with the rhythm of the universe.

As among the Bambara, there is a 'science of cloths' which is an account of the mechanism of creation. In the Dogon mind this knowledge is identified with its subject and therefore the possession of the complete number of cloths in the form of a blanket represents the ideal form of wealth, the acme of riches. It is possible to exceed this number, but to acquire twice the ideal number of twenty-two kinds of cloth would be excessive. A man in such a case would surpass the god *Amma* and draw down disaster on his people.

For this reason men are reluctant to display the family heritage of cloths, for this would be to reveal to the common gaze both the supreme expression of wealth and the symbols of cosmic knowledge. These possessions are never shown except at the death of the family head, at a moment when, in theory, the social upheaval would forbid anyone to count the goods or detect hidden motives. To exhibit cloths at a funerary ceremony is evidence that death has 'gathered up'[3] the whole universe under the form of the symbols which also constitute wealth.

Mangu: An International Alliance

The original situation of the ideal couple—twins enclosed in the same egg—is also illustrated in a religious and economic relationship maintained between the Dogon and the Bozo which has existed, it is said, from the earliest times. This institution, which flourishes over a wide area, is

[1] For the myth of the invention of weaving see ibid., pp. 35 sq.

[2] It may be simply a piece of cloth inset in a garment made of plain strips.

[3] This word may bear the meaning 'to receive for the purpose of hoarding or treasuring' as well as 'to sustain the moral burden' of the knowledge represented by the objects.

known as a 'joking relationship', though the term 'cathartic alliance' has been suggested for it.[1] A Dogon myth relates that when the reorganization of man first began, Dogon and Bozo, represented by the *Nommo* spirits, had in their clavicles eight seeds and eight fishes respectively. 'The most important thing in the world for the *mangu* (ritual partner)' say the natives, 'is the seeds in his clavicles'.[2] By this means the Bozo are marked out as fishermen and the Dogon as cultivators. When they came down to the newly made world together, they made a pact whereby they became mutually complementary. This solemn act, at once a consecration and a recognition of the contents of their clavicles, took place on the original field in which the iron-worker's anvil was embedded. His hammer was beating out the rhythm of the first operations and, since hammer and anvil participated in the form and nature of the universal system—in this instance regarded as a granary—the pact was bound up with the rhythm of those two symbols. By the oaths which they exchanged the two eponymous ancestors, who were already twins, confirmed their complementary relationship; each, by the words he spoke, penetrated the other, depositing within his partner something of himself. This 'bridgehead' formed by energy proceeding from himself enabled each to act effectively and with impunity on the other, more especially in that essential action which directly or indirectly effects purification, and which seems to be one of the chief aims of the alliance.

This complementary state is deeply felt and is expressed in two typical instances in the material life of the two peoples. For the Dogon cultivator the double ear of millet, and for the Bozo fisherman the fish *izu ya*[3] represent this relationship of twin-ness.

If a cultivator finds in his field an ear of millet (*yu*) with two tufts, he immediately cuts it, takes it to the family shrine, and, at the next sowing, the family head will distribute four grains to each member of the family in order to ensure him an abundant harvest. At the same time one grain is thrown in the direction of Bozo territory,[4] which amounts to giving them half the ear, that is, half the good fortune and the abundance, as one would do for a twin.

In the same way, if a Bozo catches an *izu ya*, he must immediately seek a Dogon to eat it with him. If he cannot find one, he simply puts a piece of the fish in with the catch he is taking to market; if he still fails to meet a Dogon

[1] See G. Dieterlen, 'Les correspondances cosmo-biologiques chez les Soudanais', *Journal de Psychologie normale et pathologique*, juill.–sept. 1950; M. Griaule, 'L'alliance cathartique', *Africa*, xviii. 4, Oct. 1948, pp. 242–8.

[2] *aduno magu dye wogo dene inne gozen togodige.*

[3] Lit. female fish; the species is *Gnatonemus Stanleyanus.*

[4] The grain is in fact thrown towards the Bamba cliffs. The *mangu* system, based on the Bozo–Dogon alliance, has, for geographical reasons, been transferred by the Dogon within their own society and applied to territorial and kinship groups. Dogon and Bozo are a considerable distance from one another; the geographical proximity of Dogon groups participating in the *mangu* relationship (by oath, alliance, or blood) enables purification rituals to be carried out without delay and without requiring the parties to make long journeys; the partners are thought to have, in relation to each other, sixteen seeds in their clavicles. In this way the people of Sanga are linked with those of Bamba.

he tries again at the next market, substituting another fish for the first, and so continues till he has been able to share his find with a Dogon. Only then will he feel that he has discharged the debt he has incurred by catching a fish which symbolizes twin-ness.

But it is not only in circumstances such as these that the two groups are under an obligation to provide reciprocal gifts and services; they normally acknowledge a wide range of obligations of all kinds, particularly in regard to food.

These relations are characterized by exchanges of insults and jests, often of an obscene nature, which may be easily observed and have often engaged the attention of investigators.[1] It might be said, indeed, that this is the characteristic method of establishing the relationship; the insult is in fact directed at that part of oneself which resides in the other and which one is trying to recover. It is as if one attempted to detach some of the seeds from the other and appropriate them for oneself. Here, acting in another direction, is a mechanism comparable to that of purification.

The relationship is attended by taboos, any breach of which will have most serious consequences: the *mangu* must never, in any circumstances, shed the blood of a partner; the penalty for transgression is impotence. Murder is thought to entail the death of the murderer. Sexual relations between members of the two groups are forbidden: they would unquestionably be incestuous, and would result in the guilty parties being completely denuded of the sustenance lodged in their clavicles. That is to say, the Dogon would lose his millet, the staple grain which no other transgression can affect, and would be, as it were, emptied of his substance.

The benefits of this institution are not confined to relations between the two peoples. Within their own society the Dogon have woven a close web of relationships all of which, in different degrees, recall the Bozo pact, and many examples could be given of alliances between groups of regions, between regions, between villages, and between kin-groups.

Traditionally, the oldest of these alliances is that which links Bamba with a number of other regions, and is explained by the story that a Bamba man was travelling through the Sanga region at a very unsettled time. On the way he was set upon by six bandits, whereupon he cried out '*Mangu! mangu!*' The brigands, disconcerted, put their heads together and asked the advice of an old man, who told them to spare him; they all thought he was a Bozo since the Bozo were the only people with whom the Dogon had relations, so the man escaped. Later the fraud was discovered, but the precedent became a rule and the alliance between the Bamba and the people of the plateau came to be included in the Bozo–Dogon system of relationships. 'All the *mangu* here (that is, all the relationships between Dogon)', said the Elder Ongnulu, 'copy the Bozo *mangu*.'

The importance of such an institution is obvious; those who participate

---

[1] It is this detail of the whole mechanism which has given rise to the name 'joking relationship'.

in it are equals in the sense that each is the product of a totality of forces to which an alien element has been added; they are complementary in the sense that each possesses the part that the other lacks. The two partners are equal; each finds himself in the other. 'When *mangu* cleanses a man it is as if he purifies himself.'[1]

[1] *Manene godijale ku womo wajalage ginuwo.*

THE MENDE IN SIERRA LEONE[1]

By KENNETH LITTLE

Introduction

IN this article I shall attempt to show how certain social values of the Mende are related to their cosmological ideas and how such values are expressed in ritual.[2] By a 'value' I follow Nadel in meaning an idea of worthwhileness governing a class of actions and imparting to each the index 'good' or 'bad', or 'desirable' or 'undesirable', as the case may be. And when I take the respective forms of behaviour to be instances of social values I understand that here such-and-such an idea of worthiness is commonly held and consistently applied to the various occasions of acting.[3] Such an idea of worthiness is also embodied in a set of normative rules which, as Talcott Parsons points out, not only serve as the ends of specific acts and chains of them, but govern as a whole or in large part the complex of actions of the individual. Thus, among the Mende there are certain rules governing relations between kinsfolk, and behaviour is 'good' or 'bad' according to whether, irrespective of other conditions, it conforms or does not conform to these rules. These rules do not define the immediate ends in relations between kinsfolk, but rather define the manner in which actions in matters of kinship should or may be performed.

The value attached to kinship and the set of rules in which it is embodied derive, as I shall show, from certain religious and magical beliefs, notably in ancestral spirits, that the Mende hold. A further system of values governs actions in the sexual field and is embodied in a set of rules which similarly have their origin in a specific cult; and the same holds good, broadly speaking, for political, economic, and educational values. What this amounts to is that moral conduct in Mende life is to a large extent regulated by a number of specific cults each of which controls a specific compartment of the common life. Thus, the *Poro*—the men's society—determines a youth's elegibility for marriage and prepares him for adult membership of the community. It also helps to regulate the harvesting of crops and the

---

[1] Some of the material presented in this study has already appeared in a slightly different form in my book, *The Mende of Sierra Leone*, 1951, and is included here by permission of the publishers, Messrs. Routledge and Kegan Paul. See also two articles in *Zaïre*, March and April 1951.

I have to thank Professor Daryll Forde for a number of helpful comments on my original draft of this article.

[2] The Mende are an agricultural people, living mainly by the cultivation of rice. They inhabit the central and south-western part of the Sierra Leone Protectorate and the adjoining part of Liberia. According to an official census taken in 1931 they number (in Sierra Leone) close on 700,000.

[3] Cf. S. F. Nadel, *The Foundations of Social Anthropology*, 1951, p. 264.

fishing season.[1] The *Humui*—a medicine society—largely controls sexual conduct and relations.

The existence of these cults, including the ancestral ones, is a function of certain ideas that the Mende have regarding the nature of the universe and the supernatural forces directing it. .This implies that the Mende have arrived at a number of conclusions of a metaphysical kind and that the various ritual and other activities of their society are the logical outcome of these. This is a convenient hypothesis but it cannot be accepted without some reservation. The fact is that the Mende are not given very much to theoretical speculation. I found it difficult to draw them out on questions of an abstract kind and am inclined to suspect that their lack of interest in this respect was due, not merely to the alien nature of some of my concepts, but to a genuine feeling of indifference. They were quite prepared, as a rule, to talk freely about themselves and their way of life in its practical applications. For example, they would discuss their farms and the technicalities of farming with some enthusiasm, and would describe with considerable warmth the commercial hazards of agricultural production and other difficulties of getting a living. They would also refer quite frequently to matters arising out of the organization of their social life, such as 'woman palaver', disputes over land, problems of political succession, &c. Additionally, there were references, more implicit than explicit, to rites and practices of a religious and magical kind. But the supernatural world hardly ever entered the conversation as a subject for conjecture without a good deal of prompting on my part. The Mende response to such overtures was, almost invariably, vague and even apathetic: and not, I think, because of any special inhibition or taboo. It is true that a specific aspect of this field concerning the activities of the various cult associations, or 'secret societies', lies completely outside the province of secular discourse. But many questions of 'religion' and 'medicine' and the sphere of ancestral spirits are a not uncommon part of everyday experience about which people can speak without much fear.

My general impression, therefore, is that the Mende have an essentially 'practical' attitude to life. They prefer to concern themselves with the problems of today rather than those of tomorrow. This, I think, explains their lack of interest in metaphysics, including the metaphysical side of popular Christianity, which in terms of its rewards in the after-life argues essentially for a 'long-term policy'.[2] I also conjecture that they extend an equally

---

[1] Nowadays, the *Poro* is probably a stronger force in Liberia than in Sierra Leone. For a detailed account of its traditional organization among the Liberian tribes the reader should consult G. W. Harley, 'Notes on the Poro in Liberia', *Peabody Museum Papers*, vol. 19, No. 2, 1941.

[2] Dr. Hofstra, who worked in Mende country in the early thirties, once attended a service held by an English missionary in a village. After the service, which the majority of the villagers attended, was ended, the opportunity was given to them to put questions to the missionary. The people, however, did not use this opportunity for discussion on relevant religious or metaphysical questions, but at once engaged the missionary in a long conversation asking him to explain why the price of palm kernels was so low. Cf. S.

practical attitude of mind to their relations with what we should term the supernatural world. The fact that their supernatural world is an extremely complex one, peopled by innumerable ancestral and non-ancestral spirits, does not invalidate this point. The situation seems to be that they regard 'super-natural' phenomena in much the same kind of way and frame of mind as they regard the material circumstances of their environment and the motives and actions of human beings. For both sets of phenomena they have their own working interpretation which also includes a method of dealing with or rationalizing what is strange or unpredictable. Such an attitude is also, within the bounds of Mende knowledge, quite empirical. They are quite prepared to experiment with new materials, and this factor helps, perhaps, to explain their readiness to assimilate creeds alien to them or, at any rate, the external trappings of such creeds. For example, in the case of Islam, which nowadays many Mende people profess, the Qu'ran is regarded and used in much the same fashion as a native medicine. It is employed to manu-facture a powerful charm by inscribing a Sura in Arabic writing upon a wooden board. The Arabic characters are washed off in water, which is bottled, and then serves to endow its possessor with a commanding per-sonality. As a further instance, some villagers with whom I discussed the notion of God, described a visit paid them by a Christian missionary. He had pointed out the merits of a Christian way of life and had been 'kind' to them, and so they had agreed to become Christians if he would build them a school.

Beliefs in a Supreme Being and in Spirits

In such circumstances, any attempt to reconstruct the Mende cosmology has its obvious dangers. The European observer is tempted, for the sake of coherence and clarity, to impute philosophical conceptions and formula-tions which are far more rigid and concrete than the actual nature of Mende belief. What does exist in this respect is a rich and varied store of tradi-tional and mythological lore descriptive of the world as the Mende conceive it and of the relationships of human beings to each other. This is lacking in doctrine and is largely **proverbial in** character.[1] Outstanding in this

Hofstra, 'The Social Significance of the Oil Palm in the Life of the Mende', *Internationales Archiv für Ethnographie*, Band xxxiv, Heft 5–6, Leiden, 1937.

[1] Here are a few examples:

If God dishes your rice in a basket, do not wish to eat soup.
(If God has made you a poor man, do not desire to be rich.)

When a child is well-fed, he looks upon a grave as an ordinary heap of earth.
(When a child is happy, he disregards serious things).

When a big tree falls, the birds in it scatter.
(When the leader falls, his followers disperse).

The sounds of a person's cry show his tribe.
(Your actions determine the kind of person you are).

If a frog has no belly when it is young, what will it have when it is old?
(If something is not good at the beginning, it can hardly be good at the end).

If an old woman says that she was once beautiful, you can verify it from the back of her neck.
(If anyone claims to have had good qualities, you can check it from his present behaviour.)

collection of tales, sayings, and proverbs is the notion of 'God', of a supreme being who created the earth and everything in it. The name for 'God' which is most commonly used is *Ngewɔ*, but he is also known by what appears to be a much older name—*Leve*. A possible explanation is that *Leve* represents a more traditional usage because, in tracing the origin of certain practices, one is frequently told that 'this is what *Leve* brought down to us long ago', and a similar expression occurs in certain prayers which are part of a social institution like the *Poro*, apparently as a sanction for the carrying on of the rites concerned.

The name of *Ngewɔ* is frequently invoked by the Mende, and the idea that he represents some kind of supreme power or force certainly seems to be strongly held,[1] but he is in no sense an immanent being. Like most African supreme beings, having made the world, he retired into the sky.[2] He has little immediate contact with the affairs of men, although he still sends the rain to fall on his 'wife', the Earth. There are numerous expressions such as *Ngewɔ jahu* and *Ngewɔ luma*, corresponding approximately to 'God willing' in European terms, which imply submissiveness: but many of them are largely proverbial or socially formal in the sense in which similar terms are used in Europe. I think that most Mende people will admit that they know very little about the actual nature of *Ngewɔ* because, as one informant put it, 'no one has ever seen him'. *Ngewɔ* is not entirely unapproachable, however, and sometimes a prayer may be addressed directly to him and his help is frequently sought over the use of medicine and, as I shall show later, in the prospering of family relations.

In addition to creating human beings, animals, plants, and inorganic matter, *Ngewɔ* is also responsible, apparently, for the existence of a certain non-material kind of power or influence known as *hale*. The latter point, however, is frequently implicit rather than explicit in Mende myth and is brought out only by direct inquiry or allusion to the phenomena in question. However, it is made quite definitely. 'The (*Poro*) *ngafa* was made by God and not by man,' was the reply of one informant, the head of a large household, to a comment of mine on the apparently secular nature of this particular 'spirit'.

Spiritual beings fall broadly into two categories—ancestral and non-ancestral spirits. The ancestral spirits, as the term implies, are the spirits of

---

[1] This is exemplified by the following expressions, viz: 'Everything is God', i.e. God permits all things; 'God is judge', He has the last word, &c.; cf. W. T. Harris, 'The Idea of God among the Mende', *African Ideas of God*, ed. Edwin Smith, 1950, pp. 277–97.

[2] The Rev. W. T. Harris reports a story that long ago, *Ngewɔ* made the earth and all things, and ended by making a man and a woman. *Ngewɔ* told them that if they wanted anything, they had but to ask him for it. But they came to him so frequently that he said to himself: 'If I stay near these people they will wear me out with their requests; I will make another living-place for myself far, far above them' (ibid.). I found it difficult, however, to obtain many precise particulars of the creative role of *Ngewɔ*. Literate members of the Mende community gave me some very elaborate and detailed accounts of the creation, but these stories were so obviously influenced by Christian or Islamic teaching and Western education as to provide very little guide to indigenous belief in this respect.

former living members of the community—both former members of the various cults as well as individual families.[1] The non-ancestral spirits comprise certain widely known spirits or genii (*dyinyinga*)[2] associated quite often with natural phenomena such as rivers, forests, and rocks, but not confined to any one locality; a host of nameless spirits associated with specific local features, such as mountains and rivers; and spirits associated specifically with certain cults. Both categories of spiritual beings are much nearer at hand than *Ngewɔ*. The ancestral spirits and the better-known genii are therefore worshipped and propitiated, both because they personalize supernatural power and because the ancestral spirits are a means of communicating with the ultimate source of that power, which is *Ngewɔ*. Their worship is organized in different ways by the various cults referred to, and as each cult embodies its own system of values it will be convenient to consider them in turn.

The Ancestral Cult

I shall deal first with the ancestral cult in whose rules, as already mentioned, are embodied the values set on kinship. This cult is based on the belief that a person survives after death and that his surviving personality goes to the land of the dead. In order to enter this new country the person's spirit has to cross a river, and certain rites, known as *tindyamei* or 'crossing the water', are necessary. These include the offering of a chicken upon the grave by the dead person's relatives—four days after burial for a man, three days after burial for a woman. Sometimes money and personal articles are deposited with the corpse. These are to provide the deceased with a present with which to greet the spirits he will meet 'on the other side' and to indicate his earthly position and rank to them. Since the spirit cannot 'cross the river' before this rite has been carried out, it is essential that the dead person should have relatives who are able and willing to perform it. To deny a person these rites is tantamount to condemning his spirit to remain on earth and, thus, to be haunted by it.

The grave itself is conceived sometimes as a big town which the deceased enters on being lowered into it. To dig a grave is spoken of as building a house. Generally, however, notions of the next world are of a rather vague kind, though it is pictured sometimes as a clean town, with white sand. Ideas which are more specific are obviously influenced by the teaching of local Moslem preachers. What is fairly significant, however, is that the conditions of this world are apparently continued in the hereafter, and the life led by the ancestral spirits seems to be similar in many respects to that of the people on earth. Some informants described them as cultivating

---

[1] I notice that Mr. Harris differentiates between the *kɛkɛni*, those ancestors whose names and feats are known, either through personal knowledge or oral tradition, and the *ndebla*, those who died in the far-distant past.

[2] The singular of *dyinyinga* is *dyina*, which suggests that the term has an Islamic origin. This may be the case, but I think that *dyina* merely represents a more specific version of the indigenously held conception of 'nameless' spirits referred to above.

rice-farms, building towns, &c. It also seems that the spirits retain an anthropomorphic character and much of their earthly temperament and disposition. An informant explained the latter point by mentioning that his brother, who died away from home without his people's knowledge, appeared in a dream to one of their neighbours. In the dream he gave certain instructions about a leopard's tooth, which was found afterwards on the body.

The cycle of an individual ancestor lasts as long as the dead person is remembered in prayers and sacrifices, and this varies with social and political status. On the other hand, as Hofstra points out, it is necessary to distinguish between the ritual and the psychological side of remembrance. Sometimes an ancestral ceremony is performed simply to indicate to the community that the family concerned is in a position to make a large sacrifice; sometimes the personal factor transcends ritual bounds.[1] Feelings of affection that the living have for the dead probably also help to explain why the appearance of ancestral spirits, usually in dreams, is not feared, though the object of such visits is probably to scold the person concerned for some neglect of his duty to the spirits. Such visits are also part of the tutelary role that the ancestors play as protectors of the family and of its individual members. In this capacity they offer guidance and counsel and are regarded and addressed in much the same way as are the living senior members of the group by their juniors. Misfortune suffered personally, or by the family as a group, is a sign of ancestral displeasure and is interpreted as a warning that the persons concerned should look closely into their recent conduct towards relatives as well as towards the spirits themselves. Not only a person's own ancestors but the ancestors of other people may be vengeful towards him if they were wronged during their lifetime. If this happens, the only thing that the victim of their revenge can do is to ask one of the nearest living relatives of the spirits whom he has offended to pray to them on his behalf. The relative's good will is secured by a present and he proceeds to make an offering at the grave at which the offending person should also be present.

This relationship between the living and the dead is expressed in a fairly regular system of rites, and a short description of them will illustrate the wide nature of the ancestral role which is, in part, disciplinary. The implication is that the spirits expect their share of whatever prosperity comes to their living relatives and the latter's households. These relatives are surviving sons, grandsons, and great-grandsons, and nephews on both sides of the family. Female relatives are usually included in the cults of their spouses unless they are themselves heads of households or sufficiently senior

[1] Cf. S. Hofstra, 'The Ancestral Spirits of the Mendi', *Int. Arch. f. Eth.*, Band xxxiv, Heft 1–4, Leiden, 1940. 'It happened in two cases that elderly women when asked for information about births and deaths in their families were hardly able to speak; they became for some moments overwhelmed with grief when they mentioned the names of the children they had lost at an early age' (p. 195). Readers desiring a detailed account of mortuary and religious customs of the Mende should consult this valuable article.

to have a direct relationship with the ancestors. Generally the approach is made by the male head of the household concerned and either he, or a special member—the *hɛmɔi* (praying man)—in a large-sized household, conducts the ceremony. Very often, there is also a special place—the *hema* (praying place)—for such activities. This is situated in the bush at the foot of a large cotton-tree between whose roots a small wooden shelter is constructed. The members of the household congregate there and a fowl and some rice are brought forward. The *hɛmɔi* then calls the name of the ancestors, taking care not to omit any, and concludes with the name of the most recently dead. He addresses them somewhat in this manner: 'Well, grandfathers, we are here now and here is your portion.' The food is then set down and the party returns to the village and partakes of a communal meal. After this there is general rejoicing. If the food left at the shrine is eaten up by birds or passing strangers, it is a sign that the ancestors have accepted the sacrifice and are pleased. A further ceremony must be performed if it has not gone by the next day. Ceremonies and sacrifices of this kind are usually carried out in the early morning, possibly on account of the implications of vigour associated with the beginning of the day.

Some families make a number of routine offerings during the year, but others do not appear to sacrifice without some special cause. Decisions to do so are generally the result of someone dreaming of an ancestor, or of a run of misfortune or illness in the family. The ancestors are angry and wish to be fed. It is assumed that the person who is sick has offended them in some way. There are several ways of appeasing them; one is by the ceremony of the 'red rice'[1] (*mbagboli*) another by 'the laying of the plant' (*howei*).

The head of the family, or the 'big wife' of the sick person, usually conducts the red rice ceremony. Two pieces of tobacco are taken to the ancestral graves and a supplication in words like the following is made on the 'offender's' behalf:

Ah, grandfathers, I have come to you: Momo is the one who is ill. The soothsayer informs me that you are angry with him because he has not 'fed' you for a long time. Do you, grandfathers, kindly pardon him. He is a small boy; he has no senses yet. I have come now to beg you. My heart is now clear. The sky above is also satisfied, and the earth below is also satisfied. Every day that passes, we ask that you people should always be our leaders and should not leave us unprotected.

Next morning, the sick man's relatives bring cooked rice and a fowl. Pepper is omitted from the offering lest it make the hearts of the *nduwumoi* (the dead) very hot and make them still more angry. The person in charge then goes up to the grave and prays: 'Old father Jina . . . let this reach you; old father, Abu . . . let this reach you. The food I promised to give you is what I have now brought. Let no bad thing happen to him (the sick person), and even to us (the relatives), let nothing bad happen to us.'

[1] 'Red rice' is rice mixed with a special red-coloured palm-oil.

The rice is mixed with the liver of the fowl and placed upon the grave. Then water is poured out for drinking with the words, 'Please, the water', and the rice is eaten. All close their eyes, and at the word of the person officiating they open them again, and say in chorus: 'In your protection let our eyes be open for something sweet in the future.'

The *howei* ceremony is customary when the graves of the ancestors are at some distance from the village. In this case, after prayers of a similar kind have been said, the rice is usually put on two crossed leaves (the *howei*) and placed upon the public highway. To test if the angry spirit is appeased, a fowl is brought to peck at some rice which has been placed on the offending person's tongue, or the palm of his hand. If the fowl refuses the rice, further offerings have to be brought and the ceremonies repeated.

A more routine approach to the ancestral spirits is in connexion with the making of rice-farms. Rice is the staple food of the Mende and the main focus of their agricultural interests and activities. New farms are made by cutting down the forest. After selecting the site for his farm during the coming year, the farmer takes a white fowl and a piece of shirting to the place he has in view. He finds an ant-hill and addresses sorrowful words to the ancestral spirits so that they may take pity on his condition: 'We have come here to make our farm. We have not come in a proud way to annoy you; do not be angry with us. Let not our machetes wound us as we work; let not the big trees fall on us and hurt us!' In due course, the trees have been felled and the farm is ready for burning. Before this can be done, however, the ancestors must be informed and so the farmer takes palm-wine down to the scene of the coming operation in order to inform the spirits ceremonially about it.

At sowing, which is the most crucial part of the work, a more elaborate ceremony is carried out. Before beginning their task the farmer and his helpers go to the entrance of the farm, where it adjoins the road from the town. Here, the farmer erects a frame of palm leaves. Two sticks, about $4\frac{1}{2}$ feet long and forked at one end, are stuck into the ground, a cross-piece is laid along the top, and a number of additional sticks are used to support the structure. A small hollow is dug in the ground underneath it and an ant-hill, which has been sliced off with a machete, is placed in the hollow with some ferns tied around it. The ceremony itself begins with the farmer harrowing the earth in front of the ant-hill with a hoe. He then scatters seed profusely in the runnels. The hoe is broken by splitting its shaft, and both head and shaft are placed against the ant-hill. The farmer and his workmen bend down and cover over the rice and smooth down the soil with their left hands, moving gradually towards the ant-hill and keeping their right hands stretched out, palms open. (Stretching out the hand in this way is a method of 'associating' oneself with the sacrifice which is taking place). While they are doing this, the oldest member of the party prays to the ancestors to prosper their work, calling upon those spirits which have a special reputation as farmers. Then a cock is handed to the farmer. He unties its wings, lays it on the ground, and cuts its throat with a knife. Then, holding the fluttering carcass in both hands, he squeezes blood over the ant-hill, the hoe, and the 'sown' ground. Then he plucks out some of the feathers, attaches them to the shaft, and scatters other feathers over the 'sown' ground. The ceremony concludes with his placing a cup containing 'red rice' beside the ant-hill. This is to 'feed' the ancestors.

Ceremonial observances in connexion with harvesting begin when the rice has ripened. Their object, also, is to retain the good will of the ancestral spirits as well as to ward off any evil spirits which may be lurking about the farm. The farmer takes a portion of newly harvested rice to the high bush surrounding the farm, and addresses the ancestral spirits in these words: 'Our rice is not yet enough, but here is your portion. When all our rice is cut, we will bring you your own again.'

The first rice to be reaped is taken from the part of the farm which was first sown and harrowed (the practice is first to sow, or rather broadcast, the seed and then work it into the soil). None of this first rice is eaten that day. The next day it is cooked and prepared with 'red' oil and given to the person who prepared the harrowing and sowing medicines. Then either he or the praying man offers it to the ancestors, calling upon those, now dead, who previously worked on the farm, with these words: 'Through you (i.e. the immediate forebears of the farming household) we go to our ancestors. We have brought you this rice. Let not the rice left in our hands be used in a bad way. Look after our children, our wives; let no bad thing fall on us.'

Everyone then takes part in a general feast, and when the food has been eaten, they go down to the harvest field. Rice is also placed on flat stones by the roadside for the ancestors, and this is consumed by the old people. Special care is taken to perform this rite if any relatives of the farmer have died during the past year.[1]

The above ceremonies suggest that the Mende believe that the ancestral spirits are in a position to help the living, even to intercede on their behalf. This does not necessarily mean that the spirits have power in their own right; the implication is rather that whatever influence the spirits possess and exercise on behalf of the people on earth is due to *Ngewɔ*. *Ngewɔ* 'made' spirits in the same sense that he made human beings and everything else on earth, and he is responsible for things being what they are. By this I mean that in a limited sense of the verb *Ngewɔ* 'helps' a human being to fulfil himself as a human being, i.e. to act and behave like a human being. He helps *hale* (medicine) to be power. He helps a spirit to behave like a spirit. Here is an illustration of what I am trying to convey. When two persons have a dispute the matter is often settled by making both parties 'swear' on a stone or 'anything else that *Ngewɔ* made'. It is believed that

---

[1] I should mention that for the sake of brevity and simplicity, I have omitted details of other rites performed in connexion with farming whose elements are magical rather than propitiatory.

the spirit in the stone will be helped by *Ngewɔ* to decide the issue and to punish the guilty or offending party. In other words, the stone 'fulfils' itself (as forensic medicine) through *Ngewɔ*.

Relationship of the Ancestral Cult to Kinship Organization

The basis of the ancestral role, therefore, lies in the ancestors occupying a position in the cosmos nearer to its creator, *Ngewɔ*, than the people on earth.[1] In other words, they are, conceptually, a link between the living members of Mende society and the final source of supernatural power. This point is implicit rather than explicit in indigenous belief; nevertheless, it seems to be sufficiently borne out by the fact that prayers offered directly to the spirits are also intended for transmission to *Ngewɔ*. The following is a good example from the final blessing of the young *Poro* initiates before they leave the bush school and return to ordinary society. In it the spirits of former members of the *Poro* are invoked;

Father Siaffa, let it reach to you; let it reach to Kanga; let it reach (lit. 'be laid down') to the head, the great one (i.e. *Ngewɔ*). This is what *Leve* brought down (showed us to do) long ago. These children whom we are 'pulling' from the *Poro* today, let nothing harm them; let them not fall from palm trees. . . .[2]

In this, both the nature of the invocation and the order of the words suggest that the ancestral spirits should be helped by *Ngewɔ* to fulfil the object of the prayer. As already explained, *Ngewɔ* himself is a long way off, the ancestors are nearer to hand and therefore more immediately able to assist. There is also a related implication, frequently occurring in Mende belief, which is expressed proverbially in the saying, 'God is the Chief'. In other words, *Ngewɔ* is too 'big' to concern himself about the ordinary person; he has to be approached indirectly. As one of my informants put it, 'If you are seeking a favour from a chief, you don't go to him yourself; you start by asking someone near him to speak on your behalf'. This is the general pattern of etiquette which reaches down to quite minor officials, and is also practised in the extended kin group. It is also customary to preface such overtures by a gift to the person from whom the favour is sought.

Sociologically, the proximity of the ancestral spirits to *Ngewɔ*, and their role as media for communication with him, is very significant. It provides an obvious sanction on relations with the living family and on the relationships that its individual members have with each other. Such a sanction adds not only greater importance to the system of formal duties which the

---

[1] The Rev. W. T. Harris (op. cit.) says that when prayer is offered at hills and rivers there is the belief that the *ndebla* (distant ancestors) convey the prayer to the original spirits of the hill and water, and these in turn take it to *Ngewɔ*. I did not myself hear of this belief though I came across many instances of prayers and sacrifices being offered to such 'nature' spirits, the declared object being to ward off danger or to propitiate the spirits concerned.

[2] The Rev. W. T. Harris records a similar prayer to the ancestors: 'O God, let it reach to *Kenei Mɔmɔ*, let it reach to *Nduawo*, let it reach all our forefathers who are in your arms' (ibid., p. 281).

living are expected to perform on the ancestors' behalf but also a deeper meaning to the rights and obligations of kinship. The latter are also given ritual expression in a type of family compact known as *kotei*, when a group of relatives come together and bind themselves to some common task or undertaking. For example, they may promise to unite as one body for the protection of each other or of family property. In reinforcement of the pledge they eat a communal meal together, promise to observe certain common taboos, and call the ancestors in to witness the compact, which then becomes a species of family law. Any infringement of it is regarded as a grave sin against the dead, as well as the living, members of the group, and is punishable by the spirits themselves.[1]

Bonds of kinship hold good on both sides of the family, and a person has obligations towards certain kin of his mother as well as towards the kin of his father. This is so, despite the fact that *ndehun* (lit. brotherhood), the term which denotes the closest possible relationship of persons, is in the strict sense limited to the patrilineal relatives of Ego. Technically, Ego's mother, as well as his wife's relatives, are the *mbondaesia*; but it is quite a common practice for Ego to include not only his own mother but any of his mother's relatives with whom the degree of personal association is strong within the category of his *ndehun-bla* (family people). This is largely because of the special relationship existing between Ego and his or her mother's brothers, the *kenyaisia*. It involves a dual system of inheritance in that a person is entitled to a share of his uncle's property in addition to inheriting from his patrilineal relatives. The nephew's privileges include the right to his uncle's daughters or to his wives after his uncle's decease; but he is not allowed to inherit the wives if he has already married or had intercourse with a daughter. He is also entitled to use his uncle's belongings while the latter is alive, and to certain perquisites, such as the head of any animal that his uncle kills. Reciprocally, the uncle is entitled to full use of his nephew's services on his farm and in a number of other ways. For example, by tradition he is allowed to offer his nephew or niece as a pawn in discharge of a debt.

Towards his *ndehun-bla*, in the wider sense, a person's obligations are well known and obvious to all concerned and, as already mentioned, are reflected in the roles performed reciprocally by the living and dead members of the family. In other words, the ancestral spirits stand, conceptually, in the same relationship to the family as do its senior members on earth to their own sons and daughters and nephews and nieces. Upon the younger

---

[1] Here is an example of a *kotei* made by the members of a chief's family in Upper Mende country:

   (a) Their town shall never voluntarily be surrendered to invaders.

   (b) No member of the family shall be left in slavery.

   (c) Members shall maintain any oath made on the *kotei*.

   (d) Membership shall be open even to their slaves who, after taking the oath and eating the rice, shall be liable no longer to be sold; any female child born of such a slave shall be married to a 'true-born person of the soil'.

   (e) Members shall tell the truth to one another.

generation falls the obligation of providing the older generation with food by working on their farms, performing other manual services, and showing them respect and deference in every way. In return, the older generation blesses the younger people, provides them with counsel, and shares its inheritance with them. Disobedience on the part of a son, and more particularly a nephew, is a grave offence bringing the most serious consequences, and the sin can only be expiated in a ritual way.

Formerly, if a son left home without his father's permission the father would stand in his house or just outside and say: '*A Ngewɔ* (O God), you know this is my son; I begat him and trained him and laboured for him, and now that he should do some work for me he refuses. In anything he does now in the world may he not prosper until he comes back to me and begs my pardon.'

If in his wanderings the son finds he has a run of misfortune, he will realize that the father's curse has fallen upon him and he will return home repentant. He goes first to his mother, who takes him to his father with a gift of rice, fowl, and money. He sits or kneels at his father's feet, holding the father's right foot with his right hand. The father then prays:

O, *Ngewɔ*, this is my son; he left me without any good fortune in the world because he knows I have cursed him; he has now come back to beg me; he knows he cannot stand behind me; he has come now to beg me to pull the curse as I am pulling it now. Wherever he goes now may he prosper and have many children.

The members of the family who are present respond: '*Ngewɔ jahu.*'[1]

If an uncle (mother's brother) should have cause to curse his nephew, it is necessary for the latter's father to intercede in order to persuade the uncle to retract his oath. The offender's brothers and sisters must also be present. The father then brings his son to the uncle to confess and apologize for his sin. He (the father) also offers the uncle money or a country cloth. If the uncle accepts the present all the nephews and nieces, including the offending person, prostrate themselves, holding on to the uncle's feet. The uncle then prays that they may all be forgiven the wrong they have done him and that the curse may be removed. Then he sucks up some water out of a bowl brought by the offender's mother and blows it in a fine spray over the heads of all the nephews and nieces kneeling in front of him. He also smears a mixture of dust and water on their foreheads. This finally removes his curse. He blesses them, and the family eat a meal together as a group.

The fact that a father intercedes with the mother's brother suggests that ritually it is most important for a person to be on good terms with the latter. There are a number of reasons for this. In the first place, the Mende consider that since a brother and sister come from the same father they may be regarded as one. Therefore, all that a mother gives her child is given also by her brother, and so her brother's pleasure or displeasure is the same as

---

[1] Harris, op. cit., p. 283. Note that in this case the prayer is made directly to *Ngewɔ* without ancestral intermediaries.

her own. Moreover, though the physical part of an individual—his bones, flesh, &c.—is provided by his father through the semen put into the mother, the child's spirit (*ngafa*)[1] is contributed by his mother.[2] This makes the mother the child's 'keeper' in a sense that is difficult to translate directly into Western terms, the concept being more analogous to 'good fortune' than to the more obvious 'guardian angel'. Unfortunately, I have no means of saying how the respective contributions of the male and female parent relate to such beliefs as the Mende have in rebirth and reincarnation. In some cases, the finger of a dead man is pricked, or a string is tied round his waist, so that he will be recognized when he reappears. Children are also named, sometimes, after a particular ancestor, especially if they bear any resemblance to him, and all this seems to suggest some idea of the life-cycle being renewed.[3] What is quite evident, however, is that the mother's contribution to her child is regarded as particularly important and that, in consequence, primary attention is paid in ritual matters to the maternal side, the paternal side of the family being secondary. Thus, in praying to the ancestors the spirits on the mother's side are first invoked and afterwards those on the father's side. Again, in the funeral ceremony of *tindyamei* it is generally one of the maternal uncles of the dead person who invokes the latter's spirit.

The Cult of Nature-spirits and Genii

I will pass now to the spirits of a non-ancestral kind. These, as mentioned above (p. 115) include various spirits associated with specific local features, such as mountains and rivers; certain more widely known spirits or genii who are also associated quite often with similar natural features but are not confined to any one locality; and spirits associated specifically with certain cults or secret societies.

As is the case with ancestral spirits, these local 'nature-spirits' are also propitiated, but the sacrifices made to them are usually limited to some important seasonal event. One brief example, from a town in Upper Mende country, must suffice. The river, on which this town is situated, regularly overflows its banks during the month of September. This is interpreted by a soothsayer as a warning that the conduct of the people has angered the spirit dwelling in the river and that the whole

[1] *Ngafa*, as mentioned above, is the general term for 'spirit', including ancestral spirits, spirits associated with the secret societies, &c.

[2] According to one of my informants, a person's character and temperament are largely influenced by the conduct of his father and mother. They are good if his mother has been obedient to her husband; bad, if she has been wayward.

[3] Hofstra (op. cit.) is more definite on this point. He recounts a fairly wide belief in the following cycle. After being created by *Levei* (God), people begin their lives in the sky. When they die there, they are reborn on earth. When they die on earth they go to a place under the earth. There is, also, the process of being reborn, of dying, and of moving to a place, which is repeated several times. In this way a human being goes through ten lives. Hofstra's informants were unable to say whether the end of the cycle would bring the total extinction of the spirit. They were inclined to think that extinction would follow.

country will be flooded if the spirit is not propitiated. A day is appointed for the necessary sacrifices, which take place at the end of the month, when sufficient rice is available. The whole countryside contributes its share of sheep, fowls, fish, palm-oil, and salt; and the cooking utensils required are carried secretly out of the town during the night before the ceremony to a spot on the upper part of the river. This contains some large stones and tall trees which are the abode of the spirit, and is the place where the cooking must be done.

No one is allowed to cross the river before daybreak lest the spirit refuse the offering. In the morning a procession moves out to the spot, carrying the food. Women are not permitted to accompany it and the cooking, which is normally the duty of women, is done on this occasion by men. They prepare two separate portions, one for the spirit and one for the company. Particular care is taken not to cut the throat of the fowl intended for the spirit's pot. This fowl is cooked together with the hearts and livers of all the sheep offered. The soothsayer acts as 'master of ceremonies' and before 'feeding the stones' he calls out three times. He then calls a fourth time, '*ngiye wai*', meaning 'big hill'. In response comes a call from the bush, usually like that of a cock. It is uttered by a man whom the soothsayer has hidden there the night before. The answer is taken, however, as a sign that the spirit is present, and the soothsayer continues with the offerings. To test if they are acceptable or not, a white kola nut is split and the two halves are thrown into the air. If the inner portions show uppermost on landing, the verdict is favourable and the people return joyfully to the town. Failing this, an inquiry is made to find out if any rules of the ceremony have been broken, a further sacrifice has to be made, and fresh auguries taken. Some days later, when the level of the water in the river has dropped, it is taken as a sign that the spirit has been successfully appeased.

Dealings with 'nature-spirits' of this kind are collective affairs in which everyone takes his full share of responsibility. With the more widely known *dyinyinga* or genii, on the other hand, the relationship is of a more individual kind, is more arbitrary, and even fortuitous. It also tends to depend upon the performance of rites which are wholly magical in character. A few examples will clarify these points.

The genii are usually encountered in lonely places, such as the side of a mountain or in the heart of the forest. Sometimes they appear to a person when he is sleeping. They often have the form of human beings and are white-skinned.[1] There is, for instance, the *Tingoi* who appears as a beautiful siren-like woman with a soft white skin. She lives in the deep water of a river and is seen sometimes perched on the brow of a rock dressing her hair with a shining golden comb. Usually she is good-willed, and she rewards

---

[1] More than one informant has suggested to me that this attribute of white skin-colour derives from the Portuguese, who were the first European people with whom the Mende had contact. It might be conjectured that such a skin-colour enhanced the magical character of the genie through being so unusual.

handsomely anyone who approaches her in the right way. But your move must be made at the right moment. You should steal upon her from behind and snatch away the comb. She will come to you entreating its return with every possible form of flattery; but to let her have it back means poverty for the rest of your life, if not death. You must flatly reject every new request and must burn the comb and place the ashes on the cooking-stones in your house. Every time the *Tingoi* visits you, you should double your conditions and find some fresh excuse for denying her.

The *Ndogbɔjusui* is the most widely known genie. He lives on the top of a mountain by day and wanders about the forest at night. To lonely travellers who have strayed from their path he appears as a man with a white skin and a long white beard. The *Ndogbɔjusui* tricks them into following him still deeper into the forest after asking them certain questions. These questions are aimed at the actual thoughts in a person's mind, but the latter must never admit what he is thinking or give a direct reply. Instead, he should always answer the *Ndogbɔjusui's* inquiries in contrary and roundabout ways. For example, if the *Ndogbɔjusui* asks 'Whence do you come?' you should reply, 'From the moon'; if he asks 'What do you want to eat?' you say, 'Stones'; 'What do you use to carry water?' you reply, 'A fishing net'. Then the *Ndogbɔjusui* takes a net and fills it with water; when the water runs away, he leaves you alone. If your answers outmatch him in subtlety, the *Ndogbɔjusui* is generous with his gifts.

The genii are specifically recognizable in anthropomorphic terms and possess, apparently, well-marked human tastes, emotions, and passions. Like human beings they are susceptible to approach and responsive to flattery, but their favour is not won in the same ordered way as is that of the ancestral spirits, and it is more fickle. The obtaining of it depends mainly on the personality of the individual encountering them rather than on precise rules of conduct. In any case, though contact and intercourse with them may be productive of great good fortune, it is also fraught with a certain amount of risk. The person who deals with them must act boldly. Either he obtains power over the genie, or the genie takes control of him. In the latter case, he may be obliged to do the genie's work; or, to retain its favour, may have to sacrifice something to which he is very much attached, such as his own firstborn son.[1] Genii appear to some persons and not to others and, as already mentioned, quite often they make their appearance at night-time when a person is sleeping. Their relationships with human beings sometimes even include sexual intercourse.

As Hofstra points out, the relations between human beings and genii bear a somewhat incidental character, at least when compared to the relations of the Mende to their ancestral spirits.[2] Only sporadic contact is

---

[1] Hofstra describes an interesting case of a Mende boy who killed his father at the instigation, the boy claimed, of two genii. According to the boy's account, the genii appeared before him with swords in their hands and threatened to kill him if he did not carry out their command. Cf. Hofstra, 'The Belief among the Mende in Non-ancestral Spirits', *Int. Arch. f. Eth.*, Band xl, Heft 5–6, Leiden, 1942.　　　[2] Ibid., p. 176.

made with the genii. Nevertheless, the elements of artifice, of boldness, and of sudden good or ill fortune involved in human experience of them are all significant of valued patterns of Mende life. The Mende approve open-handed generosity, which they frequently combine with extreme secrecy over private affairs. They also respect feats of hardihood and nonchalance in the face of difficulty or danger, but the conduct they particularly admire is strongly tinged with bravado, and boastfulness is generally condoned. Even an adventurer will be courted and flattered so long as his success lasts, but once unfortunate he is likely to be reviled or forgotten, whatever past service he has rendered. It is also a special point of honour that a Mende man should get the better of his opponent, preferably without revealing his anxiety to do so. Likewise, Mende women are expected to drive a hard bargain, whether in trading or in relations with their husbands or lovers.

This suggests that the Mende attitude towards the genii has an allegorical character. Broadly speaking, relationships with this category of spirit are on an individual rather than a group basis. Unlike relations with the ancestors, a person deals with the genii on his own initiative and responsibility; the matter is of no concern to the group. A farmer, perhaps, is out working in the bush and finds some special object, such as a red stone, on his way. This may be a sign that some genie wishes to get into touch with him and that if he takes it home the genie may appear to him and reveal some special knowledge. But he also knows that the genii often expect something very precious in return for their favours and that if he decides to deal with them it will be at his own personal risk. In other words, the methods of regarding and treating these spirits are an expression of some of the values which motivate and guide the Mende in their personal relations with each other.

The Non-ancestral Cults and Use of 'Medicine'

The non-ancestral cults, or so-called secret societies, involve a somewhat different notion of, and approach to, supernatural power. In this case, spiritual beings are actually impersonated by means of carved wooden masks, raffia capes, and other accoutrements, which are worn by the senior and hereditary officials of the groups concerned. These 'spirits' leave their secret enclosure only on special occasions, and there is the strictest prohibition on non-members seeing or coming into any kind of contact with the more sacred of them. Thus the *Gbeni*, the principal spirit of the *Poro*, 'comes out' only to mark some important or crucial event in the common life. It may be at the opening of the annual *Poro* 'school' for fresh initiates, or at the coronation or death of a paramount chief or other high political figure. During the *Gbeni's* appearance all women and children must be kept out of sight and it is 'dangerous' even for initiates of the society itself to cross the *Gbeni's* path. Similar prohibitions are attached to the sacred spirit of the *Humui*.

These 'spirits' personalize supernatural power, but they are not in themselves the apparent object of cult activity. Their role, in the main, is to impress initiates and to create the necessary condition of awe among the general public. The cult members and devotees enter into relationship with the supernatural world in other ways. The *Poro*, for example, 'works' mainly through the spirits of its deceased members in a manner analogous to the ancestral cult proper, and the immediate object of the *Njayei* and *Humui* seems to lie rather in the cultivation of powers held to inhere in certain inanimate things, such as 'medicines'. To a lesser extent there is identification with certain animals; for example, the *Njayei* society has a sacred boa-constrictor whose flesh is taboo to all members, and this animal is given the same kind of ceremonial burial as a senior member of the association. But more generally interest centres in 'medicine', and this applies particularly to the *Humui* and *Njayei* societies and also in a lesser degree to the *Sande*. Each of these societies has its special medicines, which are lodged in the houses of the respective cult leaders. These medicines are the principal source of cult authority and influence and the means whereby the ritual and other functions of the cults concerned are performed. It is necessary, therefore, to explain in some detail the part of 'medicine' in Mende belief.

The general Mende term for 'medicine' is *hale* and, in a rather limited meaning of the concept, a medicine is simply any physical object or instrument which is capable of magical use. Such objects range in physical form from old razor blades and faded ribbons to bundles of rags, feathers, and cowrie shells. Subjectively, however, *hale* is something more than the mere object itself. It represents a special kind of supernatural power or quality which becomes attached to the object through the influence of *Ngewɔ* because a connexion with *Ngewɔ* is implicit in the notion of *hale*. Thus, in the frequent use made of medicines for all kinds of social purposes, the name of *Ngewɔ* is invoked so that the medicine itself may be effective. This is apparent in the use of medicines to check the veracity of witnesses in court, to settle disputes, to protect property from thieves, to detect criminals, &c. Taking the last case as an instance, the procedure is somewhat as follows. A person whose goods have been stolen takes out his medicine and makes a tour of the village, calling out publicly that if the wrongdoer does not confess his misdeed he will 'submit the matter to God'. But if there is no answer to this apparently charitable action, the aggrieved person proceeds to the cross-roads and invokes his medicine, calling upon it to seek out the thief and take revenge on him, the implication being that the medicine itself will serve as the instrument of justice. A curse is placed in this way upon the malefactor, which can be removed by an equally direct process. All that is required is that the person employing the medicine shall reverse his original injunction. He commands that the various penalties and misfortunes with which the culprit has been threatened shall not take effect.

This example suggests that medicine is a means of maintaining a sense of moral equilibrium within the community. It provides a way whereby an aggrieved party can feel that the person who injured him is not going unpunished even though it is impossible to bring the malefactor personally to book. It would be misleading, however, to assume from this or from the association of *hale* with *Ngewɔ* that all medicines are necessarily 'good' in the sense that they serve socially approved ends.[1] On the contrary, there are a number of powerful medicines in Mende society which are put to definitely anti-social purposes. These include the *ndilei* which enables its owner to assume the personality and role of a vampire feeding on human blood, and the *bɔfima* which is compounded out of the flesh and other parts of a human being. The use of such 'bad' medicines is a serious crime, and if discovered the medicine is usually confiscated. But what is particularly significant in this respect is the fact that such 'bad' medicines can also be put to a 'social' purpose. Thus, various chiefdom medicines which are employed for the purpose of swearing witnesses in court frequently consist of such confiscated material, which is kept in a special box. The fact that privately owned and otherwise very harmful medicines can be 'municipalized' in this way for the public good suggests that there is also a quite impersonal or 'neutral' quality about *hale*. Of course, the Mende themselves usually distinguish clearly, if pressed, between 'good medicine' and 'bad medicine'; but from the point of view of the observer *hale* is 'good' or 'bad' simply according to the way it is used and the person who uses it. A further point which bears on this is the fact that the various properties of *hale* are denoted specifically in terms of the way and the purpose for which it is used. Thus, *mumu bao hale* is a medicine 'that can care', i.e. one intended for protective purposes; *kpoi hale* is a drinking medicine, i.e. for prophylactic purposes; *sondu wa hale*, a medicine for swearing.[2]

Theoretically, any grown person in Mende society is capable of using medicine,[3] but the conditions require people who are specialists in its production and employment because *hale* is potentially dangerous as well as potentially helpful. Mishandling of it may bring down harm on its manipulator and those associated with him. The more powerful medicines might be compared to electric batteries of high voltage: they are charged with energy. Hence, it is very risky for an inept or unauthorized person to tamper with them, even to go anywhere near them. For example, such a person intruding into the corner of the house where the leader of the women's society keeps

---

[1] There is also the problem of witchcraft to be accounted for. The Mende believe that there are certain persons who are 'hosts' to 'witch-spirits'. These 'witch-spirits' travel about independently of their human 'hosts' and can cause sickness and disease and kill a child by 'eating' the child's own spirit. If the Mende theory of creation is consistent, these 'witch-spirits' presumably owe their existence to *Ngewɔ* in the same sense as everything else 'that *Ngewɔ* made'. I do not imagine, however, that the Mende themselves would formulate the matter in this way, and it seems to pose a proposition analogous to the Christian problem of evil.

[2] A medicine used specifically for certain types of purification is *sawei*; the word is linguistically different from *hale* but involves psychologically the same concept.

[3] The common use of *hale* is rationalized by the popular saying that since 'God' is so far away, it is up to everyone to adopt what means he can to help himself.

the special *Sande* medicine would in all likelihood incur a severely swollen stomach. It is also believed that a medicine becomes very closely connected with, even assimilated to, the personality of the owner. Thus, the *ndilei* medicine becomes an integral part of the person using it. He becomes virtually the slave of the *ndilei* in return for the vampire-like work it does for him, and is slavishly subject to its will.

In one sense the operation of *hale* is quite automatic, from the point of view of the person using it as well as from that of anyone falling foul of it. A protective medicine left hanging over your door 'stabs' the witch the moment he enters it; a person trespassing on bush declared out of bounds by a *Poro* sign is immediately afflicted with some injury or pain. In other cases the action is delayed, but is equally mechanical. Yet at the same time it is believed that knowledge and skill are helpful both to obtain the best results from medicine and to avoid its consequences. A powerful medicine has to be tended and 'nurtured' as carefully as a child, and part of the technique in the case of specific medicines consists in 'talking' to them in a certain way every day. The more powerful the medicine, the more harm it is liable to cause, but it is also capable of greater benefits to all concerned; hence the need of properly qualified and responsible people to look after it.

The Secret Societies as Controllers of Morals

This brings us back to the secret societies, which, as already mentioned, are the owners of the most powerful medicine in Mende society. These are the people who, by heredity, training, and other special circumstances and qualifications are best suited to the task. These societies, and more particularly their senior members, are the experts in such matters and hence the official specialists and practitioners of medicine in Mende society.[1] In this connexion therefore, it needs to be emphasized that these secret societies work essentially in the interests of the community. The ends they seek and the 'medical' and other activities undertaken under their aegis have social approval, irrespective of whether their activities are carried on for some communal purpose or are performed for the benefit of individual members of the public. In general, as mentioned earlier, their task is to propagate

---

[1] I am omitting reference, for the sake of brevity and simplicity, to other categories of person 'legitimately' concerned in one way or another with the interpretation or use of supernatural power. These include soothsayers, diviners, medicine men, witch-doctors, and owners of private medicines. The activities of these persons are quite 'unofficial' compared with the activities of the secret societies. By this I mean that the medicine man, witch-doctor, and others like them, work mainly as private individuals, though they may sometimes be employed for a purpose which has communal implications, such as the preparation of a farming medicine. On the whole, however, they are engaged for, and serve, individual and personal rather than public ends. Their knowledge is their own personal property and they can pass it on to whom they will and at whatever price they can obtain for it. Moreover, as private practitioners, they are under less obligation to consider the social results of their work, which means that the kind of engagements they fulfil are not necessarily altruistic. A medicine man, for example, may undertake anything from a love potion to a cure for a headache, or from a talisman to secure successful candidature in a contest for the chieftaincy to a 'swear' which will bring about the downfall of his client's rival.

values socially important to the community. The duty of the *Sande*
(women's society), for example, is to further womanly character and virtue
as the Mende construe such things. But the aims are practical as well as
ideal and include the cure of sickness and disease, in some cases by physical
as well as ritual methods.

What these considerations imply, in other words, is that the role of the
secret societies is somewhat analogous to that of a national institution performing various kinds of public function. The attitude taken towards re-
munerating society officials for their services substantiates this. In theory,
payment is made to the society itself for any work done by its members, the
implication being that the latter's skill is something they owe to the cult. It
is a form of cult property which can be used or imparted to an outsider only
in terms of the society and under its auspices.

Naturally, this position of the secret societies and their relation to *hale*
has results which, sociologically, are far-reaching. By their possession of
this particular aspect of supernatural power and their ability to manipulate
it, the secret societies are in a position to monopolize a large part of the cultural life. Like the medieval church in Europe, they are able to lay down
rules of conduct and prescribe certain forms of behaviour. Any such regulations made are sanctioned by the belief that to break them will involve
serious consequences not only to the individual concerned but to other
persons connected with him. It is believed that he may incur some illness
or disease, or suffer some misfortune or accident. A woman may become
barren. The rules laid down mostly take the form of prohibitions and affect
certain kinds of actions and social relationships as well as physical objects.
For example, not only is much of the paraphernalia of the cults, including
the apparatus used in their secret ceremonies, their special meeting-places,
&c., strictly taboo to non-members, but the medicines of secret societies
operate as sanctions to enforce certain prohibitions; for example, sexual
intercourse is forbidden in certain places, a man may not marry any close
relative of his wife while the latter is still living, a man may not sit on his
sister's bed, &c.

Quite a large number of these prohibitions have the effect of a moral
code whose infraction produces psychological as well as physical consequences. A person may break it wittingly or unwittingly, but in either case
the only people who can help him are the controllers of the particular cult
concerned. This means that, like the medieval church, the secret societies
are also the only agency capable of remitting certain 'sins'. Remission involves a series of rites which usually include initiation of the 'guilty' party
into the cult concerned. On the other hand, the role of these cults in this
respect is to some extent departmental and even a matter of specialization.
That is to say, particular sections of the common life and their control tend
to fall within the provinces of specific societies. Thus, as mentioned earlier
(pp. 111, 112), the *Humui* has charge of sexual behaviour and relations; the
Poro and the *Sande*, respectively, decide when a boy or a girl is old enough

for sexual experience and are responsible for inculcating and safeguarding the kind of public conduct considered appropriate by and towards men and women. In addition, the *Poro* largely controls questions of political succession, and helps to regulate the harvesting of certain crops; the *Sande* has charge of all matters concerning childbirth.

These considerations, including the ritual aspect of the matter, can be illustrated most conveniently by the *Humui* society. The rules of the *Humui* constitute, to all intents and purposes, the rules of marriage and mating. Sexual relationships in Mende society are governed primarily by these rather than by the recognition of consanguinity, which enters into the matter almost as a secondary consideration. Breach of certain of these laws is known as *simongama* and necessitates the fining and washing of the offending parties.

The nearest European equivalent of *simongama* is incest, and it goes without saying that *simongama* is a particularly serious offence. In general terms, it is *simongama* for a man to have sexual relations with any close relatives on the patrilineal side; with any descendants of his own mother, irrespective of the paternity of such descendants; and with any close relatives of his existing wives. By special dispensation of the *Humui* he may, in some cases, have relations with and marry his wife's sister after his wife has died. Generally, marriage with father's brother's daughter is regarded as reprehensible and no children are expected to result from the union.[1]

In addition to restricting marriage between certain categories of persons, the rules of the *Humui* prohibit specific kinds of sexual behaviour for the community as a whole. It is forbidden to have sexual intercourse with a girl under the age of puberty,[2] or with any person, irrespective of age and social and biological relationship, in the bush at any time during the day or night. It is also forbidden to have intercourse with any woman who is nursing a child, or with any woman who is pregnant. Other sexual offences are for a

---

[1] Nevertheless, this kind of marriage is practised fairly often by chiefly houses in order to maintain property and position.

Specifically, *Humui* regulations prohibit relations on the part of the man with the following categories of person, viz:
- (*a*) His own mother, or maternal grandmother.
- (*b*) His own daughter, or granddaughter.
- (*c*) His own sister, or half-sister.
- (*d*) His paternal and maternal aunts.
- (*e*) The daughter of his brother and sister, and the daughters of his brother's and sister's children.
- (*f*) His wife's sister, and any immediate descendants of his wife's sister.
- (*g*) The descendants of his wife's brother while that wife is still alive.
- (*h*) The daughter of his wife's father's brother.
- (*i*) The sister, or any close relative, of any woman with whom he has had relations at any time, so long as that woman is still alive.
- (*j*) Any woman, irrespective of relationship, with whom his brother or half-brother has had relations.
- (*k*) Any woman, irrespective of his relationship to her, who has suckled him.

[2] As implied above, there is, however, one important qualification in this respect. To have intercourse with an uninitiated girl, i.e. one who has not passed through *Sande*, is an offence against that society and should be expiated through its medium.

brother to sit on his sister's bed, or a sister on her brother's bed. A man may not shake hands with his mother-in-law or with the mother of any woman with whom he has had sexual relations. A wife may not visit her parents on the same night after intercourse.[1]

The *Humui* also has rules of sexual hygiene. For example, a woman is forbidden to speak to, or to remain in the presence of, any of her relatives or any members of the family of the man with whom she had intercourse, until she has washed in the morning. If she comes into physical contact with any of her own or his female relatives the offence is more serious and is treated as *simongama*. Apparently the implication is that the sexual act itself is extended by her action to proscribed relatives and affines of the man. If a woman has had sexual intercourse during the night she must wash before she cooks any food the next day.[2]

Breaches of these rules and regulations, whether deliberate or not, are regarded, in the case of *simongama*, as very injurious to the relatives of the persons concerned, as well as offending the *Humui* society itself. It is believed that all concerned are in danger of sickness or disaster. The guilty party himself must recompense the woman's family as well as the *Humui*, and, as mentioned above, the offence has also to be expiated in a ritual way. *Simongama* is regarded as a particularly atrocious and disgraceful offence when a person of note, such as a paramount chief, is involved, and if such an occasion arises the native authorities deal with it as secretly as possible. It may involve a tribunal of neighbouring chiefs to adjudicate in the matter.

As already mentioned, sometimes an individual forgets about a *Humui* rule or breaks it unknowingly. Then suddenly he becomes ill or something disastrous happens to a member of his family. The immediate step in that case is to consult a soothsayer. The soothsayer has a bag of stones, each of which represents one of the various misfortunes to which humanity is heir. He spreads these stones out on a mat on the ground and, while manipulating them, questions his client closely. He asks him if he remembers having done such and such an act or broken such and such a rule. He tries to get his 'patient' to confess some great or small misdemeanour which might be interpreted as a concrete offence against known society rules and regulations. If the 'patient' denies any such offence, he is told that he is lying or has forgotten the matter. Finally, the soothsayer names the particular society against which his patient has transgressed and tells him that the only way to right things is to offer the members a full confession.

The person reports there, and the final stage is for him to be ritually

---

[1] Denise Paulme describes a similar set of prohibitions among the nearby Kissi of French Guinea. The Kissi concept of *ma* is apparently analogous to, if not identical with, *simongama*. Cf. 'Fautes sexuelles dans une société africaine', *Journal de Psychologie normale et pathologique*, Oct–Dec. 1950, pp. 507–24.

[2] Another rule of *Humui*, which has no obvious connexion with sex, is that cold ashes in the hearth should be swept away before preparing food, and that stale food or drink should never be used. The latter rule is going out of use with the adoption of European dietary customs. (See also Paulme, op. cit.)

'washed' or to be made a member of the society and formally initiated. It depends upon the nature of his offence and the rules of the society. Initiation usually follows if he has trespassed on society bush or come into physical contact with any of the secret paraphernalia. Through such contact the person concerned is considered to have acquired a measure of the society's own special knowledge and power. This, perhaps, explains the reason for initiation. It means that he is placed under oaths and obligations which effectively prevent any further leakage of the society's special secrets. It also obviates the possibility of his making independent use of society knowledge and setting himself up among the public as an unauthorized practitioner. Once initiated, on the other hand, the fame of any medical work he does redounds to the credit of the society as a whole rather than to him as an individual.

Assuming that one of the sexual laws of the *Humui* has been broken, the whole family of the 'sinner' may be considered guilty. The head of the society, who is an old woman, is given a fowl, a quantity of rice, a mat, some native thread, and, nowadays, a shilling.[1] The family are told to seat themselves on the mat in a circle, and the *Humui* woman winds the thread round the neck, feet, and hands of each of them so that all are tied by the same thread. They then extend their hands, palms upwards. The *Humui* woman, who is inside the circle, places some of the rice on their palms and on the tops of their heads. She has a bowl containing a mixture of water and leaves which is the special *Humui* medicine. Into this she dips the fowl and with it purges the family. This is done three times. Then she takes the fowl to each person in turn, having prayed that they will all be released from their sins. If the fowl pecks at the rice on the hand and on the head then the person concerned has nothing to confess, but if the fowl jibs at any one of the piles of rice, he must make further confession. When the fowl has pecked at all to the satisfaction of the *Humui* woman, she scatters the leaf-medicine over the whole group, using the fowl as a sprinkler. She then declares the family to be free. They eagerly tear away the thread binding them, jump up from the mat, and go down to the river to bathe.

Space does not permit description of the rites of other cults which, in many cases, also involve forms of purification. For example, if a pregnant woman miscarries, the women of the town go out into the bush under the direction of a senior official of the *Sande* society and collect herbs.[2] Returning, they sprinkle all the houses in the town with this lustral medicine. This must be done before further procreation can proceed with success. Insanity and other forms of mental complaint are put down to breaches of the *Njayei* society. They result from the sufferer having trespassed on *Njayei* bush or seen the dead body of an important member of the society before it was ritually purified.

[1] Compare the role of the *sarino* among the Kissi. Among them this person is sometimes a man, sometimes a woman. Cf. Paulme, op. cit., p. 510.
[2] Among the Kissi such matters are dealt with by the *sarino* (ibid.).

It must suffice, therefore, to conclude this article with a brief examination of the main factors dealt with and to say something about the present trend of Mende belief and values in this respect. It may be noted that certain rites of both ancestral and non-ancestral cults specially emphasize the solidarity of the kin group. The nephew who wrongs his uncle, or the person who breaks a sexual rule, is not left alone in his guilt. His sin affects everyone closely connected with him, including his brothers and sisters, even his whole family. Moreover, not only do the latter share the individual's 'guilt', but the 'sinner' himself can only be absolved if his relatives also are pronounced free. Apparently they are all involved. This suggests two things. First, not only is the group as a whole expected to take responsibility for certain acts, but extra value of a negative kind is attached to these acts.

A further conclusion of a psychological kind might be drawn, but it is more arbitrary. It is this: that in both ancestral and non-ancestral cults, 'wrong' behaviour is regarded as a breaking of some specific rule of conduct, not as the flouting of some divine or absolute law of the universe. True, the ire of the ancestral spirits is feared and their displeasure is cause for anxiety, but there is always a means of salvaging things. It may mean some inconvenience or personal sacrifice, but the ancestors can be flattered, propitiated, and soothed out of their anger. Similarly, the penalty for offending one of the non-ancestral cults is severe, but there are also the appropriate remedies which can be obtained through the secret societies themselves. All this might imply that the effect upon personality in terms of feelings of guilt and sin is less significant than in communities which have assimilated the Christian notion of personal responsibility for moral action. In other words, from the point of view of individual psychology the problem of personal responsibility is largely 'externalized' rather than 'internalized', as it is among those who have been imbued with the Christian doctrine. This is not to suggest that the Mende fail to experience guilt and sin as we understand the terms. There is little doubt that they do. What I am implying, however, is that guilt and sin can be expiated more readily, and perhaps more effectively, among them than among those members of European society whose evaluation of moral conduct is based upon absolute standards of 'right' and 'wrong'.

The Changing Values of Mende Society

It is obvious to the observer that the system of Mende values thus briefly outlined is undergoing rapid change. The factors responsible are numerous, but among the more important must be included the extended use of Western currency and opportunities to gain possession of it. In former times, the younger men as well as most of the women were almost entirely under the control of senior members of the family. They had to rely on their elders not only for economic support, but for most of the available ways of attaining extra social status and other forms of social benefit.

Nowadays, a young man need not wait until his father and relatives are ready to provide bridewealth on his behalf. He can earn the money by taking a labouring job with the Government, by moving to the mines, even by working on his father's own farm. A woman can set up as a trader, can travel on the railway from one market town to another, and can make herself relatively independent of her husband for economic purposes. During the recent war the Government adopted the practice of paying monthly allotments to the wives of soldiers serving overseas. Sometimes, individual wives were able to double the amount allowed them by making 'friendship' with another soldier and sending along a sister, or some other woman, to pose as his wife at the District Commissioner's Office. Some women took the opportunity, with the connivance of soldiers, to repay bridewealth, and followed their new 'husbands' when they were removed for training to other parts of the country.

Another factor is the slow but gradual spread of education which, in casting doubt on the older ideas and beliefs, also affects mostly the younger generation. There is also the teaching of the Christian Missions and, more important, the social influence of the Christian-taught Creole community[1] in spreading part European, part Creole notions of respectability and canons of 'civilized' behaviour which depreciate the indigenous way of life. This group attaches particular importance not only to monogamy but to wearing European clothes, following Western eating and dietary habits, and adopting English names.

It is easier to assess the effect of all these various processes on overt behaviour than on the actual content of indigenous belief. There is little doubt, however, that the authority of the older generation, including that of heads of families, is much less than it was. This is partly because the size of the individual household, particularly in the more urbanized areas, is much smaller, partly because the women as well as the younger men are economically more independent. The fact that women have become accustomed not only to the use of money but to regular money payments affects their attitude to marriage. They say, 'We can't marry a farmer who works to earn only by the year!' and they prefer someone who, like a clerk, is paid by the month or by the week. In consequence many of the younger men are driven, if not to leave the farms, at any rate to supplement their earnings by doing part-time work in the nearest town. Another result of the greater freedom of the younger generation and their movement about the country is the growing popularity of unsanctioned forms of 'marriage' which lack the formal consent of the parents of both parties demanded by indigenous law.

All this social disruption and mobility obviously militates against the ceremonial observance of kinship, but less strongly than might be expected.

[1] This Creole community is descended from the original settlers of Freetown and the Sierra Leone Colony. Its members have been engaged in a variety of professional, clerical, trading, and industrial occupations for something like a hundred years, with consequent effects on their social differentiation.

I gained the impression that family sentiment and loyalties are still quite firm among all sections of the community, including the newly literate one. One reason is that it is difficult for a literate person to realize his ambitions without family support. He needs their help financially to obtain further education, and both financially and morally if he has any political aspirations, such as a chieftainship. Another and more important reason which affects the much greater mass of non-literate people is the fact that the indigenous faith has already been largely taken over by Islam. Islam, as generally followed in Mendeland, includes the older rites and has even added fresh ones of its own. Funerals are a good example of this, because Moslems commemorate the seventh and the fortieth day after burial, as well as the fourth day as in the ancestral cult. They also celebrate a number of important feasts including, in particular, the ending of the fast of Ramadan. All these occasions call kinsfolk together and stress their obligations to exchange gifts and services. As mentioned earlier (p. 113), Islam as popularly practised by the Mende also seems to encourage the use of magic, and the *mori-man* is a well-known figure in nearly every town and village. He manufactures a large variety of charms and amulets by means of Arabic writing and prepares a special protective device, known as the *kpakpa*. This is popularly termed a 'sacrifice', but it consists simply of any odd scraps of available material and its use is entirely magical, not propitiatory.

But it is not only the 'islamicized' section of the Mende community which has abstracted elements of the older religion and put them to individual and magical purposes. Most of the newly converted Christians practise the ancestral cult only when political or other special circumstances demand it;[1] but many of them turn instead to magic. They rely quite often on special talismans. Others are regular clients of medicine men whose help they seek in love affairs and to further personal careers. A charm that is much in demand in the latter respect is the invisible but powerful Kono 'witch's cloak'. This 'garment' is supposed to give the person 'wearing' it an impressive and commanding personality, and so it is particularly valuable to anyone, such as a candidate for the chieftainship, desiring to take a prominent part in public affairs.

Modern conditions have also curtailed or modified the practices of the non-ancestral cults in certain ways. The *Gbeni* 'spirit' of the *Poro* no longer 'comes out' in the larger towns, because a substantial section of the population there, including literate and semi-literate native people as well as Colony Creoles, would disregard the customary taboos of such an occasion, thus giving cause for a public disturbance. Nowadays, new initiates rarely

---

[1] For example, one of the traditional duties of the Chief is to uphold the ancestral and other cults of his chiefdom, and most chiefs who are professing Christians also have an ancestral shrine in their compounds. The Chief is also the official patron of the *Poro* society.

A number of other individuals who are nominally Christians continue the ancestral practices at the same time, and on one occasion I was formally 'introduced' to the ancestral spirits by a person who combined the office of 'praying man' in the ancestral cult with a leading position in the local Mission church!

remain in the *Poro* bush for more than a few weeks, and in the case of schoolboys the time may be even shorter. But although initiation itself seems to have become largely a fee-paying rite, boys entering the bush are still forbidden to take anything European in the way of clothes and equipment with them. The *Sande*, on the other hand, is readier to adopt modern innovations. The girls re-emerge from the bush dressed in the most up-to-date Creole fashions, and the *Sande* custom of excising the clitoris in initiation has been largely replaced, it is claimed, by a small token incision. It is also significant that in certain parts of Mendeland the *Sande* leaders have been willing to allow young women trained in modern methods of mothercraft and hygiene to take part in the initiation procedure as a Government-sponsored welfare measure.[1]

Beliefs and practices in connexion with the genii appear to continue and to have a particularly firm hold upon numbers of the younger literate people. Some of the most graphic descriptions of *dyinyinga* that I received were from boys at a secondary school. Possibly this is explained by the strong element of magic in this cult rendering it specially suitable to the individual needs of people coping with a new and unpredictable culture.[2]

Conclusions

The net result of all these changes in custom and outlook is that an increasing number of people in Mende society no longer acknowledge the tribal and traditional sanctions to which they were formerly subject. The older values and forms of social prestige, which hinged largely on kinship and membership of institutions like the *Poro* and the *Sande*, are being gradually superseded by new ones. This means that although the moral core of Mende life is still largely intact, there is a growing tendency for an individual's position to be socially assessed with reference to the community as a whole rather than to the particular kin group from which he originates. More specifically, increasing value is placed on Western forms of social behaviour in matters ranging from religion to dress, and on the performance of occupations demanding Western forms of education and skill. A new set of normative rules is also evolving, but for the present the rules governing interpersonal relations are still largely derived from the older culture.

[1] The *Poro* elders have generally been very hostile to analogous forms of educational experimentation in their own 'school' on the grounds that the *Poro* function is to be regarded as symbolical rather than utilitarian. They have also strongly opposed the extension of the *Sande* experiment to areas up-country.

[2] According to Hofstra, however, the genii appear less frequently than they used to do, at least in the neighbourhood of towns. This is supposed to be due to the European custom of increasing the number of bridges. The noise which is caused by bridges, especially by those of the concrete type, compels the *dyinyinga* to retreat to quieter places, where they are able to continue their lives less disturbed (op. cit., p. 177).

THE SHILLUK OF THE UPPER NILE

By GODFREY LIENHARDT

THIS essay is based primarily on literary sources,[1] which contain un-usually full references to the religious and cosmological ideas of the Shilluk. In places, I have reinterpreted earlier writings on the Shilluk in the light of my own knowledge of the related Dinka, and of other Nilotic studies. The concepts of these Nilotic peoples are alike in many ways, and the Shilluk and Dinka have for long been considered as related, from the point of view of anthropological theory, by the presence among them both of different forms of the institution of 'divine kingship', studied by Frazer and Seligman.[2] Upon this institution much of their interpretation of the universe and of their own place in it depend.

Lack of definition and dogma in their religion and cosmology makes it possible for Nilotic peoples to accept many different versions of their mythology and history, and also permits some syncretism of belief. I do not consider here speculations about the possible influences of ancient Egypt, the Fung, Islam, or the early monophysite Christianity of the Sudan, on Shilluk belief.[3] It is, in fact, remarkable that contact with foreign peoples and ideas, over a long period, should have left so little mark on Shilluk thought. Some of the stories which Hofmayr[4] attributes to Christian in-fluence are widely known among other Nilotic peoples and elsewhere, in places farther removed from probable contact with Christianity. Lack of formal definition of beliefs and notions about the universe also makes the study of Shilluk cosmology necessarily a study based on inferences from myths, hymns, and other texts, collected piecemeal from informants, none of whom can speak with any final authority. It is clear that Shilluk cosmology is not present to the mind of any one Shilluk as a single, orthodox system, abstracted from the narrative flow and imaginative detail of myth. Even one man may tell slightly different versions of the same story,[5] for the telling is

---

[1] References throughout are to the Shilluk bibliography appended, the dates being the dates of the publications cited. Some of the sources contain many texts in the Shilluk language, and where these are translated into a language other than English, I have given an English version after examining the Shilluk text. I should like to thank all writers on the Shilluk, upon whose observations this summary and representation entirely depend. Their publications, however, are not all easily accessible, nor are they specifically concerned with the analysis of the Shilluk ideas here studied. This must be my excuse for writing about a people of great ethnological interest and importance, who have already been described in detail by writers who have known them well.

[2] J. G. Frazer, 1911. C. G. Seligman, 1911, C. G. and B. Z. Seligman, 1932.

[3] Discussion of Shilluk contacts with some of these will be found in W. Hofmayr, 1925, and D. Westermann, 1912. For general cultural and conceptual similarities between ancient Egypt and negro Africa, the reader may be referred to C. G. Seligman, 1934, and H. Frankfort, 1948, among others.

[4] 1925, pp. 195-6, the stories of a fall of man, and of a woman's bearing a god.

[5] D. S. Oyler, 1918 (i).

partly a creative process, and there is no writing to establish a preferred and approved text. Shilluk experience and knowledge of their world, which we here try to understand by analysis and systematization, is by them synthesized in an imaginative whole, at the centre of which are their early leader and hero, Nyikang, and the divine being which they call *juok*. Though *juok* is thought ultimately to dispose what happens in the universe, Nyikang, who created the Shilluk kingdom, is the subject of most mythology. There is nowhere any indication that the Shilluk have formulated elaborate ideas of the general order of all creation. Their notion of cosmogenesis is of the creation of that order which, as they see it, was built up by Nyikang, and has been maintained by his successors, the Shilluk kings. Before considering the wider significance of Nyikang and *juok*, it is convenient to give a brief account of the land of the Shilluk, the life they lead in it, and the general outlines of their social organization. With these in mind, it is possible to analyse their cosmological ideas in the broad outline to which an essay of this length is necessarily restricted.

Environment and History

The Shilluk live along the west bank of the Nile in the south of the Anglo-Egyptian Sudan, where their hamlets are built in close succession, following the line of the river from around Kaka to Lake No. They are about 110,000 people,[1] densely settled on a narrow strip of savannah country nearly 200 miles long, and four to five walking-hours in width. The soil is black and fertile near the river and its inlets, becoming sandier towards the neighbouring Arab country in the north and the Arab and Nuba country of Kordofan to the west. On the east bank of the Nile are the related Dinka, the Shilluks' neighbours to the east and south, and there are Shilluk settlements, bounded by Dinka and Nuer, on the east bank and on the lower reaches of the Sobat. Though their values are predominantly those of a cattle-herding people, the Shilluk lead a less pastoral, transhumant life than the Nuer or Dinka.[2] Their cattle are estimated at 25,000, and they keep sheep and goats. Since their settlements are strung along the bank of the Nile, they can find grass for their herds near home in the dry season, from January to April, and cultivation seems to receive more time and attention among them than among less sedentary Nilotes. From June to September the rains fall, and much of the country becomes flooded. The early rains are the time for sowing the staple crop of millet, of which many varieties are grown, along with maize, sesame, and various beans and pumpkins. These depend upon the rains, and are harvested between September and November. Tobacco, also called 'the grass of the ancestors', depends on hand-watering from the river, near which it is grown in the dry season.

[1] The authorities vary considerably in their estimates of the human and cattle population. The figures given here are quoted from those given by Mr. John Donald, of the Sudan Political Service, and published by Professor Evans-Pritchard, 1948.

[2] P. P. Howell and W. P. G. Thomson, 1946.

Linguistically, the Shilluk belong to the Luo-speaking people, amongst whom are also the Anuak of the Baro and Pibor rivers between the Anglo-Egyptian Sudan and Ethiopia, the Lango and Acholi of Uganda, the Alur of Uganda and the Belgian Congo, and many scattered groups in the Bahr-el-Ghazal Province of the Sudan, of whom the Luo (Jur) are the most important. Some of these claim some slight contact, in comparatively recent times, with the Shilluk kingdom. Amongst the Luo-speakers the Shilluk are unique in their possession of a single royal dynasty, in relation to which all are members of one Shilluk kingdom, with well-defined territorial and social limits. By this also they are chiefly set apart from the other Nilotic negroes, the Nuer and Dinka, with whom they otherwise have much in common in physique, character, and culture. Perhaps more than the other Nilotes, the Shilluk have for long been in intermittently hostile contact with foreign enemies and foreign governments. The traveller Schwein-furth, who visited them in 1869, says that at that time little or nothing remained of the original condition of the Shilluk, who of all Nilotic negroes 'used to uphold the most perfectly regulated government', which, he says, can only be properly appreciated by reference to the registers of the expedition of Mohammed Ali earlier in the century.[1] We cannot now know what the Shilluk were really like at that time, and it is certain that some of their indigenous custom, particularly that concerning the election and disposal of the Shilluk king, has been interfered with to such an extent that the Shilluk themselves are uncertain about some details of the old belief and practice. Nevertheless, until the present day the Shilluk have retained a consciousness of their national identity and integrity, and have been slow to modify their ideas to accord with those of the various strangers in their land. The main features of their social structure remain, and under the present government, versions of their ceremonies for the funeral and installation of the king have been carefully observed and described.[2] Enough of the traditional practice and belief remains, and has been recorded, to make unnecessary too much speculative reconstruction of the Shilluk past; unfortunately the absence of historical records makes it impossible to study the development of the kingship, which might explain some apparent anomalies in accounts of the present situation.

Social Organization

The Shilluk are divided, on the basis of descent traced in the male line, into about 100 different descent groups, which have been called both clans and lineages. They are exogamous, and some of them, at least, are totemically affiliated with natural or artificial species of various kinds. Members of these descent groups may be found living in any part of Shilluk country, and the main groups are themselves dispersed in smaller groups throughout Shilluk country. The largest descent groups are without any corporate

[1] G. Schweinfurth, 1873, p. 93.
[2] P. Munro, 1918, and Howell and Thomson, 1946.

existence. The smallest unit of Shilluk social structure is the family (*gol*) living in a homestead of one or two huts. From one to fifty or more such homesteads built together form a hamlet, the members of which keep their cattle together, and are gathered round a headman; a group of hamlets forms a settlement, of which there are about a hundred in Shilluk-land. The settlement is composed of branches of different descent groups, one of which is dominant within the settlement and forms a nucleus around which the others form themselves into a distinct community. This dominant descent group or lineage provides the leader or chief of the settlement. Settlements are politically opposed to each other, though there have been in the past loose confederations of settlements, which have been used, and sharpened in outline, for administrative purposes. The whole of Shilluk land is divided into two provinces, Ger in the north and Luak in the south. All the Shilluk recognize a common head of their whole land, the *reth*, who is here called the king; the king always comes from the royal clan, the *kwareth*, founded by the first Shilluk king, Nyikang; it is the largest clan in Shilluk land, and may have representatives in any settlement. There is now a royal capital at Fashoda. In Shilluk tradition the earliest Shilluk kings had no fixed capital, but reigned from their natal homes. Now, although the capital at Fashoda has been long established, the wives of the king are sent away from Fashoda to various parts of Shilluk land to bear their children, and the children of the king (*nyireth*) are brought up away from the capital. Only those princes whose fathers have been installed as kings of the Shilluk can themselves claim to be installed and, in theory at least, princes who are thus eligible may at any time advance their claims by killing the reigning king. Besides the royal clan, and the lineages of 'commoner' clans, known collectively as the *colo*, there is a distinct clan called *ororo*, originally a branch of the royal house, but said to have been disinherited and cut off by an early Shilluk king. Members of this clan have special duties to perform in connexion with the king, but do not have royal status. In addition, there are the *bang reth*, servants of the king, composed of wives of previous kings, descendants of personal attendants of the king, people possessed by the spirit of Nyikang or of some other king, and others who in one way or another have become retainers dependent on the royal house. From these come the guardians and priests of the shrines of Nyikang, of which there are several in various parts of Shilluk country, and the shrines and graves of other Shilluk kings. Offerings are made at these graves and shrines as part of the religious cult of Nyikang and the royal house, which is the main cult of the Shilluk, though offerings are made to their own ancestors also by the heads of the commoner lineages. Their totemic observances seem to amount to little more than not eating the totemic species, and both totemism and the cult of ancestors of commoner descent groups are said to figure less largely in Shilluk religion than the cult of Nyikang and the kings. Shilluk totemism may in fact be of Dinka origin. Besides the priests of the Nyikang cult, and operating apart from them, there are diviners of various sorts, seers and holy men, called *ajuogo*. Such people may also be priests of the Nyikang cult, but in themselves they do not form part of any organized religious system embracing the whole kingdom. There is said to be no cult of the divine being *juok*, who is approached through Nyikang and the Shilluk kings.[1]

Myths of Origin and Traditional History

In considering the Shilluk apprehension of order in their universe, we may first suggest how they classify themselves and other people with whom they have been in contact. The name 'Shilluk,' used by most authorities, seems to be an Arab form of their own name for themselves, *Col* or *Ocolo*, or 'the children of *Col*'. They call their country 'the land of *Col*',[2] but it is also spoken of as 'the land of Nyikang', and they may refer to themselves as Okang, which is possibly derived from the name of their leader. All those who now are Shilluk and live in Shilluk country do not think that they had a common origin. Some of them think that they came originally with Nyikang, and others that they are descended from people who in one way or another Nyikang eventually incorporated into his kingdom. The most detailed and circumstantial of Shilluk myths are about the origin of the present internal organization of the Shilluk kingdom. Less detailed stories, which nevertheless seem, for the Shilluk, to have something of the intrinsic validity which we attach to history, are told in order to assimilate to the Shilluk world their knowledge of other Nilotic peoples. In their accounts of their own history, and of their relationship with other Nilotes, we find an interest in process, which is absent from their accounts of their relations with other peoples outside their system. This in itself might be expected, though it might have been supposed that the long period during which they have been in contact with non-Nilotic peoples would have generated more elaborate aetiological stories to explain the presence and customs of quite foreign human beings. Even within the Nilotic world Shilluk stories of their relationship with the Luo of the Bahr-el-Ghazal, with whom they can have had only the most casual and occasional contact for many years, are a great deal more circumstantial than those of their original relationship with the Dinka, who are among their nearest neighbours. They thus have traditions of relationship which do more than account for their social relations at the present day, and which have not been modified to accord with them. There is some indication that they value the knowledge of historical tradition for its own sake.

Shilluk classification of the peoples with whom they have been in contact, or of whom they know, may briefly be described as follows. Differences of function, status, and origin within the Shilluk kingdom are ultimately attributed to Nyikang, or to one of his successors, the early Shilluk kings.

---

[1] This very brief survey of those features of Shilluk social organization necessary for an understanding of their cosmology is drawn from many sources, which I have not thought it necessary to cite individually. [2] Westermann, 1912, *et al.*

Differences and divisions between the Shilluk and other Nilotic peoples are attributed to differences between Nyikang and others who are thought to have been once closely associated with him. Differences between the Shilluk and people whose culture and system of thought are quite unlike their own are attributed to an ubiquitous God, *juok*. Leaving aside for the moment the Shilluk classification of people within their own kingdom, I mention briefly some of the stories referring to the relationship between the Shilluk and some other Nilotes, and between the Shilluk and foreign invaders.

According to one Shilluk tradition,[1] in the original migration from their first homeland, 'the land of Duwat', the Shilluk were with their leader Nyikang, and with them were the Dinka led by Dengdit, the Anuak led by Gilo, and the Luo led by Odimo. There are various versions of this story, and the presence of Odimo in it is inconsistent with other stories about him. The kin relationship supposed to exist between the leaders also varies from one account to another. In this version, the Anuak first broke away, and then the Dinka, and finally, when the Shilluk were on the fringes of the country they now occupy, the Luo turned away towards the Bahr-el-Ghazal. The story shows some idea of successive developments in a necessary chronological order, and the stories of the relationship of the Shilluk with the Luo contain circumstantial details, some of which are confirmed in independent accounts given by the Luo themselves.[2] These are people who are thought to have been involved in Shilluk history from very early times; we are not given any indication that the Shilluk attempt to account for their existence, but only that they themselves account for their relationship with the Shilluk. It is not so with the stories about white and brown people. One tells, for example, how it was that God (*juok*) came to help the *turuk*, the Turk or European,[3] rather than others of his sons, the people of Darfur, the Abyssinians, and the Shilluk, who were afraid or refused to approach him.[4] Another version, found also among other Nilotic peoples, attributes the success of the light-skinned people both to superior guile on their part, and to some preference shown them by God. We are also told that when God began to make men, he made them from light-coloured clay, until his hands became dirty towards the end of his task, and he then made the Shilluk, who lost their equality with the light-skinned people.[5] Like other Nilotes, the Shilluk seem to have singled out writing and guns as the gifts with which God gave supremacy to the foreigners;[6] and Shilluk songs recorded by Hofmayr[7] suggest that circumcision has come to stand for much that is contemptible in foreign custom and

---

[1] Hofmayr, 1925, p. 14.

[2] J. P. Crazzolara, 1950, has tried to build up the traditions of the Luo (Lwoo)-speaking peoples into a connected history.

[3] Though Turks, Arabs, and Europeans can be verbally distinguished from each other in Shilluk, Europeans, particularly when they are officials, are often called *turuk*.

[4] Hofmayr, 1925, p. 241.   [5] Ibid., p. 207.

[6] Westermann, 1912.   [7] 1925, pp. 460 ff.

behaviour. Although there are many Shilluk names by which non-Nilotic foreigners may be distinguished from each other, they are also classed together as *obwonyo* (foreigners), a word also used for a reddish millet,[1] and as such they are distinguished collectively from Nilotic peoples who are not included in this category. The Nuba (*dongo* or *dhongo*)[2] seem to occupy a special position among foreigners, for Nyikang himself established a relationship with them by marrying his daughter to a Nuba.

As the Shilluk see it, the other Nilotes were separated from them in the course of a common history. To explain the presence and dominance of foreigners from outside their Nilotic world, they have stories of a metaphysical kind, positing some special act of God. These stories have clearly been invented in recent times for purely explanatory purposes. Shilluk interest in foreigners, as shown in myth and song, centres primarily on the way in which they have been opposed by Nyikang and the Shilluk, and the more they can be subordinated to Nyikang, the more they are assimilated to Shilluk tradition. Thus, it seems that the fighting with the invaders of their country in fairly recent times has, for the Shilluk, little of the imaginative significance which they attach to superficially trivial incidents in the lives of their early kings. If Hofmayr's derivation[3] of the word *obwonyo* (foreigner) is correct, the Shilluks' first national enemy, whom Nyikang urged them to resist, gave their name to others who followed. Nyikang and his successors, the Shilluk kings, are thought to have been the leaders of opposition to such national enemies. Nyikang both relates the Shilluk to other Nilotes whom they know, and focuses their hostility to attacks on their national integrity and exclusiveness. He represents, in this and other ways which may later be considered, the specifically Shilluk way of life and thought.

The Order of the World and Society

The order of Shilluk society is best approached by a consideration of the myths of migration under Nyikang, for some features of Shilluk society are thought to have originated in that period. Some of the details of these myths cannot be fully understood without a preliminary knowledge of the main natural divisions of the Shilluk world. Writers on the Shilluk do not report any story of an original state of chaos, in the strict sense, when man, earth, and sky were together in one undifferentiated whole, though such stories exist among the Dinka. There are Shilluk stories which do seem to suggest that at one time the world was not differentiated as it now is. For

[1] J. A. Heasty, 1937; Westermann, 1912, p. 248, transliterates the word for red millet slightly differently from the word for foreigners. Hofmayr, 1925, says that the word is derived from *ya puny*, the name originally given by the Shilluk to the Fung, with whom they were in early contact. Another word for the Fung, said to include the people of Sennar generally, is *cai*.

[2] Heasty, 1937, *et al. Dongo* probably means 'hill-people'. In a hymn quoted by Hofmayr 1925, p. 7, the Fung or the people of Sennar are referred to as *dongo cai*.

[3] See note 1.

example, it is said that[1] originally God (*juok*) had the people in his land, until they ate fruit which made them sick, and God therefore sent them away. Another story tells that there was once a road to the moon which men could use, but they became too heavy to do so, in circumstances which are not here relevant.[2] Yet another story[3] tells how the sun and moon used to live together, until they quarrelled and therefore are no longer together. In some Shilluk myths (to be considered later) it is said that some men were not differentiated from animals and other creatures. There is thus the implication, though it may be conveyed in stories which are perhaps not told very seriously, that some things which were once together are now apart. The broadest division of the space around them recognized by the Shilluk is between what is above (the sky) and what is below (the earth). There is a Shilluk riddle which runs: 'What are the two half-round things (in Shilluk, *opunne*, literally 'loaves') of God (*juok*)?' and the answer is 'heaven and earth'. Hofmayr gives the explanation that 'the form in which this is figured is that of a loaf of bread'.[4] Besides sky and earth, there is the river, a third main region of the Shilluk spatial ambient. This tripartite division of the universe into earth, sky, and river, corresponds, of course, to the real categories which anyone in Shilluk country is bound in some way to acknowledge, and in which he is bound on some occasions to think. The savannah country is without mountains, ravines, forests, or other distinctive natural features which might diversify its general contours, and strike the imagination forcibly enough to modify the clarity of the simple, primary distinctions which a man observes in the natural world around him. In such a land, where there is nothing of any size to break the horizon, the sky does indeed become apparent as separate region, almost a place, in relation to the earth. Besides these, there is the river, reflecting both earth and sky. The crops and grass, on which the Shilluk and their herds depend, require that the sky should send rain and the river should rise, and they also need the fish which the river contains. The three regions of earth, sky, and river have values and associations which make the division significant in Shilluk religion and cosmology, as well as in their economy. Their Nilotic neighbours live in a country which, generally, is not unlike their own. The real foreigners come from country of different and inferior quality. Among the Dinka and Nuer also it is thought that the real foreigners come from a country different in nature from their own.

Legends of Nyikang

Legends of the birth and wanderings of Nyikang do not suggest that they occurred in a country very different from that in which the Shilluk now live, but it was a long way away from the present Shilluk kingdom. We are told that the land of Duwat, or the land of Kero, from which the Shilluk

---

[1] Hofmayr, 1925, p. 238. The details may be Christian.
[2] Ibid., p. 366.   [3] Ibid., p. 364.   [4] 1925, p. 399.

originally came, was to the south of their present home, but whether south-west or south-east varies from one account to another. This homeland was 'at the end (or "head") of the earth,'[1] and near a great lake.[2] Apart from this, we hear only that in that land there was a king, called Okwa, and that he was the father of Duwat, Nyikang, and other sons. Also, there was then no death, for as people became old, they were trampled by cattle, and became infants again.[3] Accounts of this first land, which also represents the beginning of Shilluk historical time, are sparse and simple. This may be consistent with the fact that in this original land and time, the Shilluk suppose that they were not differentiated from others of the Luo-speaking group. Their accounts of this early period are like their other most general cosmological ideas, in showing little of the development and systematization which come from meditation and reflection; elaboration and detail appear in their myths with the emergence of Nyikang, and therefore with the beginning of the Shilluk royal house and the Shilluk nation. Of the time before that, they know only the little which has here been stated.

There are various accounts of the birth of Nyikang. In one, it is said that he was the son of Okwa, who was the son of Omara, who came from heaven.[4] In another he is the son of Okwa, but Okwa traces descent through several forefathers to a great white or grey cow, which was created by God in the river.[5] Nyikang's mother, Nyakaya, was either a crocodile, or partly crocodile, and is now associated with the crocodile in Shilluk thought, though she is also a woman. In all versions of the story of Nyikang's ancestry, his descent is traced through his father to a man who came from heaven, or from a special creation of God in the form of a cow, and his mother is a creature of the river with the attributes of the crocodile. Nyakaya, the mother of Nyikang, represents in Shilluk thought the totality of riverain beings and phenomena, and offerings are made to her on the river bank, at the grassy spots where the crocodile emerges. She is also especially associated with birth and with new-born babies.[6] Seligman was told that 'unusual behaviour on the part of almost any land animal would lead the Shilluk to look upon the creature as a temporary incarnation of Nyikang', while 'unusual behaviour on the part of a water animal would be put down to the animal incarnating the spirit of Nikaiya (Nyakai)'.[7]

Nyikang and his followers started their wanderings from their original home as a result of a quarrel between Nyikang and his half-brother, sometimes said to be his 'brother', Duwat.[8] They quarrelled about who should succeed their father, Okwa, as leader and king. Since Duwat was elected, Nyikang left with his faction. According to one story, he took the royal

---

[1] Oyler, 1918 (i). This is also a common Dinka idea, though they say that this land was 'at the foot of the earth'. It has for them not only the suggestion of remoteness, but also of being the time and place from which their traditions start.

[2] M. E. C. Pumphrey, 1941.
[3] Oyler, 1918 (i).
[4] Westermann, 1912, p. 157.
[5] Ibid., pp. 155 ff., et al.
[6] Hofmayr, 1925, p. 159.
[7] C. G. Seligman, 1932, p. 86.
[8] Westermann, 1912, p. 159.

emblems.[1] The story shows that, from the earliest times, the Shilluk suppose the kingship to have been a source of rivalry between the sons of the previous king. Nyikang is not thought to have been the elder of the brothers, and there is no account of any superior claim on his part, except that he also had a following. There is no emphasis in the myth on any customary order of succession, and so today any son of a king who has once been installed is theoretically eligible to become king if he can press his claim. In the past, at least, a man could retain the kingship only if he was able to defend himself against rival claimants. Rivalry over who shall be king is intrinsic to the Shilluk type of kingship, and may perhaps be seen as the most extreme form of the separation of the person from the office consistent with hereditary right to succession.

In the course of their wanderings, Nyikang and his followers came to a country occupied by Dimo,[2] where they lived for a while, and Nyikang married Dimo's daughter. She bore children, of whom the most important was his son Dak. Dak then quarrelled with Dimo, whose people wanted to kill him. Nyikang made an effigy of Dak, which was speared in Dak's place by the followers of Dimo. Effigies of Nyikang, Dak, and another son of Nyikang called Cal, are now used, as will be described, in the ceremonies for the installation of the Shilluk king. This is the first mention of an effigy, which was thus an idea of Nyikang. In one story Dak is a mischievous and quarrelsome figure, who grew to a tremendous size. He is also very intelligent, and there are accounts of how he and Nyikang, in contest with Dimo, were able to blind Dimo's people and his cattle, thus forcing Dimo to give up the fire, which he had hidden, and to release the rain, which he had stopped. The significance of this power of Nyikang and Dak to cause blindness will later be suggested. Here we remark that the effigy of Dak, used in the ceremonies for the installation of the king, is now a long figure made from bamboos and surmounted with black ostrich feathers, and that Dak is still a symbol of the warlike qualities of the Shilluk king. He is the fighter while Nyikang is the leader. The third son, Cal, who is also represented in effigy in the ceremonies for the installation of the king, is made not of ambatch, like Nyikang, nor of bamboo, like Dak, but of rope, and the feathers which form his head are the grey feathers of the female ostrich.[3] He plays a less important part than Dak or Nyikang in the ceremonies. We are told that Cal was a coward, and therefore Nyikang thought it safe for him to remain with him and Dak, while he sent away another of his sons, Buro, because he was as headstrong as Dak.[4] It is said that Cal succeeded his father as king, but did not reign for long and disappeared, to be succeeded by his brother

[1] Hofmayr, p. 14. The emblems then were a skin for slinging across the shoulder of the king, and a hoe of some kind. Other emblems were later acquired. The story shows how Shilluk ideas of kingship are bound up with the possession of distinguishing emblems by the king.

[2] Who is sometimes said to be a brother of Nyikang. The relationship varies with the context of the telling of the story.

[3] Howell and Thomson, 1946, p. 68.　　　　　　　　　　[4] Oyler, 1918 (i).

Dak. In this story, and in the weaker, female associations of the effigy of Cal, I think we may see represented by contrast the value which the Shilluk attach to courage and warlike qualities in their king, for the aggressive, headstrong Dak supersedes in importance the weaker eldest son, Cal. In songs Dak is the symbol of fighting.[1]

As a result of Dak's and Nyikang's quarrel with Dimo, Nyikang's wife's father, Nyikang and his followers set off once more on their wanderings, while Dimo and his people went in the other direction towards the Bahr-el-Ghazal. It may be noted that Dak, in quarrelling with his mother's people and cleaving to his father, showed in an exaggerated form the nature of the loyalties of the royal sons today, as they should ideally be. Their claim to importance for the whole kingdom is through their father the king and his agnates, and not through their mother's people. A conflict of loyalties between the father's and the mother's people, implicit in other Nilotic societies, is here resolved in a myth of the Shilluk kingship by the aggression of Dak against his maternal uncle Dimo. The main incidents in the further migration of Nyikang, Dak, and their followers, are a fight with Garo, the son of the Sun, Cang, and the crossing of a river, said to have been the Bahr-el-Ghazal, beyond which Nyikang settled his people in their present kingdom. Between them and their present home, there was a river covered with the floating vegetation, the *sudd*, which even now accumulates on these reaches of the Nile and its tributaries. One of Nyikang's followers, an albino, asked Nyikang to clear a way for the people to cross by spearing him in the river. Nyikang did so, and this letting of blood cleared a way for the Shilluk to reach their present home.[2] Hence one of Nyikang's many praise-names, or titles of honour, means 'crosser of the river' (the Bahr-el-Ghazal). The fight with the Sun and his son, an incident which seems to suggest to Hofmayr[3] some early contact between the Shilluk and the Galla, occurred when the Shilluk were temporarily settled on the river bank, before crossing. Nyikang then lost a cow. It was reported to be in the herd of the Sun, and Dak set out with his followers to reclaim it. He fought with Garo, the son of the Sun, and cut off Garo's hand or finger in order to get a silver ring or bracelet. In the course of the fight, Nyikang drove the Sun back into the sky, and revived his army by sprinkling them with water, or by touching them with the silver bracelet. Another version is that Nyikang made the Sun shine at night so that the fight might go on.[4] Others of Nyikang's titles of honour refer to this victory over the Sun. The silver from the ring or bracelet is said to have been used for silver emblems—a bracelet and spear

[1] Hofmayr, 1925, p. 63.

[2] Westermann, 1912, *et al.*

[3] Hofmayr, 1925, p. 61, where the Shilluk names for the Sun and his son, Cang and Garo, are said to be similar to those for a division of the Galla, *Yangaro, Tsangaro,* or *Djindjiro,* and other details of the story are said to connect with the Galla. If this is so, there must have been some contact between the Western Dinka of the Bahr-el-Ghazal and the Galla, since they have the same story.

[4] I do not give all the details of this story, of which there are many versions. The résumé here given follows Hofmayr, 1925, pp. 60–62, and Westermann, 1912, pp. 159–61.

ornaments—which are among the royal emblems of the Shilluk at the present day, and are given to a new king at his installation.[1] The crossing of the river and the fight with the Sun seem to be occurrences of great imaginative importance for the Shilluk, as they are for the Western Dinka, in whose mythology they appear in a different form, and by whom they are associated, though in different ways, with a mythical leader who in many ways resembles Nyikang. It may be mentioned that the sun, in Shilluk country, seems to be at its hottest at the end of the dry season, just before the rains, and its heat is in a sense overcome when the rains fall. Nyikang is believed to bring the rain, and in that sense still revives his people by sprinkling them with water. At this time, too, those who have been herding cattle for the dry season on islands in the river or in pastures on the east bank of the Nile, must return to their homes on the west bank to cultivate, crossing the river in order to do so. The subduing of the Sun, and the crossing of the river by Nyikang and his followers, thus recur in different form in the lives of the Shilluk. They still have to take their cattle to pasture across the river during the dry season, and return home with them when the rains start. Westermann says that:

The Shilluks along the White Nile cross over to the east bank; likewise the cattle of the Sobat Shilluks descend to the lagoons south of the Sobat. So in both cases they have to cross the rivers, which is, on account of the many crocodiles living in them, not undangerous, and is therefore done with much care and accompanied by weighty ceremonies in order to keep the crocodiles away; this forms an important part of the duties of the witch-doctor.[2]

In the account he gives of such a river crossing, it is said that the cattle are led behind ambatch canoes which the Shilluk use.[3] It will be remembered that the effigy of the 'crosser of the river', Nyikang, used in the installation ceremonies for the king is also made of ambatch.[4] Nyikang is important for that crossing on which the Shilluk herds depend for their grazing. In another Shilluk text Nyikang asks his mother, Nyakaya, to dry up the river in order to help his people against foreign enemies.[5]

In the stories here summarized, Nyikang, the leader and first king of the Shilluk, is able to affect celestial phenomena—he may also raise winds and bring rain—and he divides the river to lead his people across. By agnatic descent he is linked either with a man from heaven or with a special creation of God, and through his mother, Nyakaya, he is linked with the river. He is also the leader by whom the Shilluk were first differentiated as a separate people, and who gave them their present land. His praise-names and titles of honour acknowledge and record his association with sky, river, and earth. Apart from those already mentioned, he has the names 'heaven'

[1] Crazzolara, 1950, p. 39.
[2] Westermann, 1912, Introduction, xxix–xxx.
[3] Ibid., p. 172.
[4] Thomson, 1948, p. 159. This is a correction of Howell and Thomson, 1946, where it is said that the effigy of Nyikang was made of bamboo, like that of his son Dak.
[5] Hofmayr, 1925, p. 55.

or 'the above', and 'cloud'; he is called 'son of the Nile' and 'son of the river';[1] and in hymns[2] he is called 'our earth' or 'master of the earth'. Thus, all three regions of the Shilluk universe are nominally assimilated to Nyikang, and he to them. It is the single person of Nyikang which gives all three regions their coherence in a single world. There is no other figure in Shilluk mythology, except his successors and representatives the Shilluk kings, who thus associates earth, sky, and river, belonging in part to all.

Significance of Nyikang in the Shilluk World View

Although Nyikang was a man, and is conceived as such by the Shilluk, he is believed not to have died, and thus he is not identified with ordinary men.[3] He is said to have disappeared. Oyler[4] gives some of the expressions which the Shilluk use of Nyikang's end; 'he was lost', 'he returned to his country', 'he went up', 'he became wind', 'he went and lives': all expressions implying that he did not die. He adds that the Shilluk say 'that if Nikawng should die, the whole Shilluk race would perish'. Even now the king of the Shilluk is not spoken of as having died, though the later Shilluk kings, unlike Nyikang and his immediate successors, are thought to have become mortal. Since, as I have suggested, Nyikang is a notion by which the Shilluk apprehend a unity and coherence in the specifically Shilluk world, it is understandable that now, when a king dies, the Shilluk say, 'there is no land— the Shilluk country has ceased to be'.[5] It is not simply that Nyikang and his successors are thought to maintain the order of the Shilluk social and natural universe as though from a position above and outside it. In Nyikang, and in the kings, the parts which make up that order are correlated, and the correlation is apprehended in a single term, Nyikang. He and his successors are thought of as real historical persons, living at their own particular times and with their own unique characteristics and legends. They also represent the idea of a timeless state, unaffected by the chronological succession of events. Every king, representing Nyikang, represents the principle which unifies the Shilluk as a nation, and brings into focus the widest range of specifically Shilluk ideas about the order of nature and of society.

It was Nyikang who first separated the Shilluk people from others of the same stock, who ordered them not to mix with their early enemies,[6] who differentiated them among themselves by associating different lineages with different territories and, where totemic, with different totems, and who made the territorial divisions of Shilluk-land. Thus, he is both a unifying and a differentiating principle in Shilluk thought. The processes of individuation and separation, attributed to Nyikang, involve the creation of the ordered relationship of the individual and separate parts to each other, as the Shilluk understand it. Myths of Nyikang are ways of apprehending that relationship. It is said, for example, that the Nuba have some right,

---

[1] Hofmayr, 1925, p. 43.   [2] Ibid., *passim.*
[3] Ibid., p. 45.   [4] Oyler, 1918 (i), p. 115.
[5] Howell and Thomson, 1946, p. 18.   [6] Hofmayr, op. cit., p. 7.

which is now not exercised, to take part in the election of the Shilluk king. This right comes from Nyikang, who originally married his daughter to a Nuba, and received from the Nuba an inlaid stool, a replica of which is now the 'throne' of the Shilluk.[1] Such a myth, for the Shilluk, gives the Nuba a customary place in the social order of the Shilluk world. There are other examples which show that Nyikang explains differentiation, as he explains the relationship between the differentiated parts. One illustration may be taken from a myth of Nyikang's making people from animals,[2] and another, from the nature of the territorial divisions of the Shilluk kingdom.

It is said that when Nyikang first arrived in his land with his followers, he made people for his kingdom out of insects, fish, and animals. These he captured and turned into human beings, and they are the origin of the Shilluk common people. After Nyikang had made these people from the animal creation, 'the parent stock was removed by death', so that their children might not know of their origin. So the Shilluk common people derive their humanity, and their separateness from the animal creation, from the action of Nyikang. They claim, however, that their totems were given them by Nyikang,[3] who thus both separated them from the non-human creation, and also established an ordered relationship between some of the descent groups of his kingdom and various non-human species. According to another account, Nyikang alone was able to recognize that men were masquerading as animals and, seeing through this confusion, he captured them and made them into the men they really were.[4] This story shows Nyikang able to distinguish between appearance and reality, and to assimilate the reality to his kingdom.

Partition of the Shilluk kingdom by Nyikang

The clearest example of Nyikang's position in Shilluk cosmology—that is, their apprehension of the differentiation and the correlation of the parts of their world—is to be found in the territorial partition of the Shilluk kingdom, and this is here described at some length. Nyikang is thought to have entered present Shilluk country in the south-west, near Tonga, and to have moved along the west bank of the river until he established the northern limits of his country near Muomo, founding villages on the way, and associating them with his followers, his clients, or himself. The dominant lineages of various Shilluk settlements thus owe their association with the land in which they live to Nyikang. Westermann says that the Shilluk themselves think of their land as a whole by referring to Tonga and Muomo, its most northerly and southerly settlements, which term 'corresponds exactly to the expression of the ancient Hebrews: from Dan unto Bersheba'.[5] Shilluk country is now divided into two provinces, Ger, or Gerr, in the north and

[1] Hofmayr, 1925, p. 31.
[2] Westermann, 1912, p. 156; Oyler, 1918, pp. 111, 112.
[3] Hofmayr, op. cit., p. 235.
[4] Oyler, 1918 (i), p. 111.
[5] Westermann, op. cit., Introduction, xx.

Luak in the south, which, in some situations, are politically opposed to each other. These territorial and political divisions are associated, but not coterminous, with two religious divisions which Howell and Thomson call 'sees'.[1] One of these is called Gol Dhiang, and corresponds to the province of Ger and northern Shilluk-land. The other is called Gol Nyikang, and corresponds to Luak and southern Shilluk-land, which Nyikang first settled. These two religious divisions are separated by a stream or inlet of the river, the ceremonial crossing of which by the king-elect forms part of the ceremonies at his installation. The theme of crossing the river, already referred to, is thus repeated in the installation ceremonies for the Shilluk kings, and we find elsewhere how important in Shilluk thought is the crossing from one bank to another. There is, for example, a riddle, the ideas contained in which must seem curious to those for whom the separation of the banks of a river does not have such imaginative value. The riddle asks 'What is a big man, who knows only one bank?' and the answer is 'an island'. Hofmayr explains that an island, unlike the river or the stream, has only one bank.[2] There can thus be no crossing from bank to bank.

Ger and Luak each comprise a number of districts, which are the loose confederacies already mentioned, and seem to have been much modified by Turkish and British rule. It is clear, however, that in the past the really important divisions of Shilluk-land were the religious moieties, Gol Dhiang and Gol Nyikang, and that the boundary between them was the inlet of the river, called Arepejur, which is said to mean 'the gathering of the peoples'. Each of these moieties was divided into settlements. Of these settlements, some of which have given their names to the administrative districts to which they now belong, four were of special traditional importance. These were Muomo and Tonga, guarding the northern and southern marches, and the two settlements divided by the stream Arepejur and facing each other across the boundary between the moieties. The leaders of these latter settlements represented their whole moieties in the election of the Shilluk king, so that in this situation the leader of one settlement was also the leader of Gol Nyikang, and the leader of the other was also the leader of Gol Dhiang.[3] Just north of the boundary between Gol Nyikang and Gol Dhiang, and therefore technically in the northern moiety Gol Dhiang, is the present royal capital, Fashoda. The king's clan seems to be well represented on both sides of the boundary between these moieties.

In describing the Shilluk divisions of their country, it is easy to introduce the notion of an administrative system, with an element of superordination and subordination in the relations between the larger territorial units and

[1] Howell, and Thomson, 1946, p. 75.   [2] Hofmayr, 1925, p. 402.
[3] The history of the boundary between northern and southern Shilluk-land has been very confused. The details of this confusion do not affect Shilluk cosmology. Some of the information here given is from Pumphrey, 1941, but the main analysis of the significance of the religious moieties is taken from the way they functioned at the installation of the King Anei Kur, recorded by Howell and Thomson, 1946, and from the analysis given in Evans-Pritchard, 1948.

the smaller units which they comprise. Such a logical model would be misleading for the interpretation of the significance of the moieties, Gol Nyikang and Gol Dhiang. These seem to function primarily, if not exclusively, in the election of the Shilluk kings, successors to Nyikang. In the election of 1943–4, of which we have a full description,[1] the two leaders of the religious moieties had first to reach agreement upon the successor of the dead king, and their choice was confirmed by a representative of the king's clan, which is not identified with either moiety. An electoral college, representing various settlements of Shilluk-land, then confirmed the choice, which, according to Shilluk custom, had to be one of the princes whose father had already been king. In this case the choice was very limited, and the electoral college at once accepted the proposal made by the leaders of Gol Nyikang and Gol Dhiang. Disagreement between these over the choice of the king is said to have led to fighting between the moieties in the past, and thus to civil war in Shilluk-land.

The division of the kingdom into Gol Dhiang and Gol Nyikang thus becomes effective at the election of the king, and the preliminaries to the installation of the new king do indeed create the division which Nyikang, the king's ancestor, is said to have created in the past.[2] When the leaders of the moieties have reached agreement, there is still a ceremonial opposition between them until the king has actually been installed, when the moieties are again put together in a single kingdom, the kingdom which Nyikang originally united under himself. The Shilluk kings conceive their country as a unity by dividing it into moieties, which separate and then unite, over the election of the king. The theme of the resolution of duality and separateness, perhaps an idea paralleled by that of crossing from one bank to another of the river, in order to make a unity consciously recognized by the Shilluk, may also be seen in other features of the installation ceremonies of 1943. The Shilluk king must be possessed by, or identified with, Nyikang, so that some writers say that he 'incarnates' Nyikang. At the installation ceremonies an effigy of Nyikang is brought from northern Shilluk-land, where Nyikang is said to have disappeared during a dance.[3] There is a mock fight between this effigy, accompanied by the effigies of Dak and Cal, and the king-elect. In this fight the king first retreats from the effigy, is then captured by it, and finally must seize from it a small girl, who plays an important part in the ceremonies. She appears to represent the wife of the king's office and, since the king is to take the place of Nyikang, who represents that office, he must also take the wife. Hostility between the king-

---

[1] The election may have been considerably modified by European and earlier rule, and the element of election by vote may have been stressed at the expense of a rather different principle, described below (p. 157).

[2] Howell and Thomson, 1946, p. 30. Pumphrey (1941) quotes a story in which the existence of Gol Dhiang, which may well be of later foundation than Gol Nyikang, is attributed to a later Shilluk king, but it is still a king who made it. This seems to refer to an earlier stage in the evolution of the kingship. Here we speak of the kingdom as it was at the election of 1943.

[3] Hofmayr, 1925, p. 45.

elect and the effigy of Nyikang then ceases, and the effigies are returned to their shrines and the king is installed. Thus, in order that the king-elect of the Shilluk shall be understood to have become one with Nyikang, separation and opposition between him and the effigy of Nyikang are created and resolved after fighting in mock battle. This resolution of the separateness of the king-elect and Nyikang is also a unification of the moieties of the Shilluk kingdom for, in the mock fighting, Gol Nyikang supports the king-elect, while Gol Dhiang supports the effigy of Nyikang. Here again Nyikang and the Shilluk king may be seen to represent the principle by which the whole Shilluk kingdom is differentiated into parts, and by which these parts are again comprehended in a whole. In the installation of the new king the unity and integrity of the Shilluk kingdom under Nyikang and the king are stressed at the same time as the *necessary* nature of its parts. The uniting of the parts is not then a function of their subordination to a larger national whole, to which their rights to separate existence are surrendered.[1] It is a function of the acceptance by all of Nyikang and the king, through whom are understood the notions of unity in diversity, which have here been briefly discussed.

The Concept of Juok (God)

There is a Shilluk proverb which says that 'the Shilluk customs come from Nyikang',[2] and I have preferred to suggest something of the general significance of Nyikang, rather than to exemplify in detail all the customs which the Shilluk say are derived from him. For, in saying that their customs derive from Nyikang, the Shilluk are speaking both of an original and supposedly historical king, and of complex notions of order and permanence which form what we should have to call a metaphysical system. When the Shilluk make an ideal correlation, whether of parts of the body social, or parts of Shilluk-land, or parts of the natural physical ambient, they introduce the concept of Nyikang. By reference to him they make the ...ost inclusive summary of the detailed order of their world and grasp that order in a single term.

Nyikang is necessary for the Shilluk understanding of their social and spatial categories, but he does not explain his own existence, nor the grounds for the reality which, for the Shilluk, he ordered in the categories by which they comprehend it. The nature of that reality is understood through the notion of *juok*, God, to which I now turn. It has already been said that the Shilluk explain the superiority and dominance of foreigners by a preference shown them by *juok*. In Shilluk story it is *juok*, not Nyikang, who created the world, and *juok* is the being who maintains it and informs it in its entirety. We have so far considered, in the Shilluk understanding of Nyikang, a notion by which a wide range of phenomena are comprehended in their interrelations and explained; to that extent we have

---

[1] In contradistinction to some European theories of the nation-state.
[2] Hofmayr, 1925, p. 376.

considered Nyikang in the form of an abstraction somewhat removed from the real person he is for the Shilluk. Even for the Shilluk there is an element of the ideal in Nyikang, who is to that extent an abstraction. Their divine being, *juok*, is a still more abstract notion and ultimately explains a wider range of diverse phenomena.

Juok is usually said to be the supreme being of the Shilluk, to be spirit, and to be 'the greatest spirit', and to be in some sense above Nyikang.[1] He is thus not inappropriately spoken of as 'God', provided that the use of this name is not allowed to introduce a more sharply defined concept of his nature than the notion of him formed by the Shilluk themselves. In many cases it would make the Shilluk texts more intelligible, and involve fewer contradictions in translation, if we were to think of *juok* not so much as the supreme being in a quasi-social hierarchy of 'beings', but as that being upon which, for the Shilluk, everything else is contingent. It is clear that if the Shilluk are asked whether God has a body or is spiritual, they answer that he is spiritual or 'like the wind', for he exists for them in no single mode, is omnipresent or multipresent, and is invisible. I do not think, however, that this separation between the material and the spiritual, by which *juok* must be placed in one or the other category, is one which would spontaneously occur to the Shilluk. They have different words for the 'spirits' of the dead. 'Spirit' generally, if it is to be distinguished from matter or body, is *wei*, which comes from the common Nilotic root meaning life or breath, and thus soul or spirit, and distinguishes what is active and alive from what is inert and lifeless. So, in translating the word *juok* as 'God', and saying that he is spirit, it is desirable not to introduce foreign conceptions of the nature of the Shilluk God as he is in himself. There is no Shilluk definition of his nature comparable to that with which those accustomed to revealed religions are familiar.

Juok, the being which created and still maintains all the world and what is in it, is one in essence, though, as it were, with many facets, which seem to refract him into a multiplicity of 'beings'. These resemble what we think of as spirits and manifestations of various sorts, and for us our use of these different words is enough to separate what they denote, conceptually, from God. For the Shilluk, who use the same word *juok* for each item in the multiplicity of forms and manifestations, and also for the principle manifest in them all, the conceptual distinction between the supreme being and other beings associated but not identical with him is not verbally made.

Hofmayr records a complex metaphysical statement made about *juok* by a Shilluk, who explained that *juok*, God, 'is from one side spirit (*wei*), and from the other side spirit, but from front and back he is body (*del*)'.[1] By this we can only understand that the human experience of *juok* may be an experience of something which takes material forms, but that these have

---

[1] The fullest account of the meaning of the word *juok* is in Hofmayr, op. cit., and most of what follows comes from that source unless otherwise indicated.

[2] Op. cit., p. 205.

a third, a spiritual or ideal, dimension. To put this in another way, the Shilluk quotation suggests that what is material has another, non-material, dimension, and we are told that *juok* is 'present to a greater or lesser degree in all things'.[1] Although *juok*, as the first principle, is the ultimate explanation for everything, the notion of *juok* seems to be particularly used to account for such phenomena as elude explanation in less abstract terms. It is a necessary logical concept for the Shilluk. Seligman quotes Dr. Heasty as saying of *juok* that 'he appears to be one, and yet seems to be a plurality as well . . . anything the Shilluk cannot understand is *juok*'.[2] That is, what the Shilluk cannot otherwise account for, they account for by this concept. So, for example, the creation of the world and of life is the work of *juok*, and he may also be an explanation for sickness and death. The presence and powers of the foreigners are explained with reference to *juok*, for those who are specially gifted are supposed to be so by virtue of the stronger flow, in them, of the being which created and animates the universe. *Juok*, therefore, is the support of Nyikang and the Shilluk kings. Since they represent, for the Shilluk, the order of the society and the world in which they live, and since *juok* has his place in that order, it is to be expected that for them Nyikang should also be an indication of the nature of God. So, in what Hofmayr says is the oldest Shilluk song, Nyikang is represented as speaking for God 'thus God says'.[3] This association between God and Nyikang is, of course, what has led to the anthropological study of Nyikang and his successors as 'divine kings'. God and Nyikang are two terms of Shilluk thought which cannot be reduced to any third term, but co-exist and participate in each other.

Relation of Nyikang to God

Examples of this are numerous. It is said that there are few direct appeals to God, and that Nyikang is usually invoked as an intermediary. Westermann quotes a prayer which 'is said to be the only prayer to *juok*', and says that the Shilluk were taught it by Nyikang. This explanation was, presumably, given him by a Shilluk, and is an example of their interpretation of God by Nyikang already mentioned. Part of the prayer runs:

There is no one above thee, thou God. Thou becamest the grandfather of Nyikango; it is thou (Nyikango) who walkest with God; thou becamest the grandfather (of man), and thy son Dak. If famine comes, is it not given by thee? So as this cow stands here, is it not thus: if she dies, does her blood not go to thee? Thou God, and thou who becamest Nyikango, and thy son Dak! But the soul (of man), is it not thine own? It is thou who liftest up (the sick).[4]

The association between Nyikang and God in this prayer is so close that it is sometimes difficult to know which is addressed. Since the Shilluk myth and tradition tell them much more about the nature of Nyikang, who is a man, than about the nature of God, who is not, it is to be expected that they

[1] Howell and Thomson, 1946, p. 8.
[2] C. G. Seligman, 1932, p. 76.
[3] Hofmayr, 1925, p. 7.
[4] Westermann, 1912, p. 171.

should understand the more abstract notion, God, by the less abstract, Nyikang. A still clearer example of the approximation of Nyikang to God in Shilluk thought is to be found in a prayer, part of which runs:

> We praise you, you who are God. Protect us, we are in your hands, and protect us, save me. You and Nikawng, you are the ones, who created, . . . and it is you Nikawng, who are accustomed to assist God to save, and it is you who give the rain. The sun is yours, and the sea (river) is yours, you who are Nikawng . . . The cow (for sacrifice) is here for you, and the blood will go to God and you.[1]

Here also may be seen the attribution to Nyikang of control of the sun and the river which, along with the rain mentioned in the first prayer, are the features of the Shilluk world upon which their prosperity ultimately depends, and which may help or ruin them.

God, Nyikang, and the Shilluk kings seem to form a continuum in the Shilluk religious system. Nyikang is thus sometimes called *juok piny* (*piny* being earth or world) while God is either simply *juok*, or *juok mal*, God above. The Shilluk king, the representative of Nyikang, is chosen ultimately by God, as he is accepted and possessed proximately by Nyikang. A long Shilluk epic begins with the lines 'Nyikang joined with God, the election was held . . .', the election being that of King Kur.[2] There are reports of a form of election slightly different from that described earlier in this essay. In Hofmayr's account the king-elect is agreed upon by the electors much in the way described, but Nuba from Liri, with whom Nyikang formed a relationship, are said to come with pebbles, which represent those who have a right to succeed. These pebbles, one of which has been prepared beforehand to represent the chosen candidate, are thrown into the fire, and the pebble representing the king-elect turns red, or white, or red and white. Red stands for prosperity in cattle, white for good crops. The chosen prince is then challenged to fight at night and, if he acquits himself well, he is told that he is a brave man, and that God has decreed that he shall be king of the Shilluk. The installation ceremonies then proceed. At one point in them, when the king-elect enters the village of Debalo on his way to the capital at Fashoda, the chief of Debalo asks him, 'What do you want here?' and the king-elect replies, 'I am the man sent by God to rule the land of the Shilluk'.[3] Despite the election there is thus a 'fiction' that it is God who chooses the Shilluk king and is the ultimate support of the Shilluk kingship. The order of the Shilluk kingdom depends upon Nyikang and the king, and Nyikang and the king derive their positions from God.

The Divine Kingship of the Shilluk

The connexion between God and Nyikang is of great importance in defining the sort of 'divine kingship' which is the central feature of the Shilluk

[1] Oyler, 1918, (ii) p. 283.   [2] Hofmayr, 1925, p. 451.
[3] Hofmayr, 1925, pp. 145 ff. Westermann, (1912, p. 122) gives an account of yet another form of election, in which sticks are placed in a fire, the one which flames most representing the king-elect.

cosmological system. *Juok* and Nyikang are the most general explanatory concepts the Shilluk have, *juok* or God accounting for the existence and nature of reality, and Nyikang for the way in which the Shilluk order and interpret it. Though Nyikang may be called *juok piny* (God below) he does not represent the totality of what the concept of God means to the Shilluk. God is also apprehended in other ways, and is addressed as God the Protector, God the Giver, God the Creator, and by other titles which correspond to the various situations in which the Shilluk need to invoke him, or explain effects which they attribute to him. *Juok* is thus a common explanation for illness, for the Shilluk seem to use this word to account for what is unknown in its nature but experienced in its effects.

The Shilluk God is the final explanation both for what is good and what is evil, from a human point of view, but he is not himself good or evil. Howell describes him as 'a remote and amoral deity . . . present to a greater or lesser degree in all things',[1] and there are many indications in the literature that it would be a mistake to understand, by the Shilluk word for God, a being which could be defined in ethical terms. It is well, in discussing Shilluk ideas, to distinguish their ethical from their religious conceptions; for though Nyikang is the foundation of and sanction for Shilluk customary behaviour, and God is the support of Nyikang, in neither case is there any emphasis on intrinsic ethical qualities. Nyikang is not the teacher or founder of an ethical system, and the attributes which he shares with God refer, not to judgements of ethical value, but to the nature of reality and its interpretation. In the biographies of the Shilluk kings their traditional reputations are not mainly founded upon whether they were just or virtuous, but upon whether the Shilluk prospered under them, whether they were effective in war, whether they were brave, and whether they were clever. Their caprices are also remembered.

Nyikang and Dak were the most important Shilluk kings and may be regarded as models of what the ideal Shilluk king should be. Some account of their lives has already been given, but it has perhaps not been made clear that the stories recorded of them emphasize their intrigues, deceptions, and intelligence, and the craftiness which seems for the Shilluk to be a sign of the particular gifts of God. Thus, in the story of the attempt by Dimo to kill Dak, when Nyikang made the effigy which was speared in Dak's stead, it is said that[2] Dimo said 'Nyikang is a fool, but Dak is full of talk', which means, says Oyler, that Dak was a man of ideas. He also says that Nyikang 'was an inventor, and many of the things in everyday use . . . were first made by Nyikang'. In their contests with Dimo, Nyikang and Dak show themselves both more powerful and cleverer, and in this cleverness they are alike. Dak particularly, the son who effectively succeeds his father and is second in importance only to Nyikang himself, is shown to be not only

---

[1] Howell and Thomson, 1946, p. 8.
[2] Oyler, 1918 (i), p. 108. In this account, it is said that Dak made the effigy, though in other accounts, e.g. Westermann, 1912, p. 159, Nyikang made the effigy.

mischievous and aggressive, but also a trickster who (vainly) attempts to deceive his father for his own advantage.[1] Westermann[2] quotes a text in which Nyikang commends a liar (perhaps a licensed jester), and another in which it is made clear that it was Dak's cunning which resulted in the catching of one of the creatures, described as a *juok*, with which the Shilluk kingdom was originally built up. The traditions of the Shilluk kings recorded by Hofmayr give details of their duplicity and cunning, their military prowess, and their cruelty and caprice. In this way they are approximated to God for these, and particularly intelligence and knowledge, are qualities by which a man manifests the power of God in him. The very nature of the election to the Shilluk kingship gives an advantage to the clever, as well as to the ruthless and brave, and the office must constantly have offered opportunities for intrigue and homicide. These features of 'divine kingship' tend to be somewhat elided in European accounts of the sacred character of the office, but some of the interest of the Shilluk kingship lies in the fact that the sort of sacredness it represents is little associated with an ethical code. Nyikang and the kings, along with God, are nevertheless for the Shilluk the sanctions for the customary rules and norms of behaviour. Thus the sanction for the customary moral order of Shilluk society is not conceived primarily in ethical terms, but as a manifestation of successful power and intelligence. So the test of kingship is success in the widest sense, and an unsuccessful king is soon killed by his rivals or disposed of by his retainers.[3]

Social Values: Cleverness and Success

That intelligence and success are attributed to the favour of God may be seen in other ways. Spirits, or those who are divinely inspired, are shown in Shilluk stories to be both clever and successful. They know more than others, and they can turn this knowledge to their own advantage. The Shilluk *ajuogo* (diviners), whose power is said to come from *juok*, are such people, and Oyler says of them that 'the Shilluks think of the witch-doctors or medicine men as good, not because their lives are good, nor yet because their practice is good, but because they are looked upon as the channels through which occult powers may be transmitted to men'.[4] They are personally prosperous because they are necessary, and they are necessary because they know better than ordinary men how to achieve success; such a divinely inspired person may therefore be approached for help in stealing

---

[1] Hofmayr, 1925, p. 61.   [2] 1912, p. 166.

[3] I have deliberately omitted any discussion of the killing of the Shilluk king, which by some authorities is said to be a ritual putting to death when the king's powers fail. The evidence for this is very confusing; in the records of the kings given by Hofmayr (1925), some clearly have died or been killed without ceremonial. It is difficult to reconcile this with the suggestion made by some authorities that the killing of the king is a ritual act performed to maintain the fertility and vitality of the land, cattle, and people, and that the ceremonial killing is believed to be essential for this, though misfortune for the whole land may later be attributed to some inadequacy in the funeral rites.

[4] Oyler, 1920.

a cow, for example. In a text given by Westermann[1] the hare is taught and saved by *juok*. The hare (or rabbit) is said by Hofmayr to be the favourite figure in many Shilluk animal stories, and the stories quoted by him and by Westermann show how clever, and how lucky, the hare is. A story given by Hofmayr[2] about the hare's eating young crocodiles appears in a different form in Westermann,[3] where this act is attributed to Dak, the clever son of Nyikang. The moral of these stories is that astuteness and trickery, like knowledge, pay, and it seems as though unusual intelligence, ingenuity, and luck associate those who possess them with the divine intelligence, and the success for which God is the Shilluk explanation. Hofmayr gives as a translation for the Shilluk expression *juoga tarr*, 'that which I have from the highest being, my soul, my lot, luck, my other self, is favourable to me'.[4] The large number of Shilluk riddles is an indication of the high value set on cleverness and ingenuity, and it is to be expected that these qualities, held up for admiration in their stories and in their daily life, should be ideally associated with Nyikang and their kings.

The kings, and all others inspired by *juok*, are sacred because they manifest divine energy and knowledge, and they do so by being strong, cunning, and successful, as well as by appearing to be in closer touch with the suprahuman than are ordinary men. The signs of this closer communion are dreams and 'hysterical' possession, or at least some outward sign of contact with a superior power. Examples of behaviour showing this are numerous. In the installation ceremonies of 1943, when the king-elect was set on the sacred stool of Nyikang at a climax in the ceremony, we are told that 'the *reth* (king) was seized with a trembling fit at the critical moment, and certainly he appeared to be in a dazed condition immediately afterwards'.[5] This form of behaviour is a common sign of possession by a power greater than human among other Nilotic peoples. Though there was some reference in these ceremonies to the king as the source of justice, and to the ethical qualities necessary in a ruler, they were clearly distinct from the central religious significance of the ceremonies. So also, though we find many references in Shilluk texts to God as the helper of the poor and the final court of appeal in trouble, his activity in these respects is not to be taken as an indication that he is only or primarily an apotheosis of ethical virtue. Many of the hymns to Nyikang and God are laments that the land is being destroyed because they are not helping, and we are told that when their prayers are not answered, the Shilluk may curse Nyikang for not assisting them.[6] A Shilluk proverb says that 'God threads good and evil men on a single string', suggesting that, in some circumstances at least, God does not seem to reward virtue and punish vice.[7] In other texts he is shown as the ultimate sanction for customary ethical behaviour, as a helper, and as a

[1] 1912, p. 180.   [2] 1925, p. 376.
[3] Op. cit., 155.   [4] Op. cit., p. 193.
[5] Howell and Thomson, 1946, p. 62.   [6] Oyler, 1918 (ii), p. 285.
[7] Hofmayr, 1925, p. 376.

judge, for, as the source of both good and evil, he can be regarded as indifferent, or friendly, or hostile, according to the judgement of the individual in any particular situation. His existence is taken for granted, and what people know or think of him does not alter nor define nor limit him. It is suggested by Hofmayr that the idea of punishment for wrong done is connected rather with the dissatisfied dead and with the ancestors than with the direct action of God. It is they who bring it about that God punishes the guilty.[1] Such beliefs are accompanied with very little elaboration of ideas about the state of the dead. Stories about the land of the dead, where all is quiet, as it is in the Shilluk capital of Fashoda, seem to represent fancies rather than traditionally formulated beliefs. The dead are in some sense nearer to God than are the living for they exist increasingly in a world of ideas, as the impressions they left upon their descendants become fainter with the passage of time; but, as another Shilluk proverb says, 'man does not think about death'. They pray that they may be helped in this life.

Association of Nyikang with Light and Knowledge

Mention was made earlier of a contest between Dak and Dimo, in which Dak struck his opponents blind, until they accepted his superiority, when he restored their sight. The same story is sometimes told of Nyikang and Duwat.[2] Since Nyikang and Dak represent the way in which the Shilluk know the order of their world, as well as being themselves examples of knowledge and intelligence, it is appropriate that the power to blind people should be attributed to them in myth. Another myth tells how Nyikang, in order to capture some sorcerers for his country, covered the earth with a shadow so that they could not see anything.[3] This association of Nyikang with seeing and light, and thus, I suggest, with knowledge and understanding, occurs again in the belief that Nyikang sometimes shows himself in dreams as a bright light;[4] he appears also, among other forms, as a white bull. Dak and other kings appear also in the form of a white egret. The logic of this symbolism is not specifically examined in the literature, but in Shilluk thought there seems to be some association between light and sight, and Nyikang and the kings. In the installation ceremonies of 1943, we are told that 'all objects of great sanctity were covered in white cloth . . . with all cattle [for sacrifice] it was evident how careful the Shilluk were to see that the animal was blindfold'.[5] At the conclusion of the sacrifices which marked the stages towards the complete installation of the king, then representing Nyikang, these wrappings were torn off. The significance of this may be partly that such objects, which are holy, are also dangerous to ordinary men who must be protected from them. In the installation ceremonies, the Shilluk fled when they supposed that Nyikang had come, and again fled from the effigy of Dak, with 'a mixture of fear and laughter'.[6] One

[1] Ibid., p. 232.
[3] Westermann, 1912, p. 168.
[5] Howell and Thomson, 1946 p. 78.

[2] Oyler, 1918, (i), p. 108.
[4] Seligman, 1932, p. 76.
[6] Ibid., p. 26.

theme of these ceremonies was the avoidance of Nyikang and a fear of his power, accompanied by the veiling of the objects particularly associated with him. The complexity of this behaviour, particularly the 'fear and laughter', demands a more penetrating analysis than is possible here.

Conclusion

In such a brief account it has been possible to give only an outline of the cosmological ideas and social values of the Shilluk, and it has been inevitable also that these should have been somewhat over-formalized and systematized. Shilluk cosmological ideas are embedded in belief and action. They are not systematized by the people themselves, who reveal them only by their sayings and their behaviour. It is impossible to give an account of them without abstracting them from the reality, formulating them as ideas with a certain degree of coherence between them, and thus constructing a system which has no exact counterpart in the thought of the Shilluk themselves. Such an account is bound to show, here and there, that effort to achieve consistency which is part of our tradition, but not of theirs. I have tried to show how the order known to the Shilluk is dependent upon their belief in a mythical hero and king, Nyikang, who is the figure to which every subsequent Shilluk king is assimilated in thought. This assimilation is enacted in the ritual for the installation of each new king. Nyikang is an analogue, for the Shilluk, of the power which created and maintains the universe. That power, which I have been content to call God, is of greater importance to the Shilluk as a source of vitality, both intellectual and physical, than as a being with ethical attributes. Nyikang and the kings similarly belong not to an ethical, but to a metaphysical system. Shilluk religion is concerned with the maintenance, as a divine order, of the order in which they live and have always lived. The kings, and Nyikang, are held to represent that order, which without them would not exist. The death of a king and the installation of his successor, are therefore of critical importance in the Shilluk kingdom, and that importance is marked by ceremonies of great imaginative and symbolic richness. The importance and uniqueness of the king is similarly emphasized by the existence of a special vocabulary used of him, and by various special observances which may be studied in the literature. They mark him off from ordinary men, no less than his titles—'first-born of God', 'child of God', 'reflection of the ancestors', 'master of the world', 'last-born of God', and others.[1] Any particular king, however, is also, as an individual human being, to some degree unequal to the office. The Shilluk have no superstitious reverence for the individual human king, and many kings have been removed by violent death when, for one reason or another, their people have tired of them. It is, perhaps, chiefly after the climax of the installation ceremonies that the dignity of the office, and the human nature

[1] Hofmayr, 1925, p. 150. The 'first-born' and the 'last-born' have special status, at least in Dinka thought, because the first 'opens the way' for the others, while the other 'closes the way'. They are, so to speak, the alpha and omega of generation.

of its occupant, are most clearly recognized. Then the elected king, wearing on his wrists the emblematic silver bracelets and followed by a bearer carrying a fan made from the wings of the saddle-billed stork, comes down from the mound of the shrine at Aturwic; he is lifted on to the sacred stool of Nyikang, and receives the allegiance of the chiefs of settlements, who stick their spears into the ground before him. Though he sits in state as a king, he is admonished by the chiefs and told what is expected of him. At the election of 1943–4, the chief of Tonga said to the king; 'Our job is not to keep order, that is your job. Our duty is to supply you with choice morsels of hippo meat.'[1] Although he was speaking of a new, administrative situation, we may see here the idea of the king as a source of social order, who fulfils his function merely by existing. The king's office keeps the Shilluk in palpable relation with an ideal order, which they hold to be the true order of their universe. There is a Shilluk proverb which says that 'the Shilluk only believe what they see'.[2] In their human king they are also able to see what they believe.

[1] Howell and Thomson, 1946, p. 71.   [2] Hofmayr, 1925, p..377.

SELECT SHILLUK BIBLIOGRAPHY

BANHOLZER, P. L., and GIFFEN, J. K. The Anglo-Egyptian Sudan (ed. Count Gleichen), 1905.
BELTRAME, G. Il Fiume Bianco e i Denka, 1881.
CRAZZOLARA, FR. J. P. 'Beiträge zur Kenntnis der Religion und Zauberei bei den Schilluk', Anthropos, 1932.
—— The Lwoo. Part I, Lwoo Migrations, 1950.
EVANS-PRITCHARD, E. E. The Divine Kingship of the Shilluk of the Nilotic Sudan, 1948.
FRANKFORT, H. Kingship and the Gods, 1948.
FRAZER, J. G. The Golden Bough, part iii, 1911.
HEASTY, REV. J. A. English-Shilluk Shilluk-English Dictionary, 1937.
HOFMAYR, FR. WILHELM. 'Religion der Schilluk', Anthropos, 1911.
—— Die Schilluk. Geschichte, Religion und Leben eines Niloten-Stąmmes, 1925.
HOWELL, P. P. 'The Shilluk Settlement', Sudan Notes and Records, 1941.
—— and THOMSON, W. P. G. 'The Death of a Reth of the Shilluk and the Installation of his Successor', ibid., 1946.
MUNRO, P. 'Installation of the Ret of the Chol (King of the Shilluks)', ibid., 1918.
OYLER, REV. D. S. 'Nikawng and the Shilluk Migration', ibid., 1918 (i).
—— 'Nikawng's Place in the Shilluk Religion', ibid., 1918 (ii).
—— 'The Shilluks' Belief in the Evil Eye. The Evil Medicine Man', ibid., 1919.
—— 'The Shilluks' Belief in the Good Medicine Men', ibid., 1920.
PUMPHREY, M. E. C. 'Shilluk "royal" Language Conventions', ibid., 1937.
—— 'The Shilluk Tribe', ibid., 1941.
SCHWEINFURTH, G. The Heart of Africa (Eng. trans.), 1873.
SELIGMAN, C. G. 'The Cult of Nyakang and the Divine Kings of the Shilluk'. Report of the Wellcome Tropical Research Laboratories, 1911.
—— Egypt and Negro Africa, 1934.
—— and MRS. B. Z. Pagan Tribes of the Nilotic Sudan, 1932.
THOMSON, W. P. G. 'Further Notes on the Death of a Reth of the Shilluk (1945)', Sudan Notes and Records, 1948.
WESTERMANN, D. The Shilluk People. Their Language and Folklore, 1912.

THE KINGDOM OF RUANDA

By J. J. MAQUET

T HE world-view of a people refers to a kind of reality which is not directly observable. We can observe things and behaviour, but not ideas or mental attitudes. These have to be inferred. Furthermore, although the concepts and propositions which make up the world-view of the Banyarwanda[1] are all arrived at by induction, they do not possess the same logical status. They are located, so to speak, on different levels of abstraction. Some are arrived at by immediate inference from observation, as when we say, for instance, that for Banyarwanda 'the invisible world is a fearful reality'. This statement may be immediately inferred from the behaviour of the Ruanda people: their words, when they tell us their beliefs about the action of the spirits of the dead, and their behaviour if they are threatened by them. On the other hand, a statement such as 'strictly contractual relationships are inconceivable for a Munyarwanda' is much more abstract because it is reached by successive stages from an analysis of the political organization of Ruanda. The validity of the two kinds of statement is not necessarily affected by their degree of abstraction. Even a proposition which seems very far removed from its factual foundation may be checked by the observation of other relevant facts.

Ideas concerning the place of man in the world, his destiny, his main values, his attitudes in relation to his fellow men, the rules of his behaviour, and the meaning of the invisible world, may find expression in many kinds of social phenomena. However, as might be expected, some of these phenomena are particularly significant, as, for instance, folk-tales concerning the creation of the world and the arrival of the Batutsi in the country, proverbs, and forms of cult. To these special attention has been given.

The validity of an unstated cultural premiss will, of course, be established with more certainty if it is found implied in several and very different cultural phenomena. For instance, an analysis of the political structure may lead to the discovery of the principle of the fundamental inequality of the three castes of ancient Ruanda. The same principle is also implied in tales explaining the origin of the three groups and the sources of their social roles.

This study refers to the period when the Ruanda cult had not yet been subjected to the impact of Western culture. This is not very far back in time, for it seems that the first white man to be seen in Ruanda was Count von Götzen, who travelled through the country with a German scientific-military expedition in 1894. The first permanent occupation of the country was not more than fifty years ago, and important changes in the culture have

[1] The inhabitants of Ruanda.

been brought only during the past thirty years. The present Ruanda culture has lost the coherence that existed in pre-European days. Those who have become more closely associated with alien activity, and have therefore felt its influence more constantly, now share a culture made up in part of their ancestral way of life and in part of their interpretation of the Belgian variety of Western culture as it operates in a colonial situation. Even those who have not been brought into direct contact with whites feel that their old patterns of life are losing their validity. But that more or less hidden part of the old culture, consisting of basic assumptions on the relationships of man with the world and with other men, has suffered the least change. To be sure, the legends of the descent of the first Batutsi meet with more scepticism than in the past, but the fundamental beliefs that this story reflects are still profoundly embedded in the Ruanda ethos. Even when new institutions; based on assumptions conflicting with the earlier ones, are imposed under external pressure and adopted, the principles shaping the older institutions will subsist and, if participation in the new institutions is unchecked, these will be completely reinterpreted in accordance with the former premises. Some manifestations of the continuing existence of the ancient assumptions in the contemporary context will be considered here, but we shall be mainly concerned with the Ruanda world-view as it was at the beginning of this century.[1]

Ruanda is a highland country in East Africa lying in the region delimited by lakes Kivu, Victoria, and Tanganyika. Its area is 24,500 square kilometres; its population amounts to almost 2 million inhabitants, the highest density in Africa south of the Sahara. Three socio-'racial' castes are to be

[1] Much of the material used in this study was collected by the author during two years' work (1950–1) in Ruanda as a social anthropologist of the *Institut pour la Recherche Scientifique en Afrique Centrale* (I.R.S.A.C.). The author was very much helped in his field research by Dr. E. Finoulst and Dr. G. De Clercq during their six-month course of training under his direction. Extensive and valuable information has been found in the published literature on Ruanda, especially studies by Father A. Arnoux, Abbé L. de Lacger, Abbé Alexis Kagame, the late Father A. Pagès, Mr. G. Sandrart, Father Schumacher, and Mr. J. Vanhove. The author is also grateful to the Abbé Kagame for having placed at his disposal some of his manuscripts. In formulating the conceptual and theoretical scheme used in this paper, the author has relied considerably on the teaching and works of Professor Clyde Kluckhohn of Harvard University. He is immensely indebted for his fundamental training in anthropology to the teaching staff of London University and particularly to Professor Daryll Forde. Mr. Lawrence Oschinsky has kindly corrected the manuscript. A short bibliography is given at the end, but it has not been felt necessary to document this study at every point, nor indeed was this possible, since it was written in the field with the use of a very restricted library.

This is an essay in the etymological meaning of the word. If the underlying configurations of a culture constitute its most important part, since they provide a key to the interrelatedness of apparently unconnected phenomena and to the meaning of apparently incomprehensible behaviour, they are also the most elusive realities. They evade direct observation and, often, direct interrogation. The anthropologist, therefore, must be sure that his inferences are logically acceptable not only to his own mind but also to the minds of the participants in the culture he studies. All this requires a thorough knowledge of the overt aspects of a culture and a long familiarity with them. The author is painfully aware that he has not gone very deeply into the ethos of Ruanda. This is only an attempt at a synthesis of the results so far obtained in researches which are still proceeding.

distinguished among its peoples: pastoralist Batutsi[1] (about 10 per cent. of the population), agriculturalist Bahutu (about 85 per cent.), and Batwa, hunters and potters (about 5 per cent.).

Man and the Material World

The world in which men are placed and which they know through their senses was created *ex nihilo* by *Imana*. The Ruanda word *kurema* means to produce, to make. It is here rendered 'to create' because our informants say that there was nothing before *Imana* made the world. This belief concerning the origin of the material world is universal and clear. To any question on this point, the answer is ready.

The Banyarwanda assert that we do not see the whole of the material world which was created at that time. The world of our experience is flat; its limits are far away and made of fences like the ones we see around kraals. On these fences there is a big rock which is the sky we see. Beyond the rock there is another world (*ijuru*) similar to our own, with hills, trees, and rivers. This world may be said to be heavenly only in the sense that it is above the sky: it is not a paradise but rather a richer duplicate of our world. Under the soil on which we tread there is yet another world (*ikuzimu*) also conceived as similar to our own. There is nothing infernal about it. The material universe is thus a kind of three-storied construction. It is not impossible to go from one floor to another: some people and animals came from the world above to the intermediate world and, according to some legends, one man at least went to the lower world.

In our world the moon and the stars (which are kinds of glow-worms) stay high up in the sky. The sun rises in the morning and in the evening reaches the end of the world where a powerful man kills it and cuts it into pieces. Then he throws the main bone across the vault of heaven to the East where it grows up and the following morning the same process begins again.

In essentials our world was created as we see it now, but there have been some changes in the course of its history. Some hills were raised up by the kings of Ruanda; the formation of Kivu Lake is accounted for in different folk-tales. Cattle, which rank so high in the Ruanda scale of values, also made a special appearance on the intermediate world. The stories give more than one version of their origin but they agree on their arrival in a world already constituted and inhabited by men. According to some tales, creatures did not originally have the same bodily form as they have now. It is said, for instance, that horns were given to animals after they had been created.

This, and a belief that the world is now slowly degenerating, getting old (people's stature is decreasing, cows give less milk), suggest that the Ruanda conception of the universe is not a wholly static one. The world does not remain the same, it is in process of evolution. However, when direct

---

[1] In this paper, following the common use, we have kept the prefixes of the Ruanda words, such as *mu* for the singular and *ba* for the plural.

questions are asked, it appears that this conception of the life of the universe has not been the subject of speculation and is not of great importance to the Banyarwanda.

Without *Imana* the world would not continue to exist and his action is necessary to maintain life. *Imana's* action, however, is not manifested in particular interventions; it is conceived rather as an underlying force which sustains the whole universe but does not interfere in the development of the life of nature. Seeds are put into the ground and after some time plants come up, the banana-trees produce their yields, the cows breed. All this is the normal course of things and we may expect the recurrence of these events at the proper times. This universal order, indeed, is not independent of *Imana*. He made plants grow and animals multiply, but he does not have to act to give fertility in each case. The scholastic distinction between prime cause and secondary causes can very well be applied to Ruanda conceptions. *Imana* acts as the prime cause of the universe and therefore any event may be imputed to him. On the other hand, nature itself includes the secondary causes which account for the regular unfolding of its course.

But this natural order is not unalterable. *Imana* remains master of the rules he has established. There are numerous stories of miracles worked by *Imana* (a stick becomes a cow, teeth are granted to a girl who had none, &c.). Other beings besides *Imana* may act on nature: the spirits of the dead and even some men, the sorcerers. They may prevent somebody's beans from growing, they may have a man or a cow struck down by lightning. In particular, rain, so important in this country where rainfall is very irregular, has been regarded as under man's control. There were rain-makers (*bavubyi*) who had the dangerous responsibility of regulating rainfall.

Natural forces—rain, wind, hail, storms—are not considered as persons having desires and intentions that could be influenced by prayers or offerings. It seems that only thunder is personalized, and is regarded as a king (*mwami*). When a person has been struck by lightning, it is said that the Thunder-King has honoured his subjects with a visit and has taken one of them with him. Lightning receives the same salute as the king of Ruanda.

Banyarwanda implicitly distinguish between the regular course of nature and more or less unexpected events. Towards the former they assume a rational attitude. They do not look to the invisible world to account for the alternation of the phases of the moon, the growth of plants, the breeding of cattle. These phenomena are explicable on the level of secondary causes. Neither *Imana* nor the occult powers interfere in the normal course of material nature. It would be misleading to conceive of the Ruanda people as 'primitives' living in an irrational world where every phenomenon is an enchantment demanding explanation in terms of an intervention of the invisible world. They look at the world in its regular course in the same way as does a product of Western culture.

Of course, a Munyarwanda could not explain the interplay and the exact action of secondary causes as a Western scientist would do. But neither

could the great majority of people in our culture. They believe that some
specialists know exactly how natural phenomena work, and they have an
idea of the type of explanation the specialists use. Banyarwanda have fundamentally the same attitude.

In relation to natural phenomena which do not appear with such regularity that they may be expected at about this or that time, the ideas of the
Banyarwanda are quite different. Because of their unexpectedness, these
events resemble the consequences of human intention. As a man suddenly
becomes angry and hits somebody, so thunder strikes. If an occurrence is
clearly an exception to natural laws, as Banyarwanda know them, they are
confused. If I have taken ordinary care of my banana-grove and it does not
produce so many or such good fruits as the trees of my neighbours on the
same hill, there must be some reason to be sought outside the normal order
of the world. Moreover, these unexpected events may often be dangerous and
detrimental. Since any Munyarwanda has, as we shall see later, many powerful enemies in the invisible world, he is easily led to suspect them. Consequently, when confronted with happenings in the material world which
do not fit into their conception of the normal order of things, the Banyarwanda explain these events as due to a special intervention of supernatural
forces. *Imana* himself may be responsible, but when the event is regarded
as harmful, ghosts or sorcerers bear the blame.

In this interpretation of unusual events, the Banyarwanda differ significantly from the people of the West. First, it should be emphasized that for
us, events which seem to be exceptions to the laws of nature are much
rarer. Those who scientifically know a certain field of spatio-temporal reality
can show that events unforeseen by laymen, such as a storm, are in fact
completely in accordance with the order of nature. When the event seems
inexplicable to the specialist, the uninitiated person is generally unaware of
the fact and indeed often displays a greater belief in physical science than do
scientists themselves. A basic assumption of our culture is that science (of
the physico-chemical type) can explain any material phenomenon. Thus
any event in that sphere of reality will be interpreted in accordance with
that belief. The event may, however, be of such a type that a 'scientific'
explanation does not seem possible. For instance, the unpredictable event
(a storm, a famine) may happen several times in the same place and no
reason can be found for that repetition. The Western mind will then usually
have recourse to the concept of chance, by which is meant, that the numerous conditions which must be realized in order to produce the event may
happen accidentally to coincide more than once. There is no inevitability in
the repetition of that constellation of conditions, it may just happen. The
concept of chance, by which we avoid recourse to the supernatural in such
cases, is not used by Banyarwanda. For them a phenomenon of the material
world is either a part of the normal course of nature and is explicable in
itself, or it is extraordinary and must be understood as a supernatural interference.

Man and the Non-material World

Imana, the Creator

Imana, the creator, is a person. He is conceived as an intelligence, a will, an emotivity. He is extremely powerful: 'the plant protected by *Imana* is never hurt by wind', '*Imana* has very long arms', '*Imana* goes above any shield'. He is non-material. His action influences the whole world; but Ruanda is his home where he comes to spend the night. He is always invoked as 'God of Ruanda' (*Imana y'i Ruanda*).

Imana is essentially good: 'your enemy is digging a pitfall for you, *Imana* prepares your exit', '*Imana* gives, he does not sell'. This is why he takes care of men and why there is no cult in his honour. He is so good, I have been told, that he does not require any offering.

There is a special creative act of *Imana* at the beginning of each person's life. Impregnation in itself would not be sufficient to produce a new human being. This is why the young wife, at evening, leaves a few drops of water in a jar. *Imana*, as a potter, needs some water to shape the clay into a child in her womb. Then, after birth, *Imana* decides what life is to be for that individual: happy or unhappy. If, later on, a man is miserable, poverty-stricken, in bad health, it is said that he was created by *Ruremakwaci*. This way of speaking has led some observers to understand that besides *Imana*, there was another creator, perhaps subordinate, perhaps an evil spirit. As a matter of fact, *Ruremakwaci* is the name given to *Imana* when he does not create very successfully, when 'he is tired', or, for some inscrutable reason, decides that a certain destiny will be unhappy. This is consistent with the Ruanda linguistic habit of assigning different names to one cause according to its different effects.

Imana's influence is thought to be always beneficial for human beings. It happens very often that obstacles are placed in the way of his action by malevolent agencies of the invisible world, but from him only good things come. This is not completely consistent with the belief in an unfortunate predestination by *Imana*. It should be noted, first, that the theory of predestination has not a very deep impact on the attitude of Banyarwanda. A person who thinks himself unhappy, and might thus suspect that he has been predestined to a miserable life, does not seem to be submerged by a feeling of doom. Unless he is brought to despair by a situation from which there is no escape, he will go on living and trying to improve his condition. Secondly, this inconsistency will be better understood if we consider the attitude of Banyarwanda towards the king (the *Mwami*) in similar circumstances. The *Mwami*, the supreme authority is good, yet he may be harmful and cruel to some of his subjects. As his power is absolute, as he is magically identified with Ruanda itself, he may never be criticized. Thus the victims of some arbitrary royal decision, and their friends, go on saying that the king is good but that his favourite counsellor is very bad and is responsible for what they suffer. As might be expected, in Ruanda God is conceived according to the image of the *Mwami*, and thus when some misfortune occurs, the blame is put on another name of God or on the ghosts or sorcerers.

The beneficent action of *Imana* is general and remote. *Imana* is the source of all gifts, but he does not interfere very much in individual lives unless he is invoked. He is not the vigilant deity whom no single detail of the lives of his creatures can escape and who, when he acts, takes into account all the antecedents of the situation. There is a story of a man who borrowed beans from different people. When repayment of the loans was demanded, he was always able by his wits to avoid fulfilling his obligations. One creditor—Death—insists on being paid and pursues him. The debtor, when fleeing, calls upon *Imana* who saves him.

Imana—as is illustrated by this tale—is not the guardian of ethics and social order. He is not offended when somebody is robbed, but only if the offence is directed against himself, as when somebody disobeys a particular order of his or abuses his name. Then he punishes the offender by sending him misfortunes during his earthly life.

The Spirits of the Dead

The spirits of the dead (*bazimu*), with whom *Imana* has no closer relationships than he has with living people, constitute the second category of non-material beings. They continue the individuality of living persons and have the same names. It is usual to say: 'when he will be a *muzimu*. . . .' Though non-material, they are localized by their activity, in contrast to *Imana* who, having a much wider range of action, cannot be so precisely localized. They live in the lower world whose ruler is *Nyamuzinda* ('the one with whom one is forgotten'). Banyarwanda have not elaborated a very detailed picture of post-mortem existence. Although, according to some informants, the deceased kings of Ruanda constitute a kind of governing body in the underworld, there are no social distinctions. Life is neither pleasant nor unhappy. The *bazimu* do not drink, eat, or mate but their existence in other respects is similar to that in the world of the living. The *bazimu* sometimes come back to this world, returning to the places where they used to live. An ancestor and some other spirits may stay permanently in the hut where their descendants live or in the small huts made for them in the enclosure around the dwelling.

Whatever their temper when they were in this world, the *bazimu* are bad. Direct ancestors in both lines (although the system of descent is patrilineal) are believed to protect their living descendants, if they showed them proper filial behaviour when they were in this world, if they observe prohibitions and avoidances and if they do not forget to make offerings. But all other *bazimu* belonging to one's patrilineage (*mulyango*) are always harmful. The *bazimu* of other families are less detrimental except where there are feuds between the families. Ghosts are thus essentially malevolent towards the living. At best they are not actively injurious.

In order not to irritate the dead various observances and interdicts must be complied with. The 'cult' of the *bazimu* is accordingly aimed at appeasing them. They are frequently offered a few drops of milk or hydromel. Sometimes they require the immolation of a goat or even a bull. A girl spends some time in the small hut dedicated to a *muzimu* in order that he may enjoy having a woman. Other practices are, however, more difficult to interpret. Water may be given to the *muzumu* while at the same time he is told very loudly that it is milk. The explanation given by most informants is that *bazimu* are rather stupid and that these mock offerings are not given to the direct ancestors, who are respected, but only to collaterals who, as *bazimu*, are hated. However, it is not very clear how one can at the same time fear the powerful *bazimu* and deceive them so grossly.

Among the *bazimu*, a small group, *Ryangombe* and his *imandwa*, is particularly powerful and important. *Ryangombe* is said to have been the chief of a small band of friends and clients. He was accidentally killed by a buffalo during a hunting party. In order not to leave *Ryangombe*, his friends threw themselves on the bull's horns. *Imana* gave them a special place, the Karisimbi, a former volcano, where they have a notably more agreeable life than the other *bazimu*. To have the privilege of joining them there, Banyarwanda have to be initiated into the sect (*kubandwa*). The members of the sect believe that non-initiates go after death into an active volcano, the Nyiragongo, where they suffer torments of fire. We have here an interesting instance of conflicting ideologies in a non-literate society: the common belief that all *bazimu* reside in the underworld and the belief of initiates, who are extremely numerous, in a mildly paradisal life for themselves and a hell for other people. During their earthly sojourn the initiates have other advantages, for the powerful *imandwa* do not harm them and indeed protect them from the injurious activities of other spirits.

The relations between *Ryangombe* and *Imana* seem to be conceived as those between a client (*mugaragu*) and his patron (*shebuja*), persons who are linked by that typical Ruanda institution called *buhake*, in which a man in an inferior situation in the scale of wealth and social power asks another to grant him his protection and the possession of some cows; in return the client becomes his patron's man and owes him various services. *Ryangombe* is believed to be protected by *Imana* and to act more or less as his intermediary with regard to the initiates. But *Imana* is not present in *Ryangombe's* paradise. The cult of *Ryangombe* has importance as a force of social cohesion. Batutsi, Bahutu, and Batwa may all be initiated. This function is quite overtly stressed: *Ryangombe* has said himself that he should be called upon by everybody.

Diviners and Sorcerers

Two categories of men have special relations with the invisible world: diviners (*bapfumu*) and sorcerers (*barozi*). The former are interpreters of *Imana's* will, which they can discern in the figures made by knuckle-bones, in the viscera of chickens, rams, and bulls, or even by intuition without the aid of any instrument. Some of them use a medium, usually female, possessed by *Biheko* (one of the *imandwa*) or are possessed themselves. Thanks to them it is possible to oppose a certain defence against the *bazimu*. They can identify the spirit who causes illness or sterility or is killing the cattle; they can tell what will appease him. Batutsi and Bahutu practise as *bapfumu*. It was formerly a very respectable calling; the techniques and methods of interpretation are often transmitted from father to son. Sorcerers (*barozi*), on the contrary, are criminals obliged to conceal their activities. If found they could be immediately killed. Some of them are believed to use poisons; for instance, a powder made from the lungs of a person who has died from tuberculosis is mixed in food. Others act by magical means: sending a *muzimu* to strangle somebody, acting through lightning or an animal, using spells. Besides a certain training in the formulae, they have to acquire a magical force handed on by another sorcerer.

Such, very sketchily drawn, is the non-material world of Banyarwanda. This world is dominated by *Imana*, essentially powerful and good. The century-old problem of evil in the world, particularly acute when there is a belief in the existence of a being who is omnipotent and infinitely good, has been solved by putting the responsibility for all evil and all suffering on agents other than *Imana*. These agents are mostly human, for *bazimu* are indeed human personalities and sorcerers are men. *Imana* himself does not cause any evil but he allows the causes of evil to act. As God's beneficent action is remote, we may say that the invisible world is on the whole malevolent. Under the serene reign of the prime cause, ill-willed secondary causes have a large freedom of action which they use to torture men. Compared with the earthly world, the invisible one is rather disquieting, our informants told us. When daily life is painful, when personal security is threatened by external dangers, the thought of the invisible world present in this one has not the psychological function of relieving anxieties.

But to what extent is the invisible world a permanent presence in the lives of Ruanda people? Not to a very great extent, it seems. Their existence is not permanently dominated by the fear of *bazimu* and sorcerers. As in the material world and its regular changes, Banyarwanda consider that there are 'natural' events in the human sphere, i.e. in the domain of human existence and the part of the world that man changes by his action (agriculture, cattle-rearing, hut-building, &c.). By 'natural' we mean that these events are understood without reference to the action of the supernatural world. Some antecedent events or acts are regarded as natural causes of others. To get a cold at the beginning of the dry or the rainy season is considered to be due to the change of weather. It is known that yaws can be got by contagion. Even death is very often accepted without seeking any magical explanation. It is expected, for instance, that people will die because of old age. If beans had been planted on poor soil, a bad crop would not mean that the field had been bewitched. Thus when recurrences have been observed or when 'causes' have been discovered in the sphere of human phenomena, events happening according to these recurrences or following these causes are considered as intelligible without any reference to the supernatural world. But when events cannot be explained by reference to natural antecedents or causes, or are surrounded by peculiar circumstances, the intervention of ghosts or sorcerers is suspected and a diviner is consulted. If somebody has tuberculosis (*igitundu*) and none of his forebears or the people with whom he lives has suffered from that disease, it is thought that sorcery is the cause. If somebody dies from an illness usually considered 'natural', but the death occurs a few days after a theft of which he is the supposed culprit, he is said to have been magically stricken at the request of the robbed person.

This attitude is in fact quite coherent. When the natural cause is known, the event is attributed to it; when it is not known, or appears extraordinary on account of the circumstances, the explanation is given in terms of beliefs concerning the non-material world. Why do Westerners not use a magical frame of reference on similar occasions? First, their wider knowledge of natural sequences of antecedents and consequents makes the residuum of naturally inexplicable facts more restricted. For instance, a sudden death appears to them quite understandable for purely medical reasons. To Banyarwanda, on the contrary, a sudden death is an event of which the physical causes are completely unknown. Second, even for residual facts not scientifically explained, there is in Western culture a faith that, given time and effort, a scientific explanation will be found. The Munyarwanda has no such belief in positive science. Third, for the disconcerting circumstances which may be coincidental with illness or death, the concept of chance, which does not appear frequently in Ruanda culture, is resorted to. However, Western believers in a provident God see in these exceptional circumstances, not an accidental constellation, but a sign of the meaning God intends to give to the illness or death.

A threat permanently dominating the mind of the Bahutu was that of being accused of sorcery. This danger was connected with the invisible world but was objective enough, for such an accusation could result in being killed and, of course, merely to refrain from anti-social magic did not ensure immunity from being called a *murozi*.

The Nature and Situation of Man

Kazikamuntu (which may mean Root-of-Men) is the common ancestor of all mankind. Created by *Imana*, he had, among other children, Gatutsi, Gahutu, and Gatwa who, as their names indicate, are the ancestors of the three Ruanda social and 'racial' groups. Gatwa killed one of his brothers and for that reason was cursed by his father. Gahutu, who had been chosen by his father as heir and successor, had been commissioned by him to accomplish an important mission. As a result of overeating, Gahutu fell asleep and could not collect the information his father wanted. Gatutsi, on the

other hand, got it by his sobriety and cleverness. Kazikamuntu then chose
Gatutsi to be the chief of the brothers. There are numerous versions of this
tale. Moreover, the stories concerning man's creation are often inextricably
mixed with the legends about the arrival of the Batutsi in Ruanda. The
same names appear sometimes in the creation, sometimes in the conquest
stories. In general the latter are better known. The summary given above is
thus only one of the various accounts of the origin of mankind.

According to a widely known folk-tale, Death, personalized as a sort of
animal, was hunted by *Imana*. He told all men to stay at home in order that
Death should not find a hiding-place. An old woman, however, went out to
work in her banana-grove. Death, pursued by *Imana*, asked her protection.
Moved by pity, she let the animal hide under her skirt. *Imana*, in order to
punish her, decided then that death should stay with men. This story might
perhaps suggest a belief that there was a time when men did not die. But
we could not find other elements to corroborate that interpretation.

On the ontological character of man two points are certain. First, an
adult human being is considered to be different from an animal by virtue
of his faculty of speech (*kivuga*), his intelligence (*ubwenge*), and his will
(*ugushaka*); but the difference, if any, between a small child and an animal
is not quite clear. Second, no one of these attributes is equated with the
surviving spirit (*muzimu*). There is something in the human being which,
after his death, becomes *muzimu*, but there is no agreement as to what it is.
According to a fairly common opinion, the *muzimu* is the metamorphosis of
the *igicucu*, the shadow cast by the body in sunshine. But according to some
informants, this shadow is only an image of the spiritual shadow which is
the essence of the post-mortem spirit. In conformity with that opinion, the
living man is said to be made of three components: the body (*mubili*) which,
after death, becomes a corpse (*murambo*); life (*buzima*), which disappears;
and the shadow (*igucucu*) from which the surviving spirit (*muzimu*) results.

The heart is believed to be the seat of intelligence and affectivity. It is
conceived as a single organ although some ways of speaking suggest that it
is double. For instance, it is frequently said: 'One heart told me this, one
heart told me that.' This is another application of the habit of attributing
opposed effects of the same cause to several causes, but this is only a verbal
habit which does not deceive anybody.

These uncertainties regarding the nature of man indicate that Banyarwanda do not make any clear-cut distinction between the concepts of body
and mind. Although they recognize parts in man, they prefer to consider
the unit rather than its components.

Whatever the culture, human experience is made up of a sequence of
events and activities, such as working, eating, sleeping, maturing, suffering,
mating, getting old, and dying. What is the Ruanda attitude in face of these
universals of human life? In many societies these happenings are considered
not in their naked reality but in terms of the beliefs held as true in the
particular culture. For instance, in a society with a Christian ideology, to

suffer is not only to be hurt but also to expiate one's sins, to purify one's soul, and to identify oneself with Christ. For serious Christians, suffering cannot be stripped of its religious meaning without being completely distorted. Banyarwanda, on the contrary, seem to take a very 'secular' view of the human condition. Their belief in the supernatural world does not greatly influence their attitude to the unavoidable hardships and pleasures of life. All our informants agree that to die means above all to quit life. They believe that they will become *bazimu* but that leaves them rather indifferent. Even initiates do not show any enthusiasm for the idea of joining *Ryangombe* and his *imandwa* at their feasts. To abandon his children, his herds, his friends, is a sad thing for a Mututsi. But it is accepted, without dramatizing it, as one of those facts which belong to the normal order of things.

If quitting this life is so unfortunate, is human existence such a cheerful experience for Banyarwanda? Enjoyments and the pleasant things of life are very unevenly distributed in Ruanda. The superior caste, the Batutsi, form about 10 per cent. of the population. But, by various means, principally by the institutionalized exchange of cattle for services and dues, Batutsi have been able to gather a much higher proportion of consumers' goods. They do no manual work and have leisure to cultivate eloquence, poetry, refined manners, and the subtle art of being witty when talking and drinking hydromel with friends. Bahutu, perhaps 85 per cent. of the population, do not enjoy such gracious living. They have to produce for themselves and for Batutsi. On a very poor soil, with technologically primitive implements, it is necessary to work hard to secure the surplus production required by the Batutsi. Moreover, the great social influence of Batutsi has given opportunities for the arbitrary exercise of power, so that there are many insecurities in a Muhutu's life. But exploitation has been kept within limits set by the wisdom and the interests of the Batutsi, and a system of protection has assured a minimum of security to the Bahutu. As to the Batwa, they are so low in the social hierarchy, and are considered so irresponsible that they have had a greater independence of action. Formerly they lived on the margin of Ruanda society. They had a reputation for grossly enjoying any opportunities for eating, drinking, making music, and dancing. It should be added that Banyarwanda, according to our standards, have been rather defenceless against disease, that starvation was a real threat for the majority when the rains failed, that ritual observances and interdicts were numerous, and that when somebody happened to be involved in a charge of sorcery he had good reason for great fear. Thus it seems that, for an ordinary Munyarwanda, life is objectively hard, often dangerous but bearable. This partly explains the Ruanda outlook upon the totality of life. It might be described as a mild optimism. As many of our informants put it: 'Existence for Banyarwanda was not easy, it was even often very painful, but on the whole, life was rather a good thing.'

As everywhere, some individuals were at some time of their lives plunged into circumstances which offered apparently no way out. A Mututsi who had incurred the king's displeasure and was for that reason left without protectors, friends, or cattle was in a desperate situation; only with difficulty could he gain a bare subsistence. A Muhutu against whom an accusation of sorcery was repeated; an unmarried girl of a noble family whose pregnancy became publicly known; all these, if they failed to escape from their predicament by skill and rational behaviour (such as obtaining the king's mercy, denying the charge of sorcery and looking for the protection of a powerful man, using abortifacients or denying the pregnancy), would have recourse to the *bapfumu*, seeking to know what spirit or sorcerer was responsible for their misfortune and how to appease the malevolent being. If all the practices and offerings recommended by the diviner had no effect, then they called upon *Imana*, and if their prayers were unanswered, only drastic solutions remained, such as exile in a foreign country or suicide. But these tragic destinies were not numerous and they did not shake the belief of the majority in the moderate happiness of living.

There is a further reason for their generally cheerful acceptance of the conditions of their existence. Banyarwanda are not inclined to speculate about the inaccessible. Westerners are given to imagining how beautiful and good life might be if humanity and the universe were different from what they are. This trend of thinking is quite alien to Banyarwanda and, when it is suggested, appears futile to them. The usual, the normal (in the sense of what we are accustomed to, and what we have reason to expect) is often self-explanatory. When a particular event fits into the normal scheme of things, there are no questions to be asked. If everybody has to relinquish this existence and die, death is no scandal or absurdity. It is the way *Imana* has arranged things. There is no further problem.

Cultural Values

Human action is determined partly by cultural values, partly by the socially recognized means of attaining them. By cultural values we mean the final or intermediate aims that are considered the proper purposes of human activity in a particular society.

In a stratified society, such as that of Ruanda, each layer is likely to have its own set of values, although some of those originating in one group may extend to others. Let us begin with the Batutsi. When a Mututsi informant is asked what the people of his group wish for above all, the answer comes immediately: 'children and cattle.' A further question, 'why?', discloses that these are not ultimate values sought for themselves, but intermediate ones, means to reach more abstract ends. The latter are power (*amaboko*) and reputation (*ugukomera*).

Power is understood here in connexion with persons (power over somebody) rather than with things (power to do something). It is, to paraphrase Lasswell's definition, the ability that a person, engaged in a human relationship with another, has to oblige the latter to do or not to do something (on pain of suffering severe privation). Power is essentially the capacity to exert a significant pressure on somebody. In Ruanda, to be powerful is to be able to exact from others tribute in labour or in kind, or support for one's claims to some advantage to be obtained from the king. In the latter case pressure may remain undefined and indirect: for instance, a threat to withold backing which may later be necessary to the person who is now asked to support a request. We desire to have cattle, say our informants, because by giving one or two beasts to a Muhutu, he becomes our client (*mugaragu*) and then has to do, to a large extent, what we ask of him. We also like to have cattle in order to get as vassal another Mututsi who lacks them. The services expected from a vassal are not manual, but he will increase the influence of his lord by his family connexions and will be useful through his diplomatic shrewdness in dealing with his lord's intrigues. Finally, we desire to become ourselves the vassals of great chiefs, or even of the king, because we are then under the protection of somebody very important, we get more cows and that allows us to have more clients.

In order to become powerful it is important, almost indispensable, to have many children. Girls, by their marriages, extend one's family connexions and bring their fathers a few cows as bridewealth. Boys at an early age begin their military training which gives them a complete education in the skills, knowledge, and virtues pertaining to their noble condition. This training is given them as *intore* (chosen ones) at the royal court or at the court of an important chief. For a father to have a son at court would reinforce his influence: through his son he knows what is going on, and the king or the chief is constantly reminded of the father by the son's presence —an important security for the father. The boy could also increase the influence of his family by becoming the client of a powerful Mututsi, and thereby getting protection and cows for himself and his parents' family (*mulyango*). Finally, the marriages of his sons could create new links between the father and the families of his daughters-in-law.

In complex societies like our own the roads to power are many. In Ruanda it does not appear that power could be readily attained except through the possession of children and cows. As we shall see, warlike valour could confer very high prestige, but not necessarily power. Great warriors were often granted herds of cattle by the king as rewards for their prowess, and could then gain power by their cattle, but not directly.

If we press our analysis farther, we may say that from the point of view of power, the significance of children is to provide cattle or connexions. On the other hand, cattle give direct power (over the Bahutu clients) or ensure connexions. In relation to Bahutu labourers, cattle have many of the social functions of money in our culture. They enable the man who owns them to exert pressure on those who have few or none of their own and who try to acquire them in exchange for services. In order to facilitate comparison with other ways of life, we may use the term wealth (as a medium of exchange) instead of cattle. As for connexions, what is meant here is that type of relationship in which one party may require something from the other under the threat of some sanction. In Ruanda, of course, it would be considered very improper to give orders or to utter a threat, but beneath the polite phrasing, the true meaning of the relationship is clear. Consequently we may say that in Ruanda, the only means to power are wealth and relationships in which sanctions are implied.

The other ultimate value of Banyarwanda, reputation, is also closely connected with children and cattle. First, because powerful men are greatly respected and everybody knows the significance of daughters, sons, and cattle as means to power. Second, because cattle have also a high prestige-value in themselves. Indeed to entertain friends properly and to maintain the superior style of living of the nobles, one must have plenty of milk. Milk is the beverage of the high caste. They also drink hydromel and banana-beer, but milk is more characteristic of the Mututsi way of life. It was considered a complete food, and true Batutsi were said to live on milk alone. As each cow did not produce much milk, it was necessary to have an important herd to provide for the needs of a well-to-do Mututsi family. Moreover, cattle had an important aesthetic value in Ruanda. To be expert in cattle-breeding was required of the nobility. A whole category of poetry was devoted to the praises of famous cows, individually identified. Very beautiful cows (called *inyambo*) were regarded as belonging to the king even if they had been produced in somebody else's herd. In many festivities cattle were presented to the king or to great chiefs. All this indicates that cattle were objects of keen interest and aroused feelings of pride similar to those associated in some Western sub-cultures with the ownership of hunters or luxury cars. Cattle were the privileged possession of the superior caste, just as in Europe, in the Middle Ages, a noble had to have some landed property. Without losing status, he could not exchange his real estate for gold or goods even if they were worth much more. Such being the feelings and emotions attached to the possession of cattle in Ruanda, their high prestige-value is readily understandable.

The antiquity of a family is highly valued in Ruanda. Almost any Mututsi is able to give the names of his ancestors for six or eight generations. A family has property which is handed on from one generation to another, common ancestors to be honoured, a set of traditions and legends. It is a living reality in which one is proud to participate. Against that background one may appreciate how children, and particularly sons, give prestige to the parents. To have many children ensures that family traditions will be maintained, that the importance of the family will increase, that its property will be kept and even enlarged, that the ancestors will be honoured. This not only makes the parents happy, but is recognized by other people and their esteem for the father is enhanced.

Besides recognition of their power, admiration for their cattle, and the respect paid to them on account of their having many children, the Batutsi seek more specific reputations. They like to be recognized as courageous. They came to Ruanda by conquest and, till the European occupation, their main social function as a caste was to make war, more often offensive than defensive. Consequently military courage (*ubutwari*) was highly praised. There are numerous and interminable poems made by official bards, telling stories of battle and commemorating military prowess. The young Batutsi, during their training, were taught to compose such poems and even to invent imaginary doughty deeds. Special signs, or badges of honour, were granted to those who had killed seven or fourteen enemies during an expedition; there was a special ceremony to honour warriors who had killed twenty-one persons in a campaign. Some informants were still able to give the names of warriors who had received these marks of honour.

It is worthwhile to note, however, that even in a society so focused on military values, great warriors could gain an extreme popularity but not, at least directly, social power. Martial valour as such was not even considered a special qualification for becoming commander of the army (*mutware w' ingabo*). During battles, indeed, the chief of the army had to stay motionless in his headquarters. He was magically identified with his army: he could not move backwards without endangering the advance of the army. This type of command did not require much courage. An army commander was, on the other hand, very high in the power scale. Members of the army had to give him cattle on certain occasions (when he was taking up his duties, when he was reviewing the herds of the army members); the king granted him cattle in some circumstances, for instance, after a battle had been won, or he entrusted to the army the care of some herds. By these means the army chief had control of many beasts: he could then increase his clientship, and thus his social power, by gifts of cattle.

A Mututsi also greatly desires to be regarded as having *ubugabo*. This means the quality of being a man (*mugabo*); it includes trustworthiness in keeping promises, generosity in treating one's friends well, liberality towards the poor, moral courage in accepting one's responsibilities. In a society where relations of inferiority and superiority are predominantly personal, in the sense that authority is rarely abstract (a law, a principle) but generally identified with a person (chief, king, lord, &c.), emphasis is laid on fidelity in any personal relationship.

Another quality that the Batutsi are extremely proud to have is *itonde*. This may be translated as 'self-mastery'. To lose one's temper, to manifest violent emotion by crying is really shameful. Anger, in particular, should not be violently expressed. The demeanour of a Mututsi should always be dignified, polite, amiable, if a little supercilious. Batutsi manners have often been called hypocritical. This would be true if such behaviour were displayed in an extrovert culture where it is considered unethical not to express to a person exactly what one thinks about him. But in Ruanda it is taken for granted that only vulgar persons reveal all their attitudes and emotions. This is understandable in a strongly hierarchical society, where the authority of a superior is not restricted to certain specific domains of the life of his inferior, and where to express any disagreement with the superior is thought inappropriate. This is the point of view alike of the inferior (and everyone in Ruanda, except the king, has a superior) and of the superior (and any Mututsi is the superior of a certain number of people). Bahutu are not, and are not expected to be, very self-controlled; they are correspondingly impressed by the external dignity of the Batutsi. An aristocratic caste usually emphasizes those differences which constantly remind others how far removed they are from the noble set.[1]

When inquiries were made as to the kind of reputation the Batutsi specially wanted to avoid, the answers given did not generally indicate qualities opposed to those thought desirable, but referred to reputations in which an external danger is involved. Above all, a Mututsi fears to be considered an enemy of the king. This is partly because he feels a genuine respect for the king, but mainly because to be reputed the king's enemy was formerly extremely dangerous. It could mean dispossession of all property, severance of all social relations, exile, or death. A Mututsi also fears to be considered a traitor to his chief. This is less dangerous but it involves sanctions: if a Mututsi has been disloyal to his lord (*shebuja*), the latter may take back from him all he gave him previously and eventually all his cattle.

All this relates to the good or bad reputations people desire or fear while living, but the Batutsi are equally concerned with their posthumous fame. To be remembered as a great warrior or a powerful cattle-owner was the normal ambition of any Mututsi. Some deaths were particularly glorious: for example, to be killed in battle or to lose one's life rather than surrender one's cattle, because this is to be deprived of the only means of living in a manner appropriate to one's rank.

The longing for fame after death seems to be deeper and commoner than in our culture. It is not unlike the Ciceronian concept of *gloria*. It is a desire to go on living in men's memory quite apart from a belief in a supernatural immortality and, like *gloria*, has nothing to do with mythological conceptions of the beyond. Banyarwanda do not think that the spirits of the dead will take pleasure from the great reputations they have on earth, or so at least our informants told us. 'If *bazimu* know perhaps the fame that the people from whom they come enjoy among the living, it is definitely not for that reason that we hope to be famous after our death.' It is possible, however, that it may be connected with the belief that the living will make more offerings to the *muzimu* of somebody who is widely remembered, though we did not find evidence of any belief that the spirits would suffer a kind of second death, and disappear completely if and when they were forgotten by the living.

To sum up, the ultimate values for the aristocracy are power and reputation. Children[2] and cattle are their main intermediate values in the sense

---

[1] There are, of course, other virtues that a Mututsi likes to be thought to possess, but the three we have mentioned seem the most important according to our informants.

[2] The preceding account might give the impression that for the Batutsi, children are only means to power and fame. This view would overlook the fact that people also enjoy

that they are the almost indispensable means for achieving these ends. The originality of Ruanda culture does not lie in its high valuation of power and fame. These are recognized ends in many cultures. What is distinctive is the paucity and the indispensability of the means provided in that society for effecting these purposes.

An ordinary Muhutu could never hope to achieve a position of power over other men comparable to that which a Mututsi could attain without difficulty. A well-to-do Muhutu could acquire a few servants either by ensuring the subsistence of other Bahutu poorer than himself or, like a Mututsi, by the gift of cattle. But this was not common. Ambition for power is proper to people who do not have to worry about fundamental human needs such as food, shelter, &c. The ultimate value for Bahutu is security, for this means protection from the things our informants say they fear above all: accusations of witchcraft, starvation, and the arbitrary actions of the powerful. There are no direct methods of protecting oneself against the first of these threats. All that can be done preventively is to be a good neighbour, not to be envied by anybody, not to have enemies. . . . But there are ways of reducing the other two dangers and these are the intermediate values which the Bahutu earnestly seek: work, children, and patronage.

Bahutu till the soil from which they have to get subsistence, the tribute demanded by the chief, and perhaps a surplus. This surplus is extremely important because it will enable them to acquire some goats, sheep, even a cow, to have the time to work for their lord, to store enough food to get a few servants who will then increase production. Surpluses may be obtained only by work. That is why, among Bahutu, the man or the woman who works hard and competently is highly considered. Work enables Bahutu to achieve some security against starvation and even to attain moderate wealth.

There is a Ruanda proverb that the dog is not feared because of his fangs but because of his master. This is the main reason why a Muhutu wants to have a patron. A peasant rich enough to own a couple of cows needs the protection of somebody more powerful than himself in order to avoid the arbitrary exactions of some member of the dominant class. Patronage was institutionalized by the *buhake* agreement mentioned above. Like the lord in medieval Europe, the patron was bound to protect his client in most of the dangerous situations of life. A second reason for seeking a patron lay in the material and moral advantages accruing from the possession of cattle.

If we wish to state Bahutu values in more abstract terms, we may say that they seek security through the production of agricultural goods and the protection of a powerful patron.

Although he is not indifferent to his reputation, the Muhutu does not seem to stress its importance as much as does the Mututsi. The reputation he desires reflects the values of his caste. He likes to be considered a

their children just because they are their children. This, of course, exists in Ruanda as in many other cultures.

mugabo (a rich man) and a *mukungu*—a very rich man possessing a few cows, many fields, goats, and bee-hives. He enjoys the recognition of his fidelity to his master and his qualities as a labourer.

The Batwa never had the stability of peasants. They were hunters, potters, dancers, buffoons, and were regarded by their neighbours as being on the margin of society. They did not possess anything that others could envy. Consequently security from exactions was not such an important value for them. As people who lived a hazardous and unsettled existence, they greatly appreciated momentary and immediate satisfactions, and among these, food, especially during periods of scarcity, was the object of their activity. Their principal means of securing food varied according to their particular occupations. Hunters depended on their ability and their courage, of which they were very proud. Dancers, musicians, and buffoons relied on their talents and on the favour of their masters, their loyalty to whom was widely recognized. Indeed it is said that one could rely upon a Mutwa much more than on anybody else.

The social and economic situation of the Batwa explains and to some extent determines the value they attach to gratifying the basic need for food. Ability in their specialized occupations and a blind faithfulness to their masters were the best means to achieve that satisfaction, but skills and loyalty were also valued for themselves.

Rules of Human Action

These values, ultimate and intermediate, were eagerly sought by Banyarwanda but, as in any society, some means for realizing them were prohibited under certain circumstances. Stealing is rarely, if ever, culturally accepted as an ordinary practice for getting rich. Socially defined values are to be reached by socially approved means. We do not suggest that, in a particular society, the rules of action appear as merely social imperatives, or that the only basis for these rules is social. We would point out that some rules of action, whatever their origin and their philosophical foundation, are part of the collective heritage in any society. In Ruanda, as elsewhere, there are such rules of action. Murdering somebody who is not an enemy of one's family is prohibited. Women are forbidden to commit adultery and, among Batutsi and Bahutu, unmarried girls may not have sexual intercourse. When an order is issued by somebody in authority it has to be obeyed.

Does submission to the rules appear only as the rational behaviour of one who wishes to avoid an external punishment or is it moral conduct? Does a prospective offender refrain from wrong-doing simply in order to avoid very probable and unpleasant consequences, or is it his conscience which tells him that he should not follow his desire?

Of course this is not an either-or problem, but the question of degree or relative stress is important. Even in cultures which lay most stress on the moral motivation to action, external social sanctions are useful deterrents from prohibited behaviour. In Ruanda these external sanctions exist. Those who steal cattle, or set fire to huts, or commit adultery are punished by the political or family authorities. Social sanctions are not only physically en- forced penalties, such as corporal punishment and compensations, but also the unorganized reactions of the people who know the delinquent: kin, neighbours, clients, and lord. For the Batutsi, for whom reputation stands high in the scale of values, this is extremely important. According to our informants, the fear of being considered a man without loyalty or without dignity, the dread of being despised by one's family, prevent many breaches of rules. To use Kluckhohn's terminology, we may say that Ruanda's is a shame-culture. But it is also a guilt-culture. When a Munyarwanda has transgressed some rule so secretly that there is not the slightest chance of his being found out and incurring punishment and shame, he nevertheless feels guilty and knows, our informants told us, that his action is bad. When a child has disobeyed his father without the latter's knowledge, he thinks not only of the unpleasant consequences that the discovery of his misbehaviour might produce but also (and some informants say 'mainly') of the wicked- ness of the act itself. The Ruanda word for conscience, *kamera*, means something that is internally felt. It is situated in the heart.

That the Banyarwanda have a 'conscience' will not be rated as a great discovery by some. But since some recent studies, such as Kluckhohn's on the Navaho, have stressed the fact that, in some cultures, submission to rules seems to be realized almost entirely through a rational concern to avoid punishment or shame, it does not seem superfluous to consider how far observance of rules is, or is not, linked to ethical principles and feelings of guilt.

Let us now attempt to indicate more precisely how moral wrong is con- ceived in the Ruanda culture. As has been already mentioned, *Imana* is not the guardian of the moral order. Sometimes he seems to be regarded as its author in the sense that he might have decided that men should not steal; but it is clear that when a man steals another man's cows, *Imana* is not personally offended. Those who are offended are those who have been wronged by the action, or those who had issued an order which has been disobeyed. When *Imana* has not been directly injured (as by blasphemies), or when the injury done to another has not been specifically forbidden by him, he is not thought to be offended. The victim could, however, ask *Imana* to punish the wrongdoer and if he then became ill, it would be said that *Imana* had punished him.

The other agencies of the supernatural world have even slighter relations with ethical values. The *bazimu* are naturally malevolent and punish only those actions which they take to be directed against themselves. A way to honour the spirit of somebody who had been a thief during his life was to simulate a robbery. *Ryangombe* and his fellows were not models of morality during their earthly existence and they did not care about the ethics of their followers. Nor was there any punishment after death. For those who believe that there are two kinds of life after death—happy or unhappy—the qualification for the happy one is not to live a blameless life on earth, but to undergo initiation into the *Ryangombe* cult.

Thus the ethics of the Banyarwanda are not integrated on a religious basis such as the will of God. What is the principle of integration, or rather, we should first ask, are their ethical conceptions integrated? On the surface they consist, like any moral code, of a multiplicity of prohibitions, orders, and exhortations. Have they achieved a synthesis of these separate elements by reducing the multiplicity to one or a few principles? Or, what amounts to the same thing, could they give a definition of good and evil?

In Ruanda a great number of particular rules are subsumed under general principles such as: do not do what is harmful to people of your group or of your country; do what people related to you would like; submit to your superiors. Principles such as these are already on a higher level of abstraction than the particular rules. When informants are asked to account for a given rule or principle they give as the final justification: 'It has always been done that way in Ruanda.' We may perhaps express the Ruanda definition of good and evil in these terms: That is good (or evil) which tradition has defined as good (or evil).

Tradition is indeed a powerful force in cultures which, as in Ruanda, have been isolated for centuries from world currents. Each generation is more conscious of the importance of what it has received from the preceding one than is possible when much of what constitutes its way of life comes not from its ancestors but from some other social tradition. Moreover, their relations with their neighbours whom they frequently subjugated have persuaded Banyarwanda of the excellence of the ways of life transmitted by their forefathers. In such a situation the traditional character of a rule appears to be sufficient justification. If the ancestors, who were so wise, behaved in that way it would be preposterous to question it.

But it would be misleading to picture the Banyarwanda as following blindly the moral rules framed in a remote past without having any idea of their purpose. Some old men have a clear understanding of the social significance of certain rules. They explained, for example, that the duality of the rules concerning adultery committed by the husband or by the wife was accounted for by the importance of the wife's function in procreation. She has thus a greater responsibility than the husband for maintaining the integrity of the family.

Does this kind of thinking extend so far as independence of tradition? Some informants told us that, apart from the authority of custom, some actions were thought of as dishonourable in themselves. But these informants were Christians and, apparently, very much influenced by their religion. Moreover, they could not quote a clear case of conflict between tradition and ethics.

No moral code can achieve an absolute character in all its precepts. Prohibitions and commands frequently relate only to certain categories of persons and situations. Even the Christian Western ethic, which realizes to a very considerable extent universality and absoluteness, qualifies some of its commands. The degree of absoluteness and universality of the Ruanda rules of conduct is much lower. We might say that most of its precepts are qualified in relation to persons and circumstances. To steal cattle was forbidden, but a Mututsi could take the cattle of a Muhutu who had no lord. For a Muhutu to rob a foreigner was not forbidden. A wife might not commit adultery, but she was allowed to have sexual relations with people when ordered by her husband to do so and, even without her husband's permission, a woman could have intercourse with her husband's brothers and parallel cousins. Killing a man was prohibited, but not if he was an enemy of Ruanda or of the family, and if the feud had not been barred by the king. Banyarwanda certainly had no idea of rules of behaviour applicable to all men in virtue of their common humanity. This is perfectly consistent with the Ruanda conception of mankind and the very significant inequalities which Banyarwanda observe between themselves and neighbouring peoples and, among themselves, between the different castes.

To conclude, the rules of human action which prohibit or enjoin the use of certain means in order to achieve the culturally recognized values of Ruanda are sanctioned, not only by organized and unorganized social reactions but also by individual conscience or guilt feelings. The foundation of this moral code is not religious or supernatural but traditional; its content is a multiplicity of rules synthesized under a few moral principles. Particular precepts do not have a universal application but are relative to persons and groups.

Human Relations

Two principles dominate the field of human relations in Ruanda: inequality of men and indefinite reciprocity.

For the Banyarwanda all men have indeed a common nature; they are ultimately the descendants of the same ancestor. But this notion does not seem to be very significant, for Banyarwanda are much more impressed by the differences displayed by the various castes. The characteristics of these castes are stereotyped and repeated in many folk-tales. Batutsi are intelligent (in the sense of astute in political intrigues), apt to command, refined, courageous, and cruel. Bahutu are hard-working, not very clever, extrovert, irascible, unmannerly, obedient, physically strong. Batwa are gluttonous, loyal to their Batutsi masters, lazy, courageous when hunting, lacking in restraint. These characteristics, with differences in stress and shading, are generally recognized by all Banyarwanda. As they reflect the Mututsi point of view, it appears that the superior caste has been able to make other people see themselves in important respects as Batutsi see them. Moreover, those qualities are considered to be innate, not acquired. A Mututsi is born clever and a Muhutu impulsive. Some tales, more widely known than those concerning the creation of man, relate how the first Batutsi came to Ruanda from the heavenly world. According to some versions of this tale, they came with their servant, Mutwa, who mated with a forest ape. From that union all Batwa are descended. Such tales clearly reveal the fundamental differences which the Banyarwanda see among their castes.

When such a picture of 'natural' differences, so significant from the point of view of power, is accepted, the inevitable consequence is that some men are born chiefs and others labourers. Inferiority and superiority are due not to personal qualities but to membership of certain groups. By belonging to different castes, people have fundamentally unequal rights. If an ordinary Mututsi kills a Muhutu, one kinsman of the murderer could eventually be killed in retaliation if the king authorized it. If the murderer was a Muhutu and the victim a Mututsi, two lives were taken.

The principle of the fundamental inequality between social groups thus established in Ruanda has spread from the original inter-caste relations to intra-caste situations. A man superior to another member of his class because of his functions or his wealth, or even his ability, tends to assume towards his inferior an attitude similar to that of a Mututsi *vis-à-vis* a Muhutu. Of course the conception of inequality between superiors and inferiors of the same class is not so rigid as that between the castes, but it permeates all hierarchical situations in Ruanda.

The theme of inequality was embodied in the indigenous political organization, so that political relations clearly express the attitudes socially expected from superiors and inferiors. They are quite understandable if one bears in mind that they originate from an inter-caste situation. Authority as such is all-embracing. According to Western conceptions, any authority is defined not only as regards the people who are subject to it, but also in respect of the matters falling within its competence. A man who gives orders to another because they are on different levels in a hierarchical scale may be considered his equal in other relations. In Ruanda, there is almost no sphere of life in which an inferior is free from the interference of his superior. Because Batutsi are considered fundamentally superior to the Bahutu, there is no field in which they can feel equal. This attitude has been transferred to any hierarchical situation. The complementary attitude of dependence is, of course, expected from the inferior. Inferiority is the relative situation of a person who has to submit to another in a clearly defined field; dependence is inferiority in the totality of life. The dependent person has to submit to his master in any question. There is no domain where he is free even to express a contrary opinion. As the dependent has always to acquiesce even when orders are quite impracticable, he has to conceal his opinions and find excuses for not doing what has been ordered. Double-dealing, politeness, or a utilitarian conception of language, are the only defences of the dependent. Some time ago, a Ruanda deliberative assembly of people of standing was asked its opinion on a contemplated reform. When the most important person had given his views, everybody voted for his proposition. But after the assembly, many expressed disagreement. At the time of the vote, they had considered it improper and impolite not to agree with their superior.

On the other hand, no superior enjoys a purely arbitrary power. There are norms which are informally enforced by social pressure; and this is particularly important for people so concerned about their reputations. Since, moreover, there are several chiefs of equal rank belonging to different political structures, it is not difficult for the subject of one superior to secure support in opposing him from another. Finally, there is the possibility of appeal to a higher authority empowered to control subordinate chiefs. All this limits, in fact, the authority of chiefs, but nevertheless the authority of a superior cannot be questioned by his subjects. They may escape, intrigue, or look for another protector, but they cannot offer direct opposition. The Western conception of contract, derived from Roman law, with well-defined obligations on both parties who are equal before and during the contract, is accordingly not understood or acted upon even by Banyarwanda who have long been familiar with our culture.

Any superior is a protector, and his protection is of the same character as his authority: all-embracing and limited only by his own convenience. In any difficulty, the inferior may ask the help of his master, and, if help is refused, it will not be on the grounds that the superior is not concerned with that aspect of the life of the subordinate. On the other hand, the superior himself will be the only judge of the limits of his intervention, for the dependent has no right to require anything from his superior.

Everywhere men in authority enjoy advantages denied to those whom they command, but it is often felt that justification is needed for these privileges. In Ruanda such rationalizations do not seem to be required. It is taken for granted by everybody, the subjects included, that superiors as such should derive profits from their position. The very high standard of living of Europeans is accepted without any criticism by 'traditional' Banyarwanda not yet imbued with egalitarian principles.

The conception of authority as all-embracing, unlimited, protective, profitable, and of inferiority as dependent, devoid of rights, fundamentally weak, and generally exploited, is exactly suited to a structure of castes composed of human beings who are thought to be fundamentally different and unequal. On these inter-caste relations all hierarchical relations have been modelled. This means that the conceptions and attitudes which have just been sketched pervade most human relations in Ruanda. Indeed, very many human interactions involve persons who, in Ruanda, are placed on a hierarchical scale: man and woman, husband and wife, mother and child, father and son, old and young, craftsman and apprentice, &c., and when there is also a superiority-inferiority situation, even though confined to one aspect of the relation, the whole of that relation is impregnated with inequality.

Another basic principle governing the field of human relations in Ruanda is that of indefinite reciprocity. Whenever somebody receives a service, whenever goods are given to someone, a return is expected. This return is not the exact counterpart of what has been provided and is not due immediately or at a precisely determined time. By the granting of a favour, an almost permanent relationship is established between two persons, extending eventually to their immediate relatives. Undoubtedly some obligations are more formalized, such as those resulting from some kinds of exchange (*kuguza*), loan (*gutiza*), &c. But many relations which, in Western culture, would result in strictly defined obligations, do not have the same consequence in Ruanda. The man who receives a service or a gift is not expected to return its equivalent immediately. Such behaviour would even be frowned upon. He should wait till he is asked to return other services or goods. This is indeed the intention of the man who grants the favour: to put somebody under an undefined obligation.

There are several reasons for these relations of reciprocity. First, in an economy in which there is no standard value in relation to which everything may be assessed, it is not easy to determine a precise equivalent for goods. Second, where there is no standard medium of exchange, such as money, which can be accumulated without deteriorating, it is usually difficult to have the required equivalent to hand. Third, in a material culture in which the technological development does not allow of specialization, one has to rely on many people. It is thus very useful to have permanent debtors. Finally, and this is very important, the principle of reciprocity is much more consistent with other parts of the Ruanda culture than are alternative methods. In that culture people are not regarded as independent and equal. Consequently any relation will be so interpreted as to magnify the elements of dependence and inequality implicit in it. Moreover, to have power over somebody is an ultimate value for the Batutsi. They will thus prefer to keep a debtor under the vague obligation to do something, some day, rather than receive immediate compensation.

BIBLIOGRAPHY

ARIANOFF, A. D'. 'Origine des clans hamites au Ruanda', *Zaïre* (Bruxelles), Jan. 1951, pp. 45–54.

ARNOUX, A. 'Le culte de la société secrète des Imandwa au Ruanda', *Anthropos* (Wien), 1912, pp. 273, 529, 840; 1913, pp. 110, 754.

—— 'La divination au Ruanda', *Anthropos* (Wien), 1918, pp. 1–57.

—— *Les Pères Blancs aux sources du Nil*, Paris, 1948.

CZEKANOWSKI, J. *Forschungen im Nil-Kongo-Zwischengebiet* (Erster Band: Ethnographie: Mpororo, Ruanda), Leipzig, 1917.

DELMAS, P. 'La vache au Ruanda', *Anthropos* (Wien), 1930, pp. 945–52.

DUFAYS, F., and DE MOOR, V. *Les enchaînés au Kinyaga*, Bruxelles, 1939.

GÖTZEN, G. A. Graf von. *Durch Africa von Ost nach West*, Berlin, 1899.

HUREL, E. *La poésie chez les primitifs*, Bruxelles, 1922.

KAGAME, ALEXIS. *Inganji Kalinga*, Kabgayi (Ruanda-Urundi), 1943.

—— 'Le Rwanda et son Roi', *Aequatoria* (Coquilhatville, Congo belge), 1945, no. 2, pp. 41–58.

—— 'Le code ésotérique de la dynastie du Ruanda', *Zaïre* (Bruxelles), Apr. 1947, pp. 363–86.

—— 'La poésie pastorale au Rwanda', *Zaïre* (Bruxelles), July 1947, pp. 791–800.

KANDT, R. *Caput Nili*, Berlin, 1921.

KLUCKHOHN, C. 'Covert Culture and Administrative Problems', *American Anthropologist* (Menasha, Wisc.), vol. 45, 1943, no. 2, pp. 213–27.

—— 'The Philosophy of the Navaho Indians', in *Ideological Differences and World Order*, ed. by F. S. C. Northrop, New Haven, Conn., 1949, pp. 356–84.

—— and LEIGHTON, D. *The Navaho*, Cambridge, Mass., 1946.

—— —— *Children of the People*, Cambridge, Mass., 1947.

LACGER, L. DE. *Ruanda*, vol. 1 : *Le Ruanda ancien*, Namur, 1940.

LASSWELL, H. D. *Power and Personality*, New York, 1948.

LOUPIAS, P. 'Tradition et légende des Batutsi sur la création du monde et leur établissement au Ruanda', *Anthropos* (Wien), 1908, pp. 1913.

NAIGIZIKI, J. S. *Escapade ruandaise*, Bruxelles, n.d. (1950).

PAGÈS, A. *Un Royaume hamite au centre de l'Afrique*, Bruxelles, 1933.

—— 'Au Rwanda. Droits et pouvoirs des chefs sous la suzeraineté du roi hamite. Quelques abus du système', *Zaïre* (Bruxelles), Apr. 1949, pp. 359–77.

PAUWELS, M. 'La magie au Ruanda', *Grands Lacs* (Namur), Oct. 1949, pp. 17–48.

SANDRART, G. *Cours de droit coutumier*, Astrida (Ruanda-Urundi), 1930 (mimeographed).

SCHUMACHER, P. 'Caractériologie au Ruanda', *Zaïre* (Bruxelles), June 1948, pp. 591–624.

—— 'Au Ruanda: considérations sur la nature de l'homme', ibid., Mar. 1949, pp. 257–78.

VANHOVE, J. *Essai de droit coutumier au Ruanda*, Bruxelles, 1941.

VAN OVERSCHELDE, G. 'Wat de bewoners van Ruanda, 50 jaar geleden, dachten over God, de schepping, menshen en dingen', *Nieuw Africa* (Antwerpen), 1939–40, pp. 321–5.

—— *Bij de reuzen en dwergen van Ruanda*, Antwerpen, 1947.

THE ASHANTI

By K. A. Busia

Introduction

THERE has been a growing literature about the Ashanti since the early years of the nineteenth century. In 1819 Bowdich, who was the first European to visit Kumasi, published his *Mission to Ashantee* in which he gave descriptive accounts of the laws and customs and the religion and arts of the Ashanti. Dupuis, who was British Consul at Kumasi in 1820, also published accounts of the Ashanti in his *Journal of a Residence in Ashanti*. In 1844 the Rev. T. B. Freeman of the Wesleyan Missionary Society wrote an account of his journey to Kumasi where he was granted a piece of land to build a church.

One of the most famous of the wars between the British and the Ashanti was the invasion of Ashanti in January 1874 when the British forces were led by Sir Garnet Wolseley. Ashanti was widely publicized, especially in Britain, through the crop of books written about the campaign by military officers and war correspondents.

But the most intimate and accurate knowledge of the Ashanti we owe to Captain R. S. Rattray whose books *Ashanti*, *Ashanti Law and Constitution*, *Religion and Art in Ashanti*, and *Ashanti Proverbs* have covered in an admirable way different aspects of Ashanti culture.

The tradition which appears to be the most generally accepted nowadays is that the Ashanti were a part of the Akan stock which migrated to the Gold Coast from what is now the French Ivory Coast. The Ashanti settled in the forest belt where they founded the town of Kumasi in about 1665. The clans in this vicinity formed a military confederation against the neighbouring state of Denkera, to which they were tributary, and defeated it in the Ashanti-Denkera War of 1669. Following this, Ashanti became a powerful nation which conquered one neighbouring tribe after another.

The desire to trade with Europeans on the coast, particularly in order to obtain flintlock guns and ammunition, led to wars with the coastal tribes, and eventually with the British who protected them. The most famous of the eight campaigns fought against the British between 1806 and 1896 were the battle of Insamankow, fought on 21 June 1824, when the Ashanti defeated the British forces and captured and killed the Governor, Sir Charles MacCarthy, and eight other British officers; the battle of Dodowa on 7 August 1826, when the British assisted by allies of the coastal tribes defeated the Ashanti; the invasion of Ashanti in 1874, to which allusion has already been made, and the capture and exile of the King of Ashanti in 1896.

The basis of the Ashanti confederation was military but, in spite of external successes, the available data support the view that even at the height of her military glory Ashanti was not a stable nation internally, for the chiefdoms of the confederation were jealous of their regional autonomy. What held them together was their allegiance to the Golden Stool which was the religious symbol of their unity. The strength of the union rested on military power as well as on religious belief.

The many wars and conquests of the Ashanti brought into their midst slaves, captives, and immigrants from different tribes of the Gold Coast. Ashanti religion was very hospitable, and the Ashanti took over the beliefs, the gods, and the rites of conquered as well as those of neighbouring tribes; from the Moslem north they bought charms and amulets which were highly prized for the protection they were believed to give in battle. None of these borrowed faiths displaced the fundamental beliefs of the Ashanti. New gods and faiths were merely additions which were believed to give more power and protection against the spirits and forces of the world.

Today the Ashanti are largely an agricultural people, though there is an increasing diversity and differentiation of economic pursuits; there are changes not only in economic activities, but indeed in all aspects of life; for as a result of the long contacts with Europe, fifty years of British rule, the rapid growth of the cocoa trade, developments in education, trade and commerce, and transport, and the introduction of new laws and political ideas, Ashanti is undergoing a social change that may be described as a revolution; it may be asked to what extent all this has affected the cosmology of the Ashanti people.

In recent years Ashanti religion has proved similarly hospitable to Christianity. But, as is shown below, the world outlook of the Ashanti and their interpretation of the universe have been but little affected by the turbulent events of the last three hundred years; they have held very largely to their ancestral beliefs and practices.

I

A World of Spirits

To the Ashanti the universe is full of spirits. There is the Great Spirit, the Supreme Being, who created all things, and who manifests his power through a pantheon of gods; below these are lesser spirits which animate trees, animals, or charms; and then there are the ever-present spirits of the ancestors (*nsamanfo*) whose constant contact with the life of man on the earth brings the world of the spirits so close to the land of the living.[1]

[1] The Ashanti form part of the larger body of Akan-speaking peoples widely distributed in the Gold Coast and Ivory Coast who have in common a number of social institutions, religious beliefs and rituals; but the traditional cosmology of the Ashanti differs significantly from that of some other Akan groups. For an account of these, and in particular of the concept of a bi-sexual godhead and its relation to ideas concerning human personality and the divine chieftainship embodied in the king and queen mother, see Eva Meyerowitz, *The Sacred State of the Akan*, 1951, and 'Concepts of the Soul among the Akan of the Gold Coast', *Africa*, xxi. 1, 1951. (Ed.)

The Ashanti conception of the Supreme Being may be gathered from the titles ascribed to him. He is, the Ashanti say, older than all the things that live on the wide, wide earth (*Asase tere, na Onyame ne Panin*). He is *Onyankopon*, Alone, the Great One; *Tweaduampon*, the Dependable One; *Bore-bore*, the First, the Creator of all things; *Otumfoɔ*, the Powerful One; *Odomankoma*, the Eternal One; *Ananse Kokroko*, the Great Spider, that is, the Wise One; he is also personalized as *Onyankopon Kwame*, the Great One who appeared on Saturday.

According to a well-known myth,[1] *Onyankopon* long, long ago lived very near to men. His abode was the sky. There was a certain old woman who used to pound her *fufu* (a meal of mashed yam or plantain) and, whenever she did so, the long pestle she used knocked against *Onyankopon*, who lived just above in the sky. So one day *Onyankopon* said: 'Because of what you have been doing to me, I am taking myself away far up into the sky where men cannot reach me'. So he went up and up into the sky, and men could no longer approach him. Whereupon the old woman instructed her children to collect all the mortars they could find, and pile them one on top of the other. They did so, till they required only one mortar to add to the pile so that it could reach to *Onyankopon*. As they could not find another mortar, the old woman advised her children to take one mortar from the bottom, and put it on the top. The children accordingly removed one mortar from the bottom, and when they did so all the other mortars rolled and fell to the ground killing many people.

The idea of the original nearness of God illustrated by this myth gains support from the Ashanti belief that everyone has direct access to the Supreme Being. This is expressed in an old Ashanti maxim: '*Obi kwan nsi obi kwan mu* (no man's path crosses another's)', meaning that everyone has a direct path to the Supreme Being. There is another saying: '*Obi nkyere abofra Onyame*', which may mean either, 'No-one shows a child the Supreme Being' (he knows by instinct) or, 'No-one shows the child the sky' (which is the abode of the Supreme Being). It is noteworthy that the Ashanti never had special priests for the Supreme Being, though every god (*ɔbosom*) has a priest. Outside many a house in old Ashanti villages were altars to the Supreme Being[2] which consisted of a three-forked stick cut from the *Nyame dua* (the tree of God) with a basin or pot or gourd placed between the forks. Into the receptacle, offerings of food or wine were placed for the Supreme Being. This did not require the offices of a special priest; anyone could place his own offering in the receptacle. Though many of these altars were to be seen in Ashanti villages some twenty years ago, they have now become extremely rare. This, however, has not affected the belief in the Supreme Being. As the myth of the old woman and her *fufu* proves, the Ashanti have for a long time held the belief that the Supreme Being has removed himself too far for man to approach directly, and can

---

[1] Rattray, *Ashanti Proverbs*, 1916, pp. 20–21.
[2] Rattray, *Ashanti*, 1923, p. 142.

only be approached through intermediary deities. Though Ashanti religious ceremonials concern these intermediary deities and the spirits of the ancestors, the people have a feeling of awe and veneration for the Supreme Being who is high above all deities and who animates them all.

According to Ashanti belief, the gods (*abosom*) derive their power from the Supreme Being. They come from him and are parts of him. A god is but the mouthpiece of the Supreme Being (*Onyankopon Kyeame*), a servant acting as intermediary between Creator and creature. There is a whole pantheon of these gods, for their number is being added to all the time. Some acquire a country-wide fame for a season and then pass into oblivion; while others, like the Ntoa gods of Nkoranza, Wenchi, and Techiman, or the Tano, have become tribal gods, having elaborate annual festivals held in their honour.

Of these deities, the most powerful are those that are the spirits of rivers. An Ashanti myth has it that all the rivers, the Tano, the Bea, the Bosomtwe Lake near Kumasi, and the mighty sea, were children of the Supreme Being. The latter decided to send these his children to the earth so that they might receive honour from men, and in turn might confer benefits on mankind. The Supreme Being himself planned where he would send each of his children. The goat got to know of these plans. He and Bea were great friends, so he told Bea that whenever their father sent for them he should go quickly so that he would arrive before his brothers. One day the Supreme Being sent for his children and Bea ran quickly and got there first; so the father assigned to him the cool and shady forest country which had been intended for Tano, the favourite son. Tano therefore was sent to the grassy plains, and each child in turn was given a place different from the original plan, owing to the goat having revealed the plan to Bea. For this reason, all the worshippers of Tano as well as those of the other sons avoid the goat as a 'hateful creature'. As the myth indicates, the Ashanti regard the rivers as having spirits which they derive from the Creator, and many gods are the 'children' of rivers. 'As a woman gives birth to a child, so may water to a god.'[1]

The god requires a temporary abode and a priest. The temporary abode may be a tree or river, or a rock; or a priest might prepare for the spirit of his god a wooden image or mound of mud daubed with blood and placed in a basin and kept in a temple. The god will not always be present in this temporary abode which he enters at will or when called there by the priest.

Rattray has told in detail how the shrines of the gods are prepared, and how the priests are chosen and trained.[2] Many an Ashanti priest would claim that he was chosen directly by the spirit of the god he serves. It may be he went into the forest and suddenly discovered a flaming stone charged with power, the temporary dwelling-place of a spirit; such was the case of *Di Amono* found at Gyansoso near Wenchi in 1935; the discoverer became

[1] Rattray, op. cit., p. 146.
[2] Rattray, op. cit., chap. xiv; see also *Religion and Art in Ashanti*, 1927, chap. iv.

the priest of the god who had thus revealed himself. This priest-to-be, after the discovery, remained in the forest alone for several days, and when found behaved in a most abnormal way; it was thought that he was going mad, until an older priest who was consulted declared that the man was possessed by the spirit of a god. A shrine containing the stone was subsequently prepared, and the novice was initiated into the mysteries of the priesthood so that he could understand and interpret the will of the god that had possessed him. A similar story is told of the priest of *Kwaku Fri*, still a powerful god at Nwoase where people from all over the Gold Coast come to consult him. The spirit of the god possessed the man who is now his priest while he was away in the forest, where he remained for several days until he was discovered.

The spirit of the god speaks through his priest, sometimes by displacing the personality of the priest, so that he becomes a mere medium behaving and speaking as compelled by the spirit that possesses him. In such instances, a trained spokesman interprets the utterances and gestures of the priest. At other times the priest may interpret the will of the god through drawing leather thongs, or throwing cowrie shells or sticks, or casting a bone or stone die, or watching the fluttering of a slain chicken and the position in which it comes to rest. The gods are besought to grant health, or children, or prosperity in business, or protection from misfortune and from witches.

Animals and trees are also believed to have souls, though not all are powerful enough to cause harm to men: but there are some plants and animals that have powerful souls, and these must be propitiated.[1] Thus an Ashanti craftsman will endeavour to propitiate certain trees before he cuts them. He will offer an egg, for example, to the *odum* tree, saying: 'I am about to cut you down and carve you; do not let me suffer harm.'

In the same way, the drummer, whenever he begins to drum on ceremonial occasions, addresses the spirit of the cedar tree from which the drum is made, saying:

> Spirit of the Cedar tree,
> The Creator's drummer announces,
> That he has made himself to arise
> As the cock crowed at dawn.
> We are addressing you, and you will understand.

A similar invocation is addressed to the 'Elephant that breaks the axe', because the tense membrane of the drum is made of the skin of an elephant's ear:

> Spirit of the Elephant,
> The Creator's drummer announces,
> That he has started from his sleep,
> He has roused himself at early dawn.

[1] Rattray, *Religion and Art in Ashanti*, 1927, chap. i.

Below the gods (*abosom*) are minor deities (*asuman*)[1] that derive their power from the *abosom*, or from the souls of plants and trees. The *suman* may be in the form of beads, or medicine balls carried on strings or in a sheep's horn or a gourd. Some of them are no more than charms or talismans that could be regarded as impersonal forces acting in obedience to secret formulae and operations; the Ashanti themselves, however, believe that ultimately all *asuman* derive their power from some other supernatural beings. A *suman* protects the wearer and guards him against harm, or assists him to gain his personal ends, and functions effectively or not, according to the care given to it.

The Earth too has spiritual power. It is her spirit that makes the plants grow; she has the power of fertility. She is not a deity, for she has no priests or priestesses, and does not divine.[2]

But offerings are made to *Asase Yaa* so that she may help the crops to grow, and guard the farmer from misfortune,[3] and the sense of dependence on the Earth is preserved in the poetry of the drum language:

> Earth, condolences,
> Earth, condolences,
> Earth and dust,
> The Dependable One,
> I lean upon you.
> Earth, when I am about to die,
> I lean upon you.
> Earth, while I am alive,
> I depend upon you.
> Earth, while I am alive,
> I depend upon you.
> Earth that receives dead bodies,
> The Creator's drummer says,
> From wherever he went,
> He has roused himself,
> He has roused himself.

There was belief too in black magic and witchcraft. The forests were believed to be inhabited by the *mmoatia* (the little folk) and by forest monsters and witches.[4] It was the little folk that taught medicine men the arts of healing, and also taught them black magic. In league with the *mmoatia* and the witches (*abayifo*) was *sasabonsam*, the forest monster that was so hostile to hunters and priests. *Sasabonsam* is 'covered with long hair, has large blood-shot eyes, long legs, and feet pointing both ways. It sits on high branches of an Odum or Onyina tree and dangles its legs with which at times it hooks up the unwary hunter.'[5] Belief in these forest monsters is on

---

[1] Ibid., chap. ii.
[2] K. A. Busia, *The Position of the Chief in the Modern Political System of Ashanti*, chap. iii.
[3] Rattray, *Ashanti*, p. 125.
[4] Rattray, *Religion and Art in Ashanti*, chap. iii.
[5] Ibid., p. 28.

the wane, but tales of hunters being taught the arts of healing by the *mmoatia* still linger on, and may be heard in remote villages. Belief in witchcraft is still prevalent.

To the Ashanti Nature is a world of spirits. It is filled with the spirits of rivers, trees, rocks, and animals and with the malignant spirits of fairies and forest monsters. Yet all spirits are subservient to the Supreme Being, from whom ultimately they all derive their power. 'Of the wide, wide earth, the Supreme Being is the Elder.'

II

Man and Society

We need to know the Ashanti conception of the nature of man and society in order to understand fully their world view.

Man is both a biological and a spiritual being. This is recognized by the Ashanti in the myth that a human being is formed from the blood (*mogya*) of the mother and the spirit (*ntorɔ*) of the father. This belief reflects Ashanti social organization. Two sets of bonds, a mother–child bond and a father–child bond, derive from their conception of procreation, and determine two sets of groupings and relationships.

It is believed that the link between one generation and another is provided by the blood which is transmitted through the mother. An Ashanti therefore traces his descent through his mother. The mother–child bond makes him a member of his mother's kin group. He is a member of his mother's lineage which consists of all the descendants of both sexes who trace their genealogy through the female line to a common ancestress. This group is a localized group, and belongs to a chiefdom which it regards as its home. It may be so large a group that the members will seldom all meet together except at the funeral of a member of the lineage. Effective kinship obligations tend to be observed within smaller segments of the lineage; such a segment seldom includes more than four generations of uterine descendants of an ancestress, and living together is important for effective co-operation This was recongized, for in old Ashanti villages the members of a lineage lived close to one another in the same ward. The lineage is also a political unit; the lineage head represents it on the chief's council. The mother–child bond therefore confers the rights and obligations of citizenship. It also determines a man's status and his title to office or property, since succession and inheritance are transmitted in the matrilineal line.

The mother–child bond, which makes a man a member of his mother's lineage, also makes him a member of a wider group, her clan. Every Ashanti lineage belongs to one of the seven clans (*mmusuaban*) of Ashanti. The number of clans is sometimes given as eight,[1] but some of the best authorities on Ashanti custom maintain that there are seven clans in

---

[1] Rattray, *Religion and Art in Ashanti*, p. 64; see also Danquah, 'Akan Society', *West African Affairs*, 1951.

Ashanti and group them thus: (1) Oyoko ne Dako; (2) Bretuo ne Agona; (3) Asona; (4) Asenie; (5) Aduana; (6) Ekuona ne Asokore; (7) Asakyiri.

It is believed that all the lineages of a clan are matrilineal descendants from a single remote ancestress. The clan system is common to all the Akan peoples, and is one of the most important indices of their cultural unity. No clan members of different local lineages can, however, show their genealogical connexion, or even give the name of the ancestress from whom they claim a common ancestry. The concept is therefore mythical, but it is nevertheless an important unifying myth, for members of the same clan behave towards one another as though they were distant kin. The mother–child bond is therefore the basis of a wide net-work of relationships. It links a man with his near kinsmen, his fellow citizens, and with his society, for wherever he travels he will find someone with whom he has lineage or clanship ties.

The biological bond has religious significance too. The commemoration of ancestors links lineages and clans and, through the chief, it links the tribe and nation. Ancestor-worship, as will be shown, emphasizes the unity of matrilineal ancestry.

The father–child bond is a spiritual one. Besides the blood which a man inherits from his mother, the Ashanti believe that every man receives a *sunsum* and also a *kra*. A man's *sunsum* is his ego, his personality, his distinctive character. It is not divine, but perishes with the man. A man's *kra* is a life force, 'the small bit of the Creator that lives in every person's body'. It returns to the Creator when the person dies. It is the Supreme Being that directly gives to a man this spirit or life when he is about to be born, and with it the man's destiny.

It was stated above that the Ashanti believe that a human being is formed from the blood of the mother and the spirit of the father. An old Ashanti informant explained the latter process by saying: '*Sunsum* is that which you take with you to go to the side of the woman and lie with her; and then the *Onyankopon*, the Great One, will take his *kra* and bless your union. You give your *sunsum* to your child, not your *kra*. He comes with his own *kra*. As the Supreme Being gives you a *kra*, so he gives your child his *kra*.' A child receives two spiritual gifts, a *sunsum* and a *kra*. A father transmits his *sunsum* to the child; this is what moulds the child's personality and disposition. The Ashanti believe that a child cannot thrive if his father's *sunsum* is alienated, and a priest sometimes says of a sick child that he is ill because his father's *sunsum* is aggrieved.

In the explanation given by the old informant, he used the word *sunsum*, the personal power, or cast of countenance, or personality of a man. But more often the Ashanti will say that a man transmits his *ntorɔ* (spirit) to his child. The two terms in this sense are synonymous. *Ntorɔ* is the generic term of which *sunsum* is a specific instance. Just as every Ashanti belongs to a clan, so every Ashanti belongs to a *Ntorɔ* group. The latter consists of a group that share the same spirit; it is a 'spirit-washing or cleansing group'.

A man's *sunsum* is a child of his *Ntorɔ*; and all who belong to the same *Ntorɔ* are believed to have similar *sunsum*. Hence it can be rightly said that a man transmits his *ntorɔ* to his children.

Owing to the fact that the practices connected with the *Ntorɔ* have ceased to be generally observed, very few in Ashanti today have clear ideas about it. Though every Ashanti belongs to a *Ntorɔ* category, there are many who cannot answer correctly the question, 'What *Ntorɔ* do you wash?'

For the same reason the answers that are given as to the total number of *Ntorɔ* groupings vary from one locality to another. In Kumasi, a group of experts on Ashanti customs gave the number as seven as follows:

1. Bosommuru:
    Sub-groups, Adufudeɛ, Akrudeɛ, Asadofeɛ, Aninie.
2. Bosompra:
    Sub-groups, Aboadeɛ, Ankamadua.
3. Atwideɛ:
    Sub-group, Agyinadeɛ.
4. Agyaadefoɔ:
    Sub-group, Nkatia.
5. Amoadeɛ.
6. Akankadeɛ.
7. Abankadeɛ.

Dr. Danquah,[1] who has carried out extensive research into the dual family system of the Akan, gives twelve principal *Ntorɔ* groups as follows:

1. Bosompra.	7. Bosomafi.
2. Bosomtwi.	8. Bosomayesu.
3. Bosommuru.	9. Bosom-Konsi.
4. Bosompo or Bosom-Nketea.	10. Bosomsika.
5. Bosom-Dwerebe.	11. Bosomafram.
6. Bosom-Akom.	12. Bosomkrete.

The constant prefix 'bosom' emphasizes the fact that each *Ntorɔ* is believed to be under the aegis of a god (*bosom*). It is also noteworthy that six of these are rivers, one is a lake, and one refers to the sea. The Ashanti myth which declares that these were children of the Supreme Being has been narrated above. In the same way that these children of the Supreme Being share his spirit, so the *Ntorɔ* are children of the rivers from whom they derive their spirits; and in the same way that the *Ntorɔ* is a child of the river, so the *sunsum* of a man is a child of the *Ntorɔ* and shares its nature; thus again, all spiritual power derives from the Supreme Being. As it is the father who is the immediate transmitter of his son's *sunsum* from the *Ntorɔ*, the spiritual bond between father and son is immediate and close.

This spiritual bond is further strengthened by the belief that all who belong to the same *Ntorɔ* manifest the same characteristics. Each *Ntorɔ* transmits a particular type of character to its members. Thus, Dr. Danquah gives

[1] Op. cit., p. 12.

the distinctive character of each of the twelve *Ntorɔ* groups listed above as follows:

1.	Bosompra	The Tough
2.	Bosomtwi	The Human
3.	Bosommuru	The Distinguished
4.	Bosom-Nketea or Bosompo	The Audacious
5.	Bosom-Dwerebe	The Eccentric
6.	Bosom-Akom	The Fanatic
7.	Bosomafi	The Chaste
8.	Bosomayesu	The Truculent
9.	Bosom-Konsi	The Virtuoso
10.	Bosomsika	The Fastidious
11.	Bosomafram	The Liberal
12.	Bosomkrete	The Chivalrous.

In addition, each *Ntorɔ* group has taboos which each member observes; thus the Bosommuru group taboo the ox, the python, and the dog; the Bosompra, the leopard and a white fowl; the Bosomtwi, the bush buck, &c. Each *Ntorɔ* group also has its own sacred day for purification or 'washing of spirits'.

Another practice which linked members of the same *Ntorɔ* was the fact that each *Ntorɔ* had a number of surnames which were commonly borne by the members, and one could tell a person's *Ntorɔ* by his surname. Examples are:

Bosommuru: Osei, Owusu, Poku, Saakodie, Amankwaa, Safo, Nti, Anin.
Bosompra: Dua, Boakye, Boaten, Akyeampon, Ofori, Bediako, &c.
Bosom-Nketea: Duko, Baafi, Adom, &c.

Members of the same *Ntorɔ* also used the same forms of response to greetings, and again the Ashanti man who knew these forms could tell a person's *Ntorɔ* from his response to a greeting. For the three *Ntorɔ* groups above, these responses were:

Bosommuru: *Akudɔnrɔ*; *Aburu*.
Bosompra: *Aku*; *Esɔn*.
Bosom-Nketea: *Essua*; *Anyaado*.

Thus the members of the same *Ntorɔ* were linked by the observance of common taboos, and the use of common surnames and common forms of etiquette. All these served to strengthen the spiritual bond between father and son. The spiritual nature of the bond between them was again emphasized by the fact that a father was held responsible for his son's moral behaviour, and although a son belonged to his mother's lineage, it was the father who was liable for any damages that were claimed if his son committed adultery with another man's wife.

Social values and filial and parental bonds are thus given meaning within the Ashanti system of belief. Man as a biological being inherits his blood from his mother; this gives him his status and membership within the lineage, the clan, and the tribe, and his rights and obligations as a citizen; moreover, as is discussed below, the concept of a life hereafter and of a spirit world, and the consequent worship of the ancestors, provides a religious link and an unbroken continuity with all one's matrikin.

As a spiritual being, a man receives a twofold gift of the spirit: that which determines his character and his individuality he receives through his father; but his soul, the undying part of him, he receives direct from the Supreme Being.

One part comes via his father from the father's *Ntorɔ* which, in turn, receives its spiritual power from one of the river sons of the Supreme Being. The blood that is transmitted through the mother, the personality that comes indirectly from the Supreme Being through intermediaries, and that 'small bit of the Creator which is in every person's body' and which he receives directly from the Supreme Being, combine to make a man what he is.

These gifts, too, define his place in the universe, linking him with the world of nature and of man. All this is what the Ashanti mean when they declare: 'All men are children of the Supreme Being, no-one is a child of the earth (*Nnipa nyina yɛ Onyame mma, obi nyɛ asase ba*).'

III

Political Organization

In the preceding section it was shown that Ashanti social organization is based on the rule of matrilineal descent, and that the mother–child bond makes one a member of a lineage and so of a chiefdom; for an Ashanti Division (chiefdom) is an aggregate of social units: the lineage, the village, and the sub-division. A chiefdom is really a combination of localized lineages inhabiting a given territory and forming a political community.

Ashanti political organization is thus based on kinship. Each lineage is a political unit having its own headman who represents it on what becomes the governing body; that is, representation is based on kinship, and each lineage head is a councillor. The lineage head is chosen by the adult men and women of the lineage.

In a similar way, the chief who rules the tribe is also chosen from a particular lineage by the heads of the other lineages. Kin-right and popular selection are thus combined in the choice of a ruler.[1]

An Ashanti Division was administered on the basis of organized kinship groups through the lineage, village, and sub-division by a system of decentralization.[2] Each unit was left to manage its own affairs under its own head or council, and to provide such public services as it needed by communal labour. Issues that affected the whole tribe were decided by a tribal council of lineage heads.

The principal administrative tasks were the keeping of law and order, the defence of the tribe from attack by other tribes, the maintenance of

[1] Busia, op. cit., chap. i.   [2] Ibid., chap. iii and iv.

amicable relations among persons and groups within the community, and between the community and its ancestors and gods. In the judicial system of Ashanti, the central authority (the chief and his council of lineage heads) took official cognizance only of offences which endangered the good relations between the community and its ancestors and gods, for the maintenance of those relations was deemed essential for the well-being of the community. Other offences were left to be settled by arbitration, but they could be brought before the central authority by swearing the chief's oath; that is, by deliberately uttering words that were tabooed; as this constituted a threat to the amicable relations existing between the living and the ancestors of the chief, it had to be inquired into; what was otherwise a private issue was thus brought under the category of offences which endangered the well-being of the whole community.

This emphasizes the close link that exists in Ashanti cosmology between the world of the living and the world of spirits. The Ashanti believe that there is a world of spirits (*asaman*), where all their ancestors live a life very similar to life on earth, and this conception is implicit in Ashanti funeral rites. The dead are given food and drink and gold-dust to help them on their journey to the world of spirits. Receptacles, bedding, ornaments, and clothing which it is believed they will require in the world of spirits are buried with them, and the newly dead are asked to convey messages to the ancestors.

An Ashanti has his ancestors constantly in mind. At meals, the old Ashanti used to offer the first morsel of food to the ancestors, and to pour libations to them daily. It is believed that success and prosperity in this life depend on the favour of the ancestors. At the grave-yard, before the coffin is finally covered, the deceased is addressed by a member of his lineage:

You are leaving us today; we have performed your funeral. Do not let any of us fall ill. Let us get money to pay the expenses of your funeral. Let the women bear children. Life to all of us. Life to the chief.[1]

That prayer expresses the sense of dependence on the ancestors. They are believed to be constantly watching over their living relatives. They punish those who break the customs, or fail to fulfil their obligations to their kinsfolk. To such people they send misfortune and illness or even death. Stories are constantly circulating in Ashanti villages of deaths caused by the intervention of ancestors, and priests of the gods also often declare that sickness has been caused by an ancestor because of some guilt or misconduct on the part of the sufferer. On the other hand, those who obey the laws and customs and fulfil their obligations receive the help and blessing of the ancestors. The latter see to it that the crops of such people are plentiful, that children are born to them, and that their undertakings prosper.

Accordingly, each lineage has its blackened stool which is the shrine of its ancestors. On this shrine the head of the lineage at the appropriate seasons

[1] Rattray, *Religion and Art in Ashanti*, chap. xii; *Ashanti*, chap. v–ix; Busia, op. cit., chap. ii.

offers food and drink to the ancestors, praying that they may protect the members of the lineage, bless them with health and long life, that the women may bear children, and that their farms may yield food in plenty.

Such beliefs and practices give chiefship in Ashanti a special significance. Every lineage is believed to be protected by its own ancestors, but it is the dead rulers, the ancestors of the royal lineage, that guard and protect the whole tribe or chiefdom.

In the central rite of a chief's installation the chief-elect is gently lowered and raised three times over the blackened stool of the ancestor believed to be the founder of the royal lineage. By this ceremony the chief is believed to have been brought into a peculiarly close relationship with his ancestors. Thereupon his person becomes sacred. This is emphasized by taboos. He may not strike or be struck by anyone; he should not walk bare-footed; and, as the drummer regularly reminds him on the talking drums, he should always tread 'gently, gently; a chief walks gently, majestically', lest he stumble; his buttocks must never touch the ground. The occurrence of any of these incidents would, it is believed, cause some misfortune to befall the community, unless the expected calamity be averted by a sacrifice.

An Ashanti chief is thus important not only as a civil ruler who is the axis of the political relations of his people and the one in whom the various lineages that compose the tribe find their unity; he is also the symbol of their identity and continuity as a tribe and the embodiment of their spiritual values. An Ashanti chief fills a sacred role as the 'one who sits upon the stool of the ancestors'.

That stool, the symbol of his power, is what the famous Ashanti priest, Anokye, described as 'the soul of the nation'. It is the sacred emblem of the tribe's permanence and continuity. The chief as the occupant of the stool represents all those who have occupied it before him. He is the link, the intermediary, between the living and the dead; for, according to the conception which the Ashanti share with other Akan tribes, the dead, the living, and those still to be born of the tribe are all members of one family, and it is the stool that binds that family together.

These sentiments are kept alive in the *Adae* and *Odwera* ceremonies.[1]

At the *Adae* ceremonies the departed rulers are recalled, food and drink are offered to them, and their favours are solicited for the welfare of the tribe. An *Adae* occurs every twenty-one days, known alternately as *Kwasidae* or *Adae Kɛse*, and *Wukudae*. The former, the Great *Adae*, falls on Sundays, and the latter on Wednesdays, so that there are six weeks between one Great *Adae* (*Kwasidae* or *Adae Kɛse*) and the succeeding Great *Adae*, and six weeks between one little *Adae* (*Wukudae*) and the next little *Adae*. So every third week, on an *Adae* day, whether it is a Great *Adae* or a little one, an Ashanti chief officiates before the ancestral stools and prays to his ancestors on behalf of the tribe, asking that the earth may be fruitful, and that the tribe may prosper and increase in numbers.

[1] Busia, op. cit., pp. 27–28.

On the eve of an *Adae* the talking drums announce to the people that the *Adae* falls on the following day. The stool treasurer and the stool carriers will already have secured the sheep and drink that will be needed. Early in the morning the chief, accompanied by his spokesmen (*akyeame*) and elders, enters the stool-house. As they enter the sacred place, they take their sandals off their feet and bare their shoulders as a mark of respect to the ancestors who are believed to be present where their stools are kept. The chief then reverently offers drink and meat from a sheep that is slaughtered there to the ancestors. Placing a piece of meat on each stool, he offers the prayer: 'Today is *Adae*; come and receive this and eat; let the tribe prosper; let those of child-bearing age bear children; may all the people get money; long life to us all; long life to the tribe.'

Then he takes a bottle of rum, pours some into a glass, and letting a few drops fall on each stool he repeats the prayer: 'Today is *Adae*, come and receive this and drink; let the tribe prosper; let those of child-bearing age bear children; may all the people get money; long life to us all; long life to the tribe.'

When the rites in the stool-house are over, a public ceremony is held. The chief takes his seat in an open space or court-yard, surrounded by his councillors, drummers, and minstrels. Each lineage head or sub-chief, accompanied by his subjects and members of his lineage, ceremonially greets the chief and takes his place in the gathering. There is drumming and dancing in which everyone is free to join. The minstrels chant the traditions of the tribe, and the brave deeds of its departed rulers. The talking drums extol the chief:

> We salute you as chief,
> We salute you as chief;
> Who is a chief?
> Who is a chief?
> He is a chief who is worthy to be called master;
> We extol you,
> Man among men,
> Hero, royal of royals.

The drums will call the chief the powerful one, the valiant one, the benefactor and mother of the tribe, the defender of his people. The ruling chief may not himself deserve these appellations, but his ancestors did, and it is as their representative that he is thus addressed and extolled. They praise him because as chief he is the embodiment of the highest values of the tribe, 'the one who sits upon the stool of the ancestors'. It is the ancestors who are recalled at the *Adae* ceremony; it is they whom the tribe seeks to propitiate in order that it may receive blessing from them.

The *Odwera* ceremony was an annual festival which lasted from a week to a fortnight. Sheep, drink, and first fruits of the year were offered to the ancestors and the gods. At one of these ceremonies, when yams, eggs, sheep, and drink were offered to a tribal god by the chief, the priest prayed:

Drɔbo [name of the god], the edges of the year have met. The chief has given you yams, he has given you a sheep, he has given you eggs, and now he has brought this drink. Let the tribe prosper; may the women bear children; do not let our children die [i.e. protect them]; those who have gone to trade, may they get money; may there be peace during the present chief's reign.

As part of the *Odwera* celebrations, the chief and his people in a long procession visited the royal mausoleum (*ban mu*) and offered sacrifices and prayers there also. At one such ceremony the prayer offered to the ancestors was:

Here is food; all you ancestors receive this and eat; the year has come round again; today we celebrate it; bring us blessing; blessing to the chief who sits on your stool; health to the people; let women bear children; let the men prosper in their undertakings; life to all; we thank you for the good harvest; for standing behind us well [i.e. guarding and protecting us]; Blessing, blessing, blessing.

The *Odwera* was also a time for the cleansing of the tribe from defilement, and for the purification of the shrines of the ancestral spirits and tribal gods. The rites of cleansing and purification usually took place in a stream where the chief took a ritual bath, and water was sprinkled on the shrines and on all who were present, as a symbolic act of cleansing. A piacular sacrifice of a black hen symbolized the removal of all that had defiled the tribe, and the new year was begun with a ritual feast which the living and the dead were believed to share. All who partook of this feast were believed to receive strength and health and blessing.

The cycle of rites observed during the *Odwera* portrayed all the elements of Ashanti religious faith: the Supreme Being, the gods, the rivers, and the ancestors were all propitiated. The offerings of food and drink to the ancestors show how human they are in the conception of the Ashanti, as do the direct simplicity and naturalness of the prayers. The dominant interests of the tribe are also shown in the prayers; these are food, drink, prosperity, and increase—those things which are needed for the sustenance of life and the continuity of the tribe. Their preoccupation is with this life, not with the next. They seek aid in order that they may achieve success in this life.

In connexion with the role of the ancestors, it may be added that the Ashanti believe that the land they inhabit belongs to the ancestors, and that the living have inherited from them only the right to use it. They in turn must hand it on to their children. Hence the inquirer is often told, 'The land belongs to the stool; or the land belongs to the chief'. They both mean the same: the ancestors own the land. The stool and the chief are their symbols.

Thus in the Ashanti conception the ancestors sustain the tribe. They have given them the land; they watch and protect them, and send them the things they need. In the ceremonies and prayers described above, the reverence of the Ashanti for their ancestors and their sense of dependence on them are apparent. The ceremonies by which these sentiments are given

expression persist in the face of the revolutionary changes taking place in
Ashanti today. The strength of an Ashanti chiefdom is founded on the
belief in the ancestors, and the sentiments of unity and solidarity associated
with their worship.

IV

The Contemporary Situation

The preceding sections have shown that Ashanti cosmology is predominantly animistic. Though, according to Ashanti belief, the Supreme Being is
remote, he is nevertheless conceived as a spirit and a person; the gods, his
children, are also spirits animated by the Supreme Being, temporarily
inhabiting a tree or rock or river or shrine; men are endowed with blood
and a twofold spirit: first, the man's own personality, second, his soul;
the latter lives on after death in the world of spirits whence the ancestors
watch over the living and protect and guard them. Animals and inanimate
objects too have spirits, and are to be propitiated according as their spirits
are conceived to be strong and potentially harmful or not.

The universe of the Ashanti is largely a personalized universe, and their
behaviour towards the supernatural conceived in animistic terms is the
same as their familiar behaviour in normal human relationships and intercourse. Attention has been drawn to the characteristic naturalness and
simplicity of Ashanti prayers. As accounts given above have shown, the
Ashanti employ the techniques of prayer, sacrifice, taboo, and divination.
The gods are treated with respect if they deliver the goods, and with contempt if they fail; it is the Supreme Being and the ancestors that are always
treated with reverence and awe, a fact which an onlooker who has seen
Ashanti chiefs and elders making offerings or pouring libations to the
ancestors can hardly fail to observe. The Ashanti, like the other Akan
tribes, esteem the Supreme Being and the ancestors far above gods and
amulets. Attitudes to the latter depend upon their success, and vary from
healthy respect to sneering contempt.

The use of charms and amulets which are believed to work automatically,
provided the correct procedure is observed, testifies to the belief in impersonal power; but animistic beliefs and ancestor-worship dwarf the importance and the exercise of impersonal power. The Supreme Being, the gods,
and the ancestors leave little place for it. This is the more so because of the
ceremonialism that has grown round ancestor-worship. It has been noted
that every twenty-one days there is the celebration of an *Adae* in which all
the people join. An *Adae* is marked not only by prayers and sacrifices, but
also by pomp and pageantry, and group dancing and singing. This is a
potent means by which belief in the presence and power of the ancestors is
constantly renewed and strengthened. The ceremonies are a binding force
for the group as a whole, as well as a means of keeping the belief in the
ancestors fresh and strong.

Mention has not been made of the existence of totemism in Ashanti, because the evidence available is too scanty for its nature to be defined with satisfactory clarity. Totemism applies to a wide range of behaviour and belief, as far as West Africa is concerned. Rattray[1] judged from the taboos observed in connexion with the *Ntorɔ* divisions that one aspect at least of the *Ntorɔ* was totemistic. Such evidence as is available shows that the relationship between man and the totem is of the 'respect for services rendered' kind. The totem animal was not eaten or killed, because the myths told how the particular animal befriended the ancestors and helped them during a critical period of their history, either to obtain food, or to escape from a pursuing enemy tribe.

The myths recorded by Rattray belonged to this class; he wrote:

It has been seen that the *ntoro* is considered as being instrumental in the conception of the embryo in the womb. A further proof that this is the belief is given in the following myth—a translation of an account in the vernacular—giving the origin of the first *ntoro* ever bestowed upon man, the Bosommuru *ntoro*.

Very long ago one man and one woman came down from the sky and one man and one woman came up from the earth.[2]

From the Sky God (Onyame), also came a python (*onini*), and it made its home in the river now called Bosommuru.

At first these men and women did not bear children, they had no desire, and conception and birth were not known at that time.

One day the python asked them if they had no offspring, and on being told they had not, he said he would cause the woman to conceive. He bade the couples stand face to face, then he plunged into the river, and rising up, sprayed water upon their bellies with the words *kus kus*,[3] and then ordered them to return home and lie together.

The woman conceived and brought forth the first children in the world, who took Bosommuru as their *ntoro*, each male passing on this *ntoro* to his children.

If a Bosommuru *ntoro* man or woman sees a dead python (they would never kill one) they sprinkle white clay upon it and bury it.[4]

Agyinadie ntoro. This *ntoro* is supposed to have been given to man in a somewhat similar manner, by the crocodile.

Bosomtwe ntoro. This *ntoro* is supposed to have been given to man by Twe, the anthropomorphic spirit god of the lake.

Akankadei ntoro. 'Nyame (the Sky God) very long ago sent down a dove to the earth to a certain man and woman there with his blessing and a promise of children. The Ashanti say that persons of this *ntoro* are to be distinguished by their peaceful natures even to this day.

The Ashanti observe taboos and avoidances not only with regard to the *Ntorɔ* but also with regard to certain curative medicines and charms. A priest may forbid a patient to eat certain foods while undergoing treatment, or to touch certain things, and may prescribe a long list of 'hateful things' (*akyiwade*) which may refer to conduct as well as food and drink. As the

---

[1] *Ashanti*, chap. ii.
[2] This dual origin of man is constantly alluded to in tradition and myths.
[3] These words are used in most ceremonies in connexion with *ntorɔ* and *Onyame*.
[4] A Bosompra man treats a leopard in the same manner.

practices connected with *Ntorɔ* taboos have become obsolete, it is difficult to obtain information that will enable the nature of Ashanti totemism to be clarified. In discussing the contemporary situation it is correct to say that totemism does not count either for practical purposes or in matters of belief or conduct.

It has often been said that Ashanti religion has no ethical content. If this means that the Ashanti do not aspire to grow like the gods, then it would be true. The Ashanti do not seek identification with the Supreme Being or the gods; their emphasis is not on becoming, and therefore there is little emphasis on morality. But the Ashanti have concepts of right and wrong, of acceptable and unacceptable behaviour, culturally defined in terms of their own life and belief and, as has been apparent in the brief accounts given, the ancestors and gods punish those who violate the traditionally sanctioned code, and reward those who keep it. Within their own culture, then, Ashanti religion is ethical. It will be seen from their prayers that the gods and ancestors are expected not only to see that the crops grow, that children are born, that the members of the tribe prosper, that they succeed in their trading ventures or wars; but also that proper behaviour is rewarded and offences are punished. The Ashanti conception of a good society is one in which harmony is achieved among the living, and between the living and the gods and ancestors, a fact that is thrown into bold relief in their judicial system.[1]

There are both Christian and Moslem converts in Ashanti today. The system of belief in a Supreme Being and a pantheon of gods, in animated nature, and in ancestors is not an inhospitable one. Nevertheless, Christianity has been a source of conflict in Ashanti.[2] The nature of the conflict was thus explained in an official report on Ashanti in 1905:

The tendency of Christian converts to alienate themselves from the communities to which they belong is very marked, and is naturally resented by the chiefs who claim their hereditary right, in which they are supported by Government, to make the converts in common with their fellow tribesmen obey such laws and orders as are in accordance with native custom, not being repugnant to natural justice, equity and good conscience.

The Christian converts refused to perform the ordinary services to their chiefs, on the grounds that being Christians they could not take part in 'fetish observances'.

In 1912 a committee consisting of the Governor of the Gold Coast, the Chief Commissioner, three other officials, and representatives of the Missions then working in Ashanti—Wesleyan, Basel, and Roman Catholic—attempted to resolve the conflict by ruling that: 'No Christian shall be called upon to perform any fetish rites or service, but shall be bound to render customary service to his chief on ceremonial occasions when no element of fetish practice is involved.'

[1] Busia, op. cit., chap. iv.
[2] Ibid., chap. v.

The committee further suggested that an 'effort should be made to draw a distinction between fetish and purely ceremonial service'.

The value of these injunctions may be seen from the account of the Ashanti world view given above. The ceremonial occasions when the services of the Christian converts were required could not be 'purely' ceremonial. The convert may indeed be required to do no more than carry a chair or an umbrella or beat a drum; but the occasion may be the celebration of an *Adae*, when the people express their sense of dependence on the ancestors, and pray to them for food and health and children and prosperity.

Though Christianity has won many converts in Ashanti, this fundamental conflict remains. The chief in Ashanti fills a sacral role. Ancestor-worship provides a unity between the political and religious authority of the chief. The Christian churches seek to oust the chief as the religious head of his people; but the office of chief is not, in the Ashanti conception, divisible into secular and sacred, or political and religious, so the conflict remains unresolved. The ceremonialism connected with ancestor-worship has made it a resilient force which Christianity has not assailed. Many Ashanti Christians join in *Adae* celebrations with their fellow countrymen and share the sentiments that the ceremonials keep alive: a sense of tribal unity and continuity, and a sense of dependence on the ancestors. This aspect of Ashanti life has suffered little change from the impact of European civilization and thought.

Nor, so far as can be ascertained, has the Ashanti world view changed. It is a commonplace to describe Christianity in Ashanti and the Gold Coast generally as a thin veneer. The description is not inaccurate or superficial if it means that the people have not taken over the concept of the universe and of the nature of man within which Christianity finds its fullest meaning. The Ashanti Christian most probably still accepts the view of the universe and of man that has dominated Ashanti thought for generations. It is part of his cultural heritage, and he has taken it on, as he has done other aspects of his culture, without much difficulty, and without subjecting it to critical analysis. To most Ashanti people the world is ruled from afar by a Supreme Being who is all-wise, all-powerful, &c., the Creator of all things; below him are lesser spirits, born of the Supreme Being, but closer to men; nearest of all are the ancestors of whom he is reminded daily by speech and action.

The Ashanti concept of man has not changed either; the observance of matrilineal descent, the definition of a man's status and role, and his political and legal rights and obligations, through his membership of his mother's group give the colour of truth to the myth about childbirth; while a man's relations with his father, the latter's moral responsibility for the child, and the part he is customarily expected to play in his marriage, together with all the evidence of daily speech and practice justify the father–child myth that it is the father's *ntorɔ* that gives his son his personality. Moreover, Christian teaching has confirmed the Ashanti conception of the soul. The Bible teaches that God made man in his own image. Long before the Ashanti knew the Bible, they believed that the Creator gave a bit of his spirit to everyone whom he sent to the earth, and that with the gift of that bit of his spirit—the man's soul—was bound up that man's destiny, what he was to become and to do in the world.

On the social level, and in certain details of conduct, Christianity is influencing Ashanti society; but in matters like birth or funeral rites, where questions of the interpretation of the universe come in, the influence of Christianity is slight; for the Ashanti to a large extent still retain their own interpretation of the universe and of the nature of man and society; and the difference between this and the European interpretation of the same phenomena constitutes the fundamental conflict between the Ashanti and the European way of life.

THE FON OF DAHOMEY

By P. MERCIER

THE Fon people constituted the nucleus of the former kingdom of Dahomey, one of the most notable kingdoms of the Slave Coast. Culturally and linguistically they belong to the Aja group—often erroneously called Ewe. The neighbouring Yoruba, who originally dominated them, have exercised considerable influence on the Fon, particularly in the religious sphere.

A dynasty of Aja-Tado origin was established, probably about the end of the sixteenth century. Its history has been known in some detail and its chronology established since the beginning of the eighteenth century, when Dahomean conquest of the coastal areas brought them in contact with the European traders who had settled at Ouidah in the previous century. The economy of the kingdom was mainly dependent on the trade in slaves of which their constant wars produced an unfailing supply.

The remarkable development of the royal organization no doubt owed something to European influence. The authority of the ruler was exercised over many varied fields. The administration was highly centralized; the appointment of all functionaries was—in theory at least—in the hands of the king. In economic matters there was a strict control, not only of exported products—palm oil—but also of food crops. There was also a permanent standing army.

Apart from the ancestral cult, which was independently celebrated by each kinship group, religious life was characterized by the existence of specialized cult groups, each devoted to one of the great groups of gods. Those who had been chosen by the gods, or who had given themselves to the cult, were initiated by the priests in the course of a long period of seclusion in a 'convent' or sacred enclosure. These groups had their own special rituals.

Social stratification was very marked. Officials and priests constituted a superior class relieved from the necessity of daily toil. It was in these circles that the philosophical and religious thought of the Fon was elaborated and preserved.

Conceptions of the Universe and of Society among the Fon

I

Every writer who discusses Dahomean cosmology and religion is confronted by serious difficulties, the importance of which is widely recognized. B. Maupoil expresses the view—which is not unduly pessimistic—that 'a complete description of the mythology of Bas-Dahomey is yet to be attempted'.[1] The multiplication of gods, cults, and myths is such that no detailed account of them has ever been given.[2] Nevertheless they have been the subject of a great number of studies by more or less competent investigators. Dahomean life has many remarkable features, but it is their religion and their concepts of the world which, for a long time, have chiefly aroused and held the interest of observers; and this is not surprising. The extraordinary number of cult centres, of institutions for religious training—'convents' as they are traditionally described—of village and house shrines, is evidence of the important place occupied by religious ideas even within the normal round of daily life.[3] This elaborate complex of religion and mythology, of notions concerning man and the world, cannot fail to challenge the attention, but there is still much to be done before a comprehensive view of it can be presented. Up to the present most of the studies have been concerned with descriptions rather than interpretations, and even these are inadequate. Few authors have attempted a complete picture of the whole. The mass of data is so great that a long time had to elapse before the information collected by Le Hérissé, revised and greatly clarified by M. J. Herskovits, made it possible to disengage certain main elements in the concepts of the gods, the world, and man elaborated by the Fon. Not that they lack the faculty of systematic thought. As Herskovits rightly observes:

In a culture as highly organized as that of Dahomey, where the economic surplus has made possible a resulting leisure for ruling and priestly classes, there was no lack of opportunity for the development of a complex philosophy of the Universe. The upper-class Dahomean does not need to restrict himself to describing concrete instances when discussing the larger concepts underlying his everyday religious practice; he is not at a loss when questions of the nature of the world as a whole, or abstract principles such as justice, or destiny, or accident are asked him.[4]

Undoubtedly, the inadequacy of our knowledge is to blame; there are still many obstacles to the construction of a satisfactory synthesis. To this fact are due the limitations of the present study, which inevitably will raise more problems than it can solve.

It is necessary, however, to study more closely the obstacles to an under-

---

[1] B. Maupoil, *La Géomancie à l'ancienne Côte des Esclaves*, Travaux et Mémoires de l'Institut d'Ethnologie, lxii, Paris, 1943. This study, together with A. le Hérissé's *L'ancien Royaume du Dahomey, Mœurs, Religion, Histoire*, Paris, 1911, and M. J. Herskovits's *Dahomey, an Ancient West African kingdom*, New York, 1938, have provided very important material, amplified and sometimes modified by my own observations. They will be frequently referred to by the following abbreviations: B. Maupoil, *La Géomancie*; A. le Hérissé, *L'ancien Royaume*; M. J. Herskovits, *Dahomey*.

[2] Important investigations into this subject have been carried out by P. Verger in his field-work of 1948–9, the results of which have not yet been published.

[3] An example of this unusual wealth of religious institutions is given by C. Merlo who, in his study of Ouidah, gives a list of all the shrines, temples, and convents. See Merlo: 'Hiérarchie fétichiste de Ouidah', *Bull. de l'IFAN*, ii. 1–2, jan.–avril 1940, pp. 1–86. See also the less factual estimate, by Herskovits, of the shrines and magical apparatus within the limits of 'a walled compound of an average householder who is, perhaps, the head of an extended family' (*Dahomey*, ii, pp. 298–300).　　　　[4] Herskovits, op. cit., p. 296.

standing of the whole system. Even the results of serious scientific inquiries
have a certain heterogeneous quality which no method of arrangement can
overcome. This wealth of religious and cosmological ideas presents diver-
gences, contradictions, double versions of myths. These may be accounted
for, more or less, by the social and historical contexts in which they have
developed and by the organization of those specialized groups which have
preserved them. On the one hand, these people who today seem to be so
conservative—at all events in the religious sphere—have always displayed
an innovating spirit, even in that very sphere. Their religion and their cosmology undoubtedly have composite origins; up to quite a recent date[1] they
have borrowed, and more or less completely assimilated, a number of very
diverse elements. But even this is a simplification: borrowings and developments have not followed the same course in the different provinces, some of
which formed part of the kingdom of Dahomey for less than 200 years;[2]
hence these well recognized local variations. On the other hand, the organization of cult groups itself militates against uniformity of religious thought.
Each of these, devoted to the cult of a certain group of deities, with its own
temples and 'convents', enjoyed a considerable degree of independence,
and possessed also, by virtue of its specialization, its own outlook on the
world and the gods. This is a variant of another kind, which does not coincide with regional variations. It is clear, therefore, that not one but several
syntheses will be necessary unless these points of view are to be reduced to a
merely arbitrary unity. Thus we must recall the historical and social framework within which the Dahomean cosmology has evolved, in order to
demonstrate the partial nature of the present study.

Among the notable characteristics of ancient Dahomey are to be found
military and aggressive qualities closely bound up with a power of assimilation. Whether in the sphere of economics, of art, or of religious thought, it
was able to gather a harvest everywhere. The ruling dynasty itself came
from outside, though, it is true, from a people of related culture; imposed by
force, it displayed on a number of occasions a remarkable power of innovation,[3] and this is an important fact. The Fon themselves are the first to
admit the composite character of their religious ideas. Their traditions re-
count the introduction of a certain god or group of gods in a certain reign
historically established. These cannot always be literally accepted,[4] but this

---

[1] These borrowings continue, but the 'true tradition' (in the words of a Dahomean) of
the period of the kings has crystallized to some extent, so that it is generally possible to
distinguish what is prior to the time of European settlement.

[2] The extensive conquests began in the reign of Agaja in the first half of the eighteenth
century.

[3] B. Maupoil rightly observes: 'the kings of Abomey, Allada and Porto-novo were
originally simply popular leaders, not kings by divine right' (*La Géomancie*, p. 65, n. 2). Le
Hérissé, referring to the group which founded the kingdom, says: 'They are seen at first
as a horde of outlaws, settling among alien tribes, forming alliances and then, under cover
of these and using both force and stratagems, spreading out like a stain of oil from the spot
where they had pitched their camp' (*L'ancien Royaume*, p. 273).

[4] Thus it seems unlikely that the cult of the dual deity *Mawu-Lisa* was introduced at
Abomey alone by Agaja (c. 1708–28) or even by Tegbesu (1728–74) since *Lisa* was already

awareness that their religious and cosmological system has been gradually built up by borrowings is something which should be borne in mind. The fact that a date is fixed, even approximately, for the introduction of a certain group of deities and the notions attached to them is one of the curious manifestations of the Dahomean propensity for referring things to history. The dynasty which built up Dahomey in three centuries, and did not shrink from making any innovations which it considered necessary, played such an important part that its history has provided the temporal framework into which all important events are fitted. This mainly secular time scale, which may be called 'royal time', is sufficiently close to our notion of historic time and is often used in the same way. It involves a certain secularization of thought which is not without interest for our thesis. For the concept of a mythical time in which the present is immersed[1] has certainly been modified to allow of the emergence of an element which may be called modern.[2] Nevertheless, it is not entirely obliterated: this mythical time continues to provide the framework within which the relationships and the actions of the gods in the world are displayed. The successive entries of gods at Abomey, apart from the description of them in historical terms, have to some extent, on the religious plane, the character of revelations designed to complete a system into which, according to the people, the gods must needs be more or less successfully incorporated. We shall see in fact that elements of systematization are at work.[3]

In what conditions are the introduction of new gods and new ideas effected? Le Hérissé sees there a result of conquest: on the one hand the king imposed his cults, on the other hand he accepted—'bought'—those of the conquered peoples.[4] 'In this way the "good serpent" (*Dangbé*) was imported into Dahomey by Agaja after the conquest of Savi; the "thunder" (*Hɛvyoso*) from Hɛvie by Tegbesu.'[5] He notes also 'marriages of kings with women from other tribes' who brought their cults with them. The influence of conquest would not appear to be in doubt. Each of the conquered groups had its own ruling gods and these were either added to the Dahomean pantheon or identified with their counterparts in that pantheon. The cultures of the conquered peoples were in no case far removed from that of Dahomey, their ideas were sufficiently similar, and thus the process of assimilation was made easy. In this way the catalogue of what may be described

known at Allada in the seventeenth century (see Labouret and Rivet, *Le Royaume d'Arda et son évangélisation au XVIIe siècle*, Travaux et Mémoires de l'Institut d'Ethnologie, vii, Paris, 1929).

[1] As it is felicitously described, for example, by M. Eliade, *La Structure des mythes: archétypes et répétition*, Paris, 1948.

[2] Maupoil shows discernment in saying: 'Abomey is in no sense the "mystery" town' (as it has been described by a journalist).

[3] It should be added, however, that not all the imported elements were adopted in their entirety, and that some of the missing links must be sought outside Dahomey, especially in the Yoruba country, which had a profound influence.

[4] 'The Dahomeans then bought (to use the classic phrase) the stolen objects of worship, such as the important gods of the conquered tribes, in order to secure their benevolence' (Le Hérissé, *L'ancien Royaume*, p. 102). [5] Ibid.

as national gods was gradually established. Their regional origins are still given today: the dual deity *Mawu-Lisa* came from Aja, to the west of Dahomey, the birth-place of the dynasty; *Hɛvyoso* from Hɛvie (he was a regional *So*—the god of atmospheric phenomena); *Sakpata* from Savalou, to the north of Dahomey, and so on. Although the origins thus traditionally assigned to them, like the dates of their introduction, may be disputed, the process cannot be denied. There is another point to be considered: though the great gods and their myths were likely to be known throughout the kingdom, each region emphasized different elements, and these regional colourings, in spite of the efforts of the kings, could not be eliminated.[1] As already suggested, there are numerous syntheses to be made.

Of what nature was the conscious action of the kings in the religious sphere? B. Maupoil speaks of the organization 'of a kind of state religion'.[2] But this is certainly an exaggeration; one can only say that there was state control over powerful groups of priests and initiates. No temple might be built without the king's cognizance. The intention was, indeed, to make the shrines 'subordinate to the throne'.[3] But it would not appear that the kings intended to control religious thought; if certain cults—such as that of *Sakpata*—were to some extent kept in the background, it was because their power overshadowed the prestige of the monarchy. The kings did, however, define and modify, in areas recently conquered, the relative status of cult groups, reserving the highest place for the specifically royal cults.[4] Control was thus exercised essentially on the social plane, but the kings made no attempt to establish an orthodoxy. The traditional mythology of each cult group and each region continued to flourish in its own particular form.

Here it is necessary to recall the problem raised by Father Williams, who regards the period of expansion in the eighteenth century as marking the complete overthrow of Dahomean religious thought. He sees in it the starting-point of a 'decadence that converted Dahomean belief from monotheistic animism to idolatry'.[5] Without accepting the terms in which this statement is expressed, which belong outside the domain of science, the problem must be examined. Has the impact of external material forces obliterated an earlier conception of the world based on quite different principles? There is no reason to think so. The data on which Father Williams bases his theory of the loss of a primitive monotheism, besides being scanty, are derived in many cases from unreliable observers. It is true that rearrangement may be detected, as well as the substitution of some divine personages for others, and an elaboration of myths, but

---

[1] G. Parrinder notes that the list given by Herskovits is mainly valid for Abomey, the capital, and less so for the provinces ('Theistic Beliefs of the Yoruba and Ewe peoples of West Africa' in *African Ideas of God*, ed. E. W. Smith, London, 1951). This is true, but one has to choose between local variants. Here we shall concentrate on the Abomey point of view.

[2] *La Géomancie*, p. 65.   [3] Ibid.

[4] For Ouidah see C. Merlo, op. cit.

[5] In *Africa's God*, II, *Dahomey*, Anthropological Series of the Beaton College Graduate School, vol. i, no. 2, 1936.

there is nothing to suggest a complete break with the past. The influence of a monarchy founded by an adventurer does indeed mark a new epoch; the era of its successes initiates a period of decadence, but not in the particular sense intended by Father Williams; it is decadent in so far as the word signifies ripeness, a spirit receptive to every new thing. The *Fa* method of divination, introduced from Yoruba country, is a notable example of the remarkable success of some of these new things. In this case it was not the result of conquest: 'It may be admitted that *Fa* was officially introduced into Dahomey in the reign of Agaja, early in the eighteenth century, by a caravan of Nago traders.'[1] The whole *Fa* complex, which is not only a collection of divining procedures, but a system of cosmology, derived, after a number of revivals, ultimately from the ancient East, had a special place in Dahomean thought. A major part of the vast mythology relating to every process of divination was simply naturalized, the names of Dahomean deities being substituted for other elements. The mythology is extremely intricate and often contradictory, as might be expected in view of the many migrations of this geomantic complex.[2] But *Fa* has been inserted into the very heart of Dahomean cosmology; it represents the expression of the will of *Mawu* regarded as the chief agent of creation: *Fa* is the word of *Mawu*, and is even identified with *Mawu*.[3] In less than two centuries the assimilation of *Fa* had reached that point. Other examples may be found of its penetration of Dahomean myths.

As we have seen, this process of elaboration took place within specialized cult groups. These were the repositories of the myths which furnished the explanation of the world. And being many, they present in a different way the problem of the multiplicity of orthodoxies. Religious training, apprenticeship in myth and ritual, were carried out within the framework of formally organized communities, directed by the priests. These, with the neophytes whom they trained, were specially dedicated to the service of one god or group of gods (*vodũ*). It would seem that a cult group originated in the first place within the matrix of a kinship group.[4] This fact is offered in explanation of regional variants. But the situation changed as cults became diffused. A man can be initiated into any cult group, and thereby enters a specifically defined world of myth, to some extent autonomous. A congregation does not despise gods other than its own but, in accordance with its own view of the universe, assigns them their places. M. J. and F. S. Hersko-

---

[1] B. Maupoil, *La Géomancie*, p. 50. In this instance, the tradition seems to be historically accurate.   [2] Ibid.
[3] M. J. and F. S. Herskovits, *An Outline of Dahomean Religious Belief*, Memoirs of the American Anthropological Association, 41, 1933.
[4] See M. J. Herskovits, *Dahomey*, ii, p. 169: 'the opinion was voiced that those who know the very core of Dahomean religion can connect all the supernatural founders of sibs with some pantheon, at whose instigation these founders came to earth, and, conversely, since each *vodũ* was revealed to an individual family, whose members were instructed how to organize its worship, and through whose teachings its corps of devotees was made larger, all the *vodũ* are, in the final analysis, to be regarded as associated with human descent-groups.'

vits rightly point out that the initiate 'identifies himself with the cult of a particular pantheon with which he is associated. In a word, he belongs to a church.'[1] The part assigned to the gods in the creation, organization, and preservation of the world of men varies according to the different perspectives adopted by the specialized cult groups. Any summary account, therefore, which attempts to stress the common elements must slightly distort the picture. In any study of Dahomean religion and cosmology, if confusion is to be avoided, these essential data must not be lost sight of. The variety of contributed elements, more or less completely assimilated, the regional variants, the multiplicity of orthodoxies, constitute the chief obstacles to a synthesis. Moreover, it is in this environment of fluidity and diversity of thought that the Fon lived in the past and still, to some extent, live today. There is no question of attempting to reconstruct an earlier system of myths possessing a completely satisfactory unity, more particularly since there are not really a number of cosmologies; there is, rather, a common conception widely diversified in its details, and modified in varying degrees among the different groups by a number of influences. In the remarkably vigorous thought of the Fon nothing is rigid—at least up to the colonial period;[2] imported notions have been able to move from the circumference to the central core of myths already fully developed and generally accepted in their main outlines. This elaboration of composite data strikes the inquirer as one of the most original characteristics of Fon thought. In this meeting-place of influences—not merely determined by historical conditions but consciously accepted—thought is always open, but not, on that account, unsystematic. A number of elements, the assimilation of which is not essential, remain on the fringe; fundamental data are adopted and used to enrich the already developed system.[3] Thus a classification of the gods has been arrived at, even though some which have been placed in the same group derive from different horizons. But at another level a remarkable stability may be discerned, and that is in the essential pattern of the myths. There are structural moulds in which very diverse material is organized, and, more important, these patterns have exact correspondences in the social sphere. M. J. Herskovits has already shown the parallels between the political and social organization and the organization of the world of gods.[4] But it would seem that the problem should be regarded from the dynamic point of view. Here we have categories of thought, instruments of systemization; for example, the principle of dualism, which may be seen in divine

[1] Op. cit.

[2] B. Maupoil describes it thus: 'In face of a body of believers, who, as a result of the upheavals of conquest, were rapidly developing, with a consequent sharpening of their critical faculty and their desire for knowledge, in face of Christian and Moslem propaganda, the priests remained confined within an immovable and obsolete world, of which all the possibilities had already been expressed' (La Géomancie, p. 66). This judgement cannot be wholly accepted. .

[3] This is a simplification; one should rather speak of systems, characterized by their own variants, elaborated by each of the great cult groups.

[4] Dahomey, ii, pp. 293 ff.

persons as well as in the chief functions of human society, and which has been applied to imported gods as well as to newly created functions. This point will be examined in detail later. It would appear that the guiding principles according to which this people, so apt to borrow from all sources, has elaborated its myths, are no less important for an understanding of its cosmology than the content of the myths themselves. A study of this problem should produce valuable results, but it has many difficulties due to the inadequacy of comparative historical material.

II

In the following discussion we shall take as our basis data concerning the adherents—both priests and laity—of the cults of *Lisa* and *Dã*, referring throughout for comparison to information furnished by the principal writers on the subject. The check thus provided, as well as the homogeneity of the group of informants, should authenticate the description. It must be admitted, however, that such a brief account cannot but result in some over-simplification of the facts. We shall note, in passing, the composite character of the whole and, at the same time, the power of co-ordination which has given it, at least as regards the main elements of the mythology, a certain coherence.

The creation and the setting in order of this present world in which men live are not regarded as unique events. There has been a series of worlds and, no doubt, a series of creators. This substratum of the cosmogony is not clearly defined but is always referred to more or less directly as a necessary preliminary. M. J. Herskovits mentions it twice: first when recounting the myth of the parentage of the dual deity *Mawu-Lisa*, said to be the offspring of *Nana-Buluku*, a myth to which we shall return later;[1] then in connexion with the difficulties he experienced when questioning his informants about the first beginnings:

For the Dahomean reasons that while it is true that the world, as he knows it, was founded by Mawŭ, some being must have existed before Mawŭ, a being who had the power of creating Mawu. . . . If pressed to explain the ultimate origin of the Universe, the Dahomean philosopher replies that there are things that men cannot explain . . . but that his own reason tells him, 'there may have been many Mawŭs.'[2]

These data are somewhat confused and are merely mentioned here before we proceed to the explanation of the existing world. But the idea of a succession of worlds and of creators should not be lost sight of, even if it does not seem altogether clear. It is the background against which appears a deity, or rather a semi-personal power, universally named *Dã*, who is present at the side of the creator, acting at once as instrument and as conscious assistant in the work of ordering the world. This organizing power, this force of life and motion, is sometimes described as the first created being; other informants claim that it coexists with *Mawu* and its origin is to be

[1] Ibid., pp. 101, 291.   [2] Ibid., p. 290.

found in the domain of earlier worlds.[1] It seems probable that in this context an answer can be found to the much debated question of the existence of a supreme deity among the Fon. It is, in fact, said that *Mawu* (the name for the dual deity *Mawu-Lisa*) was created by *Sɛ* or *Sɛgbo* or *Sɛmɛdotɔ*[2] and also that *Mawu* is *Sɛ*; or even that all the gods (*vodũ*), including *Mawu*, were created by an earlier deity, and at the same time that *Mawu* gave birth to all the *vodũ*. I think it is simply that this truth has two aspects; if one is considering only the existing world, or the sequence of successive creations,[3] *Mawu* is the creator; but it is possible to go farther back, either to *Nana Buluku* or to an earlier *Mawu*. There is here a dilemma which has been made vastly more complicated by the attempt to explain it away in accordance with European notions. The difficulties experienced by missionaries illustrate another aspect of the problem. At the outset they translated God as *Mawu*—and Catholics continue to do so—but they had to oppose the cult of *Mawu* along with other 'fetishes'; this they did in the name of another *Mawu* whom they called *Sɛgbo*. This means detaching *Mawu* from the polytheistic complex in which he is simply *primus inter pares*, or rather it means passing unintentionally into the confused sphere of successive creations.[4] Protestants are aware of the difficulty and prefer to adopt a specially invented name.[5]

At the beginning of the present world, then, there are the pair *Mawu-Lisa*. They are at the head of the group of sky gods who are their offspring, as are also the other gods, of earth, &c. A number of points must be noted here. We have already seen that *Mawu-Lisa* did not represent an absolute beginning. The most clearly defined expression of this fact introduces an androgynous deity *Nana Buluku*, the progenitor of the dual creator. Although there is no specific cult of this divinity in Dahomey his pre-eminence in relation to all the heavenly deities is recognized.[6] But after reference has once been made to him at the beginning, he does not appear in the myths of the ordering of the world. It would indeed be better to speak of the 'ordering' of the world rather than of 'creation'. When *Mawu-Lisa* 'create' they seem indeed to use pre-existing material. They are demiurges rather than creators, and this is not surprising in the light of what has been said in the preceding paragraph. We may note, on the other hand, that in all the Dahomean myths of origin an essential element is the genealogy of the

[1] Cf. Herskovits: 'Aido Hwedo [the principal manifestation of *Dã*] . . . belongs to no pantheon. Instead, he pervades them all as the personification of those deities who lived before man existed and who, though individually unknown to man, must not go collectively unworshipped' (*Dahomey*, ii, p. 291).

[2] These are abstract terms used to denote the Creator.

[3] An informant represents 'the first *Mawu*' as coming to explain to the actual *Mawu* that this world is only the replica of another. This is probably an individual interpretation, but it is significant.

[4] The needs of missionaries do not concern us here, but the fact that these positions should have been adopted, without analysing them, in describing the facts, has produced the most unfortunate confusion.

[5] For example, *Ji-xwe-yɛhwe*, 'spirit of the heavens'.

[6] Cf. M. J. Herskovits, ibid., pp. 102-3.

vodũ; this is of primary importance; the intention is, in the first place, to take into account the distribution among the gods of the different forces which act on men. They speak of the world of the *vodũ* rather than of the relations between the *vodũ* and this world. In this hospitable pantheon the dominant preoccupation is to place in a suitable order the borrowed divine personalities. We have already pointed out that the multiplicity of cult groups has militated against the establishment of a generally accepted hierarchy and genealogy.

In the dual *Mawu-Lisa*, *Mawu* is female and *Lisa* male. In reference to their birth, in which *Nana Buluku* is concerned, they are regarded as twins, and their union is indeed the basis of the organization of the world.[1] Sometimes their connexion is expressed more definitely by the conception of an androgynous, self-fertilizing being. Herskovits never heard this notion spoken of except among the priests of *Sakpata*, but it is to be found elsewhere: 'Mawŭ . . . is envisaged as a Janus-like figure, one side of its body being female, with eyes forming the moon, and bearing the name of Mawŭ . . . . The other portion is male, whose eyes are the sun, and whose name is Lisa.'[2] Nevertheless, in all descriptions, after *Mawu-Lisa* has once been mentioned, the name *Mawu* alone is used. This pair is nowadays connected with the two most important heavenly bodies: the moon (*Mawu*) and the sun (*Lisa*).[3] On the other hand, their dual and conflicting nature expresses, even before the world of men was organized, the complementary forces which were to be active in it. *Mawu*, the female principle, is fertility, motherhood, gentleness, forgiveness; while *Lisa* is power, warlike or otherwise, strength and toughness. Moreover, they assure the rhythm of day and night. *Mawu* is the night, the moon, freshness, rest, joy; *Lisa* is the day, the sun, heat, labour, all hard things. By presenting their two natures alternately to men, the divine pair impress on man the rhythm of life and the two series of complementary elements of which its fabric is woven.[4] The notion of twin beings, to which we shall return, expresses the equilibrium maintained between opposites, which is the very nature of the world. The ideal birth is a twin birth; the first men always reproduced themselves thus, and the fact that this is more rare now is evidence of a fall. The cult of twins (*xoxo*) has an important place in Dahomean life.

[1] Here again a problem of origins arises. Some modes of representing this union would suggest that *Mawu* was an earth god, fertilized by *Lisa* the sky-sun. Though both are now heavenly deities, the *Sakpata* group represents earth gods. Referring to the symbolism of *Gbaadu*, J. Bertho writes: 'the black powder of charcoal of Dou, yekou-medji, would be the symbol of the earth gods: Mahou (odoudoua, a word suggesting the notion of blackness in Yoruba) and Sakpata . . .' (J. Bertho, 'Le culte du Gbadou chez les Adja du Dahomey et du Togo'). There might be a displacing of divinities here.   [2] *Dahomey*, ii, p. 129.

[3] A statue in the museum at Abomey represents *Mawu* in the form of a woman wearing the insignia of the initiates of the god, and holding a rod which supports the moon. According to popular opinion the lunar eclipse is the sexual union of *Mawu* and *Lisa*.

[4] Summing up the opposing qualities of *Mawu* and of *Lisa* Herskovits says: 'in Dahomean thought coolness symbolizes wisdom, and wisdom comes of age, and thus it is that in Mawŭ is concentrated the wisdom of the world, and in Lisa its strength (ibid., p. 103). I have myself never heard these ideas expressed in so abstract a form.

It is necessary to give in outline the diagram of the universe according to the Fon, before describing the successive stages in its organization. The universe is a sphere which may be compared to two halves of a calabash, the edges of which match exactly; the join is the line of the horizon. The surface of the earth, which is flat, lies on this horizontal plane. The first sphere is enclosed in another larger sphere, and between the two are the waters. The smaller sphere is mobile: 'The little calabash floats in the large one.' The waters outside it are the source of the rains. But within the smaller sphere there are also waters—they form the sea. It surrounds the earth, not only on the plane of the horizon, but also beneath it. 'This is why one finds water if one digs deep into the earth', says B. Maupoil, adding, 'Water surrounds the earth, covering the whole surface of the half-calabash.'[1] The heavenly bodies revolve on the inner surface of the smaller calabash. The process of ordering the world before the creation of man consisted essentially in gathering together the earth, determining the place of the waters, securing the welding together of the whole. This is where *Dã* plays a decisive part in the process. We have already pointed out that he has the character of a force rather than a divine person: he controls all life and motion and without him *Mawu-Lisa* could not have organized the world. It is only popular belief which has made him, in the same way as the other *vodũ*, a son of the divine pair.[2] *Dã* manifests himself in the world in a number of ways; it is said that there are many *Dã*, or rather manifestations of *Dã*, but the chief of them is *Dã Ayido Hwɛdo*, most commonly seen as the rainbow. In this form he appears in the myths of creation and 'gives birth to' all the other *Dã*. We may note that the name of this power means 'serpent', and it is always conceived as a serpent, the symbol of flowing, sinuous movement; but not all serpents are identified with *Dã*.

Without this life-force, which they made use of to give form to the world, the creative pair could not have carried out their task. *Dã Ayido Hwɛdo*, coiling himself round the inchoate earth, enabled it to be gathered together. '*Dã Ayido Hwɛdo*, gave us a place to live in.' When *Mawu* was creating beings to cover and people the world, it was *Dã Ayido Hwɛdo* who carried him through the length and breadth of the universe. He was to encircle the world when it was made and keep it firm. It should be pointed out that *Dã Ayido Hwɛdo*, like *Mawu-Lisa*, has dual aspects, one male, one female, and these also are sometimes conceived of as twins. All the other *Dã* are their offspring. He is, however, one being with a dual nature rather than a pair.[3]

---

[1] Maupoil's description is accurate on the whole (*La Géomancie*, pp. 62–63).

[2] In expansion of the foregoing account cf. the information given to Herskovits: 'At the beginning of the world, before Mawŭ had borne children, and before Sogbo existed, Aido Hwedo, the serpent, had been created by whoever created the world' (*Dahomey*, ii. p. 248). It is clear from this text, also, how impossible it is to speak of one absolute beginning.

[3] He is compared to the hyena (*hla*) which, in Dahomean legends, is at the same time male and female. In the shrines of *Dã* there are two pots on the altar, one representing the male *Dã* and the other the female; but another pot, buried underneath the altar, is the true representation.

When he appears as the rainbow 'the male is the red portion, the female the blue'. Together they sustain the world, coiled in a spiral round the earth which they preserve from disintegration—if they slackened it would be the end of the world—and under the sky which they uphold, with the world of gods. There are said to be 3,500 coils (*xasa-xasa*) above and 3,500 coils below. There is also another form of the myth according to which *Dã* set up four iron pillars at the four cardinal points to support the sky, and twisted round them in spirals threads of the three primary colours, black, white and red, to keep the pillars upright in their places. Black, white, and red are the colours of the garments which *Dã* puts on at different times: night, day, and twilight. Whatever the form of the myth, the coils made by *Dã* around the earth are not stationary. '*Dã Ayido Hwɛdo* revolves round the earth.' In this way he sets in motion the heavenly bodies. We have already noted that his nature is motion; it is also water. Beneath the earth *Ayido Hwɛdo* is submerged in the waters.[1] He may still be recognized today in standing pools (*tã*), which recall the memory of the primordial waters: he is seen cleaving the waters like a flash of light, his voice is heard and then an altar is raised to him close by. In the last great phase of the ordering of the world, when it acquired its present form, *Dã* also plays a necessary part. When he carried the creator from end to end of the earth, wherever they rested a mountain arose: some say they are *Dã's* excrement; but this name (*dã mi*) is chiefly given to metals and stones found nowadays in the earth. In his quality as excretor of metals *Dã* is said to partake of the nature of the sun.[2] On the other hand, in his travels over the earth *Dã* traced out the courses of the streams; till that time there were only stagnant waters (*tã*); he dug out channels in which the waters were to move. Thus the world was made ready to receive life. But the activity of *Dã* did not end there, as we shall see.

Dã has a necessary function in relation to *Mawu-Lisa*, though a subordinate one. B. Maupoil writes: 'He is always the servant of *Mawu* and *Lisa* because motion is subjected to life.' But an informant corrects this statement: 'It should rather be said: *Dã* is life and *Mawu* is thought.' At all events, at the time of this process of organization the other *vodũ* are not yet present, though it is not universally agreed that they were not born till afterwards. There may well be some confusion here, as was pointed out at the beginning of this paper. The *vodũ* are assigned their parts in the government of the world; creation is not regarded as their function. Their power may be so great and their punishments so greatly feared that their cults become of the first importance; for example, *Hɛyvoso* (*Sogbo*) and *Sakpata*, whom Maupoil describes as 'heroes of the popular pantheon': the first is lord of atmospheric phenomena, thunder is his weapon; the other rules

[1] Cf. B. Maupoil, *La Géomancie*, p. 74: 'If it is said that *Dã* dwells in the ocean (*xu*), this is because he represents for man the greatest conceivable power in ceaseless motion.'

[2] B. Maupoil raises the question: 'What is the relation between this source of life and the sun?' and he points out, in an earlier passage: 'Is it not said that *Dã* causes the Sun to move?' '*Hwɛdo* is gold, that is *hwe*, the sun' (ibid., pp. 74–75).

the earth, his weapon is smallpox.[1] There are many versions of the
genealogy of the *vodũ*, and any attempt to reconcile them would be highly
artificial.[2] There is general agreement, however, that *Mawu-Lisa* gave birth
to all the *vodũ*.[3] When the world had been put in order, each of the great
vodũ was given one of the 'domains' of which it was composed. Each of
these is head of a group of *vodũ*, genealogically related to him, and his name
is applied to the whole group. The earth is assigned to the dual deity
Sakpata; atmospheric phenomena to the androgynous *Sogbo*; to *Agbe-
Naetɛ*—twins of opposite sex—the sea and the waters (this last group is
linked with that of *Sogbo*); to *Agɛ* the wild, uncultivated land where no men
live. Each of these 'domains' is subdivided: a high degree of specialization
is an essential quality of the *vodũ*, and the differentiation of function is continued indefinitely. Each group of *vodũ* has its own language which is un-
intelligible to the others. At this point appears the last of the *vodũ* born of
Mawu-Lisa, *Lɛgba* whom we shall discuss more fully later. He has no
special domain, but acts as observer and interpreter between the *vodũ*.[4]
There is, however, another *vodũ* without a domain who also has an important function in the cosmogony, and that is *Gu*, generally referred to as
the *vodũ* of iron and having the character of a culture hero. He is the only
one whom we shall describe in some detail. He is one of the group of sky
gods directly under the authority of *Mawu-Lisa*.[5] One genealogy shows him
as the eldest son of *Mawu-Lisa* and the twin of *Hɛvyoso* who, like him, is
lord of iron. *Gu* is lord of the domestic hearth and of crafts.

Having set the universe in order and created, in the course of his wanderings, the vegetation of the wilds and the animals—the first of which was
azũi, the hare—*Mawu* formed the first human beings from clay and water,
'the mixture being worked over in the same manner that clay and water are
worked to provide building-material for the walls of a house.'[6] We shall refer
to this later when discussing the relations between the souls of men and the
creative powers. Man thus created was to receive instruction from the gods.
When the order of creation is related to the Dahomean week of four days,[7]
it is said that the world was put in order and man was formed on the day
ajaxi; on the next day, *miõxi*, the work was interrupted, but *Gu* appeared who
was to be the agent of civilization. On the third day, *odokũi*, man was given
sight, speech, and knowledge of the external world; on the last day, *zobodo*,

---

[1] He is commonly known by the name of 'small-pox fetish'.

[2] See the introductory section, pp. 211–17 above.

[3] I have on one occasion heard this disputed: an informant asserted that the *Sakpata*
group of *vodũ* are not the offspring of *Mawu-Lisa*. This supports the view that *Mawu* is an
earth deity who was supplanted in this function by *Sakpata* (who is, moreover, not female
but a pair of twins of opposite sex). The problem has not yet been solved.

[4] He is one of the powers, like *Dã* and *Fa*, to which all the specialized cult groups give a
place alongside the one to which they are directly attached.

[5] His importance is recognized by G. Parrinder (op. cit.) who notes: '*Gu* . . . is often
added as third of a triad (*Mawu, Lisa, Gu*).'

[6] Herskovits, *Dahomey*, ii, p. 232.

[7] It is possible, but by no means certain, that this may be a recent adaptation, due to
European influence.

he was given technical skills.[1] Herskovits rightly says, 'it is Gŭ who was charged with making the earth habitable for man, and this work he has never relinquished'.[2] There are two different accounts of the nature of *Gu*. He is regarded either as a person or as an instrument in the hands of *Mawu-Lisa*.[3] As a person, he is the heavenly blacksmith,[4] patron of the blacksmiths of the earth and inventor of all crafts (except weaving, which is not mentioned: clothing was made of bark-cloth). He is identified with iron and with his emblem the *gubasa*, a kind of ceremonial sword.[5] In relation to *Mawu-Lisa*, *Gu* is specially linked with *Lisa*, strength and the sun. Man was given technical skills at the time of a journey taken by the creator, like the one he made when putting the world in order. But this time it is the creator in his character as *Lisa*, accompanied by his helper or instrument, *Gu*, who travels over the earth. I have heard the same version of the myth as that given by Herskovits but with this difference that *Lisa* is not regarded as the son of *Mawu*—evidently a mistaken conception which surprises him.[6] *Lisa* comes down to earth holding *Gu* in his hand in the form of a *gubasa*.

. . . when Mawŭ gave it to Lisa, he told him to go to earth and clear the forests, and show human beings the use of metal so that they might fashion tools with which to enable them to obtain food, and to cover their bodies, and to make shelters. Therefore, when Lisa came to earth with Gu, he cut down the trees, taught men how to build shelters and instructed them how to dig the ground.[7]

He gave man tools and taught him the art of the smith. Herskovits's informant adds: 'Therefore it is held that Lisa re-established the world.' This is indeed a second creation, equal in importance to the first: 'Men had been blind and their eyes were opened.' At the same time, *Hevyoso* caused the first fall of rain, and *Mawu*, source of fertility, sent down the first seeds which were sown in the fields prepared by *Lisa* and *Gu*.

These are the main elements of the Fon cosmogony. Two great labours: the ordering of the natural world and of the world of men. The two persons of the dual deity *Mawu-Lisa* each have a special function in the process. The first task is primarily the work of *Mawu*, the fertilizer, assisted by *Dā*; the second that of *Lisa*, strength and fire, assisted by *Gu*. But how is the preservation of the world secured? That is where the other *vodŭ*, offspring of *Mawu-Lisa*, appear, each ruling his own domain. But underlying their activity is that of *Dā*. In some cases he acts explicitly as the intermediary between the *vodŭ* and the world: for example, he casts on the earth

---

[1] And with these, according to an informant, happiness. For this reason *zobodo* is the chief ceremonial day.   [2] Ibid., p. 105.

[3] M. J. Herskovits: 'Some of the tales hold that Gŭ is not a sentient being in the way that his brothers and sisters of the Sky pantheon are conceived, but that he is a "force", with a body of stone and a head of iron, though in very early times the head itself also was stone'. Ibid.

[4] M. J. Herskovits: 'Gŭ is also spoken of . . . as a smith himself, and because he is thought of as always at work in his smithy, he is conceived as living only in the open.' Ibid., p. 107.

[5] The blade is pierced with holes of various shapes symbolizing the various sky gods.

[6] Ibid., p. 106, and note 2.   [7] Ibid.

Hɛvyoso's thunderbolts. This is clearly seen in the cult; the shrines of most of the *vodũ* contain an altar dedicated to *Dã*. We have seen that *Dã* is essentially motion. It is necessary to add, as Maupoil says: 'Life is one of those mysterious motions, the pre-eminent motion, which it is the function of *Dã* to maintain.'[1] As the mobile sustainer of the universe which he enfolds in his coils, he is also responsible for all relationships and for continuity. Rather than a person, he is a force which the *vodũ* are constrained to make use of. He ensures the perpetuation of species and in particular of humanity. *Dã* is man's penis, the sperm is the 'water of *Dã*', *Dã* is the umbilical cord, the object of a special cult. It is in this sense that an informant could say: 'It is *Dã* who created man.' In the task of preserving the world *Dã* is the universal servant: of himself he does nothing, but without him nothing can be done.

We must now consider the manner in which mankind was organized—to whom the teaching of the gods was given so that to man was assigned the supreme place on the earth. There are two series of myths which give an account of this organization; one series tells of a division into peoples and countries, the other of the constitution of clans. They need not be regarded as contradictory, but it is not easy to arrange them chronologically. Local myths referring to the division of the known world among the chief nations have no doubt been modified under the influence of the emerging power of Dahomey. It is probable that in the list of the four great countries or nations Dahomey might have been substituted for another.[2] The fact that the versions disagree in certain points is evidence of considerable disturbance, and what we now have certainly represents remains of earlier versions. The only authors who have pointed this out are Le Hérissé, who did not see the implications of it and merely recorded a song which alludes to it, and Maupoil who mentions 'four clans (?) distributed according to the four points of the compass'.[3] Nevertheless these myths—modified in order to make a place in them for the young Dahomey—must long have maintained their vigour, as is shown by the action of Agõglo (*c.* 1789–97). When the Oyɔ (Yoruba) came to demand tribute from him, he set two pigs, one black and one white, to fight each other; the white one prevailed, which was taken as a sign, needing no further explanation, of his refusal to submit and of his certain victory. He had chosen the colours associated with two of the four great countries into which the creator had divided the world, and the defeat of the black pig represented the defeat of Oyɔ. When *Lisa* traversed the earth as the dispenser of civilization, he made four halts in the four quarters of space, thus distributing men over four countries. These original countries are called *sɛdoto* (god-makes-country); they are Aja, Ayɔ (Oyɔ), Ke (Ketu), Hũ. Each was founded on a different day of the week: Aja on the

[1] *La Géomancie*, p. 74.
[2] Cf. B. Maupoil, where Savé takes the place of Dahomey. I am not acquainted with this version, which, it may be noted, was given to him by a diviner of Yoruba origin. In a number of points my information does not agree with that of Maupoil.
[3] *La Géomancie*, p. 65, n. 2.

day *ajaxi*, Ɔyɔ on *miõxi*, Ke on *odokïwï*, Hũ on the day *zobódo*.¹ Dahomey (*Hũ*) was the last born, though called to a noble destiny.² Aja was situated in the west, Ke in the east—these two names are still commonly used to denote the cardinal points—Ɔyɔ in the north, Hũ in the south. In each country *Lisa* placed a stone object as its symbol: a stone in the form of a man in Aja, one resembling a bottle in Ɔyɔ, one having the shape of a calabash in Ke, and one like a *gubasa* in Hũ. Moreover, he linked each country with a colour, an element, and a sign of *Fa* representing its destiny.³ It is not easy to get a consistent picture, and rearrangement may be suspected. Aja is linked with the colour red, the element of fire, and the symbol *Loso-Mɛji*;⁴ Ɔyɔ with the colour black, the symbol *Yɛku-Mɛji*;⁵ Ke with the colour brown (*asãmya*, a mixture of the three primary colours, white, red, and black) and the symbol *Weli-Mɛji*: Hũ with the colour white and the symbol *Gbe-Mɛji*.⁶ Into such categories the Dahomeans distributed the peoples of their world. They are still used as terms of reference even though their range had been extended.

But what is much more significant from the social point of view is the division of humanity into clans founded by divine persons. Each of the original great countries or peoples was composed of a certain number of clans, and the gods assured their continued existence as they had been, in the last analysis, their founders. During the stage when the world was being civilized, the art of living in society was taught to man. According to the myth, the basic structure of all social life is the clan, all the members of which share a common essence and practise the same cult—that of their founder (*tɔhwiyo*). The task of organizing humanity was thus brought to completion by the advent of divine persons who, forming unions with human women, originated human clans.⁷ At this point there first appears *Fa*—the word of *Mawu*—with whom is bound up the destiny of each clan as of each individual. This is no doubt a modification of an earlier myth.⁸ We will quote here Herskovits's account which summarizes the facts very well: 'The earth, however, was as yet but sparsely populated when still later

---

¹ An informant adds: this is why in Dahomey the ceremonial days are *zobodo* and *ajaxi* (because the Dahomean dynasty came originally from Aja).

² See A. Le Hérissé, *L'Ancien Royaume*, p. 47.

³ The *Fa* symbolism comprises sixteen great signs and 240 secondary signs constructed according to the usual rules of geomancy (see especially B. Maupoil's study). Each expresses a universal destiny and is the centre of a series of related myths. Each sign (*du*) is personified in a 'son of *Fa*'.

⁴ Although in general the west is linked with *Yɛku-mɛji*. But my informants were explicit on this point—the only instance in which the attribution of one of the four elements was not disputed. For the rest, there is no certainty, but it should be remembered that this myth has undoubtedly suffered degradation.

⁵ This sign corresponds to the earth, but Maupoil says that Ɔyɔ is connected with water.

⁶ Dahomey is assigned the first of the signs, the one which is 'chief of all'. It should be noted that Ashanti (*asante*) is identified with the same sign and the same colour as Dahomey; the two kingdoms were related.

⁷ Herskovits records: 'It is . . . said that Gǔ and Lisa are to be regarded as the first founders of sibs, since on their visits to earth they mated and pointed the way toward an organized social life' (*Dahomey*, i, p. 159). The first part of this statement would appear to be doubtful.   ⁸ We have seen (p. 215) that *Fa* was a recent introduction.

the sons of Fate [*Fa*] came from the sky to preach the doctrine of Destiny, and to foretell that supernatural beings would appear and found family lines.' These sons of *Fa* are the *du*, personified symbols of destiny, to which reference has already been made. We may add that each of the clans—or perhaps only the chief ones—is linked to a *du* which determines its destiny. 'As had been predicted, these beings did appear, springing from rivers, emerging from great holes in the earth, rending a mountain-side, falling from the sky with the rain, or climbing down the *loko* tree.' These beings are represented under the form of animals, plants, inanimate objects or natural phenomena, but they were, however, to appear in human form.[1] 'Each of these supernatural beings or phenomena mated with a human woman, and from such matings, in each instance came the founders of the sibs.'[2] These are the *tɔhwiyo*, supernatural founding ancestors, who completed the social instruction given to man. Each gave to his own group its laws, the organization of its cult, and the distinctive symbols corresponding to its own essential character, as well as food and other prohibitions. The myth does not give a list of the original clans, and this may be readily understood since the Dahomean kingdom, growing by conquest, absorbed into itself an increasing number of clans; on the other hand, the royal clan itself would have had no place there; tradition assigns to it a comparatively recent origin, within historical times.[3] Neither is the ideal number of clans determined; only the fact of their organization is stressed.

The cult of the *tɔhwiyo* is important; not only does it predominate over that of the ancestors, but it has shrines and initiates similar to those of the great gods of the pantheon. A more than usually famous *tɔhwiyo* may draw initiates not only from his own, but also from other clans.[4] But the particular function of the *tɔhwiyo* is to govern his own clan according to the laws which he has established. Herskovits rightly observes: '. . . the role of the *tɔhwiyŏ* in influencing the behavior of his descendants is a great one. He figures with special force in matters of marriage and divorce, and constitutes a court of highest recourse in any situation of stress resulting from a breach of faith between two sibs.'[5] Above all they ensure the continued existence of the clan, acting as intermediaries between men and the dual creator. This is one of the chief aspects of the preservation of the world. The sequence of generations was secured from the beginning by the creator himself who formed men from the same clay from which the bodies of their predecessors had been moulded. Thereafter he delegated this power, under his own control, to the *tɔhwiyo* and to the ancestors gathered about them, who are responsible for the human groups thus constituted: as in so many other spheres, the activity of *Dã*, the element of continuity, is implicit here also. We must now summarize the conception of the nature of man in order to see

---

[1] For a list of these founders (*tɔhwiyo*) see Herskovits, *Dahomey*, i, pp. 165 ff.
[2] Ibid., p. 159. [3] Le Hérissé, *L'Ancien Royaume*, p. 274.
[4] In the case of the royal *tɔhwiyo*, all the initiates belong to other clans, since members of the royal clan may not form part of a cult group.
[5] *Dahomey*, i, p. 160.

how the perpetuation of the species is assured. The human soul (sɛ) has many forms, although its essential unity is insisted on: there is the jɔtɔ, the soul handed on from the ancestor of whom each living man is the representative, and who is his guardian; the sɛ, which strictly speaking is a portion of *Mawu*, the great *Sɛ* of the world; the sɛlĩdõ, which is life, feeling, personality, the individual's peculiar qualities[1] with which *kpɔli*, the destiny revealed by *Fa*, is identified; finally, there is the yɛ; this is the term most commonly used, and denotes the shadow, the indestructible portion of the individual, which, at the time of burial, becomes invisible and leaves the body.[2] The ancestor who is to become a man's *jɔtɔ*, with the permission of the *tɔhwiyo* goes to find the earth from which the man's body is to be made: while doing this he is the sɛmɛkɔkato; he becomes the jɔtɔ to which the man's soul is bound. Thus every dead member of a clan is replaced by a new living member, and in normal circumstances a soul is reincarnated as guardian spirit only within the clan.[3] *Sɛ* is the animating principle; every living man has a sɛ which is 'his *Mawu*'. This animating principle is brought to earth by *Dã*, and thus the work of the ancestors of the clan is confirmed and completed. The sɛ has an individual character, but at death it is reabsorbed into *Mawu*. The sɛlĩdõ, however, is peculiar to the individual man. It is his spiritual faculty, the preserver of his identity, the vehicle of his fate; it cannot enter into another man. The yɛ, on the other hand, the man's shadow, returns to earth as jɔtɔ, which is why a child may be the exact image of an ancestor, because the yɛ preserves its bodily form. The soul always returns to earth in the same clan[4] because the gods have guaranteed the fundamental social value which inheres in the clan. And within the clan, by the return of the yɛ in the form of jɔtɔ, the union of the dead and the living is perpetually assured. The tɔhwiyo maintains the government of the whole group; he it is who indicates to the gods those who are to die and he directs the return of souls in new living beings. It is within the framework of the clan that the perpetual movement of souls takes place; this is the real basis of the ancestor cult, which, according to Herskovits, 'must be regarded as the focal point of Dahomean social organization. In order that a sib and its component parts may exist and be perpetuated, the worship of its ancestors must be scrupulously carried out.'[5] The power of the ruling dynasty is constantly reinforced by the presence of the soul of a dead king as the jɔtɔ of the reigning king; thus the jɔtɔ of Agaja was Gãñe-xɛsu; that of Kpẽgla was Akaba;

---

[1] One of Maupoil's informants points out that to send the sɛlĩdõ back to earth is to 'create the self-same person over again'.

[2] Herskovits refers to the sɛmɛdo which he compares to personality in the European sense of the term. In fact, *Sɛmɛdo* is the name for *Mawu* in his function as creator of souls. He also wrongly identifies the sɛ and the sɛlĩdõ, and does not describe the yɛ. Maupoil's account (*La Géomancie*, pp. 378 ff.) is on the whole more accurate.

[3] Souls may seem to be 'lost', but, as Maupoil observes, 'everyone has relatives whom he does not know about. Consultations of *Fa* have made it possible to discover relationships and sometimes to ensure the continuity of families.'

[4] My informants, like those of Maupoil, contradict Herskovits's account (*Dahomey*, ii, p. 233).

[5] Ibid., i, p. 194.

of Agõglo, Agaja; of Gezo, Wegbaja; of Gbehãzĩ, Agõglo. And the *tɔhwiyo* of the royal clan, *Agasu*, whose cult was given the highest place by the kings, secures their glory and the perpetual existence of the kingdom.

We have already described the activity of *Fa*, the word of *Mawu*, and the lord of man's destiny. A symbol of *Fa* (*du*), representing its destiny, is attached to each of the great nations of men. Each clan, the foundation of which was signalized by symbols of *Fa* coming down to earth, may also have its own symbol. Finally, every individual is born under a double sign, that of his *jɔtɔ*, and the one peculiar to himself, and these are not necessarily identical. It is not within the scope of this paper to describe the system of *Fa*,[1] but some reference must be made to it in attempting to determine the Dahomean conception of man's place in the world. Maupoil defines it thus.

Fa is an actual communication from the supreme deity *Mawu*. It is an abstract, indirect, and deductive mode of interpreting or revealing the past or the future, whereby an enquirer receives, through the medium of a specialist, an answer to the problem which is exercising his mind. Above all, it offers to everyone the possibility of learning the fate which *Mawu* had appointed for his soul before giving it its earthly incarnation, and enables him to practise the cult of that soul.[2]

Human destiny is not left to chance. Every man has his place in the world and the course of his life is determined by a series of pronouncements by *Mawu* which fix the destiny of his clan, of the head of his family, and finally of the man himself. This may be revealed to him for he has his *kpɔli*, the material representation of which is a bag containing sand in which has been traced the *du* which *Fa* has made clear to him in a special rite. Thus it may be said that there are categories of fate apportioned to men as individuals, and not as members of a social group.[3] Two people who have the same *du* may be said to be identical. There are as many kinds of destiny as there are signs; they may be favourable or unfavourable. Here again may be seen the influence of *Dã*, the source of all prosperity, the lord of wealth, who guides to success and good fortune those destined to enjoy them. Nevertheless, we are not confronted with absolute determinism. In this connexion we must consider the function of *Lɛgba* already referred to as the intermediary among the gods, the envoy of the dual creator to gods and men. He introduces into destiny the element of chance or accident. Man is not a slave. Though his fate binds him strictly to the structure of the world, it is no more than the guiding line of his life. He is not debarred from all freedom, and *Lɛgba* ensures this in the world of the gods. *Lɛgba* has stratagems and tricks to evade the rigid government of the world. It is clear that the mythology of *Lɛgba* is connected with that of *Fa*, of which it is in some sort the reverse. He is not the power of evil,[4] he may be the bearer of

[1] Besides Maupoil's study already referred to, see R. Trautman, *La Divination à la Côte des Esclaves et à Madagascar*, Mémoires de l'IFAN, i. 1939.

[2] *La Géomancie*, p. 17.

[3] The gods also, offspring of the dual creator, are linked with a *du*; for example, *Hɛvyoso* is said to have been born under the *du Akla-Mɛji*.

[4] Missionaries have erroneously made him 'the devil'.

evil or of good, he may protect man but equally he may make his lot harder. *Legba* is universally venerated in all the cult groups and in every home. Each man has a *Legba* as he has a destiny, and he must propitiate him lest his destiny becomes worse.

It was necessary to refer to this divine personage, and to give a sketch of the conception of human destiny, but we shall not enlarge on it in this paper. In fact the whole concept of the world order displays a flexibility which cannot, in this brief account, be sufficiently clearly shown. Evidence is, however, provided by the existence of many groups of gods who, in spite of their subordinate status in relation to the dual creator, enjoy a high degree of independence in their use of the natural forces which they control.

The Dahomeans are conscious of the unpredictable, the novel, and this may be felt in the social sphere. They constantly emphasize the progressive expansion of their monarchy. It is true that, when describing its working, they always refer primarily to the 'great century'—the nineteenth. But they are ready to talk of the difficult beginnings, and of their hard-won liberation from the Yoruba. They think in terms of history, the history of their kings, as we have already pointed out (see section I, p. 213). They know that their ruling dynasty was self-made. Thus they never represent the kingdom as emerging fully armed and organized in mythical times. I never heard a mythical origin attributed to the organization of the kingdom, nor of divine orders concerning the constitution of the monarchy. The four *sedoto* would seem to be four groups of clans, four categories of men, only some of which formed unified kingdoms at different periods of history. Any parallels between the divine and the human on the plane of the organization of kingship can only be drawn, as the Dahomeans themselves draw them, from quite a different point of view. In the myths the climax is reached with the creation of clans.

Not only did the gods, through their intermediaries, create the clans, but they also provided the pattern for the basic units which their envoys were to establish. If they taught men to live in communities, it was because they themselves already formed social groups. They had, by effecting it, given an example of the constitution of kinship groups governed by the senior generation. It may be noted that, in this connexion, our informants seemed to bring the gods nearer to men, and to make of them a sort of prehuman generation of beings subject to the same needs as themselves. Popular versions of the myths tend to attribute to the gods very human experiences: disputes about precedence, rivalries concerning women, adulteries, &c. The gods indeed founded families and their genealogies are recounted. In these divine families, different generations are distinguished, the order of seniority, from which precedence derives, is specified. We have observed, indeed, that in general Dahomeans lay more stress on this aspect of their myths than on the successive stages in the organization of the world: the gods intervene in daily life, to reward or to punish, to exalt the man who has been initiated by 'entering his head' and possessing him.

The clans, constituted by divine activity and in accordance with the divine pattern, continue to be related to the world of the gods through the *tɔhwiyo* who rule them and through the community of the dead who still form part of them. We have seen how the myths account for the continuity of the clans by the regular passage of souls from the world of the dead to the world of the living. Even though scattered in space and divided into sub-groups, the clan preserves its unity as mythically established. In the world of the dead the *tɔhwiyo*, who mediates between gods and men and has his part in sending souls into the world and recalling them thence, is the centre of a community which constitutes the pattern and the guarantee of the earthly community, and possesses an historical depth which the latter has not.

All the ancestors appear in it in the order of their generations and their seniority, even though the oldest of them are no longer known to men by their names. An unbroken link is maintained between the clan above—which is essentially the real clan—and its incomplete manifestation on earth. The chief of the clan—*xɛnugã*—is said to be 'between two worlds': being as a rule very old, he is ready to rejoin the ancestors. The cult of the ancestors has as its first object to secure a place for them in the divine world, in the real clan, by means of rites of 'deification'.[1] Secondly, the periodic ceremonies, by paying reverence to the ancestors, ensure their continuing help for the living. This cult is one of the essential factors maintaining the cohesion of the kinship group. The *tɔhwiyo*, who exercises, in the name of the gods who sent him, the function of culture hero, in addition to giving their laws to the clan taught them also the principles of the ancestor cult. When he withdrew, the original pattern of community life provided by the gods was replaced by the invisible clan which he still directs in the world of the dead.

Even if the actual power of the ruling dynasty was derived from the enterprising actions of those whom Maupoil calls 'leaders of men', nevertheless the king soon assumed a semi-divine character in conformity with the usual cultural pattern of the Bight of Benin. We have seen how the ordering of the universe and the civilizing of man are linked not so much by the activity of the demiurge as by the mysterious power of *Dã*, the guarantor of all life. But these two activities are also regarded as simultaneous or even identical. Dahomey—where the king is the security for social harmony although he has not created it, and must respect those pre-existing elements, the divinely constituted clans—is represented, in some symbolic objects, by the double calabash of the world.[2] Similarly, the king is compared to *Dã Ayido Hwɛdo*, who sustains the world as well as society; representations of Gezo contain the serpent of the rainbow arranged in a circle and biting its own tail. One of the minor courts of the palace in Abomey is called *Ayido Hwɛdo*; there the king, resting among his wives, came

---

[1] Described in detail by Herskovits, *Dahomey*, i, pp. 194–208.
[2] See also B. Maupoil, *La Géomancie*, p. 63, n. 4.

'like *Dã*, to change colour', that is, to renew himself. In another manner also
the king is identified—or possibly merely compared—with *Dã*; he is the
'king of beads,' the 'father of riches'; as *Dã* is the assurance of fecundity,
of good fortune, success, so the king and his ancestors, whose cult provides the occasion for the most important ceremonies,[1] ensure the prosperity of the country. Strictly speaking the king is not a divine being; he
was always a war-chief; his ancestors are deified, but for the same reason
as are the ancestors of all the clans. But the authority which he exercised
over every aspect of the country's life[2] could not but result in his being
compared to a god.[3]

On the other hand, the people themselves are continually aware of the
relation between the pattern of the monarchical system and those types
and patterns of social organization which exist in the world of the gods and
ensure the order of this world. Even if no instruction had been given, and
no plan specifically laid down and confirmed by a myth, the divine world
would provide a model for the world of men.

There is an awareness of a direct connexion between the two worlds;
in the words of an informant, 'men must live in accordance with the life of
the gods'. It should be added that when new gods are introduced they are
made to conform to the nature and the pattern of the old gods. It is in this
sense that we have spoken of instruments of systematization which work
in two directions.

Among the patterns which are to be found in the divine world and in the
system of kingship, the most characteristic is the dualistic pattern. At the
head of the Dahomean pantheon we have seen the dual divinity, creator or
rather demiurge, *Mawu-Lisa*, a pair of twins or, according to some, described as twins simply in order to express both their unity and their dual
nature. The ideal type of every group in the divine world is a pair of twins
of opposite sex or, more rarely, of the same sex. We have pointed out that
among men also the ideal birth is a twin birth and that in the beginning
every birth was of that kind. This twin structure of the gods is the rule,
even though, in the present stage of its elaboration, not everything has been
integrated into this framework; it is typical that in many cases they speak
of androgynous beings, to such an extent does the double nature seem
entirely reasonable. Thus *Dã Ayido Hwɛdo* is two in one. An informant suggests that all the gods who sprang from the supreme pair came in a series
of twins, although his later statements did not fit in with that notion. Let us
consider the case of the group of earth gods—the *Sakpata*, whose inclusion
in the pantheon probably took place after the event. At the head of this group
is a pair of twins, *Da Zoji* (male) and *Ananu* (female). There may be some
doubt about *Hɛvyoso*, though many of his initiates affirm that he is andro-

---

[1] The 'customs' described by travellers.
[2] For a detailed description see Herskovits, *Dahomey*, *passim*.
[3] He is also compared to *Gu* in his function as ruler, and especially as warrior. Moreover,
he attached much importance to the cult of *Gu*.

gynous, while those of *Mawu-Lisa* connect him with his twin *Gu*. Instances
could be multiplied. The systematizing of the composite elements is not
always completely achieved, but the tendency to group the divine beings
into pairs as if that were the only perfect mode of existence, is always at work.

To dwell on the importance of the cult of twins in Dahomey is outside
the scope of this article.[1] But there is one sphere in which duality is immediately apparent and that is the sphere of political organization. At the
head is the king, and he is two in one. R. F. Burton was the first to point
this out: 'one of the Dahomean monarch's peculiarities is that he is double;
not merely binonymous, nor dual, like the spiritual Mikado and the temporal Tycoon of Japan, but two in one.'[2] It is a good definition. There is
only one royal personage, but there are two courts, two bodies of exactly
similar officials, two series of rituals in honour of the royal ancestors. The
reigning king bears two titles: 'king of the city' and 'king of the fields'. The
significance of this duality is, however, not easy to determine. Burton, and
Skertchly after him, see in it a means by which the king, to whom commerce was forbidden, could engage indirectly in trade. This seems highly
improbable. Our informants relate him to the twins who reigned in the
earliest days of the kingdom: Akaba and his sister Xãgbe, who ruled jointly
in accordance with the doctrine that twins must always be treated alike.
The dual monarchy did not perpetuate itself, until it was revealed to Gezo
that the prosperity of Dahomey depended on its revival. Thus Gezo installed Gãpke, and Glɛle, Adokpõ, and everything that was done for the one
had also to be done for the other. A remarkable resurgence of the concept that
dual nature is the condition of completeness. Officials in the same way are
doubled; here again Burton was the first to report it accurately in speaking
of the 'she *Migã*' and the 'she *Meu*', &c. Every title and every administrative office is conferred simultaneously on a woman within the palace and
a man outside it. Clearly this arrangement had a practical value: a man
could not live in the palace or govern the women; while the woman official
acted as the king's memory and his inspectorate in each administrative
department. But the Dahomeans in general, not content with this practical
explanation, remove it to the metaphysical plane. Moreover, titles, already
dual in themselves, are organized in pairs—one left and one right; prime
ministers *Miga* and *Meu*; war-chiefs *Gau* and *Kpɔsu*, &c.[3] There are numerous examples, for the significance of the principle of duality is expressed
in many ways.

Cf. A. Le Hérissé, *L'Ancien Royaume*, pp. 233–5, and Herskovits, *Dahomey*, i, pp.
263, 270–2.
   [2] R. F. Burton, *A Mission to Gelele, King of Dahome*, London, 1864, ii, p. 86. Skertchly
also mentions it; Le Hérissé says nothing of it. Herskovits quotes the earlier authorities but
adds: 'no indication of this dual role and function of the king was given in descriptions of
the monarchy obtained from present-day Dahomeans in the course of the field-work being
reported here.' My informants, however, spoke of it spontaneously, though disagreeing
about the interpretation.
   [3] All the military functions go in doubled pairs: men, women: left, right. It should be
remembered in this connexion that there were masculine and feminine battalions.

The identity of the divine and human patterns of organization is seen again in their hierarchical and specialized character. The continued existence of the world and of society is maintained in accordance with the same principles. Herskovits rightly observes: 'Dahomean culture is based on control by an officialdom, which, under the monarch, was of an essentially hierarchical character similar to that ascribed to the gods . . .' and 'just as each principal chief who governed a region had minor chiefs under his direction who were responsible to him, so each pantheon-head has minor deities under his control who are responsible to him.'[1] If the community of gods is regarded both as a family and as the diagram of world society, this is due to the specialized functions of its members. Reference may be made to the work of Herskovits who has given an excellent description,[2] the main features of which he summarizes as follows:

In the Sky pantheon, for example, one deity is entrusted with command over the animals and birds, two guard the possessions of their father, Lisa, whose domain is the sun, two play the same rôle for their mother, Mawu, who lives in the moon, one is the guardian of trees, one is goddess of the hearth. In the Earth pantheon, one god cares for drinking water, one is the messenger of his father and brings illness to man, one watches over fields, one distributes sunlight to the growing cereals.[3]

III

This account of some of the central concepts concerning the place of man and society in the world is necessarily partial and over-simplified for the reasons indicated at the beginning of the paper. One may, however, venture to describe some aspects of the connexion between concepts concerning the ordering of the world, and social values. There is a remarkable correspondence between the government of the universe and that of human society, between the structure of the world of gods and that of the world of men. These two essential aspects of the cosmogony are complementary and comparable: the king, who sustains society, is naturally compared to the divinities who sustain the world. This has not produced a mythology and a ritual of control of natural forces by a divine king: the recent origin of the monarchy—established by war-chiefs, 'popular leaders'—as well as the lively sense of history characteristic of the Dahomeans, would prevent it. But the growth of the royal prestige, and the increasing control exercised by the king—acting through specialist intermediaries—over all aspects of Dahomean life even to the organization of production, resulted in an incipient deification of the king, who was spoken of in 'accents of veneration mingled with fear'.[4]

The monarchy no longer exists. It is true that a measure of the royal prestige has devolved on the canton chiefs, who are all members of the former royal dynasty and who, under the present colonial administration,

---

[1] *Dahomey*, ii, p. 294.
[2] Ibid., chaps. xxvi–xxviii.
[3] Ibid., p. 293.
[4] Le Hérissé, *L'Ancien Royaume*, p. 5.

rule some areas of old Dahomey. But though the chiefs maintain the ancient royal ritual and the former court etiquette these are becoming increasingly only empty forms. The chiefs allow to the new élite of educated Africans the right to be independent of them. Except to the older generation, the kingdom of Dahomey is a thing of the past. Its glories and its prestige, acknowledged even by Europeans, are still and will long remain the pride of the whole people. As a memory it has a part to play, but it is no longer a social reality.

On the other hand, kinship groups, clans, and subclans, though not immune from contemporary influences, have continued to exercise an important function, even in the town of Abomey. We have seen that, to the mind of the people, they represent the original social grouping. Cultural development had two aspects: the acquiring of skills and the organization of clans. Cultural development, according to the myths, was prior to the state, in spite of the latter's vigorous growth in Dahomey. The authority of the heads of kinship groups of all grades, integrated as it is in the strongest cult system, in that complex of myths which is most widely accepted today, is still an essential factor of social cohesion. It has, of course, already suffered some injury: the administration takes account of individuals rather than communities, the younger men break away and scatter. If one discusses recent developments with the people, this seems to them to be more serious perhaps than the suppression of the monarchy. Clan organization, supported and justified by a close-knit mythology, and presenting an exact reproduction of the divine pattern, provides the type of all social life. As the clan system becomes weaker, the myths lose their significance. The very foundations of Dahomean culture are being shaken.

INDEX

THE present volume consists of nine studies, each describing the
world outlook of an African people as expressed in their myths
of creation, traditions of origin, and religious beliefs. The studies
are concerned with such widely divergent systems of thought as
the complex metaphysical system of the Dogon of Mali, the
magical cults of the Abaluyia of Kenya, the religious practices of
the Lele of Kasai, in which the forest plays a dominant part, the
secret societies of the Mende, and the ancestor cult of the
Ashanti. The authors show how closely concepts of the divine
ordering of the universe are related to the organization of society
and the everyday activities of man, so that the enthronement of
a king or chief, the brewing of beer, the building of a granary,
the organization of a hunt, all have symbolic significance and are
accompanied by appropriate rituals. The wealth of imagery and
symbolism displayed in many of these myths, and the subtlety of
the metaphysical concepts, will be a revelation to those who have
not studied the thought of so-called primitive societies.

Cover illustration: Figure of a Luba woman (Katanga Region) with a bowl.
Reproduced by permission of the Musée royal de l'Afrique centrale, Tervuren, Belgium

AFRICAN POLITICAL SYSTEMS
Edited by M. FORTES *and* E. E. EVANS-PRITCHARD

AFRICAN SYSTEMS OF KINSHIP AND MARRIAGE
Edited by A. R. RADCLIFFE-BROWN *and* DARYLL FORDE

Published on behalf of the International African Institute

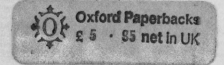

Oxford Paperbacks
£ 5 · $5 net in UK